W9-CPE-204

An Introduction to the Bible: A Journey into Three Worlds

Christian E. Hauer

William A. Young

Westminster College

Prentice Hall, *Englewood Cliffs, New Jersey 07632*

Library of Congress Cataloging-in-Publication Data

Hauer, Christian E. (Christian Ewing)
  An introduction to the Bible: a journey into three worlds/
  Christian E. Hauer, William A. Young. —2nd ed.
    p.   cm.
  Includes bibliographical references.
  ISBN 0-13-471384-2
  1. Bible—Introductions. I. Young, William A.
  II. Title.
BS475.2.H325 1990
220.6'1—dc20
                                        89-39604
                                           CIP

Editorial/production supervision and
   interior design: Patricia V. Amoroso
Cover design: Lundgren Graphics, Ltd.
Manufacturing buyer: Mike Woerner

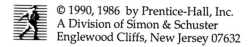

© 1990, 1986 by Prentice-Hall, Inc.
A Division of Simon & Schuster
Englewood Cliffs, New Jersey 07632

Cover illustration: The Lindisfarne Gospels, Cotton MS Nero D. IV (seventh century
C.E., Latin), folio 211, first text page of the Gospel of John. Courtesy of the British
Library.

Our cover illustration is a dramatic example of our "three worlds" concept. It is
from the Lindisfarne Gospels, the work of Celtic monks, who came to Britain to
evangelize the pagan Saxons of Northumbria. The text is Jerome's Latin Vulgate
translation. This page is the first text page of the Gospel of John, which consists of
John's meditation on the first chapter of Genesis. Manuscript illumination was one
of the great art forms of the Middle Ages. So we see the Bible move through time
and space and in the process inspire an expression of the art of yet another age.

Printed in the United States of America
10 9 8 7 6 5 4 3 2 1

ISBN 0-13-471384-2

PRENTICE-HALL INTERNATIONAL (UK) LIMITED, *London*
PRENTICE-HALL OF AUSTRALIA PTY. LIMITED, *Sydney*
PRENTICE-HALL CANADA INC., *Toronto*
PRENTICE-HALL HISPANOAMERICANA, S.A., *Mexico*
PRENTICE-HALL OF INDIA PRIVATE LIMITED, *New Delhi*
PRENTICE-HALL OF JAPAN, INC., *Tokyo*
SIMON & SCHUSTER ASIA PTE. LTD., *Singapore*
EDITORA PRENTICE-HALL DO BRASIL, LTDA., *Rio de Janeiro*

For

Chris, Sr., Ann Lee,
Liz, John, and Anna

and

Art, Rhoda,
Sue, Rachel, and Matthew

Contents

PART FOUR: THE WRITINGS

Abbreviations of the Books of the Bible

Acts	Acts of the Apostles	Jude	Jude
Am.	Amos	1 Kgs.	1 Kings
1 Chr.	1 Chronicles	2 Kgs.	2 Kings
2 Chr.	2 Chronicles	Lam.	Lamentations
Col.	Colossians	Lev.	Leviticus
1 Cor.	1 Corinthians	Lk.	Luke
2 Cor.	2 Corinthians	Mal.	Malachi
Dan.	Daniel	Mic.	Micah
Dt.	Deuteronomy	Mk.	Mark
Ec.	Ecclesiastes	Mt.	Matthew
Eph.	Ephesians	Nah.	Nahum
Est.	Esther	Neh.	Nehemiah
Ex.	Exodus	Num.	Numbers
Ezek.	Ezekiel	Ob.	Obadiah
Ezra	Ezra	1 Pet.	1 Peter
Gal.	Galatians	2 Pet.	2 Peter
Gen.	Genesis	Phil.	Philippians
Hab.	Habakkuk	Philem.	Philemon
Hag.	Haggai	Pr.	Proverbs
Heb.	Hebrews	Ps.	Psalms
Hos.	Hosea	Rev.	Revelation of John
Is.	Isaiah	Rom.	Romans
Jas.	James	Ru.	Ruth
Jer.	Jeremiah	1 Sam.	1 Samuel
Jg.	Judges	2 Sam.	2 Samuel
Jl.	Joel	Song	Song of Songs (Solomon)
Jn.	John	1 Th.	1 Thessalonians
1 Jn.	1 John	2 Th.	2 Thessalonians
2 Jn.	2 John	1 Tim.	1 Timothy
3 Jn.	3 John	2 Tim.	2 Timothy
Job	Job	Tit.	Titus
Jon.	Jonah	Zech.	Zechariah
Jos.	Joshua	Zeph.	Zephaniah

Foreword

What! Another introduction to the Bible? Isn't that what Koheleth had in mind when he wailed, "Of the making of books there is no end...?" The answer to the first question is, indeed yes. The reply to Koheleth's plaint is: there are books and books. This book is one he would not, or at least should not, have complained about. In the field of textbooks, the difference between books and books is the difference in attitude of the author, or in this case, authors. Some write what they are certain is the definitive statement, the last (not the latest) word in the field. The student is swept away and buried under an avalanche of absolute certainties. Others, and such is the case with this volume, offer a forthrightly relativistic approach: This is what is known and this is how we have come to know it. Tomorrow something may turn up—an archaeological find, or a brilliant literary analysis—that may set some (some, but not all) of what we have written on its ear. They have prepared for that possibility, and they want you to be prepared for it as well.

Perhaps the best way to sum up the attitude pervading this work is to quote the old Latin phrase *vade mecum*, walk along with me, for that is its invitation. Come along, and together let us see what there is to be learned about one of the most influential collections of literature ever put together, the Bible. Let us see what there is to be learned and how we can learn it. The program this book provides is straightforward and clear: the three worlds of the Bible, the historical, the literary, and the contemporary. Under these three headings, the authors first approach the context of the Bible, its place within the known historical past of the ancient Near and Middle East; what the archaeological and literary remains of ancient civilizations tell us about the traditions and events reported in the Bible, and what it tells us about them. They then turn to the Bible as a literary event and examine its own history, and the history claimed for it by various schools of thought. While they have not ventured too far from the beaten tracks of contemporary scholarly opinion, they have been fair and honest in their assessments. Finally, they have turned their attention to the contemporary role of the Bible. What can it, what does it mean to us, and how does it touch and affect the lives of those who stand in some connection, positive or negative, near or remote, to it?

In each instance, the authors are at pains to help the reader understand how these three worlds have come into being and how they interrelate. The technical language of scholarship has not been eschewed, but it is meticulously explained so that the insights and methods that lie behind the terms are given their due. The student, the reader, is given every consideration as well. The illustrations, maps, charts, and tables are designed to complement the text so that the biblical worlds take on a concrete presence; they are not words alone.

What lies behind this volume is, I am certain, a conviction on the authors' part that students are important, teaching is important, and the Bible is important. Those who use this text will, I am confident, come to the same conclusions.

Lou H. Silberman

Hillel Professor of Jewish Literature
 and Thought, Emeritus
Vanderbilt University

Visiting Professor, University of Arizona
Oriental Studies Department

Preface

An Introduction to the Bible: A Journey into Three Worlds is an introductory text for college students and general readers who have had little or no previous exposure to the academic study of the Bible. The "three worlds" are the *historical world* out of which the Bible emerged and through which it came to us; the *literary world* (or worlds) created by the Bible itself; and the *contemporary world* in which we read and try to understand the Bible.

The first two worlds are likely to be strange and possibly confusing for a person entering them for the first time. The historical world involves not just the history of events to which the Bible alludes. It also encompasses the original historical context surrounding the Bible; the literary history of the Bible, which means the writing, collection, copying, passing on, and interpretation of the books through time; and the process through which the books became Scripture. The literary world is equally complex. The Bible is not so much a book as it is a library. The biblical collection contains various types of literature.

Like someone traveling in a foreign country for the first time, a student embarking on an initial study of the Bible deserves an orientation before beginning the journey. Chapter 1 can be compared to an orientation to the geography, customs, and language of a new country. We will acquaint you with a few basics about each of the three worlds into which you will be venturing. Chapter 2 is like the practical preparation a student about to go abroad receives concerning such matters as how to rent a room, get to the bathroom, use the telephone, or travel on trains. We will introduce you to the methods of analysis used in the academic study of the literary and historical worlds of the Bible and to some of the ways the Bible is interpreted in the contemporary world.

However, as is the case with travel, orientation is no substitute for the journey itself. In Chapters 3 through 15 we will guide you through the literary and historical worlds of the Bible and raise questions that stimulate you to consider the contemporary world of the various books.

We have tried hard to avoid the latest academic jargon. Where technical terms were necessary for clarity, we tried to state clearly what they mean.

In our discussions of the literary and historical worlds, our intent was to describe, not to evaluate. We hope that persons of a variety of religious backgrounds, or no religious background, will feel comfortable with our descriptions. Our purpose was to create a basis for people of various convictions about the Bible to examine its literary and historical worlds. This will, we hope, create a common ground for meaningful discussion of the contemporary world. Often, when people engage in conversation about the Bible without such a foundation, they end up talking past one another.

An Introduction to the Bible combines two of the major recent trends in biblical scholarship with more traditional concerns of biblical study. One new trend is the application of social scientific models and general history of religions models in biblical study. The second is intrinsic literary interpretation of biblical texts. We have tried to make a very clear distinction between literary inquiry and historical study. On the basis of our classroom experience, we have found that introductory students benefit from an approach that keeps the historical and literary worlds separate. It will become obvious to even the most naive reader that this dichotomy cannot and should not be pushed too far. We have also tried to make greater use of recent research in Jewish studies than is common in introductory texts, particularly in our treatment of postexilic Israel and the New Testament period.

Ideally, a student should read the entire section of the Bible along with the discussion of it. We hope that the general reader, uncoerced by the time limits of an academic schedule, will be able to do just that. At the very least, our analyses of certain materials will require students to consult those particular passages. We have very deliberately tried to write a book that introduces the Bible without becoming a substitute for reading the Bible itself. Our reason for this is quite simple. No secondary text, however excellent, can replace the experience of the primary text itself. A book about Shakespeare is no substitute for *Hamlet*, nor is a book about the Bible a substitute for Genesis.

Preface to the Second Edition

The response to the first edition of *An Introduction to the Bible: A Journey into Three Worlds* from both faculty and students has been very gratifying. We are pleased that the book has proven useful in introductory classes in religion departments throughout the United States and abroad, and that teachers in other disciplines such as English, history, sociology, and anthropology have found our approach to introducing students to the Bible one they too can endorse.

We have received a number of very helpful suggestions on how to improve the book, many of which we have incorporated into this second edition. In particular, we have added study aids—chapter-ending summaries and a quite thorough glossary of terms. We have also edited the text to reflect several developments in literary and historical study and included recent works in the bibliography. However, our fundamental three-worlds approach remains the same. Students and faculty alike have told us that distinguishing the literary, historical, and contemporary worlds of the Bible has given them a new and enlightening structure for their study of the Bible.

We would particularly like to thank our colleagues in the Central States Region of the Society of Biblical Literature and American Schools of Oriental Research, who participated in a special symposium on the first edition of this book. We would also like to thank Mrs. Barbara Knife for her help in preparing the second edition. Professor Harold W. Attridge of the University of Notre Dame, Professor Ron Farmer of the University of Missouri-Columbia, Professor James Moyer of Southwest Missouri State University, and Professor Christopher Begg of Catholic University reviewed the second edition for Prentice Hall. The text now reflects a number of their helpful suggestions.

ACKNOWLEDGMENTS

Any major publication project involves the work of many persons. We would like to express our particular appreciation to the following:

Wayne Spohr, Prentice Hall field editor, gave early guidance and encouragement to the project; and Pattie Amoroso, Prentice Hall production editor, saw both editions through to completion.

Professor Lou Silberman generously provided the foreword.

Professor Robert Seelinger, Messrs. Dan Engle and Bill Wilson, and the Rev. Arthur Young assisted with photographic illustrations. Dean Richard Mattingly and Westminster College made a small grant available during the summer of 1983, which assisted in the production of the first draft of the book. Liz Hauer, interlibrary loan librarian at Reeves Library, Westminster College, provided access to documentary sources otherwise unavailable in central Missouri.

It would be quite impossible in this limited space to acknowledge the contributions of all those scholarly colleagues whose works, and whose comments and advice on our own research, made the book possible. Nor can gratitude be restricted to merely our own generation or even our own century. However, we do wish to acknowledge the special debt of gratitude we owe to those teachers whose instruction, encouragement, and example contributed to our lives in a singular fashion. Chris particularly remembers the late Dean John Keith Benton, the late Professor J. Philip Hyatt, and Professor Lou H. Silberman. Bill particularly remembers Professors John Gammie, Edward F. Campbell, Jr., and J. Kenneth Kuntz. Chris also expresses appreciation of a decade-long collaboration with Professor John Page (anthropology) in the Westminster College Field Archaeology Project, and many helpful discussions of the theory and method of archaeology and anthropology that flowed therefrom.

Both authors also acknowledge happy associations (albeit at different times) with field excavation projects of the Institute of Archaeology of Tel Aviv University, and the opportunity to learn from the late Professor Yohanan Aharoni, and from Professors Anson Rainey and David Ussishkin.

Finally, each of us wishes to thank his coauthor, whose encouragement, cooperation, and personal scholarly contribution made the production of this volume a great deal easier and a whole lot more fun than a job this size has any right to be. Any errors in this work are his fault!

CHRIS HAUER, JR.

WILLIAM A. YOUNG

CREDITS

The Scripture quotations in this publication are from the Revised Standard Version of the Bible, copyrighted 1946, 1952 © 1971, 1973 by the Division of Christian Education of the National Council of the Churches of Christ in the U.S.A., and used by permission.

Map 1, *The Fertile Crescent*, on p. 18, is from B. W. Anderson, *Understanding the Old Testament*, 3rd ed. (Englewood Cliffs, N.J.: Prentice-Hall, 1975), p. 25. Reprinted with permission of the publisher. It was adapted from *The Westminster Historical Atlas to the Bible* (Revised Edition), edited by George Ernest Wright and Floyd Vivian Filson. Copyright 1956, by W. L. Jenkins. Adapted and used by permission of The Westminster Press, Philadelphia, PA.

Map 2, *Major geographic divisions of Palestine*, on p. 19, Map 3, *Possible routes of the Exodus*, on p. 77, and Map 4, *Traditional locations of the tribes of Israel*, on p. 90, are from John Tullock, *The Old Testament Story*, © 1981, pp. 30, 77, and 110. Reprinted by permission of Prentice-Hall, Inc., Englewood Cliffs, N.J.

Map 5, *Roman world of the first century*, on p. 205, is from the frontis piece of the book *Fishers of Men*, photographs by Gordon N. Converse, text by Robert J. Bull and B. Cobbey Crisler. © 1980, text by Robert J. Bull and B. Cobbey Crisler, photographs by Gordon N. Converse. Published by Prentice-Hall, Inc., Englewood Cliffs, N.J. 07632.

Map 6, *Palestine in 30 A.D.*, on p. 206, is from Howard C. Kee, *Understanding the New Testament*, 4th ed. (Englewood Cliffs, N.J.: Prentice-Hall, 1983), p. 83. Reprinted with permission of the publisher. It was adapted from *The Westminster Historical Atlas to the Bible* (Revised Edition), edited by George Ernest Wright and Floyd Vivian Filson. Copyright 1956, by W. L. Jenkins. Adapted and used by permission of The Westminster Press, Philadelphia, PA.

CHAPTER 1

The Three Worlds of the Bible: An Orientation

Courtesy of the Israel Museum, Jerusalem

The Dead Sea Scroll of Isaiah. Two scrolls of the Book of Isaiah from the Hebrew Bible were among the first scrolls to be discovered at Qumran, near the Dead Sea. This one, known to scholars as 1Q Isaiah A, is the oldest known complete copy of a biblical book in Hebrew, or in any language. It was copied about 200 B.C.E. Its text closely resembles that of the traditional rabbinic (masoretic) text, proving that the masoretic text (with the oldest existing manuscripts from about 1000 C.E.) accurately preserves an ancient form of the Hebrew text.

INTRODUCTION

The basic assumption of this introduction to the Bible is that there are three complementary paths a modern reader can take in a serious study of the Bible. We call these three paths and their destinations the three *worlds* of the Bible, for, although interrelated, they form separate spheres that are complete in themselves. The three worlds are the literary world, the historical world, and the contemporary world.

By *literary world* we mean the world of the biblical text itself, apart from anything outside the text. This is the world created by the stories, songs, sayings, letters, and other literature that comprise the Bible. In looking at the literary world we are setting aside questions of references in the text to the world of events, situations, or things outside the literature. Instead, we are looking for the way in which the language of biblical texts creates unique worlds of meaning.

To introduce readers to the literary world of the Bible, in this chapter we will describe the literature of the Bible in general. In the next chapter we will orient students to a literary approach of the study of the Bible.

The literary world is not the only world of the Bible. In the Bible there are numerous references to the world outside the text. And it was composed in, and became a part of, history. Because the Bible is historical and because it can be interpreted in terms of the historical contexts in which it came into being and developed, we can speak of a *historical world*. By historical world we mean the events and situations that form contexts for understanding the Bible as it was being written and interpreted. The original setting is the world of the ancient Near East in general, and the world of ancient Israel in particular, from approximately 2000 B.C.E. until 200 C.E.[1] To introduce readers to the historical world of the Bible, we will present a brief overview in this chapter and an orientation to the historical study of the Bible in the next.

Modern biblical scholars use the term *synchronic* when speaking of the literary world; for synchronic means a perspective that is not concerned with the causes and effects involved in something, but is concerned, rather, with the thing itself. To view the Bible *synchronically* is to look at the biblical text itself. The term *diachronic* is used with reference to the historical world; for diachronic means a perspective that observes the web of causes and effects, the process of which a thing is a part. To see the Bible *diachronically* is to look at it in terms of the historical process of which it is a part.

However, there is more to a study of the Bible than simply describing the literary and historical worlds. The first two worlds imply a third—the *contemporary world* of the Bible. None of us reads the Bible as a totally neutral observer. We are interested to varying degrees not only in what the Bible meant, but also in what it means today. To focus on the contemporary world

---

[1]Dates are designated as B.C.E. (before the common era) and C.E. (common era).

of the Bible is to be sensitive to its impact on people and situations today. It is also to raise the personal question of its relevance to an individual and to that person's life.

In one sense, there are as many contemporary worlds of the Bible as there are readers. In another sense, each age has its own unique set of questions and approaches to determining what the Bible means. In this chapter we will survey the concerns about the Bible shared in our time. In the next chapter we will describe several approaches to understanding the impact of the Bible on our age.

AN ORIENTATION TO THE LITERARY WORLD

The Jewish and the Christian Bibles

The word *Bible* derives from the Greek *biblia*, which means "books." The Bible is not a single book but rather a collection of writings. It is a library of diverse pieces of literature that were collected together as the Scripture of the Jewish and Christian communities.

For the Jewish community, the Bible is composed of twenty-four books divided into three sections: Torah (Law), Prophets (divided into Former Prophets and Latter Prophets), and Writings. An acronym drawn from the first letters of the Hebrew name for each section yields the name often applied to the Jewish Bible: Tanak. We will use *Tanak* or *Hebrew Bible* when referring to this collection. Thus, as Figures 1–1 and 1–2 illustrate, there are three different canons of the Old Testament, only one of them identical to Tanak. Our preference for the term *Tanak* should remove some possibility of ambiguity.

Some Christian groups (Roman Catholics, Eastern Orthodox Catholics, and a few Protestant groups) add six or seven additional books (plus additions to the books of Esther and Daniel) to the twenty-four books of the Tanak. These additional works are called the *Deuterocanon* (second canon) by these groups and the *Apocrypha* (hidden writings) by other Protestant groups, whose Old Testament has the same contents as the Tanak, although arranged somewhat differently.

The Christian community added twenty-seven early Christian writings to the Jewish Bible, which they had formerly called simply *Scripture*. The addition became known as the *New Testament*, with the Jewish Bible becoming known as the *Old Testament* to Christians.

Overview of the Tanak

The Torah has a narrative framework. Indeed, much of it is narrative, so that *Law* is not a very descriptive name for it. The narrative includes a

FIGURE 1–1

The Tanak

English Name	*Hebrew Name*
TORAH	TORAH
Genesis	Bereshith
Exodus	Shemoth
Leviticus	Wayiqra
Numbers	Bemidbar
Deuteronomy	Debarim
PROPHETS	NEVIIM
Former	
Joshua	Yehoshua
Judges	Shofetim
Samuel	Shemuel
Kings	Melakim
Latter	
Isaiah	Yeshayahu
Jeremiah	Yirmeyahu
Ezekiel	Yehezqel
Book of the Twelve	Tere Asar
WRITINGS	KETHUVIM
Psalms	Tephillim
Job	Iyyob
Proverbs	Mishle
Ruth	Ruth
Song of Solomon (Songs)	Shir Hashirim
Ecclesiastes	Qoheleth
Lamentations	Ekah
Esther	Ester
Daniel	Daniel
Ezra-Nehemiah	Ezra-Nehemyah
Chronicles	Dibre Hayamim

prehistory (see Chap. 3) that sets the stage for the story of Israel's origins; the adventures of the fathers, or *patriarchs*, of Israel; and an account of Moses, the Exodus, Israel at Mount Sinai, and forty years of journeying that ended with

FIGURE 1–2

The Books of the Christian Bible

OLD TESTAMENT

Roman Catholic
(with traditional names
from the Vulgate in parentheses)   *Protestant*

Pentateuch (Torah)	*Pentateuch (Torah)*
Genesis	Genesis
Exodus	Exodus
Leviticus	Leviticus
Numbers	Numbers
Deuteronomy	Deuteronomy

Historical Books	*Historical Books*
Joshua (Josue)	Joshua
Judges	Judges
Ruth	Ruth
1 and 2 Samuel (1 and 2 Kings)	1 and 2 Samuel
1 and 2 Kings (3 and 4 Kings)	1 and 2 Kings
1 and 2 Chronicles	
(1 and 2 Paralipomenon)	1 and 2 Chronicles
Ezra and Nehemiah (1 and 2 Esdras)	Ezra and Nehemiah
Tobit (Tobian)*	
Judith*	
Esther (with additions*)	Esther
1 and 2 Maccabees*	
(sometimes put after prophets)	

Poetry and Wisdom	*Poetry and Wisdom*
Job	Job
Psalms	Psalms
Proverbs	Proverbs
Ecclesiastes	Ecclesiastes
The Song of Songs	
(Canticle of Canticles)	Song of Solomon
Wisdom of Solomon*	
Ecclesiasticus (Wisdom of Jesus	
the Son of Sirach)*	

Prophets	*Prophets*
Isaiah (Isaias)	Isaiah

FIGURE 1-2 *(cont.)*

The Books of the Christian Bible

Jeremiah (Jeremias)	Jeremiah
Lamentations	Lamentations
Baruch* (including the Epistle of Jeremias)	
Ezekiel (Ezechiel)	Ezekiel
Daniel (with supplements*)	Daniel
Hosea (Osee)	Hosea
Joel	Joel
Amos	Amos
Obadiah (Abdias)	Obadiah
Jonah (Jonas)	Jonah
Micah (Micheas)	Micah
Nahum	Nahum
Habakkuk (Habucuc)	Habakkuk
Zephaniah (Sophonias)	Zephaniah
Haggai (Aggeus)	Haggai
Zechariah (Zacharias)	Zechariah
Malachi (Malachias)	Malachi

Eastern Orthodox

It may be said in a general way that Eastern Orthodox Christianity offers a third Old Testament canon. However, Eastern Orthodoxy is a family of autonomous linguistic-ethnic churches (Greek, Syriac, Coptic, Russian, Ethiopic, etc.) in communion with the Ecumenical Patriarch. It is thus impossible to deal simply with the varied usage of each member of the family. The Holy Synod of the Greek Orthodox Church, perhaps the Orthodox communion best represented among likely readers of this text, has endorsed a canon that includes the canon of Tanak and the deuterocanon, plus 1 Esdras (3 Ezra), the Prayer of Manasseh, 3 and 4 Maccabees, and Psalm 151. Readers desiring fuller information are referred to the articles on "canon," "apocrypha," and "deuterocanon" in one of the Bible dictionaries or encyclopedias mentioned in the Annotated Bibliography.

NEW TESTAMENT

Gospels

Matthew
Mark
Luke
John

FIGURE 1-2 *(cont.)*

Acts of the Apostles

Letters Attributed to Paul

Romans
1 and 2 Corinthians
Galatians
Ephesians
Philippians
Colossians
1 and 2 Thessalonians
1 and 2 Timothy
Titus
Philemon
Hebrews

General (Catholic) Letters

James
1 and 2 Peter
1, 2, and 3 John
Jude

The Revelation to John

*The Deuterocanon (Apocrypha)

Israel on the border of the promised land. Almost all of ancient Israel's surviving religious rubrics, ritual customs, legal materials, and customary lore have been collected together and assigned to the Moses-Mount Sinai setting in Exodus, Leviticus, and Numbers, or to the rhetorical recapitulation of Deuteronomy.

The Prophets consists of eight scrolls in Hebrew, divided into two sections. The *Former Prophets* (Joshua, Judges, Samuel, and Kings) recount Israel's history from the death of Moses through the occupation of Canaan; the rise and varied fortunes of first one, then two, Israelite kingdoms; and the Babylonian conquest of Judah, the longest surviving Israelite kingdom. This history is interpreted in the light of basic prophetic religious convictions. The *Latter Prophets*—Isaiah, Jeremiah, Ezekiel, and the Scroll of the Twelve (*minor prophets*)—contain collections of the words of Israel's proph-

ets, many in poetic form, collected from the eighth through the fifth centuries
B.C.E. They also include some anecdotal material about the prophets.

The Writings are a varied collection of literary types. There is religious
poetry (Psalms and Lamentations), love poetry (Song of Songs), conventional wisdom lore (Proverbs), and skeptical wisdom lore (Job, Ecclesiastes).
Chronicles, Ezra, and Nehemiah are, like the Former Prophets, history
interpreted in religious terms. Ruth and Esther are short works of edifying
fiction. Jewish liturgical custom selected five of these documents, the
Megilloth, or festival scrolls, to be read on important religious holidays (Ruth,
Esther, Song of Songs, Ecclesiastes, and Lamentations). Daniel is the only
apocalyptic book in the Tanak; the English Bible places it among the prophets.

The deuterocanonical books evince the same variety and many of the
same literary types as the Tanak. Ecclesiasticus and Wisdom of Solomon are
Jewish wisdom books of high quality. First and Second Maccabees are
historical books. Tobit and Judith are short stories. Susanna and Bel and the
Dragon are edifying tales appended to Daniel. The Prayer of Azariah and
the Song of the Three Young Men are psalm poetry added to Daniel.
Additions to Esther provide elements of more conventional piety. The
deuterocanonical materials are discussed in Chapter 10.

Overview of the New Testament

The gospels (Matthew, Mark, Luke, and John) are narrative works
offering teachings of Jesus and accounts of events in his life. They were
apparently crafted for a dual purpose: to encourage conversions to Christianity and to instruct the converted. The Acts of the Apostles is also a
narrative work, taking up where the gospels leave off. It gives a schematic
history of the early spread of Christianity.

Letters are the most numerous literary form in the New Testament.
Thirteen or fourteen letters were eventually attributed to the Apostle Paul.
Others are attributed to the apostles Peter and John and to James and Jude,
brothers of Jesus. So popular was the letter form that some treatises or essays
(Hebrews, First John, and James) were regarded as letters. The Revelation of
John is the only apocalyptic book in the New Testament.

AN ORIENTATION TO THE HISTORICAL WORLD

Introduction

The historical world of the Bible includes the history of the writing of
the biblical literature, the history of the period in which the Bible was
composed, and the history of the interpretation of the Bible. All are recon-

structions by modern scholars using evidence from within and outside the Bible.

A literary history of the Bible is an account of its composition and its parts, from their earliest inception within history to their final written form. The earliest stage was most likely oral, as stories, sayings, and songs were spoken by storytellers, clan leaders, and religious leaders. Not all biblical literature was composed orally, but much of it was. Gradually oral traditions were written down, forming the sources used in the composition of biblical books. These sources were collected together and combined to create the books as we have them today. Finally, the books were edited as they were transmitted. In other words, there are a variety of layers in the Bible representing different stages in the history of the literature. In the last two centuries there has been a great deal of study of this process by scholars. We will survey the nature of this study and its results in the next chapter. In subsequent chapters we will draw on the reconstructions of literary historians in describing the historical worlds of biblical books.

A history of the biblical literature need not stop with the final writing of the Bible. The next stages were the canonization process and the transmission of the written texts, including their translation into other languages. The interpretation of the Bible through the centuries is also a part of the history of the literature. We will present in this chapter brief surveys of the process of canonization, transmission, and translation of the text of the Bible and of the interpretation of the Bible before the contemporary period.

A history of the biblical period uses the Bible as a historical source, alongside other evidence, to reconstruct the history of the period in which it was written. To establish a historical context, an understanding of the cultures of the ancient Near East and the Mediterranean world is essential. Therefore, this chapter includes an overview of the great empires of antiquity, whose actions impinged on the biblical experience. We will also present a survey of the history and geography of the land of Israel, to establish a framework within which particular historical questions can be addressed in subsequent chapters.

Canonization

The books of the Bible did not all attain their authority at one time. They were accepted as the Scripture of the Jewish and Christian communities only after a long process that we call *canonization*. The term *canon* means "measuring rod" or "standard." The process was complex, and scholars today disagree on details of just how and why it happened. We can give here only a very general overview of the process.

There were several distinct stages in the canonization of the Hebrew Bible, reflected in the three divisions of the canon. By about 400 B.C.E. the first section, the Torah, had gained authoritative status. By about 200 B.C.E. the second section, the Prophets, was considered canonical. By about 130 B.C.E. there is evidence that the first two sections were fixed and that the third (which became the Writings) was in the process of developing. This situation continued until about 100 C.E., when the three sections were fixed. The evidence suggests that some books (Ezekiel, Song of Songs, Ecclesiastes, and Esther) that became canonical were the subject of dispute. Other books not included in the Hebrew canon were thought by many to have a valid claim to the same authority as many of the books that were included. The Jews of Egypt in the last two or three centuries B.C.E apparently developed a different ordering of the Prophets and Writings (reflected in the Septuagint, the Greek translation of the Tanak, and in the Christian Old Testament) and included other books not found in the Hebrew canon (the Deuterocanon or Apocrypha). However, the Palestinian Hebrew canon finally attained acceptance in the entire Jewish world, and it is today also accepted by Protestant Christians.

The Greek translation of the Hebrew canon (the Septuagint) was the authoritative Scripture of the first Christians. This is demonstrated by the numerous quotations from the Old Testament that appear in the New Testament. References in the New Testament to the "law and the prophets" (Mt. 5:17; Acts 28:23) and one to the "law of Moses and the prophets and the psalms" (Lk. 24:44) suggest that the third section of the canon was still in flux.

The process of canonization of the New Testament began with the preservation of the sayings of Jesus and stories about him that were considered authoritative for the communities that sprang up and proclaimed him Lord. Gradually these were collected and adapted, creating the gospels. The gospels were probably written by 100 C.E.

Meanwhile, the Apostle Paul was writing letters to the churches he had founded or intended to visit. These letters were apparently read publicly and exchanged among churches. By 100 C.E. it is very possible that the thirteen letters attributed to Paul in the New Testament had been gathered as a collection and had attained wide authority.

The four gospels then emerged as a group, perhaps as a result of an "ecumenical compromise" among churches that favored different of the gospels as the authoritative interpretation of Jesus. By 200 C.E. the gospels, the Pauline letters, and some other writings were held to be of equal authority with the Hebrew canon (and Apocrypha). Yet the authority of other writings (Hebrews, Second and Third John, Second Peter, James, Jude, and Revelation) was still being disputed. Some books ultimately judged not of canonical status were deemed authoritative in some Christian communities.

It was not until the fourth century that the New Testament canon, as we know it, was closed. Even then controversy continued. Canonization was still a concern in the sixteenth century, when the Protestant reformers decided to exclude the books of the Apocrypha from the Old Testament, and the Roman Catholic Council of Trent (1546) reaffirmed the canonicity of most of the Apocrypha (see Figure 1–2).

Textual History

A textual history of the Bible focuses on the copying of the Bible in its original languages (Hebrew, Aramaic, and Greek) and the translation of the Bible into other languages. One principal concern is to reconstruct the "original" texts (called *autographs*) of the Bible. Unfortunately, none of the original texts of biblical books have survived. We are dependent on manuscripts in the original languages copied from earlier manuscripts and scrolls and early translations from the original languages into other ancient languages (called *versions*). These "witnesses" must be meticulously compared with one another in the effort to determine the most probable original reading of the text.

Until the late 1940s, the oldest complete Hebrew manuscript available for textual study dated from around 1000 C.E. The only other evidence came from the early translations, principally into Greek, Aramaic, and Latin. The main Greek translation preserved was the Septuagint (abbreviated as LXX),

The Shrine of the Book, Jerusalem. A special building was constructed at the Israel Museum, Jerusalem, to house the Dead Sea Scrolls and other important archaeological finds from the caves of the Judean wilderness. It is designed to suggest both the caves and the jars in which some of the scrolls were found. The great Isaiah scroll, a complete manuscript of the Book of Isaiah, is displayed here, topped by a replica of a scroll spindle.

Courtesy of the Israel Museum, Jerusalem

which was begun in the third century B.C.E. In the late 1940s, the discovery of a set of ancient scrolls in caves along the shore of the Dead (Salt) Sea made available an important new body of textual evidence. These scrolls, which include at least portions of every book of the Tanak except Esther (see chap. 10), give us Hebrew manuscripts fully a thousand years older than those previously available.

The textual history of the New Testament is also complex, with at least 5,000 known handwritten Greek manuscripts, 10,000 ancient versions, and thousands of quotations in early Christian writings. There may be as many as 200,000 differences in readings among all these sources. Fortunately, nearly all of these differences are of minor significance in determining the basic meaning of the texts.

The earliest textual evidence for the New Testament comes from fragments of papyri (paper made from reeds) that date to the second century C.E. These have all been discovered within the last century. Manuscripts written in capital Greek letters (called *uncials*) constitute the basic and longer known body of evidence, though their importance was not appreciated until the nineteenth century. The most important are known as *Codex Sinaiticus, Codex Vaticanus* (both fourth century), and *Codex Alexandrinus* (fifth century). Other manuscripts, written in a smaller, cursive style (and called *miniscules*), date from the ninth century C.E. and later. Textual history is the domain of specialists knowledgeable in the ancient languages and texts. Thanks to the skills of such scholars, the texts of the Tanak, Deuterocanon, and the New Testament can be reconstructed with great confidence. Readers today should know that good modern translations rest on critical texts that the final author–editors of biblical books would recognize as very close to the works that left their hands.

Translation of the Bible into English

Because students using this work are probably dependent on an English translation in their study, we will survey the basic stages in the development of the English Bible. The first complete English version of the Bible dates to around 1382 and is the work of John Wycliffe, who worked from the Latin Vulgate translation rather than the original Hebrew and Greek. Although it was enthusiastically received by the public in England, Church and State authorities responded by banning Wycliffe's Bible and condemning to death any who used it. Nevertheless, 170 copies have survived.

About 150 years later, William Tyndale translated the New Testament from Greek. Denied support by the Bishop of London, Tyndale received funds from a London civic official. He had to complete his work in Germany due to church pressure. When the translation reached England it was attacked by Church authorities, who said that it would lead to vice, corruption, and moral depravity. Only a few copies of the original Tyndale translation have survived. However, until the advent of modern translation, all English versions of the New Testament were essentially revisions of Tyndale's work.

The first complete English Bible to be printed was translated by Miles Coverdale and published, with the apparent blessing of King Henry VIII, in 1535. Coverdale then published the Great Bible (1539), under the license of the King and with a foreword by the Archbishop of Canterbury, Thomas Cranmer. It was ordered set up in each church, to the dismay of many priests, for people noisily crowded around it during services. The negative reaction of many Church leaders caused King Henry to restrict Bible reading to members of the aristocracy. Under his daughter, the Catholic Mary Tudor, Cranmer and other advocates of the Great Bible were executed, and Coverdale was forced to flee. However, the Great Bible gained popularity and was revised as the Geneva Bible (1560) and the Bishops' Bible (1568).

In response to the growing popularity of English translations, Roman Catholic leaders joined together in support of a new English version, the result being the Douay Version (1606–1610).

In an effort to bring unity to an increasingly divided English church, King James I ordered a new translation of the Bible by the best scholars in the land. Apparently, forty-seven were involved, divided into several working groups. The result was a work based on the Tyndale-Coverdale versions, but with greatly heightened literary polish. The new Bible was not immediately accepted, but gradually the King James Bible (Authorized Version, 1611) acquired the status it still enjoys as the most widely used English Bible among Protestants.

In the nineteenth century important new manuscripts of the Bible in the original languages were discovered, making new translations desirable. A revision of the Authorized Version (AV), based on new evidence, was produced by an interdenominational group of scholars in England and published in 1885. An American revision, called the American Standard Version, appeared in 1901.

The discovery of papyrus letters and other everyday documents of Greco-Roman life showed that the Greek of the New Testament was nonliterary and conversational. This sparked a surge of translations in the twentieth century that attempted to use a simpler style than the AV. For example, in 1976 the United Bible Societies published the Bible in *Today's English Version*.

A revision of the 1885 and 1901 Standard versions was carried out in America during the 1930s and 1940s and published in 1952 by the National Council of the Churches of Christ in America. Intended to embody the best results of modern scholarship while retaining the classic English style of the King James Version, the Revised Standard Version (RSV) was an immediate success and continues to be widely used. A continuing Standard Bible Committee of outstanding scholars periodically revises the RSV to keep it current with recent findings.

The discovery of the Dead Sea Scrolls was another impetus for new translations. In the last few decades there have been a number of new English translations by scholars, none of which has yet attained the popularity of the AV or the RSV. These include the New English Bible (1970), prepared by British scholars in an effort to produce a literary translation as suited to the twentieth century as the AV was to the seventeenth; the New American Bible (1970), prepared by members of the Catholic Biblical Association and sponsored by the American bishops; the Jerusalem Bible (1966), an English translation from a French version produced by Catholic scholars; the New American Standard Bible (1975), a revision of the 1901 version quite popular among some Protestant groups; and the New International Version (1978). A revised edition of AV 1611 in modern English was issued in 1979 as the New King James Version.

The Jewish Publication Society in the United States produced an excellent English translation of the Tanak, the Holy Scripture, in 1917. The same organization launched a new translation project in the 1950s. The Torah appeared in 1962, the Prophets in 1978, and the Writings in 1982.

For students not familiar with the original languages, it is often fruitful to compare several alternative readings of difficult passages in modern translations to see the possible range of meanings.

A problem for biblical translators is that different names for God were used in the Hebrew Bible. The general term for god in Hebrew and other similar languages is *El*. The traditions of the Tanak use this singular form and the plural form (*Elohim*) as designations for the God of Israel, as well as for other divine beings. Translators reflect this difference by capitalizing the term and translating it "God."

Another divine name presents more difficult problems for translators. It is the proper name for the deity used in the Hebrew Bible, usually transliterated into English as *Yahweh*. The problem is that the earliest Hebrew manuscripts were written without vowels. Thus, the proper divine name appeared as YHWH. By the time vowel signs were added to the Hebrew manuscripts of the Tanak, the custom had developed of not pronouncing the proper name of the deity. Instead wherever YHWH appeared in the Scripture, the Hebrew word *Adonai* (Lord) was pronounced in its place. Early translations adopted this act of reverence. Thus, YHWH was read in Greek as *Kyrios* and in Latin as *Dominus*. The major English versions have followed this custom. However, Hebrew has several words of respect that may be translated "lord." To make clear where the proper divine name was used in the original Hebrew, most editions of the English Bible set the initial L in large capitals and the rest in smaller caps, yielding LORD, wherever YHWH appears. We will follow this convention by using LORD wherever YHWH appears in the Hebrew text.

The term *Jehovah* appears in some translations and has become a popular name in English for the God of Israel. This form probably originated when scribes attached the vowels from *Adonai* to YHWH in biblical manuscripts to remind readers to say Adonai when they saw YHWH. Early translators mistook YHWH written with the vowels from Adonai as the intended name and wrote the combination to yield "Jehovah."

Interpretation

The historical world of the Bible also includes the interpretation of the Bible from the time of its writing until the present. Interpretation began even as the Bible was being written. Later books of the Tanak explained the significance of earlier writings. For example, Daniel 9 is an interpretation of the references to the seventy years of punishment after the destruction of Jerusalem in Jer. 25:11–12; 29:10. In Nehemiah 8, Ezra is described as not only reading the "Book of the Law" (presumably the Torah or some part of it) but also explaining what he read.

In the New Testament there are over 1,600 citations of the Old Testament. Because the New Testament community viewed itself as living in the final age of history, it is not surprising that the Old Testament was viewed as full of prophecies now being fulfilled. Because Christians believed Jesus was the Messiah (Christ) of Israel announced in the Tanak, the New Testament often sees predictions about Jesus in Old Testament passages and shows how they have been fulfilled.

Another type of New Testament interpretation of the Old Testament is typology, in which Old Testament persons, events, or things are seen as having counterparts in the new age that began with the coming of Jesus Christ. For example, Christ is called the New, or Second, Adam. Related to this is allegorical interpretation, in which an Old Testament narrative is said to have a hidden meaning that relates to a Christian theme. For example, Paul claims in Gal. 4:21–31 that the relationship between Sarah and Hagar (Genesis 16) was an allegory for the conflict between the slavery of the old covenant and the freedom of the new. The New Testament also collects quotations from the Old to illustrate given themes (e.g., Rom. 3:10–19).

Before, during, and after the New Testament period, Jewish scholars (rabbis) were developing their own methods of interpreting the Tanak. In general, interpretation was either for the purpose of *halakah* (understanding the meaning of a text as it relates to observance of the law) or *haggadah* (amplifying the text for devotional and inspirational purposes). Set rules to govern halakic interpretation were developed, but haggadic interpretation was freer. The rabbis believed that Scripture could have a multiplicity of meanings unless a matter of halakah was involved, and there they debated what the one meaning was. As one rabbi wrote, interpreting Jer. 23:29, "just as a rock is split into many splinters, so also may one biblical verse convey many meanings."

In subsequent centuries interpreters typically stressed one of four levels of meaning in Scripture—literal, allegorical, moral, or mystical. For example, medieval Christian scholars interpreted Jerusalem in the Bible as either the earthly city (literally), the Church (allegorically), the soul (morally), or the heavenly city of God (mystically).

The Protestant Reformation in Christianity caused an explosion of interest in the Bible among ordinary people. Reformers like Martin Luther (1483–1546) and John Calvin (1509–1564) said that, approached with faith, the Bible yields to ordinary readers the living Word of God. The Bible, they said, is the preeminent authority for believers. They both stressed the plain meaning above the allegorical or the mystical sense, unless the passage in question was clearly meant to be taken as symbolic. Two of the results of the Reformation were translations of the Bible into the language of the people and commentaries intended for general audiences.

In response to the Reformation, the Roman Catholic Church reasserted at the Council of Trent (1545–1563) an interpretation of Scripture that stressed the authority of the church. After the Reformation, a movement called Protestant Scholasticism developed the doctrine of the *inerrancy* of Scripture to counter the Catholic emphasis on tradition. Inerrancy means that the Bible was dictated by God to human writers in a manner that overrode the human personality of authors. Therefore, the interpretation of Scripture must come from Scripture and not from the church or other human agency, for that would dilute its divine meaning. For the first time, *literal* meaning was equated with the view that the Bible is the actual, direct word of God. This approach to interpretation is called *literalism*.

The Enlightenment of the seventeenth and eighteenth centuries, which stressed reason as the test of truth, brought renewed emphasis on rational interpretation of Scripture. The Jewish philosopher Baruch Spinoza (1632–1677) argued that the Bible must be interpreted using rational and scientific principles. In particular, he said that an interpreter must take into account the original historical situations in which the biblical authors wrote. Especially in the nineteenth century, the *critical movement* (called *higher criticism* or *historical criticism*) burst forth with profound impact. Scholars devoted themselves to the effort to reconstruct the history of the composition of Scripture, setting aside in the process such traditional notions as the view that Moses wrote the Pentateuch. In general, this movement, which continues to be very influential today, is based on the assumption that the task of interpretation is to place a document in its most likely original historical context. Higher criticism (in contrast with lower criticism, which is concerned with reconstructing the original text) thus tries to determine when and how the books of the Bible were written, to whom they were written, and why they were written. This approach draws on as many sources of evidence as possible about the Bible and the period in which it was written.

Throughout the nineteenth and twentieth centuries, there has been a vigorous response to higher criticism by proponents of literalism. In more recent years those who recognize the value of historical criticism have questioned its almost total dominance of the academic study of the Bible. As this introduction maintains, it is important to interpret texts not only historically (diachronically) but also in terms of their structure and meaning (synchronically).

Geography of the Ancient Near East and Israel

At its greatest extent, the land of the Bible includes the area from what is now Turkey in the north to Egypt in the south, and from Italy in the west to Iran in the east. More specifically, the geographical area with which we are concerned is the narrow strip of land at the east end of the Mediterranean Sea. The larger area was the arena of the empires of the ancient Near East—Egyptian, Assyrian, Babylonian, Persian, Greek, and Roman. The smaller area, which became known as Palestine, was a land bridge across which these empires passed during military campaigns and trade excursions. This area is a coastal corridor connecting the continents of Asia and Africa. To the north and east lay the empires of Mesopotamia (the land between the Tigris and the Euphrates rivers). Here, at different times, the Babylonians (in southern Mesopotamia) and the Assyrians (in northern Mesopotamia) flourished, exercising dominance over the area. To the south, beyond the Sinai Desert, was Egypt, located along the banks of the Nile. The area from Egypt through Palestine into Mesopotamia is called the Fertile Crescent. Western civilization was born within this crescent-shaped swath of arable land, sandwiched between sea and desert.

The land called Palestine was known by a variety of names in the ancient world. In some texts it was called Canaan. In the Bible it is often "the land of Israel." The name *Palestine*, which derives from "land of the Philistines," was applied to the whole area by the Romans in the second century C.E.

Although small in size (150 miles from north to south and an average of 60 miles from east to west, about the size and shape of Vermont), Palestine has many contrasting features. The land is divided by two north-south mountain ranges that are intersected by east-west valleys, creating four geographical regions: the coastal plain, the central highlands, the Jordan Rift, and the Transjordanian Highlands.

The coastal plain, along the shore of the Mediterranean, is narrow in the north but broadens in the south as the coast swings to the west. The plain

MAP 1

begins in the north at Tyre and continues until it is broken by Mount Carmel, where the important Jezreel valley begins. This triangular-shaped very fertile plain (also known as the Plain of Esdraelon) is the only valley that cuts across Palestine all the way from the coast to the Jordan valley. Thus it was heavily traveled and of great strategic importance in ancient times. It was controlled by the city of Megiddo. South of Mount Carmel lies the Plain of Sharon, a

MAP 2 The major geographic divisions of Palestine

forested area during the biblical period. At the south end of Sharon was Joppa, Jerusalem's seaport. To the north, Herod the Great built another port, Caesarea, which during New Testament times was the official center for the Roman governor of the province of Judea. The southern stretch of the plain was named after the Philistines, who inhabited it and built five main cities (the Pentapolis): Gaza, Ashdod, Ashkelon, Gath, and Ekron. Through these plains ran a road as important as any modern highway—the Way of the Land of the Philistines or the Way of the Sea (Via Maris). It was the major thoroughfare between Egypt and Mesopotamia and therefore of great commercial and strategic importance.

Between the southern coastal plain and the central highlands is a range of low hills (the Shephelah). Through this area, full of olive and sycamore trees, ran a series of valleys that led toward Jerusalem. Therefore, it was full of important and often fortified cities during the Israelite period—Lachish, Beth-shemesh, Gezer, and Beth-horon, to name a few.

The central highlands are the spine of Palestine, formed by a mountain range that begins with the Lebanon range to the north and continues all the way to the desert, broken completely only by the Jezreel valley. The northern

Photograph by the senior author

Israel: land of contrasts. A modern road winds down a steep mountainside, while other mountains rise to the north. The traditional boundary between the tribes of Benjamin and Ephraim, and hence the boundary between the northern and southern Israelite kingdoms, ran through this area. Judas the Maccabee scored one of his victories over the Seleucid army nearby on this steep ascent in the second century B.C.E.

part of this region is Galilee, which was sparsely populated and isolated in the biblical period. In the foothills of Galilee was Nazareth.

The area around Mount Ephraim became known as Samaria. Because it was connected to the Jezreel valley, it was accessible and full of important cities such as Shechem, Tirzah, Dothan, and Samaria.

Further south was Judah. Bounded by steep slopes east and west, Judah was defensible and relatively isolated. Although crops could be grown in some areas, the rocky terrain was more suitable for vine culture and for grazing sheep and goats. Judah's major road was along the east slope, and along this road were the important cities of Hebron, Bethlehem, and Jerusalem.

South of Judah lay the Negev (which means, in Hebrew, "dry land" or "south"), a wilderness area suitable only for seasonal shepherding. During the biblical period, Beersheba was the main town and marked the traditional southern boundary of Israel (Dan was the northern). In the first century B.C.E. and the first century C.E., the Nabateans, with their capital at Petra, lived in this area.

The Jordan Rift is a huge geological fault between the two mountain ranges. It is a deep depression running from Mount Hermon in the north (9,232 feet above sea level) to the Dead Sea (1,300 feet below sea level) in the south and beyond. It is dominated in the upper half by the Jordan River (from the Hebrew for "descend"). The Jordan begins in several streams near the foot of the snow-peaked Mount Hermon and flows through a swampland (called Lake Huleh) into the Sea of Chinnereth (also called the Sea of Tiberias or the Sea of Galilee). Near Lake Huleh was the important city of Hazor. Along the shore of the Sea of Galilee (which is actually a freshwater lake) lay the important New Testament cities of Capernaum and Tiberias. The sea is surrounded by steep hills that create a funnel effect for the winds that can quickly whip up into a serious storm on the water.

South of the Sea of Galilee is the Jordan Valley, which in biblical times was full of dense vegetation and predatory animals. The most important cities of the valley were Bethshan, at the juncture of the Jordan and Jezreel valleys, and Jericho, near the Dead Sea. The Jordan River enters into the Dead Sea (also known as the Salt Sea or Sea of the Arabah), the lowest point on earth. Because the sea has no outlet, its waters evaporate, leaving a salty brine in which no marine life can survive. Along the banks of the Dead Sea, the Judean mountains are pocketed with caves. On the northwest edge of the sea lies the ancient site of Qumran, where most of the Dead Sea Scrolls were found. The Jordan Rift continues south, forming the Arabah. At the southern end of the 100-mile-long Arabah was the seaport of Ezion-geber (the modern Elath), from which sea trade was carried out, with the copper mined in the region a prime commodity.

The mountains across the Jordan to the west (the Transjordanian Highlands) form a plateau. This area was roughly divided into four districts by four streams. From north to south these were Bashan, Gilead, Moab, and Edom. A trade route ran the length of this plateau (the King's Highway).

History of the Ancient Near East

The great empires of the ancient Near and Middle East developed in the valleys of the Nile in Egypt, the Tigris and Euphrates in Mesopotamia, and the Indus in India. These river valleys were all suited to large-scale irrigation agriculture, which leads to urban civilization. During the period known to archaeologists as the Bronze Age (ca. 3300–1200 B.C.E.), great urban cultures arose in each of these valleys. We shall pass over the Harappan (Indus Valley) civilization because it was overrun by Aryan invaders before the biblical period was well under way and because (despite some trade relations) it was peripheral to the cultures in which biblical history transpired.

FIGURE 1–3

Archaeological Periods in Palestine

Stone Age

Paleolithic (100,000–8000 B.C.E.)
Mesolithic (8000–5500 B.C.E.)
Neolithic (5500–4000 B.C.E.)
Chalcolithic (4000–3300 B.C.E.)

Bronze Age

Early Bronze (3300–2000 B.C.E.)
Middle Bronze (2000–1500 B.C.E.)
Late Bronze (1500–1200 B.C.E.)

Iron Age

Iron I (1200–900 B.C.E.)
Iron II (900–600 B.C.E.)
Iron III (600–300 B.C.E.)

Egypt. The culture along the Nile exhibits one of the longest unbroken strains of ethnic and cultural continuity in the world. From the time of the Old Kingdom until the Muslim Conquest of the seventh century C.E., Egypt had basically a single civilization. There was change and adaptation (especially with the infusion of Greek culture after the conquest of Alexander in the fourth century B.C.E.), but things Egyptian remained recognizably so for over 3,000 years.

Egypt is sometimes called the *gift of the Nile*. Indeed, the habitable land is a narrow strip along the Nile with desert on either side. Egyptian agriculture depended on the annual Nile floods and on irrigation from the river. Egypt was a difficult land to invade, and there were relatively few infusions of new populations. Only once during the entire Bronze Age was Egypt successfully invaded. The conquerors were Asiatics (the Egyptian name for people to the northwest, from Sinai and beyond). They became known as *Hyskos* ("aliens"). The Hyskos kingdom in lower (northern) Egypt lasted from about 1700 to 1550 B.C.E.

The native Egyptian dynasty that followed forced out the invaders and brought the Egyptian empire to its apogee. The brilliant pharaoh Thutmose III (1490–1435) campaigned northward and extended his dominion to the Euphrates. Once again, under Ramses II (1290–1224), Egypt projected its power that far northward, only to be blocked by the Hittites. Sheshonk I's invasion of Israel (ca. 920) marked the last successful Egyptian incursion into Asia. Egyptian influence declined during the first millenium B.C.E., though the empire remained a power to be reckoned with until the Persian Conquest (sixth century).

Egyptian culture was permeated with an optimism rooted in elaborate hope for an afterlife. There was an opulent life-style for the rich; yet ordinary people seemed to fare well in Egyptian society in most periods. The slave-driven hordes building the pyramids are a product of Hollywood imagination. It is more likely that the great pyramids were built by agricultural workers during slack seasons.

Egypt had a large and generally benevolent pantheon of deities. Not surprisingly, a sun god headed many of the early local pantheons. Later Amun-Re (actually a combination of two sun gods) and the falcon-headed Horus emerged as central deities. Khonsu (the moon god) and Nut (the sky goddess) joined Amun-Re to form the divine triad of the great cultic center at Thebes. Still later Osiris, god of the underworld, and his wife Isis became central deities. The pharaoh was considered to be the son of Amun-Re and thus himself a god. Pharaohs generally enjoyed great popular affection.

Mesopotamia. Whereas the Nile floods were beneficent, the floods of the Tigris and Euphrates were dangerous and destructive, a fact reflected in Mesopotamian mythology. Mesopotamia was much more open to foreign influences than Egypt. Conquests by warrior aristocrats who installed themselves atop the existing hierarchy were fairly common. Still more common was the peaceful diffusion of cultural innovations.

The basic character of Mesopotamian civilization was laid down by an Indo-Aryan people, the Sumerians, in the early Bronze Age. They may have been displaced by Semitic peoples. Certainly the language that succeeded Sumerian, Akkadian, was Semitic.

Mesopotamia was the seat of great empires from late in the third millennium B.C.E. onward. Often there was more than one great power between the rivers or on the fringes, and several of these have bequeathed artifacts and records that illuminate the earliest biblical traditions. But prior to the encompassing Persian conquests of the sixth century B.C.E., the major northern influences on biblical history were three: the Hittites, the Assyrians, and the Babylonians.

The mutual exhaustion caused by the confrontation between the Hittite and Egyptian empires, climaxing in the Battle of Kadesh in about 1286 B.C.E., set the stage for the rise of the nation of Israel. Assyria became the dominant influence in the Near East from the ninth through the seventh centuries. Less durable was the Neo-Babylonian Empire that replaced the Assyrian, only to perish at the hands of the Persians in the middle of the sixth century.

Persia was not really a Mesopotamian empire, because it arose in what is now Iran. But Mesopotamia was the center of its wealth and power, and Babylon was its hub during its dominance in the sixth and fifth centuries. Babylon was also the center of operations of the Macedonian conqueror Alexander during the fourth century. The death of Alexander and the division of his empire to some extent re-created the situation of the pre-Persian world. The Seleucids of Babylonia and Syria and the Ptolemys of Egypt vied for control of the lands between. This unsettled situation continued until Rome moved east. For biblical history the crucial date is 63 B.C.E., when the Roman general Pompey occupied Jerusalem.

Mesopotamian civilization had more influence on Israel than Egyptian culture. Like the Israelites, most Mesopotamians were Semites, and during most of biblical history the empires of Mesopotamia were the dominant power. The Bible traces the origins of the people of Israel to Mesopotamia, whereas in Egypt they were resident aliens.

Like the Egyptian culture, the Mesopotamian was feudal in organization. Unlike Egypt, there was no optimistic hope of an afterlife. The souls of the dead were thought to go to a disembodied existence in the underworld, the fate of all, rich and poor alike. Unlike the Egyptian, the Mesopotamian kings were not considered divine. At best, the king was thought to be the adopted son of the chief god and an agent of the gods.

Assyria was one of the most militaristic powers in history, directing a great deal of energy to the development and use of the technology of war. The Assyrians showed great cruelty to the people they conquered. Their practice was to decimate the societies they conquered through exiling the most important people, if they had not died in battle.

From the very beginnings of biblical history, the lands between Egypt and Mesopotamia were pawns in the power games of these empires. It was only when the great empires were in a temporary eclipse early in the Iron Age (ca. 1100–850 B.C.E.) that Israel and her neighbors flourished. Otherwise, Egypt was the dominant power through the second half of the second millennium, and Mesopotamian empires (first Assyrian, then Babylonian) dominated in the first millennium, until the Persians took over.

From the Assyrian and Babylonian conquests of Israel and Judah in the eighth and sixth centuries through modern times, excepting the brief Maccabean interlude, the land of Israel was under the control of a succession of empires. It was not so much their resources that made Israel and the other lands between the empires so important. Rather it was, as noted, their strategic location on the routes of trade and conquest that it was essential to control.

FIGURE 1-4

Major Social and Cultural Periods in the History of Israel

The Patriarchal Period (Disputed. Perhaps ca. 1750–1500 B.C.E. or 1500–1350 B.C.E.)
The Mosaic Period (Disputed; perhaps ca. 1350–1300 B.C.E.)
The Entry of the Exodus Group into Canaan (Disputed. Perhaps between 1300–1200 B.C.E.)
The Period of the Judges (ca. 1200–1020 B.C.E.)
The United Kingdom (ca. 1020–922 B.C.E.)
The Divided Kingdom (ca. 922–721 B.C.E.)
The Judean Kingdom (ca. 721–587 B.C.E.)
The Babylonian Period (ca. 597–539 B.C.E.)
The Persian Period (ca. 539–333 B.C.E.)
The Hellenistic Period (ca. 333–63 B.C.E.)
The Roman Period (63 B.C.E.–end of the biblical period)

History of Ancient Israel

The history of the people of Israel begins sometime during the second millenium B.C.E., when their ancestors (remembered in the stories of the patriarchs preserved in Genesis) left Mesopotamia and moved to the area we call Palestine. This is called the *patriarchal period*. Sometime between the fourteenth and twelfth centuries, their descendants, who had migrated into

Photograph by the senior author

The Valley of Jezreel from Megiddo. This view to the east helps one to grasp the strategic importance of both this very fertile valley and the great citadel, Megiddo. The main north-south route between Egypt and Mesopotamia passed through the Carmel mountain range to the coastal plain here. Great warriors, from Thutmose III in the fifteenth century B.C.E. to Allenby in the twentieth century C.E., have won victories here. The Hill of Moreh (Judges 7) rises in the center middle ground, while Mount Tabor (Judges 4–5) stands in the distance on the left.

Egypt, were enslaved, later escaped, and returned to Palestine through the Sinai Desert. Because of the role attributed to Moses, this is often called the *Mosaic period.*

Then follows the occupation of the land of Canaan (Palestine). During the twelfth and eleventh centuries the tribes that made up the people Israel were apparently loosely organized, joined together by kinship claims and by a commonly held allegiance to their covenant God. Charismatic leaders emerged to head coalitions of tribes against common enemies. Because these leaders are called judges in the Bible, this is known as the *period of the Judges.*

In the eleventh and tenth centuries the tribes gradually organized themselves into a state-level society, with a centralized bureaucracy under a king (Saul, David, then Solomon). This is the period of the United Kingdom. A period called the Divided Kingdom followed, with a division of the land into two nations—Israel in the north and Judah in the south. The Divided Kingdom continued until Israel was conquered by the army of Assyria (completely by 722 B.C.E.) and Judah was dominated by the Babylonians (by 589–587 B.C.E.)

Then followed the Babylonian Exile, when the Judean King and many other leaders were forced to live in exile in Babylon. When the Persians replaced the Babylonians, there was a return of some leaders to Palestine, beginning the period called the *Persian period*. The Babylonian Exile began a phase of Jewish history called the *Diaspora* (Dispersion), in which Jews established communities outside Palestine.

The Persian period continued from about 538 B.C.E. until 333 B.C.E., when the Macedonian conqueror Alexander the Great gained control of Palestine. This began the Hellenistic (Greek) phase. Alexander's successors, the Egyptian Ptolemies and the Mesopotamian Seleucids, eventually took control of Palestine in turn. The vicious repression practiced by the Seleucids sparked a revolt among Jews, headed by a family called the Hasmoneans, or the Maccabees. Their victory led to the creation of an independent Jewish state in the second century B.C.E., which lasted until the Romans took over in 63 B.C.E.

Throughout the New Testament period Rome continued to maintain control over Palestine and the Mediterranean world. All of the New Testament was written against the backdrop of the *Roman period*. Several dates are especially important. During a Jewish revolt in 70 C.E., Jerusalem was leveled by the Romans, a traumatic event in both Jewish and Christian history. This was about forty years after the death of Jesus. Paul had conducted his missionary activity and written his letters in the 40s and 50s. During the development of the Christian Church and the period of the writing of the New Testament, there existed relative toleration, interspersed with periods of persecution of Christians by Roman authorities (for example, in the 60s under Nero, possibly in the 80s and 90s under Domitian, and twenty years later under Trajan). The period before the 70s is usually called the *apostolic age*, and the period after that, which continued until the middle of the second century, is called the *postapostolic age*.

As we have now seen, the historical world of the Bible has a number of possible realms. Given the limitations of an introductory text, we will not be able to devote separate attention to each area in every chapter. Subsequent chapters will focus on the original historical contexts of biblical books and the reconstruction of biblical history.

AN ORIENTATION
TO THE CONTEMPORARY WORLD

Throughout the history of interpretation of the Bible, readers have been affected by the times in which they lived. Their approach to Scripture was in large part determined by the concerns and assumptions of the cultures and communities of which they were a part. We are no different. We must be aware that, as we study the Bible, our understanding is guided by the contemporary world. This is not to say that all modern readers read the Bible the same way. Within the contemporary world are a variety of different realms, some diametrically opposed. For example, a student who is a member of a Jewish or Christian community that takes a literalist approach to Scripture will read the Bible in a way considerably different from a student who comes from a nonreligious background or one in which the Bible is not seen as the literal word of God.

However, there are issues unique to the modern world that affect the questions we raise as we study Scripture, whatever our presuppositions. For example, the scientific theory of evolution has raised questions for the contemporary interpreter of Genesis that are unique to the modern world. Interpreters disagree on how to answer these questions, but no modern reader of Genesis is completely unaffected by them.

Nor can a reader of the Bible today be divorced from the reality of the threat of nuclear annihilation. This threat conditions how we view biblical passages on war, peace, and the end of history, as well as the Bible in general. The worlds of science and technology, with their emphasis on natural causes and effects, invariably elicit questions with which the contemporary person wrestles in reading of the involvement of God in history and nature. Likewise, the conflict among modern political systems and the various "third world" liberation movements shape our understanding of the biblical prophets, the sayings of Jesus on wealth, and the description of the life-style of the early Christians in the Book of Acts.

The now familiar picture of the earth as a small blue marble floating in a sea of black, which was taken from space by astronauts, is a graphic symbol of the new consciousness that is emerging. We are more aware than ever before of the interdependence and fragility of life on "spaceship earth." This new, global perspective is bound to affect our reading of the Bible in ways that are just now beginning to take shape.

So far we have viewed the contemporary world of the Bible as the determiner of the concerns modern readers bring to reading it. There is another way to look at this world. The only situation to which the Bible speaks is the present. This is to raise the question of the relevance of the Bible to the twentieth century, and of the uses to which the biblical text is put today. This will be discussed in the next chapter.

Our approach in this text to the contemporary world of the Bible is to raise questions for reflection and discussion at the end of each chapter. In that way, the different points of view of readers can be brought to bear. Our assumption is that reflection and discussion, informed by a study of the literary and historical worlds of the Bible, will be most fruitful.

THE PROBLEM: JOURNEYING INTO THE FIRST TWO WORLDS

In studying the Bible it is possible to become trapped in one of the three worlds we have now identified. There is the danger of subjectivity for those unable to look beyond the contemporary world. If this world only is included in a study of the Bible, it can become a mirror for our own attitudes and prejudices. In the nineteenth century a number of biographies of Jesus were written. But, as Albert Schweitzer, who was not only a missionary to Africa but an eminent New Testament scholar, showed, most of these biographies portrayed Jesus as the reflection of the biases of the author. To a romantic writer, Jesus was an idealist; to a political radical, he was a revolutionary. Needless to say, we must be careful to avoid forcing Scripture into the mold of our own preconceptions.

A reader can also become locked into the historical world. As we have noted, it is extremely important in studying a text to become aware of its context. But the Bible is literature, with meanings not necessarily dependent on historical setting. For example, some scholars have become so wrapped up in trying to determine the original contexts of the Psalms that they have neglected them as poems with meanings apart from the situations in which they first appeared.

Similarly, the literary world can become a place to hide from the hard questions of historical context and contemporary impact. The Book of Job, for example, should be viewed not only as a literary masterpiece, which it is, but also in terms of the context of the Wisdom Movement of Israel and the ancient Near East and from the perspective of modern events that spotlight the question of the relationship between God and evil, such as the various holocausts of modern history.

The challenge we face is to set aside our own questions, concerns, and preconceptions, shaped by our experience of the contemporary world, long enough to travel into the timeless world of the text itself and into the historical world in which the text came into being and through which it has passed. If we are diligent and patient in this effort, we will be rewarded with a more informed basis from which to make judgments about the relevance of the Bible today. This is not an easy journey; no one likes to travel without at least some baggage. There are no certain safeguards to avoid becoming trapped in one of the worlds. Healthy doses of humility and self-criticism are the best antidote.

Let us now gear up for the journey with an introduction to the methods of studying the first two worlds of the Bible and a discussion of its uses in the contemporary world.

SUMMARY

The approach followed in this introduction to the Bible is to distinguish three worlds of the Bible for study: literary, historical, and contemporary.

By *literary world* we mean the biblical texts themselves. To describe this world is to relate the images, stories, insights, and questions we as readers see in these texts.

By *historical world* we mean the events, places, and people that form the context in which the Bible was written, transmitted by copyists and translators, and interpreted through the ages. To study the historical world is to use evidence within as well as outside the biblical texts themselves to better understand when, why, how, where, and by whom they were composed. To focus on these tasks is to work on the *literary history* of the Bible. In addition, study of the historical world of the Bible involves using the biblical texts as historical sources in an effort to reconstruct the general history of Israel and the ancient world.

By *contemporary world* we mean the assumptions, points of view, and questions modern readers bring to the Bible whenever they encounter it; the ways in which the Bible confronts and challenges us today; and the various uses to which the Bible is put in the present by individuals and communities.

In this chapter we introduced you to each of the three worlds through an overview of the types of literature in the Bible; the history of the Bible's composition, translation into English, and interpretation; the geography and history of the ancient near East and Israel, the lands of the Bible; and the issues at stake as modern readers confront the Bible. Finally, we warned of the dangers of too much emphasis on one of these worlds to the exclusion of the others.

The three-worlds approach is a tool, not an end in itself. The Bible, after all, is not neatly divisible. We recognize that a unified reading of the Bible, blending literary, historical, and contemporary concerns, is best. The challenge to any student of the Bible is to develop for himself or herself a mature, holistic understanding of what is unquestionably one of the most important and influential collections of writings in human history. Our conviction is that a journey into the three worlds of the text will assist a serious student in reaching that goal.

QUESTIONS FOR DISCUSSION AND REFLECTION

1. How does a study that distinguishes among the literary, historical, and contemporary worlds differ from the way you have approached the Bible previously?

2. Do you agree that the study of the literary and historical worlds of the Bible is an important foundation for the study of the contemporary world of the Bible? Why or why not?

3. What potential value do you see for yourself in a study of the three worlds of the Bible?

4. What are the three most important issues of contemporary life in your opinion? In your opinion, how is the Bible related to them?

5. It has been said that individual readers have a *private canon*, that is, biblical books and passages that they personally find most meaningful. If you have a private canon, what is it? If you do not, raise the question with someone who does.

6. Which is the more precise descriptive term, Tanak (or Hebrew Scripture), or Old Testament? Why? What accounts for this?

CHAPTER 2

Gearing up for the Journey: An Orientation to the Methods of Biblical Study

Photograph by Bill Wilson

Archaeology in Israel. These workers on the 1980 excavation of the biblical city of Lachish are meticulously preparing to remove the bones of an infant found beneath the collapsed wall of a house in the Canaanite city, which was destroyed in the late thirteenth or early twelfth centuries B.C.E.

INTRODUCTION

Many people who try to journey into the worlds of the Bible become confused by the variety of study methods they encounter, and they wonder which way they should proceed. What are the differences among the various approaches, and how do they relate to each other? The intent of this chapter is to clarify, using the perspective of the three worlds, the various stances from which the Bible can be studied.

First, we will examine the type of study appropriate to a journey into the literary world. The goal of this approach is to understand the meanings of the literature itself, apart from anything outside of it. Therefore, we call this type of study *intrinsic*. The assumption of intrinsic study is that biblical texts create unique worlds through their language. The goal is to re-create through description, as faithfully as possible, the dynamics of these worlds. Because each interpreter inevitably reads texts from a certain point of view, which cannot be completely divorced from the description, and because the world's texts are rich and multifaceted, intrinsic study yields not one, but numerous possible readings of texts. There is no right or wrong description of the world of a text, but rather readings that are more or less faithful to what is actually created by the literature. Thus, the criterion for judging intrinsic study is the text itself.

Next, we will turn to the method of study related to the historical world of the Bible, focusing our attention on the search for the original historical contexts of biblical literature and the effort to reconstruct the history of the biblical period. Because the historical world focuses on establishing settings external to the Bible, we call the methods associated with it *extrinsic*. The basic assumption of extrinsic study is that the Bible is part of the historical world and can be better understood in terms of the contexts in which it came into being (and through which it passed). This type of study draws on a wealth of available information outside the Bible, provided by archaeology, anthropology, and other disciplines. It also treats the Bible as a historical source.

A principal value of extrinsic study is that it helps us understand what the Bible meant when it was written, by exploring how it was written, for whom it was written, and what situations motivated the writing. For example, seeing Genesis 1 in the context of ancient Near Eastern creation mythology helps clarify what this text meant in its original historical context.

Like intrinsic study, extrinsic study can distort texts. Zealous interpreters sometimes describe contexts that the available data do not support when other investigators check them out. The test for extrinsic study is to ask how well the reconstructed context suggested by the interpreter "fits" the available evidence—inside and outside the Bible. Your task as a reader in assessing our historical interpretation will be to analyze whether the contexts we describe are supported by the evidence we present. As with all extrinsic interpretation, we are stating what we consider the most probable reconstructions. You must ask whether we make too much or too little of the evidence.

If intrinsic study is the path to entering the literary world of the Bible and extrinsic study opens the way into the historical world, how should we explore the contemporary world? In a word, *carefully!* There are a variety of approaches to determining the contemporary impact of the Bible and very strong opinions as to which is best. In this chapter we will describe some of the ways the Bible is used today.

INTRINSIC STUDY: JOURNEYING INTO THE LITERARY WORLD

Introduction

Various methods of study of the literary worlds of biblical texts have developed in the last decade. Most adapt various modes of contemporary literary analysis that reflect particular theories of literature. For example, *reception* or *reader-response criticism* assumes that the meaning of a text results from the effects it has on readers and studies how texts create these effects.

Interpreters influenced by a theory known as *deconstruction* contend that readers actually create texts in their encounters with literature. According to this method of analysis, no reading of any text is fixed or final, since each reader's re-creation of a text is different.

Structuralism holds that beneath the surface features of texts are "deep structures" that contain the most important meanings to be discovered by readers. Structuralists look for recurrent patterns in texts, usually polar opposites, in which they believe the deeper messages are encoded.

This study of the intrinsic world of biblical texts will not follow a particular theory of literature. Instead, we will simply observe basic, generally recognized literary features of biblical texts such as genre, theme, and structure. Our comments result from a reading that involves the following steps:

1. Establishing the boundaries of the text being studied
2. Distinguishing the type(s) of literature found in the text
3. Observing the prose and poetic qualities of the text
4. Searching for the theme(s) of the text
5. Identifying the "surface" structures of the text
6. Presenting an integrated reading of the text.

1. Establishing the Boundaries. A photographer can stand in one place and use one camera but take a variety of pictures of the same subject merely by changing the lens of the camera. In the same way, an interpreter of the Bible describing its literary worlds can present a variety of readings simply by narrowing or widening what is in view. It makes considerable difference whether the world being described is the entire Bible (Jewish or Christian), one section (such as the Torah), one book (such as Genesis), one collection of literary units within the book (such as Genesis 1—11), one single literary unit (such as Gen. 1:1—2:4), or one passage within the unit (such as Gen. 1:26–31). It is legitimate to study any of these worlds and to try to describe their unique characteristics. However, the more limited the boundaries, the more specific and detailed the description can be. Sometimes it is fruitful to compare two worlds, such as the two different accounts of creation in Genesis 1 and Genesis 2 (see chap. 3).

In reading an intrinsic study of a biblical text, be aware of the limits of the world being described. In this work our primary attention will be on books of the Bible and the major collections of literary units within them. However, we will sometimes change the lens and look for characteristics of sections of the Bible (such as the Torah), and sometimes even venture comments on the Bible as a whole. On a smaller scale, we will sometimes examine individual literary units as examples of recurrent types. For more detailed discussions of individual passages, readers should consult commentaries on the books, such as those recommended in the bibliography at the end of this book.

2. Distinguishing the Type of Literature. Intrinsic study also describes the types of literature present in the world being analyzed. As a framework for this step, we will outline some of the forms of literature found in the Tanak and the New Testament.

In the Hebrew Bible we encounter many different types of literature, among them myths, legends, historical narratives, short stories, sermons, genealogies, chronicles, songs, meditations, oracles, blessings and curses, legal sayings and codes of law, prophetic sayings, proverbial sayings, poetic dialogue, and apocalyptic visions.

Although today we use the term *myth* to speak of stories that are assumed to be false, we must set that definition aside if we are to understand the myths in the Bible and in other ancient literature. In general, myths are stories about actions of divine beings. In the Bible there are allusions to myths of this type, such as the reference to the deeds of the "sons of God" in Gen. 6:1–4. However, because the Bible acknowledges only one god, the use of myths (which dominate other ancient Near Eastern religious texts) is restrained. Rather than developing new myths, the Bible adapts the myths of other cultures to its unique view of God. For example, as we shall see,

Genesis 1 adapts a myth about creation that was common in the ancient world to a belief in one all-powerful creator. Myths often answer some of the most basic human questions, such as, Why are we here? Where are we going? What is the meaning of life—and of death? To call a text a myth does not mean that it is false, but rather that it is a story centering on divine action outside the realm of history. Because the Bible is primarily historical in its orientation (that is, concerned about the world of time and space), myths are usually adapted to historical settings. For example, as we shall see, Exodus 15 adapts a myth of divine combat to a historical situation.

Many modern interpreters of religious literature use the concept of myth in a more general sense, to refer to any narrative that establishes the world views for a people whether or not divine beings are involved. From this perspective, myths are foundational stories that establish basic values, goals, and acceptable modes of living. The interpreter who applies this broader understanding will see many myths in the Bible. For example, the stories about the ancestors of Israel in the Torah establish models of faith and practice for the people who preserved them. And the Gospel accounts of Jesus might be called mythic in the sense that they provide paradigms for disciples of Jesus to follow. Although we recognize the validity of this understanding of myth, in this textbook we use *myth* in the narrower, more traditional sense just explained.

The common definition of a *legend* is an account regarded as historical, but not verifiable. Unlike myths, legends focus on human characters (but often with divine involvement). Formally, legends focus on a single event or series of events, and on a single character, pair of characters, or family. Sometimes, legends are combined into *cycles* to tell a connected story. Although concrete in form, legends often have broader implications. One type of legend focuses on ancestors who reflect in their lives the qualities the people descended from them either have or should have. The stories of the patriarchs in Genesis (see chap. 3) include such legends and cycles of legends. Other legends explain why something is the way it is. They are called *etiological legends* (legends about origins). For example, the account of the Tower of Babel in Genesis 11 is an etiological legend that explains why there are so many languages. *Hero legends* describe the exploits of memorable leaders, such as the deliverers known as "judges" (see chap. 5).

Historical narratives are developed accounts of events and people of the past. The historical narratives of the Bible deal with events and people in the development of the nation Israel (Tanak) or early Christianity (New Testament). There are no historical narratives in the Bible in the modern sense; that is, accounts that intend an objective, verifiable description of the past. In the Bible, historical narratives always relate the past in order to highlight an underlying meaning, usually in terms of the divine purpose. For example, the historical narrative in the early chapters of Exodus describes the deliverance of the descendants of Jacob from Egypt from the perspective of a divine plan for this people. Disasters such as the Babylonian conquest of Judah narrated in Second Kings are presented as divine judgment on the sins of the people. Historical narrative weaves other types of literature into accounts of the past—legends, songs, stories, sayings, and so on.

The *short stories* of the Bible are distinguished from legends in that they are narratives in which a sustained plot is developed through a series of closely connected scenes. They are not historical narratives, because, although they may relate to questions of history, they move behind the scenes to focus on a more individual story. Their style is more refined and polished than the usual historical narrative. Typically, short stories do not present the deity as an onstage actor. The stories teach a moral or religious "lesson" or "lessons" in an entertaining manner. Among the short stories of the Bible are the Joseph story in Genesis 37—50 and the stories of Ruth, Esther, and possibly, Jonah.

A *sermon* is an address by an individual that speaks of God and the divine involvement with, and purposes for, people. Sermons usually exhort people to action and challenge people to be obedient to God. In the Tanak, Deuteronomy takes the form of a sermon.

Genealogies are lists of names purporting to record the pedigree of an individual or the relationship among families, clans, tribes, or nations. Genealogies linking Adam ultimately to Abraham are found in Genesis 1—11, creating continuity in this collection of literary units.

Chronicles, like historical narratives, give accounts of past events and persons. However, unlike historical narratives, chronicles simply list, usually using a formula, the events and persons, with no attempt to highlight underlying causes or meanings. The Books of Chronicles are, in fact, more historical narrative than chronicle. In Kings, short excerpts from chronicles and references to the chronicles are used as a source for the narrative (e.g., 1 Kgs. 14:29).

The types of literature described so far tend toward prose. The rest that we will discuss are more poetic. *Songs* are poetic compositions that give indication of having been put to music or performed. For example, Exodus 15 is presented as a victory song used at the time of the Exodus from Egypt.

Meditations are long poems that do not seem to have been sung, but rather seem to reflect on various themes. Some meditations are on the Torah (such as Psalms 1 and 119). Other poems reflect on the nature and role of Wisdom (Proverbs 8 and Job 28, for example), times and seasons (Ec. 3:1–9), old age (Ec. 12:1–8), the justice of God (Psalm 73), or creation (Job 38—39).

Oracles are utterances or pronouncements from an authoritative source about what is going to happen in the near or distant future, introduced by a formula. In the Tanak, oracles are from God. There are many prophetic oracles introduced by the formula "Thus says..." (see chap. 6), and a few are scattered elsewhere (as in Numbers 23—24).

Blessings and their opposite, *curses,* are also pronouncements with the formulaic introduction "Blessed be..." or "Cursed be...." They announce well-being or disaster for persons or groups. Blessings and curses are rooted in the belief that, once uttered, they carry effective power that cannot be revoked, because they invoke the power of the divine. An example of a blessing formula is Dt. 28:6, a curse is found in Dt. 27:15–26. One recurrent type of blessing, developed into an extended poem, is the deathbed testament in which a father blesses his children (e.g., Genesis 49).

Other types of literature found in the Tanak will be described as they appear: legal sayings and codes (chap. 4), prophetic sayings (chap. 6), proverbial sayings (chap. 8), the poetic dialogue of Job (chap. 8), and apocalyptic visions (chap. 9).

In the New Testament we find many of the same types of literature as in the Tanak. There are no *myths* as such in the New Testament. However, some contend that the Gospel of John adapts a myth in its portrayal of Jesus and that the Resurrection accounts and the story of the Transfiguration of Jesus are mythic. There is also dispute over which New Testament accounts should be called *legends.* The birth narratives about Jesus in Matthew and Luke seem to be the strongest candidates. The only sustained *historical narrative* is the Book of Acts, although the Passion narratives in the gospels might also be so considered. *Sermons* are found throughout the Book of Acts (e.g., 2:14–36). There are *genealogies* of Jesus in Mt. 1:1–17 and Lk. 3:23–38. *Songs* in the New Testament are usually hymns in praise of Christ (e.g., Col. 1:15–20). There are no legal codes in the New Testament, but *legal sayings* are found in the Sermon on the Mount (Mt. 5—7). Although sometimes called a hymn, the prologue to the Gospel of John (1:1–18) might also be considered a *meditation* on the Word (Logos) of God made flesh. The gospels have a number of *proverbial sayings* attributed to Jesus (such as Mt. 5:13–15). The beatitudes in the Sermon on the Mount (Mt. 5:3–12) are a *blessing* formula. The Book of Revelation includes *apocalyptic visions.*

However, the New Testament also introduces new types of literature. There is no precedent in the Tanak for the two most dominant literary forms of the New Testament: *gospel* (see chap. 12) and *letter* (see chap. 14). Within the gospels and letters of the New Testament there are several other types of literature not encountered to any significant extent in the Tanak. Many of the teachings of Jesus in the gospels are in the form of *parables,* brief narratives that forcefully illustrate a point. There are but a few such narratives in the Hebrew Bible (as in 2 Sam. 12:1–6). However, parables and other sorts of anecdotes were a favorite teaching device of the rabbis of Jesus' time and later. In the letters, we find other literary forms not paralleled much in the Tanak. Paul uses *allegories,* usually as a device to interpret the Hebrew Bible (e.g., Gal. 4:21–31). He also adapts *lists of virtues and vices* similar to those found in Greek ethical treatises (e.g., Col. 3:5–17).

3. *Observing the Language.* In addition to distinguishing the type of literature, an intrinsic study requires sensitivity to the nature of the language of the biblical text. Because the Bible was written in languages quite different from modern English, students dependent on translations need to make a special effort to become familiar with the characteristics of biblical language that can be observed in translation.

The basic distinction to be made is between poetic and prose styles. This distinction should not be too closely drawn, because the style of biblical language defies such neat categorization. Often it is difficult to say whether a text is poetry or prose. Rather than being categories, we should think of the distinction as two points on the same spectrum. Some texts have language that tends toward the *poetic* side; others have a style that tends toward *prose*.

Poetry can be distinguished from prose by the regularity of its style. Prose language tends to have sentences of irregular length and rhythm. In general, poetic language observes conventions that give it uniformity of line length and rhythm (although the rhythm or meter of biblical poetry remains largely an unsolved mystery).

The principal convention of biblical poetry has come to be known as *parallelism*. It might better be called *balancing, seconding,* or *extending.* Biblical poetry is almost always composed of two-line (sometimes three-line) units in which the elements of the second (and third) line(s) balance the elements of the first by reasserting, strengthening, or in some other way completing them. For example, Ps. 24:3 asks

> Who shall ascend the hill of the
>   LORD?
> And who shall stand in his holy
>   place?

Notice how the second line balances the first, by repeating the thoughts in different words. The phrase "Who shall ascend" is balanced by "Who shall stand," and "hill of the Lord" is repeated as "his holy place."

Biblical poetry is composed then of *thought units*—words or phrases—that are structured in two (sometimes three) lines of roughly equal length. There is no rhyming. Rather, the lines are related through balancing of thought units.

Sometimes, as in the example from Psalm 24, the thought units of the first line are balanced by their repetition, in the same order, in the second line.

In other couplets the second line contrasts the thought of the first, as in Pr. 20:29.

> The glory of young men is their
>   strength,
>   but the beauty of old men is their
>   gray hair.

Another type of balancing is *stairlike;* one part of the line is balanced in the second, but the thought is developed further. Psalm 74:23 is an example.

> Do not forget the clamor of thy foes,
>   the uproar of thy adversaries
>   which goes up continually!

As this example shows, parallelism often has a function other than simply patterning the language. Here the notion of the rising clamor of enemies is expressed in the building, crescendo effect of the verse. It is not enough merely to categorize the type of parallelism in a biblical poem. It is important to ask how the balancing contributes to the world being created.

The larger sections of biblical poems, consisting of groups of two- or three-line units, are often called *stanzas* or *strophes.* There is no set length for the stanzas of biblical poems, although they are usually short. Sometimes a refrain marks the end of a strophe, as in Psalm 107 (vv. 8–9, 15–16, 21–22, 31–32). On occasion there is an acrostic (alphabetic) arrangement of strophes, in which each stanza begins with a subsequent letter of the Hebrew alphabet (e.g., Psalm 119). Usually changes in strophes are more subtly indicated by changes in subject or grammar. A reader should examine a poem to determine the stanzas in it. Each presents a scene that blends together to paint a world of words and images. By the way, *selah,* found in many psalms, does not seem to demarcate stanzas. We wish we knew its meaning!

As we shall see in our analyses of some biblical poems, there is often a parallelism among the stanzas of a poem, with one balancing another (see, for example, our discussion of Psalm 8 in chap. 7).

In one sense, biblical poems are like musical compositions. The arrangement is really not linear. Rather, there is a concentric ordering in which themes emerge, slip away, then come together again. Or, similarly to paintings, poems create pictures, using words instead of lines and colors. Like a picture, a poem may have a subject, but not one that can be reduced to a neat summary. One might say that poems are like butterflies—if you try to pin them down, they die.

Because biblical poetry draws on the stock of images of ancient Israel and the ancient Near East, some of the poems need clarification. For example, "pit" is not a hole in the ground, but a metaphor for Sheol, the dwelling place of the dead. Water imagery is often a way of speaking of the chaos that opposes the divine ordering of life and therefore threatens humanity.

Unfortunately, many of the poetic devices of biblical poetry are lost in translation. Biblical poems make frequent and effective use of alliteration (repetition of sounds at the beginning of words or syllables), paronomasia (word plays), assonance (repetition of sounds in accented vowels), and onomatopoeia (words that sound like what they describe). Other devices, such as irony, can be noticed in translation.

Biblical poetry was meant to be spoken and heard. Even in translation its impact can be felt. When you read biblical poems, do so aloud. Try to capture the mood or feeling you find in them.

The other type of language to be observed in the Bible is *prose*. This is used principally in historical narratives and stories. It is also found in legends, myths, sermons, gospels, and letters.

We can generally discern in prose a movement of thought from A to B to C, more so than in poetry. The reader observes a flow to prose and tries to understand the place of individual scenes in that movement. In narratives a tension is usually established, heightened, and perhaps mitigated in succeeding moves until it attains a climax; then in some way it is resolved. This basic pattern can be observed again and again in biblical stories and historical narratives.

By modern standards biblical prose is very simple and straightforward. In describing or narrating scenes, biblical stories get right to the point. There is a minimum of the background information and asides so typical of modern stories. Biblical narrative does not very often present what characters are thinking or feeling. In fact, the biblical narrator does not intrude into the story at all (again unlike modern stories). The plot is developed through straightforward descriptions of actions, or, frequently, through reported dialogue of characters. The pace is quick. Stories are brought rapidly to a climax through a series of juxtaposed scenes, sometimes with little or nothing to connect them. For example, in the gospels, Jesus seems to "jump" from place to place with the focus on the action within the scenes rather than on the connections among them.

Given the terseness and brevity of biblical prose and its refusal to look into the thoughts and feelings of characters, readers must infer motives and intentions. Instead of telling us about the divine plan to create the nation Israel, the narrative simply begins with the LORD speaking to Abraham (Gen. 12:1–3). From this utterance, one infers the divine intention. And instead of telling us that Abraham was a man of faith, the narrative follows the divine address simply by stating what Abraham did, which implies his faith.

Another characteristic of biblical narrative prose is *foreshadowing*. Often the outcome of a story is indicated at the beginning (as when Rebecca learns that her younger son Jacob will supplant his older brother Esau). The action then revolves around how everything falls into place to bring this about. Often there is a tangled web of events that makes the outcome seem impossible. There are also interludes that heighten the tension, usually just as it seems the inevitable will be thwarted.

An important characteristic of biblical prose and poetry is *repetition*. Key words, phrases, and scenes recur, giving an indication of something to which the poem or story wants to draw our attention. Repetition also serves to build tension or add a nuance by balancing two elements. An obvious example is Psalm 150, which reverberates with the call to "Praise!" no less than twelve times. The prologue to the Book of Proverbs (1:2–6) leaves no doubt that the concern of the book is with "wisdom," but it contains a number of subtle nuances on the meaning of "wise" and "wisdom." The patriarchal narrative repeats the scene of a patriarch's wife being taken by a foreign ruler no less than three times (Gen. 12:10—13:1, 20; 26:1–11), but with a different twist each time. Within a story, the repetition of a word is a clue to a central concern of the narrative, as, for example, the repetition of the word *blessing* in the Jacob story in Genesis.

Having made the distinction between poetry and prose, and described some of the major characteristics of each, we should reiterate the point with which we began. This distinction should not be pushed too far. Much prose has a poetic quality in the Bible, and much poetry has the character of prose. Nevertheless, asking whether a text is more poetic or more proselike can be helpful in trying to understand its world.

4. Searching for Themes.   In an intrinsic reading of a text, an interpreter should look for the theme or themes. A theme is an organizing unit that dominates a literary unit. It is not the same as the subject of a unit, but rather is a perception of how the subject is handled. In other words, a *theme* is an interpreter's word for what is seen to be dominant. It is the interpreter's responsibility to show how the perceived theme accounts for the work as it is.

An example of a theme should help clarify this tool of intrinsic study. A reader might ask "What is the theme of the Pentateuch?" One study suggests that it is

> the partial fulfillment—which implies also the partial non-fulfillment—of the promise to or blessing of the patriarchs. The promise or blessing is both the divine initiative in a world where human initiatives always lead to disaster and a re-affirmation of the primal divine intentions for man.[1]

The themes of particular books can also be perceived. For example, the principal theme of the Song of Songs has been stated in a recent study as "the paradox of love in the world."[2] In some cases, a book may even state its own theme. The theme of Paul's letter to the Romans, for example, might be

---

[1]David J. A. Clines, *The Theme of the Pentateuch* (Sheffield, England: Journal for the Study of the Old Testament, 1978), p. 29.

[2]Marcia Falk, *Love Lyrics from the Bible: A Translation and Literary Study of the Song of Songs* (Sheffield, England: Almond Press, 1982), p. 97.

drawn from 1:16, where Paul states that the gospel is the "power of God for salvation to every one who has faith, to the Jew first and also to the Greek."

In an introductory study, the identification of themes can be a very helpful way for readers to enter the literary world of the Bible.

Related to themes, but distinct, are *motifs*. These are images that recur in texts but do not constitute the theme. Observing the principal motifs in a text is often important. For example, in the story of Joseph in Genesis, clothes, and their being put on and taken off, is a recurrent motif.

5. Identifying the Structures. The language of texts forms patterns that can be observed, which then become maps to their literary worlds. We have already begun to discuss structure in talking of the phenomenon of parallelism or balancing, by which poetic language is patterned. In alluding to types of literature, we have also begun to speak of structures, for each literary form has a typical structure. We should discriminate between *typical structures*, that is, patterns shared by literature of a certain type (e.g., hymns), and *unique structures*, which are the individual patterns of separate texts. We will identify a unique structure when analyzing the literary world of Genesis 1 in the next chapter.

We should also discriminate between what might be called the formal or surface structures of texts, either typical or unique, and what have come to be known as *deep structures*. These are the implicit structures in the texts that manifest culturally determined or universal patterns of life and thought. In recent years a movement called *structuralism* has developed, and many structuralist interpretations of biblical texts have been attempted. They go beyond the scope of an introductory study (see the bibliography).

6. Presenting an Integrated Reading. The final step in an intrinsic study is offering a reading of the text being interpreted, drawing together observations gathered from the steps just discussed as well as others. The point of intrinsic study is not merely to analyze texts, but also to offer synthetic readings of them. Therefore, in our intrinsic discussions of biblical literature we will not "run through" the steps of intrinsic study. Rather, we will present synthetic readings that draw on the various insights of this type of research.

EXTRINSIC STUDY:
ENTERING THE HISTORICAL WORLD

There are two types of extrinsic study of the Bible, one that focuses on the historical development of the literature itself and another that uses the Bible as a historical source (along with others) in an effort to reconstruct the history of the biblical period. They are obviously related. However, in the first area of extrinsic study, a variety of specific methods of analysis have developed.

Those methods that attempt to reconstruct the stages in the development of biblical texts can be identified as *literary history*. Although they do overlap, each type of "criticism," as they are called, focuses on a different stage in the history of biblical literature: the oral or preliterary stage, the written sources, the editing of sources into their final written form, the transmission of texts in their original languages, and the canonizing of texts. To reconstruct the history of the biblical period, we will use the empirical method of historiography.

Literary History

Two methods of extrinsic study aim at uncovering the earliest stage in the composition of the Bible. *Traditions criticism* seeks to reconstruct the development of individual elements (traditions) within texts to find their point of origin and to trace how they have been adapted as they have been transmitted. Although traditions criticism carries an interpreter into the written stages in the circulation of traditions, the central concern is the preliterary stage, in which traditions circulated orally. That tradition (the handing over or passing on of beliefs and practices) was important in the development of the Bible is evident in such texts as Dt. 6:20–25, where a father is instructed to pass on the Exodus tradition as an explanation of why it is important to keep the Torah, and 1 Cor. 15:1–11, where Paul writes about receiving the tradition about the Resurrection of Jesus and passing it on in his preaching.

The traditions critic looks for evidence of such traditions as the Exodus and the Resurrection in other texts and tries to trace the process of development of these individual traditions, probing back as far as possible into the preliterary stage. For example, the Resurrection tradition Paul preserved can be compared to the adaptation of the same tradition in the sermons in Acts. The interpreter can then speculate on how the Resurrection tradition was shaped as it circulated orally in sermons in the Christian community before being written down in the letters of Paul and the Acts of the Apostles.

Form criticism is related to intrinsic study in that it examines biblical literature to determine the variety of typical literary forms. However, the objective of form criticism goes beyond the identification of literary types, to search for the "situations in life" in which these types developed. Form criticism assumes that typical social settings give rise to typical literary forms. For example, a typical literary form found in the Psalms and elsewhere—the lament—suggests a ritual of fasting in which people mourned a loss. Thus, form criticism uses biblical literature as a means to learn about the social history of the people of the Bible.

There has been a great deal of form critical analysis of the Psalms (see chap. 7), as well as other literature of the Tanak. New Testament form critics have applied themselves to the process of discovering the situations in the life of the early Christian Church in which the various literary forms of the gospels especially, but other New Testament literature as well, arose. For example, form critics studying the "pronouncement stories" in the gospels, in which Jesus is confronted with a question, then makes a pronouncement on the issue raised (see, for example, Mk. 12:13–17), have speculated that this type of literature gives us insights into the types of disputes that plagued the early Christian Church. Form criticism helps us see more clearly the social, cultural, and religious settings in which the Bible developed. However, it is a speculative endeavor, which can give rise to theories that are not sustained by the evidence.

Source (or documentary) criticism is a type of analysis that seeks to identify the various written sources used in the writing of the Bible, as part of the effort to reconstruct the history of the literature. The first result of this type of study was the so-called *documentary hypothesis*, which claims that behind the Pentateuch in its final form were a series of written sources and/or cycles of oral tradition combined together. This theory has undergone vigorous discussion since it was first proposed nearly 200 years ago, and it has since been refined.

On the basis of changes in vocabulary and style, proponents of the documentary hypothesis maintain that there are four major sources evident in the Pentateuch. Early advocates of this view assumed that the sources were written documents. But some or all of them may have been cycles of oral tradition before their incorporation into the books we know as the Torah. The earliest was J (the YHWHistic source or strand), so named because it used the divine name YHWH (which begins with a J in German). Because this theory was propounded by German scholars, it is called J. The next was E (the Elohistic), from the divine name Elohim used in this source or strand. Then came D, from Deuteronomy. Finally, the P (priestly) source or strand arose. It is called P because of its interest in cultic matters. According to this theory, the J source was in existence in written form by about 1000–900 B.C.E. Then E followed about 100 years later. D was a product of the seventh or sixth centuries, and P was written after the Exile (sixth century or later). By dating the sources, we can place them in specific historical settings and reflect on how, why, to whom, and by whom they were written. We can also inquire how the sources were combined to create the final version of the Pentateuch. Although the documentary hypothesis is still assumed by many biblical interpreters, it has come under increasing criticism for its sometimes arbitrary divisions of the literature. Source critics assume that repetition (for example, of the story of Sarah being taken by a foreign ruler) is an indication of different sources. As an intrinsic study shows, such repetition may have other explanations. Perhaps these positions need not be seen as mutually exclusive.

For the New Testament, source criticism has resulted in hypotheses about the sources used by the writers of the gospels (see chap. 12) and other books.

Redaction criticism focuses on the final written form of a text, presupposing the work of the other types of extrinsic study so far discussed. The term *redaction* refers to the editing of materials. Redaction critics study how traditions, forms, and sources have been combined together in the final written form of a work. The method works best when there is clear evidence of the editing of materials. The first three gospels, for example, have many of the same episodes, so a redaction critic can compare the different versions of the same incident and the ways in which they are used in Mark, Matthew, and Luke. The goal of redaction criticism is to discover the perspective of the final compiler(s) of a writing as a step in the process of reconstructing the stages of composition of the Bible. With its concern for the final shape of the work, it has similarities with intrinsic literary study. Besides comparison of parallel versions to determine editing, redaction criticism depends on other indications of this final stage in a work's composition. Introductions, conclusions, and "seams" between episodes offer evidence of redaction, as does repetition.

Redaction criticism has been applied to the books of the Tanak on a more limited basis. Because Chronicles almost certainly uses Samuel and Kings as sources, we can deduce the point of view of the compiler of Chronicles. The final verses of Ecclesiastes seem to come from the hand of an editor, who leaves a distinctive mark on the final version of the book (Ec. 12:9–14).

Textual criticism examines the transmission of works once they have been written and seeks to reconstruct the most likely original texts. This method and its results have already been discussed in Chapter 1.

Canonical criticism examines works in terms of their place in the collections deemed authoritative in the Jewish and Christian communities. The historical process did not end when books were written, but continued as they were selected and ordered canonically. For those within the communities that consider the Bible authoritative, this opens the door to seeing the Bible not merely as literature but also as Scripture. Even for those who do not recognize the authority of the Bible, canonical criticism is a reminder that the whole is more than the sum of its parts.

The Empirical Historical Method

The American comedian Jack Paar used to end his monologues with the question, "How was that?" To which a disembodied voice would respond, "As compared to what?" This is an illustration of the concept of *control*, which is fundamental to all scientific inquiry. Control means the introduction of a standard that permits ideas and evidence to be evaluated

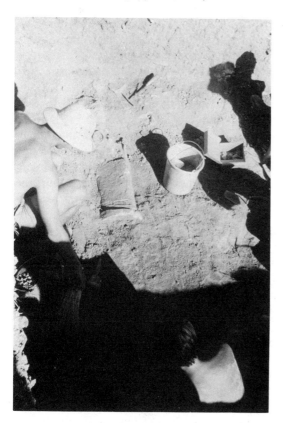

Iron Age shrine at Lachish. Student archaeological volunteers carefully excavate a column-shaped incense altar from a small early Iron Age (probably Israelite) shrine. Fragments of the pottery vessels in which the incense was actually burned are scattered around it. The shrine was probably razed during Pharaoh Sheshonk I's invasion after the death of Solomon (late tenth century B.C.E.).

Photograph by the senior author

in an orderly manner. It is the cornerstone of any *empirical* method, that is, one which depends on observable evidence. The use of control prevents subjective preference from displacing objective discussion. Generally speaking, control permits investigators to keep their bearings.

Historians ordinarily apply a form of the empirical method in the following manner. They develop a hypothesis, a statement of what may be the case (or, in history, what may have been the case). Then they examine the available evidence. In historical research, evidence (or data) often means documents. But the historian studying the ancient world (including the biblical period) must take into account archaeological data as well. Both positive and negative evidence are examined, and then judgments concerning the truth or falsity of the hypothesis are made. Alternatively, a historian can survey the available evidence and ask what is the most likely explanation for its existence. That is, the historian might try to frame an explanatory hypothesis that does the best possible job of fitting the evidence into a meaningful pattern.

One element of the empirical method is the use of models borrowed from the social sciences, particularly sociology, social psychology, and anthropology. The advantage they provide for biblical history is a variety of models of human behavior valid in different cultures. This is especially true of anthropology. We shall use anthropological models in addressing issues in biblical history, so the method we are using might also be called *historical anthropology* in some contexts.

The empirical method results in probable, not absolute, conclusions. There is always the possibility that new evidence will prove an accepted hypothesis false; suggest new, more probable, hypotheses; or raise totally new issues. The appeal of this method is always to "public information," that is, data that can be evaluated by anyone who has developed the basic skills and information required to study the subject at hand.

USES OF THE TEXT: TRAVELING
INTO THE CONTEMPORARY WORLD

Religious texts such as the Bible have typically been put to at least two types of uses. These might be described as the *theological* and the *devotional*. The theological is the derivation of authoritative religious teaching from the text, as when theologians derive the doctrine that the world was created out of nothing from the biblical accounts of creation, or the doctrine of the Trinity from the New Testament description of the relationship between God the Father, Jesus, and the Holy Spirit. The derivation of *ethical* teaching is also a theological use of the Bible. The devotional use of religious texts may be either communal or individual, but its purpose is personal and experiential rather than intellectual. That is, persons are led to some sort of religious experience or insight through devotional study.

In addition to theological and devotional uses, some religious texts are suited to *liturgical* use, that is, use in worship. Lessons from the Bible are read in Jewish and Christian services. Psalms and other sections of Scripture may be sung, chanted, or read. At the most intense level, biblical texts may serve as the basis for the re-creation of the events they describe. For example, the Jewish Passover makes liturgical use of the biblical account of the deliverance from Egypt so that worshipers can sense themselves in the same situation as those who were a part of the original Exodus. The Christian sacrament of Holy Communion (the Eucharist, or the Lord's Supper) makes liturgical use of New Testament passages to reenact the Passover meal Jesus ate with his Disciples before he died. Liturgical use can "remember"; it can also "anticipate." Both Passover and Communion have dimensions of looking ahead to a time of future deliverance, giving participants a foretaste of the Messianic Age or the Kingdom of God.

Another use of the Bible may be called *political*. Whenever interpreters appeal to Scripture to support a particular action by, for, or against governing authority, they are using the Bible politically. For example, opponents of abortion have used the Bible to support action aimed at ending legalized abortions. And proponents of government action to assist the hungry and homeless have drawn on the Bible to support their positions.

All these uses of the Bible that attempt to derive a contemporary meaning from texts have their proper place. They "misfire" when their uses or appropriate places of application are confused. There will be no deliberate theological, ethical, devotional, or political use of the biblical texts in this work, because our concern is to describe objectively the literary and historical worlds of the Bible. However, we recognize that theological and devotional questions are important and of great interest to many readers. Therefore, we will conclude each chapter with questions for reflection and discussion, some of which will raise issues of theological and devotional interpretation. If this book is being used in a group setting, we suggest that the various views of all participants as to the proper theological and devotional interpretation of texts be heard and respected. However, on questions of literary and historical interpretation, we suggest you be less cordial. You can and should discuss vigorously various alternative literary and historical interpretations of texts, those in this work and others. But the bottom line in descriptive study is, "What does the *evidence* support?" That should always be the question.

We have now surveyed the three worlds of the Bible and the methods appropriate to studying them. We have distinguished the literary, the historical, and the contemporary worlds and charted a course for entering them. Now let us begin the journey.

SUMMARY

Having introduced the reader to the literary, historical, and contemporary worlds of the Bible in Chapter 1, in Chapter 2 we outlined the methods of study appropriate to the first two worlds and the range of contemporary uses of the biblical texts.

We called examination of the literary world *intrinsic study*, since the focus is *within* the biblical texts themselves. In an intrinsic study, one must establish the boundaries of the text being described, distinguish the type(s) of literature within the text chosen for analysis, pay attention to the poetic and/or prose character of the text, identify the theme(s) present as appropriate, and analyze the structure of the text. The goal of intrinsic study is a synthetic reading of the text, drawing together the various observations made of the text itself.

Study of the historical world is *extrinsic,* focusing on the relationship between the text and evidence *outside* the text. Scholars have developed a number of methods of study useful in reconstructing the history of the composition of the Bible. In this chapter we briefly described each of these methods and their role in reconstructing the *literary history* of the Bible: traditions criticism, form criticism, source criticism, redaction criticism, textual criticism, and canonical criticism. In this chapter we also discussed the way in which historians and social scientists use the *empirical method* in an effort to reconstruct the historical world of the Bible.

Finally, in this chapter we identified some of the contemporary uses of the Bible—theological, devotional, ethical, liturgical, and political. We encouraged readers to engage in open, respectful discussion of the various meanings of the Bible for contemporary life. Our hope is that the descriptions of the literary and historical worlds of the Bible in the remaining chapters will provide helpful background information for such discussion. We intend the questions at the end of each chapter to provoke both individual reflection and group discussion of the contemporary world of the Bible. These questions are suggestions and certainly do not exhaust the possible issues serious readers may wish to raise about the meanings of the Bible for our time.

QUESTIONS FOR DISCUSSION AND REFLECTION

1. Which seems most important to you, intrinsic or extrinsic study of the Bible? Which seems easiest for you to understand? Which is more difficult?

2. Practice a little intrinsic criticism on an art form you have recently experienced and enjoyed: a movie, a song, or a book. Describe the world created by this art form, without reference to anything outside the piece. Now attempt an extrinsic description. What do you know about how it was composed, who brought it into being, why it was created, for whom it was composed, and its relationship to other events or situations outside its intrinsic world?

3. A prominent twentieth-century religious thinker said, "I cannot take the Bible literally, but I try to take it seriously." What is the difference between taking something literally and taking it seriously? Do you think the attitude of modern Christian and Jewish groups toward the Bible is too literal? Too serious? Not literal enough? Not serious enough? Could a person who was not a Christian or Jew take the Bible literally? Seriously?

4. As noted in this chapter, the literary history of the Bible is complex. The relationship between the Bible and historical events is also complex. The literary history of the Bible is longer and more complex than that

of most modern literatures of any sort. But modern examples may clarify our understanding. Reflect on the literary history of a story in your daily newspaper, the process between an event's transpiring and the report's appearing in print. Also discuss the various types of literature in the newspaper, ranging from front-page, lead stories to editorials to comics to satirical columns, and so on.

CHAPTER 3

Origins: The Book of Genesis

Courtesy of The University Museum, University of Pennsylvania

Great Ziggurat of Ur. Located in southern Mesopotamia, Ur was an important city from Sumerian times. The ziggurat was a great earthen pyramid or artificial mountain used in rituals to symbolically connect heaven and earth. Shrines were situated on top and at the base. A ruined ziggurat may underlie the Tower of Babel story in Gen. 11:1–9. Genesis 11:27–31 identifies "Ur of the Chaldeans" as Abraham's ancestral home.

52

The Book of Genesis is an account of the creation of the universe (Genesis 1—2), the origins of human communities (Genesis 3—11), and the beginnings of the people set apart by God (Genesis 12—50). The focus gradually narrows from the entire cosmos to one man, Abraham, and then begins to widen again. In this chapter we will examine the literary and historical worlds of each of these sections before raising questions related to the contemporary world of Genesis.

PREHISTORY: COSMIC ORIGINS (Genesis 1—2)

The Literary World: Balance in Genesis 1—2

The theme of the first two chapters of Genesis is the creation of the heavens and the earth by the one God. A subtheme is mankind's special place in this creation. However, there is not one creation account, but two, different in both content and style. To describe the literary world of Genesis 1—2 is to compare and contrast these two narratives.

The first account (1:1—2:4a) is patterned as six "days" of creation followed by a seventh day on which the Creator "rests." Then there is a transitional statement (2:4b) that sums up the first account and introduces the second. In the second account, creation is described again, with the focus on the origins of mankind and other living creatures.

There are significant differences in the content of the two creation stories. In Genesis 1 the order of creation is light, heaven, earth, vegetation, sun, moon, stars, sea creatures, birds, land animals, and humanity. In Genesis 2, the stage is entirely the earth. Unlike in the first account, the creation of humanity precedes the creation of vegetation and animal life. In Genesis 1 the creation of humanity is a single act, with the suggestion that male and female were created simultaneously. In Genesis 2 the creation of man and woman are separate acts. In the first chapter creation is preceded by watery chaos and begins when these waters are divided. In the second chapter the precreation situation is a dry desert; creation begins with the land being watered. In the first account the creator is identified simply as God (Elohim). He is present in the account only through the commands that cause the creative acts to occur. In the second account the creator is called LORD God (YHWH Elohim), adding the proper name of the deity to the general designation. YHWH Elohim is intimately involved in the happenings; creation is a hands-on experience for the deity. Like a potter, he forms man from clods of earth. He breathes the breath of life into man. He shows concern about man's solitude. Like a surgeon, he takes a rib from man to make a helper suitable for him. A careful reader will find other differences in the content of the two chapters.

The two accounts also differ stylistically. The first is precisely choreographed. The days are numbered, like the scenes of a drama. Each day is carefully patterned, beginning with the divine utterance ("And God said…") and ending with a refrain ("It was evening and it was morning…") and, on all but one day, the phrase "And God saw that it was good," or, on the sixth day, "very good." Each act of creation results in a pair of opposites: darkness and light, night and day, evening and morning, water and sky, water and dry land, sun and moon, grass and trees, birds and sea creatures, beasts of the field and creeping things of the earth, human male and female.

The six days of creation are likewise balanced into a pair of three-day sets. In the first set a context is established for creation. In the second set the actors appear, climaxing with the entrance of the lead character on the earthly stage—humankind. The following outline shows how Genesis 1 is structured:

Setting	Characters
Day 1: Light	Day 4: Luminaries
Day 2: Sea and heaven	Day 5: Sea creatures and birds
Day 3: Dry land	Day 6: Land animals and
	humankind

Set apart from the creative process is a static situation before and after creation. Before the creation there is a formless chaos. The presence of the Spirit of God (perhaps better translated "mighty wind") foreshadows the change. After the creation there is a return to stasis, but without an indication of chaos. Now there is order, and the Creator rests.

The second account (2:4b–24) has a narrower focus and a much different style. It is a story, not a description. Everything takes place more or less at once, "in the day that the LORD God made the heavens and the earth." There is no ordering, no balance, no careful symmetry. Man is created; then the Creator goes about developing a place for him (the Garden), food, and companions. There is a spontaneity in this account, as though the Creator is pursuing an experimental process. In the first account the divine architect-engineer lays out the blueprints and watches as his commands are carried out, saying as each step is completed, "That's just the way I planned it!" In the second account the divine artist starts with a central theme (man), then fills in the background to complete the picture. In the first account there is no real tension; everything is in its place, balanced and harmonious. In the second account tensions are quickly established. The man is commanded not to eat of the fruit of one of the trees of the Garden. He is alone, in need of companionship. The second tension is resolved with the creation of woman. But the first tension is left unresolved. Will man and woman eat the forbidden fruit? The way is opened to the next, connected, scene.

To the modern mind, schooled to look on contradictions as errors, the two different creation accounts cause a dilemma. If there are two, which is correct? However, this is to impose a foreign standard on biblical literature. As noted in Chapter 2, two of the basic techniques of both biblical poetry and prose are repetition and balancing. This is the way emphasis and nuance are achieved. To include two accounts of creation is to emphasize the importance of cosmic origins. To set different accounts side by side is to give a broader perspective, which reflects the ambiguity in trying to speak of such a basic mystery as the creation of everything. By itself each account is narrow. Is the Creator as austere and distant as Genesis 1 implies, or as intimate and casual as Genesis 2 suggests? The two accounts together give a balanced view of the Creator. And the order and harmony of Genesis 1 is balanced with the trial-and-error world of Genesis 2. Do we not experience the creation in both ways, at different times? A modern writer would probably blend the accounts to form a single, qualified version. To respect the world of Genesis 1—2 is to recognize how the two separate accounts complement and balance one another.

The Historical World: Creation Accounts of the Ancient Near East

Literary History. From the perspective of literary history, a near consensus has emerged among scholars that the first creation account is part of the P (priestly) stratum-source of the Pentateuch. P is concerned with matters of worship and the priesthood (the seventh day of rest in Genesis 1 validates the Sabbath from the creation on). Most literary historians think that P was written during or shortly after the Babylonian Exile (that is, between 550 and 450 B.C.E.), in response to the situation faced by those who were taken into exile in Babylon.

The second creation account is usually identified with the J (YHWH-istic) stratum, so named because of its use of the special divine name YHWH. The most widely accepted date for the J stratum is the time of Solomon or shortly after (tenth to ninth centuries B.C.E.). Genesis 1 was added to the J (or JE) account. This editing (or redaction) was by the author(s) of P or by another editor. The recognition of these various sources or strata is the result of the documentary hypothesis of source critics (see chap. 1).

Many ancient peoples developed creation accounts. These were not meant to be bad substitutes for science, but were statements about the meaning of the cosmos and the status of things in it. Often they justified some political or social order.

The stories told by Israel's predecessors and contemporary neighbors presupposed polytheism and often lodged creation in a dispute or struggle among the gods. The world after it was created remained infused with divinity. In the Babylonian *enuma elish*, the cosmos was formed when Marduk, the patron god of Babylon, killed Tiamat, the threatening dragon of watery chaos, and divided her corpse to form the dome of heaven and the dry land. Marduk's victory justified his headship of the pantheon and Babylon's role as the imperial city. The sun, moon, stars, and so forth, and the various natural phenomena were regarded as gods and goddesses, or their abodes.

The status of humanity in these narratives is often problematic. In *enuma elis* and the *Atrahasis Epic* (another Mesopotamian story), humans were created to be the slaves of the gods, providing offerings so the gods (and their priesthoods) wouldn't have to work. These accounts were often closely tied to the annual agricultural fertility cycles, and they suggested that the cosmos might come unhinged without the repeated creative acts of the gods, sustained by the cultic acts of humans. Events in the human realm had to be foreshadowed by divine actions in the spirit world.

The Israelites used the combat-creation theme as a poetic metaphor (see p. 175 on Job), but not in their creation narratives. Their creation accounts do, however, share common motifs with their cultural matrix. Creation begins in chaos (water in Genesis 1, desert in Genesis 2). Tiamat, the Babylonian chaos dragon, underlies the Hebrew word *tehom* (translated as "deep," Gen. 1:2), though the Hebrew version is simply water. The flat earth and heavenly dome of Babylonian cosmology persist. But the Hebrew accounts are monotheistic. The one God creates a stable material universe requiring no ritual supports. Humanity holds a high status in both Israelite accounts; indeed shares with God in creative activity. Male and female exhibit God's image and likeness in Genesis 1. The center of focus shifts from the spirit realm to the plane of human experience. The climactic event, the goal of the narrative, in both Israelite accounts is the creation of a humane institution. In Genesis 1 it is the Sabbath, the universal day of rest for people and domestic animals. In Genesis 2 it is marriage. The Israelite stories thus reinforce the world-affirming optimism and humanitarianism characteristic of the Torah traditions.

PREHISTORY: COMMUNAL ORIGINS (Genesis 3—11)

The Literary World: Separation in Genesis 3—11

The Garden of Eden (Genesis 2—3) In a word, *harmony* is the theme of Genesis 1—2 as a whole. As a result of divine creation, there is harmony between the Creator and his principal creation—humankind; between humanity and nature (expressed, for example, in the pun involved in the creation of man [*adam* in Hebrew] from the ground [*adamah*] and between male and female (expressed in the unity implied in 1:26 and more explicitly in 2:24). The one source of tension in the harmonious creation is the prohibition against eating the fruit of the tree of knowledge of good and evil (2:17).

That tension is exploited in the next scene, which can be considered part of the Garden of Eden story begun in Chapter 2 (3:1–24). The harmony of creation is broken by the rebellion of humankind, and the result is alienation and separation.

As is the case with Hebrew narrative style, the story moves very quickly. With no introduction, the action begins. The serpent, identified only as the most subtle of the wild creatures in the Garden, plays the role of the trickster. Tricksters in literature are figures who use psychological ploys and distortions to encourage others to do what they know they should not. They are not so much evil as they are devious manipulators of others. In this case, the trickster exploits the human desire to be "like the gods" or "like god." That is apparently what "knowing good and evil" means, although the meaning of the phrase is admittedly ambiguous. Many commentators feel that "knowing good and evil" is like saying "knowing it all." This perspective has been denied humankind, yet humans are unwilling to accept the limitation.

With the serpent as catalyst, the desire to be "like god" proves too strong to resist, so the woman and then the man eat the forbidden fruit. The result is the replacement of harmony with separation. First, there is estrangement between the man and the woman; they become aware of their nakedness, are ashamed, and hide. Next, there is separation from the LORD. The man and woman try unsuccessfully to hide from him and deny their guilt. The man blames God for giving him the woman. This leads to a heightening of the tension between man and woman (She made me do it!) and introduces a distance between humankind and the animal world (the serpent is to blame!). Finally, the harmony between humankind and the earth is disrupted. "Cursed is the ground because of you; in toil you shall eat of it all the days of your life" (3:17). As a result of their disobedience, the man (now called Adam, "everyman") and the woman (now called Eve, "lifegiver") are expelled from the Garden. The original harmony is irrevocably broken, it seems. And humankind is aware of the basic source of alienation in human life: death (3:19).

The elements of the story can be outlined as follows:

Catalyst: The serpent tempts the woman.

Rebellion: The woman and man eat the forbidden fruit.

Confrontation: The man and woman hide, but the LORD finds and confronts them.

Rationalization: The man blames the woman (and, by implication, God); the woman blames the serpent.

Result (Alienation): The harmony of humankind with the Creator and with nature, and the harmony of male and female, are broken.

Despite the swift reaction of the LORD to this act of disobedience, and despite the pervasive sense of alienation, there is a new tension introduced, which balances the negative tone. Despite their estrangement, there is a glimmer of persistent harmony between man and woman. The man names the woman Eve because she is the mother of all living. They leave the Garden together, not apart. Even though the LORD expels the pair from the Garden, lest they exploit their newfound knowledge and eat of the tree of life and become immortal, he clothes them, suggesting that the LORD still has compassion for humanity. And although the pair has experienced a sort of "spiritual death" as a result of eating the fruit, the LORD does not kill them, as his command had implied he would.

Cain and Abel (Gen. 4:1–16). The next story is the account of two brothers, Cain (a farmer) and Abel (a herdsman). It too is a story of alienation. Here the *catalyst* is the LORD's unexplained preference for Abel's offering over Cain's. Probably it just meant that Abel's burned better. Despite this external motivation, a comment makes clear that the real problem is not the LORD's preference, but Cain's inability to master sin. The *rebellion* is fratricide; Cain murders Abel. There is a *confrontation* by the LORD, but Cain offers a *rationalization:* Am I my brother's keeper? The result is *alienation* for Cain: from nature (4:12), from other people (Cain will be a fugitive), and from the LORD (4:15). However, again there is a qualification. To protect Cain from being slain while he wanders, the LORD places a mark on him, a "brand" to warn whoever might try to do violence that Cain belongs to him.

The links among the narratives are genealogies that connect the stories from creation onward (Gen. 5:1–32; 10; 11:10–32).

The Flood (Genesis 6—9). The next extended narrative, the Flood story (chaps. 6—9), follows the same pattern we have observed in the earlier stories. The pace is quickened. The sons of god (divine beings) are the culprits, indicating that rebellion has spread to the divine realm. They saw the daughters of men (*catalyst*) and had intercourse with them (*rebellion*). This sets the stage for the observation that humankind is completely evil. The *confrontation* is an inner one for the LORD, who must admit the mistake he has made. The consequences are severe. *Alienation* has run its course; now there is a complete reversal in the creation process. Creation has been so disrupted by rebellion that a new start is necessary. In this story the *qualification* becomes the central element. The blameless Noah will be spared, along with representatives of the animal kingdom. In a graphic return to precreation chaos, the chaotic waters burst through the firmament and rise up from below. That sets (or resets) the stage for a new beginning. Dry land again "emerges," and a new command to be fruitful and multiply is given. The new creation is marked by a covenant between God and all flesh and a promise not to destroy life again with a flood. Yet the hope of a fresh start is quickly shattered by Noah's curse upon a grandson for something his father did while Noah was passed out drunk.

The Tower of Babel (Gen. 11:1–9).   In the final story in the Prehistory, the Tower of Babel (11:1–9), there is again a *catalyst* (one language), an act of *rebellion* (building the tower in the heavens, a ziggurat, to facilitate human access to and control of the heavenly realm), a *confrontation* ("Come, let us go down!"), a *rationalization* (lest we be scattered), and the resultant *alienation* (confusion of languages). What is missing is any indication of divine compassion qualifying the alienation.

The Theme of Genesis 1—11.   Considering Genesis 1—11 as one literary unit (the Prehistory), we can observe a general theme. It is the tension between the harmony present in the created order and the alienation that occurs as a result of the human refusal to accept the prescribed limits of creation. The estrangement deepens until God decides to start over again, but even the purging of creation does not work, for the one blameless man does not turn out to be as righteous as billed. As alienation grows, the divine compassion balances it, until the failure of the new beginning after the Flood. With the confusion of human languages, there is no sign of divine mercy. As the Prehistory ends, the question of the continued place of humankind in God's creation is open. Having tried and failed twice to have a harmonious creation, with humankind at the center, perhaps God will find someone else to play the lead or simply give up on the whole mess.

The Historical World:
Setting the Stage for History

The Prehistory sets the stage for history and tries to render comprehensible the Israelite understanding of nature and history.

This does not beg the question of the ultimate historicity of some of the traditions in Genesis 1—11. Some of them may in fact have roots in historical objects and events. The mark of Cain (4:15) may well have been a Kenite tribal tattoo. The list of heroes who lived before the Flood (chap. 5) has a counterpart or predecessor in a list of Sumerian kings who lived before a flood and who, like the biblical heroes, lived to substantial ages. The etymology of Babel in Gen. 11:9 seems to connect it with Babylon, and a ruined Mesopotamian ziggurat (temple pyramid) seems to constitute the physical basis of the story.

One of the dramatic news bulletins generated by early Mesopotamian archaeology was the discovery of silt deposits at various locations, patently the work of great floods, which were quickly associated with Noah's flood.

The *Gilgamesh Epic*, with a flood interlude narrated to the hero by Utnapishtim, the Babylonian Noah, probably has Sumerian roots. Another Sumerian story, in which the Noah figure was named Ziusudra, has also come to light. The biblical flood story, which itself is a composite of traditions, almost certainly traces back to Mesopotamian origins. The sort of horizon-to-horizon flooding presupposed by the Noah story simply has no archetype or precedent in the experience of people living in Israel, a country lacking the huge rivers and the broad valleys or deltas required for such a phenomenon. The Israelites must have brought this tradition with them as they moved southward from Mesopotamia, or acquired it from Mesopotamian sources at a later time. The story may coalesce a folk memory of a succession of great floods of the sort experienced in Mesopotamia. Or it may embody the memory of one particularly catastrophic flood. In any case, the Noah story is grounded in history in the sense that its authors were not creating it out of whole cloth, but rather, were reworking an ancient folk tradition that itself rested on actual human experience.

However, given the current state of evidence, we simply cannot talk about history when discussing Genesis 1—11. No drawing or description of a Kenite tattoo survives. The long-lived hero kings cannot be anchored in any historical contexts. The ruined ziggurat cannot be pinpointed. Which flood or floods, and when or precisely where, cannot be specified. Thus, not all materials that ground in history are necessarily historical. These stories do not seem to function in a historical fashion, to convey information about people and their experiences in space and time. Rather, the stories in Genesis 1—11 seem to be trying to answer basic questions about why things are as they are. The technical term for this type of story is *etiology*. An etiological story explains the origin of something, in response to the perennial human question, "Why?" For example, Why is there hostility between the human and the divine, between human beings and nature, and among humans? The story of the Garden of Eden relates the reason. Why are there so many languages? The Tower of Babel explains the reason. Searching for a historical context for Genesis 1—11 leads not to actual events, but to the human longing to know why things are as they are—what they *mean*, not their efficient causes—and to Israel's need to know why the Creator of the universe involved himself with Abraham and his descendants.

There has been a great deal of literary historical study of the sources used in the composition of Genesis 1—11. This section is a composite of at least two literary strata, the J and P previously noted. The alternation of the divine names YHWH and Elohim, differences in literary style and interest, and otherwise inexplicable repetitions and contradictions all point in this direction.

ORIGINS OF THE PEOPLE OF GOD (Genesis 12—50)

The Literary World: Promise and Journey in the Patriarchal Legends

The Prehistory has set the scene. In Genesis 12 we center in on the lead characters in the subsequent drama. The Prehistory also establishes the basic dilemma (human rebellion) and foreshadows the resolution (divine mercy) in the narrative, but it leaves the situation in a seemingly hopeless state.

Against this background Gen. 12:1–3 establishes a new theme, which will in some respects dominate the biblical narrative throughout. In a word that theme is *promise*. It is the promise of the LORD, first expressed to a Mesopotamian named Abram (whose name is later changed to Abraham), and his wife, Sarai (later changed to Sarah). With the barest of introductions to the man Abram, the promise is immediately brought to center stage.

> Now the LORD said to Abram, "Go from your country and your kindred and your father's house to the land that I will show you. And I will make of you a great nation, and I will bless you, and make your name great, so that you will be a blessing. I will bless those who bless you, and him who curses you I will curse; and by you all the families of the earth shall bless themselves." (12:1–3)

This threefold promise of a land (see also 12:7), progeny (a great nation), and blessing (not only for the nation formed from Abram, but also through this nation for others) is the thread woven throughout the stories of the patriarchs (the "first fathers" or forefathers of Israel): Abraham (Genesis 12—25), Isaac and Jacob (Genesis 26—36), and Joseph (Genesis 37—50). This theme also connects the patriarchal stories with what follows. Throughout the narrative, the promise is renewed, endangered, and reaffirmed in an intricate web of scenes.

Related to this primary theme is a secondary one: *journey*. The story of the promise is told as a series of journeys—Abraham to Canaan; Jacob to Paddan-aram and back; Joseph (and the rest of his family) to Egypt; Moses to Midian and back; the tribes of Israel out of Egypt, through the wilderness to the border of Canaan, and finally into the promised land.

Although we follow the tradition of calling these stories "patriarchal," we should not ignore the crucial role of women in the narrative. A more descriptive title might be "ancestral narratives," for both forefathers and foremothers are principal characters.

Abraham (Genesis 12—25). Even before the promise is given to Abram, a tension in its fulfillment is introduced, foreshadowing the major concern of the Abraham narrative. Sarai is barren (11:30). How can the LORD make of Abram (meaning "father of many") a great nation, when he is already seventy-five years old and his wife is unable to have children? As they later recognize, there is more than a little bitter humor in their situation.

We gain insights into biblical characters through their words and deeds; unlike the characters in modern literature, we are rarely given access to their thoughts or feelings. In Abraham's case, his actions speak. Despite the seeming absurdity of a childless septuagenarian becoming the father of a great nation, he leaves his own country without question and heads off for a new land. Through his actions we are told that Abraham is a man of faith, willing to trust the word of a deity previously unknown to him. Abraham is also clever. His wife Sarah—and the promise—are endangered when the "beautiful" Sarah is taken to Pharaoh's house while they are in Egypt. With foresight, Abraham has told her to claim to be his sister, so that the Egyptians will not kill him (12:10–20). To make the point of the patriarch's cunning (and the LORD's protection) more forcefully, the wife-sister motif is repeated in the Abraham story (20:1–18). Abraham is also materially successful (13:2). He is a good host (Genesis 18) and a mediator among men (Genesis 13).

Abraham is also portrayed as a military hero, successfully leading a small guerrilla force against an alliance of raiding kings (Genesis 14). Thus, he is not a crazed wanderer who follows divine voices through the desert. He is a skilled, successful, and wise leader. Because Abraham symbolizes the nation that remembers him as "father of the country," this characterization is part of the development of a positive Israelite self-image.

Most of the Abraham narrative is devoted to portraying Abraham as a man willing to trust the LORD totally. In Genesis 15 the promise is renewed, Abraham responds in faith (15:6), and the promise is sealed with a covenant ceremony. Even though Abraham still has no heir, he trusts the LORD to fulfill the promise. The scene is repeated in Genesis 17, for emphasis, but this time the deity is called El Shaddai (God Almighty), and the sign of the promise is circumcision. The promise (called here a *covenant*; see chap. 4) is said to be "everlasting," that is, unconditional. Finally, after years of waiting, a son, heir to the promise, is born—Isaac (Genesis 21).

When his faith is tested, Abraham endures. In one of the most sublime stories in the Bible, Abraham is told by God to sacrifice Isaac, with no explanation why (Genesis 22). There is no hint of reluctance by Abraham to kill his son and, thereby, the promise. Not until Abraham demonstrates his willingness to take Isaac's life is the boy saved. This story functions to make crystal clear the depth of Abraham's devotion to God. His loyalty to God conditions every other loyalty. But he is not passive in his relationship with the deity. He is willing to challenge the LORD's plan to destroy Sodom and Gomorrah and to bargain for the salvation of the people (18:22–33).

The character of Sarah is also developed in the story. She is a woman who, at age seventy-five, remains beautiful. But she does not rely on her attractiveness. She uses her wits to try to assure that the promise will be fulfilled (16:1–6). Like her husband, she shows skepticism about their having a son in their old age (18:9–15). In this collection of vignettes about Abraham and Sarah, we see not flat, lifeless characters who walk through a divinely ordained drama like robots, but complex persons, with strengths and weaknesses, to whom a promise is given, put in jeopardy, and renewed.

Isaac and Jacob (Genesis 25—36). In the patriarchal narrative the stories of Isaac, Abraham's son, and Jacob, Isaac's son, are woven together. Isaac is a transitional figure. The stories in which he is the central character repeat, and therefore connect him with, similar incidents in the life of Abraham (Genesis 26). Jacob looms larger. The story of Jacob serves to balance the Abraham narrative and to prepare the way for the Joseph story, as we shall see.[1]

As in the Abraham cycle, Isaac's wife (Rebekah) is barren (25:21). But unlike Sarah, Rebekah does not have to wait years for a son. The problem is almost the opposite. Twins are born, creating a conflict as to who shall be the principal heir. Because Esau is the first to emerge from the womb, he has the right of the firstborn—a double portion of the inheritance and the office of family head. The basic tension in the story is introduced when we are told of an oracle received by Rebekah: "the elder shall serve the younger." And at birth, the infant Jacob ("supplanter") is already trying to fulfill the oracle, grabbing his older brother's heel.

The friction between the brothers is compounded by their opposite natures. Esau is a ruddy, hairy outdoorsman. Jacob is a smooth-skinned, contemplative boy who likes to stay inside. Esau is a fool, willing to sell his birthright for a bowl of pottage. Jacob is clever, taking advantage of his brother's hunger to buy the birthright. Later, prompted by his manipulative mother Rebekah, he exploits his father's age and blindness to steal the blessing intended for Esau. Abraham was introduced as a man of faith, who trusted God. Jacob is introduced as a conniver who collaborates with his mother in deceit. They are unwilling to trust God to fulfill his promises.

Now Jacob's journey begins, in prudent flight from Esau's wrath (not in faith, like Abraham). It takes him to the home of his Uncle Laban in Paddan-aram and back home again. It is a journey not only of time and space, but within Jacob himself. Ultimately, his journey transforms him. In Abra-

---

[1]For observations on the literary world of Genesis 26—36, we are indebted to Michael Fishbane, *Text and Texture: Close Readings of Selected Biblical Texts* (New York: Schoeken, 1979), pp. 42–62.

ham and Jacob we have two patriarchal types, one whose faith is evident at the outset, the other for whom the journey to trust in God is a slow, agonizing process.

In his initial flight, Jacob has an encounter with the LORD at a place that he names Bethel (House of God). There the LORD gives him the promise made to his father and to Abraham. Jacob's response is to place a condition on his trust in the LORD (28:20).

In his years with Laban, Jacob is tested. First, the tables are turned on the deceiver, and the deceit ironically turns on the matter of birthright. Jacob has fallen in love with Laban's younger daughter Rachel ("ewe") but, after working seven years to earn the right to marry her, he is tricked by Laban into marrying the firstborn Leah ("cow"). The right of the elder daughter to marry first is the basis of a comeuppance for Jacob. But Jacob is not only clever, he is also persistent. He works another seven years to marry Rachel. Through hard work, and the clever use of magic, Jacob becomes wealthy at his father-in-law Laban's expense. And the promise of a "great nation" begins to seem realistic as eleven sons are born to Jacob.

Now the journey starts to be reversed. In a series of scenes that balance step-by-step the journey away from home, Jacob returns to Canaan. On the way, Rachel demonstrates her cunning by stealing her father's household gods, a symbol of family leadership.

The unresolved tension in the story is the conflict between Jacob and Esau. As Jacob prepares to meet his brother, hoping that he can win his favor through gifts, the climax in his inner journey is reached. He has another encounter with the divine, near a border, this time in a wrestling match near the Jabbok River (32:22–32). After an all-night struggle, the fight is a draw. Jacob receives the blessing he has demanded, but he is also given a new name, Israel, which means "he who strives with God" or "God strives," and a limp in his walk. These indicate that Jacob has changed. There are a number of levels of meaning in this story of Jacob's wrestling match, but in its present context it indicates that in an encounter with God (symbolized in the name Jacob gives to the place, *Peniel*, which means "face of God"), Jacob has undergone a transformation. He resolutely limps out to encounter his brother.

In a clever twist, when Jacob meets Esau, it is the "fool" Esau who takes the initiative in reconciling the hostility between the brothers. Esau's warm reception moves Jacob to recognize that "to see your face is like seeing the face of God" (33:10). He has not earned Esau's favor, yet Esau has accepted him with open arms. Apparently that causes Jacob to realize something about the God he has been attempting to manipulate and the nature of the relationship he should have with him. In another clever reversal, Jacob bows down before his brother.

After an interlude, the journey of Jacob continues (Genesis 34) with a return to Bethel, the site of his first encounter with the LORD. Now Jacob is a man of faith. He puts away all foreign gods and builds an altar. Here at Bethel the change in Jacob is reaffirmed as again he receives the name Israel. In the final scene of Jacob's journey, Jacob and Esau together bury their father, who has been lingering all these years on his deathbed, waiting for the conflict between his sons to be resolved.

The structure of the story of Jacob is that of a story within a story, what we might call an *envelope structure*. The story of Jacob's relationship with Esau is the frame, or envelope, for the story of his stay with his Uncle Laban. Despite the fact that the narrative is composed of a series of seemingly independent legends about Jacob, it has been woven together into a carefully crafted composite around the theme of the journey of Jacob. Jacob's journey balances Abraham's. Abraham's journey is that of a man of faith, whose faith is tested; Jacob's journey is of a man who comes to faith after finally seeing the face of God in his brother's compassion.

Joseph (Genesis 37—50). From a literary perspective, the Joseph narrative is much more integrated than the earlier patriarchal stories. Instead of individual incidents woven together, the story is a sustained tale with clear plot development. It has been called the first example in the Bible of a short story or novella. In the Joseph story the dominant promise theme moves into the background. The deity, who plays such a crucial role in the Abraham and Jacob stories, speaking from time to time, moves offstage. There are no indications of God's playing a direct role in the Joseph story. Nevertheless, a principal conclusion in the story is that the divine intention underlies the web of events in this drama of conflict among brothers.

We are introduced to Joseph as a spoiled, arrogant, and foolish seventeen-year-old. Favored by his father, he is naturally despised by his older brothers. And when he foolishly tells his brothers of his dream that they will serve him, they hate him all the more. Not surprisingly, when they have the chance, they plot to get rid of him, first deciding to kill him, then (at Judah's urging) making a profit from their crime by selling him into slavery.

Then follows an interlude involving Judah (chap. 38), in which Judah is tricked by his daughter-in-law Tamar into fulfilling the kinship responsibilities he has been neglecting. As in the Jacob story, this interlude interrupts the principal story just as the tension is heightening. Although unrelated to its setting, it plays a crucial role in foreshadowing later developments, as we shall see.

Once in Egypt, Joseph is tested. He is tempted by his master's wife and imprisoned unjustly, but throughout remains steadfast. Although the LORD is not directly involved in the story, the narrator points out that "the LORD was with him" (39:2, 23). Using his ability to interpret dreams, but attributing the power to the LORD, Joseph wins release from prison and quickly rises to power as a high official in Pharaoh's administration. The distance Joseph has come from his family is symbolized by his marrying an Egyptian wife and taking an Egyptian name.

Now the reversal begins. Joseph does not journey home (like Jacob); instead, his family journeys to him. Driven by famine, the brothers are forced to go to Egypt, paralleling the forcing of Joseph into Egypt. Like Joseph, they are tested by being unjustly accused and imprisoned. Unwittingly they fulfill the dream by bowing before Joseph but show they are unchanged by claiming to be "honest men." One brother (Simeon) is endangered, as Joseph had been, and apparently they are willing to leave him in prison. Now the tension is at its height. How can reconciliation occur when the brothers have not changed? Once again, they come to Egypt, and now Joseph places them in precisely the same situation they had been in with him years earlier. The fate of the youngest, favored brother (now Benjamin) is in their hands. They can leave him to die if they choose. But now Judah, who had contrived to sell Joseph and had learned his lesson from Tamar about fulfilling kinship responsibility, takes the initiative (as did Esau in the Jacob story). He asks to take Benjamin's place in prison. With this act of compassion, the way to resolution is opened, and the journey is completed as Jacob and his sons are reunited in Egypt, where they settle in the land of Goshen.

Genesis ends with the promise to Abraham renewed but not yet fulfilled. The descendants of Abraham are still few in number. They are now living outside the land promised to Abraham. In the journeys of Abraham, Jacob, and Joseph the narrative introduces several types of persons of faith. However, if the promises to the patriarchs are to be fulfilled, there will have to be a journey of the people.

The Historical World: The Patriarchs in History

Finding the Original Context. The narratives concerning the patriarchs Abraham, Isaac, Jacob, and Joseph seem more characteristic of ordinary human experience than those encountered in the Prehistory. The people who move through the stories are recognizably human, and they exhibit consistent character and at times even signs of growth, as the literary analysis has shown. Thus, readers might get the subjective impression that when we move into the patriarchal narratives, we come into the realm of history.

But subjective impressions, however strong, fall far short of historical demonstration. Is there any firm data showing that the patriarchal narratives are historical in nature?

Outside of the Bible itself, there is no direct evidence that the Israelite patriarchs existed. Some researchers profess to be able to connect the four kings of Genesis 14 with Bronze Age monarchs. Others believe that the recently discovered Ebla archives name the "cities of the plain" in the form and order known from the Abraham story in Genesis. But both of these

FIGURE 3–1

Political Situations in the Ancient Near East
Before the Exodus

Date (B.C.E.)	Egypt	Canaan (Palestine)	Mesopotamia
3200		Protourban culture (Jericho)	
2800	Old Kingdom (ca. 2900–2200)	Seminomadic invasions	Sumerian ascendancy (ca. 2800–2360)
2400	First Intermediate Period (ca. 2200–2100)		Empire of Akkad (ca. 2360–2180)
2000	Middle Kingdom (ca. 1950–1750)		Sumerian resurgence (ca. 2206–1950)
1800	Second Intermediate Period Hyksos rule (ca. 1700–1550)	Patriarchal Period (?)	Old Babylonian Dynasty (ca. 1830–1530) Hammurabi (ca. 1728–1686)
1600	New Kingdom (ca. 1550–1100) Hyksos expulsion (ca. 1550–1525) Thutmose III (1490–1435)	City states under Egyptian control	Hittite invasion and decline of Babylon
1400	Amarna Era (ca. 1400–1350)	Weakening of Egyptian authority; *Habiru* active	Old Assyrian Empire (ca. 1356–1197)

findings have been vigorously disputed by other scholars familiar with the data. Even if verified, neither of these propositions, among others that have been advanced, would confirm that a man named Abraham ever existed.

Archaeological data do seem to illuminate the patriarchal narratives, particularly in terms of marriage and inheritance customs. The storytellers of ancient Israel had no way of recovering or reconstructing forgotten customs of the past. That certain customs appear in the narratives suggests that they were contained within traditions handed down from an earlier period. This is illustrated by references to a type of surrogate motherhood known from archaeological discoveries. Both Sarah, the wife of Abraham, and Rachel and Leah, the two wives of Jacob, compensated for periods of personal infertility by giving their slaves to their husbands to bear children. This was important in a world where offspring constituted a person's retirement annuities. The Torah provided for young widows under the levirate law (Dt. 25:5–10) and permitted polygamy and concubinage. It had no provision for surrogate motherhood. Had it done so, there would have been no grounds for the Samson and Samuel birth stories (Jg. 13:1–25; 1 Sam. 1:1–28).

The importance of Rachel's theft of her father's household gods is similarly illuminated. The patriarchs are portrayed as de facto YHWHistic monotheists. The images *were* taken by a wife, not by the hero himself. The significance of the theft, beyond the opportunity for a bit of humor, is not clear in the Israelite story. Bronze Age Mesopotamian custom made possession of the family gods the sign of the firstborn, the next family head. Rachel was thus feathering her husband's, and her own, nest.

Much of our knowledge of family law in the Bronze Age comes from adoption papers. In a culture where family ties were paramount and land title was closely tied to family (and clan) membership, adoption was used by men without male heirs to provide for their old age security and for the continuity of family and property. Because real property was frequently not transferable outside the kinship circle, adoption was also used to secure loans with real property.

A comparison of this material with the Jacob stories, especially Genesis 29—31, shows many close parallels in the customs. It has even been suggested that Laban adopted Jacob before he had sons of his own. Jacob's departure, and Rachel's theft of the household gods, would then be connected with the birth and growth to maturity of Laban's natural sons, with a consequent decline in Jacob's family status (Gen. 31:1–2). Adoption is not a factor in the Abraham-Sarah-Hagar tale. But it is likely that customs we know from adoption contracts were a part of the general complex of family law and customs through many parts of Bronze Age culture.

The general location of the patriarchs in the environing culture is also consistent with what is known of Bronze Age society in Mesopotamia and the Levant. It was, as described earlier, a feudal and largely agrarian society. Documents from various times and places in that world contain references to a people who are called *habiru* or *'apiru*. The resemblance of these words to *Hebrew* is quite obvious. These habiru appear as outsiders ("men without a master"), persons who do not have a place in the feudal order. In times of disorder they appear as raiders and cohorts of rebels. The biblical word

Hebrew comes from a root meaning to "cross over," a likely term for people who came from someplace else and lacked a proper knowledge of and respect for boundaries. In this connection, down to the rise of the monarchy, the term *Hebrew* may not have been a compliment among the Israelites themselves (e.g., see 1 Sam. 13:3; 14:21, and Gen. 39:14). In the earlier biblical traditions, the Israelites do not use the term among themselves, but only to identify themselves to outsiders, as outsiders use it to designate them. They see themselves as "strangers and sojourners." They use land in Canaan, but they do not own it; Abraham has to buy the cave of Machpelah for a family burial place (Gen. 23:1–20). The Israelites do not consider intermarriage with the indigenous population of Canaan to be a good thing (Gen. 24:1–67; 26:34–35; 27:46—28:9).

The patriarchal narratives begin with a migration, but this does not mean the people were nomads. When the patriarchs moved, it was for a good reason.

Where in the Bronze Age did the Israelite patriarchs fit? Until recently there was a fairly strong consensus in favor of the middle Bronze Age (ca. 2150–1550 B.C.E.). This view is now being questioned with increasing frequency. Some scholars date the patriarchal period earlier. Some argue that the patriarchal stories did not originate until after 1000 B.C.E. and are not historical.

However, as we will see in the next chapter, there *is* compelling, if not incontrovertible, evidence for dating the Exodus from Egypt in the thirteenth century B.C.E. Any reconstruction of patriarchal history should therefore begin with the most firmly anchored event, and that is the Exodus. This makes the late Bronze Age the most likely chronological setting for the patriarchal period.

Patriarchal Religion. A careful reader of the patriarchal stories notices that alongside the typical names for the deity, YHWH (LORD) and Elohim (God), there are some other names: God Almighty (El Shaddai) in Gen. 17:1; 28:3; 35:11; and 48:3; God Most High (El Elyon) in Gen. 14:18–20; and God of Seeing (El Roi) in Gen. 16:13, for example. These names all include the divine name El with various epithets. Archaeological research has shown that *El* was the general Semitic name for the "father of the gods" (like Zeus in Greek mythology). El could be addressed by a variety of epithets, often reflecting different sanctuaries.

It may be that the different divine names mentioned reflect patriarchal contact with Canaanite religion. We know from later periods that Israelite writers adapted Canaanite mythology to speak of the LORD. That practice may have begun earlier. Or it may be that the patriarchs were polytheistic, and that the references to belief in and worship of one god are anachronistic. The revolutionary factor in patriarchal religion may have been not the worship of a single god but the close ties between the deity of the patriarchal clan and the patriarch. In a time when gods were thought of as localized beings, often dwelling in one temple, the patriarchs apparently believed in a deity who journeyed with them and was related to them not via a sanctuary but through a covenant.

Conclusion. Taking into account all we have observed, we can conclude that the patriarchal stories are authentic folk memories passed down from the Bronze Age, probably the late Bronze Age. The precise nature of these materials, whether accounts of actual exploits, tribal activities narrated under the name of eponymous heroes, etiological tales, or whatever, must be determined by the analysis of each story in question. Individual analysis is also needed to distinguish the accretions added as the stories were transmitted. It is certainly not unreasonable to assume both that some of the ancestors of Israel were remembered in some circles in Israel and that the memories of them were used to advance Israelites' understanding of the world around them.

SUMMARY

The Bible begins with a portrait of cosmic and human origins, as the backdrop for the story of the ancestors of the nation Israel. Genesis 1—11 constitutes a Prehistory to the story of Israel, which begins with the patriarchal narratives (Genesis 12—50). Genesis is part of the Torah, the first section of the Tanak or Pentateuch.

From a literary perspective, two creation accounts in Genesis 1—2 combine to give a balanced picture of the mystery of origins. Examined historically, these two accounts seem to be the product of different writers or schools. Study of their original context leads the reader to other ancient near Eastern accounts of origins, from which these stories seem to draw imagery even while they interpret the meaning of creation in unique ways.

We detected a recurrent literary pattern in Genesis 3—11. The human breaking of the divinely created order causes a tension between harmony and alienation. Historical study suggests that although some of the traditions in Genesis 3—11 have roots in history, their principal function is to set the stage for history.

Our literary analysis of Genesis 12—50 stressed the themes of promise and journey. A threefold divine promise of land, progeny, and blessing comes first to Abraham and Sarah, then to Isaac and Rebekah, Jacob and his wives, and Jacob's twelve sons. Each of these first ancestors of Israel pursues a journey, with both external and internal consequences. The weight of evidence in the search for the original historical context of the patriarchs seems to point to the Late Bronze Age (about 1500 B.C.E.). A careful reading of Genesis 12—50 reveals hints of the religion of the ancestors of ancient Israel, although the significance of these clues is far from clear.

Questions of origins are timeless, equally as fascinating to us as to those who first heard and read the stories of Genesis. We turn now to questions about the relationship between Genesis and contemporary discussions of origins.

THE CONTEMPORARY WORLD: QUESTIONS FOR DISCUSSION AND REFLECTION

1. Some people today claim that the creation accounts in Genesis were primitive prescientific attempts to explain the origin of the world. But because they are not identical with the accounts of modern astrophysics and biology, they should be dismissed. Others argue that modern scientific views (especially the biological notion of evolution) are mistaken unless they can be harmonized with a fairly literal understanding of the Genesis accounts, especially the six-day creation. The discussion in this book takes the historical position that modern science did not emerge until the seventeenth century C.E. Thus it would be unreasonable to expect the Genesis accounts to anticipate or reflect it. It is suggested that the Genesis accounts affirm the meaning of the created order (it is good; it represents the Creator's intention) and affirm certain states of affairs in it (humanity has a high and responsible status; marriage is good, etc.) rather than offering pseudoscientific explanations of it.

   Having read the Genesis creation accounts, can you conceive of any additional plausible functions or meanings for them beyond the options just noted? Discuss the various options. Which seem more viable, and why?

2. Is it important whether Adam and Eve, Noah, and the other characters in the Prehistory (Genesis 1—11) ever existed as historical persons? How does your conclusion affect the contemporary significance of the stories about them?

3. Read the interpretation of the story of Abraham's encounter with the LORD in Romans 4. Is this a legitimate use of Scripture? Are there other, equally legitimate, ways to use the story of Abraham's encounter with the LORD theologically?

4. The patriarchal promise states that not only will Abraham's descendants be blessed, but they will also be a source of blessing for all people. What implications does this have for the moral responsibility of persons who enjoy some special benefit, advantage, or privilege today?

5. The patriarchal stories make it clear that the patriarchs were not perfect people. Still, they served God's purposes in important ways. Do you see any contemporary significance in this insight?

6. Does the promise to the patriarchs in Genesis give the contemporary state of Israel a claim to the "promised land"?

CHAPTER 4

Covenant: Exodus, Leviticus, Numbers, and Deuteronomy

The Winston S. Churchill Memorial and Library in the United States.
Photograph by the senior author.

Reredos of the Church of St. Mary, the Virgin, Aldermanbury, Westminster College, Fulton, Missouri. The Ten Commandments are inscribed above the altar of this London parish church, rebuilt by the great architect Sir Christopher Wren in the seventeenth century and reconstructed according to Wren's design on the Westminster College campus. The commandments are on stylized tablets, and the reredos, in the style of Wren's woodcarver Grinling Gibbons, is modeled on the ark found in a Jewish synagogue. This shows the importance placed on the Decalogue not only in seventeenth-century English churches but also in Western culture.

INTRODUCTION

In the remaining four books of the Pentateuch, the theme of fulfillment of the patriarchal promise continues to dominate the narrative. At the beginning of Exodus, the first element of the threefold promise of progeny, land, and blessing is well on the way to fulfillment. With the deliverance of the people from bondage in Egypt and the subsequent wandering in the Sinai wilderness, attention turns to the second element—the promise of a land. With the covenant at Sinai, and especially with the speech of Moses in Deuteronomy, the theme of blessing is central. At the end of the Pentateuch, each of the promises is on the verge of fulfillment. Within the framework of the narrative there are several types of literature—legends, poems, legal codes, and speeches.

These books also raise a number of important historical questions such as, How did the Exodus take place and who was involved? When were the law codes included and when were these books actually written? Was Deuteronomy, or a portion of it, the lawbook found in the Jerusalem Temple in the seventh century B.C.E.? What is the literary history of this material? How does the law found in these books compare with similar legislation in other ancient cultures? These questions will concern us in our historical analysis.

LET MY PEOPLE GO (Exodus 1—18)

The Literary World: Pharaoh a God?

The narrative in Exodus 1—18 tells the story of the enslavement of Jacob's descendants in Egypt by a Pharaoh who "did not know Joseph" (1:8); the birth, early career, and commissioning of Moses by God, who reveals for the first time (to the characters in the story) the special name YHWH (The LORD); the confrontation of Moses and his brother Aaron with Pharaoh with the demand to "let my people go"; the ten plagues visited upon the recalcitrant Pharaoh and his people; and the miraculous deliverance of the fleeing Hebrews from Pharaoh at the Red Sea.

The story gives us an opportunity to observe the role of irony in a biblical tale, especially in the portrayal of Pharaoh, whose attempts to oppress the people of Israel and keep them from escaping are thwarted at every turn. Pharaoh lays heavy burdens on the people; they multiply all the more. He plots to kill the sons of the Hebrews, but he is outsmarted by Hebrew midwives. His own daughter adopts Moses, causing Pharoah to take to his bosom the very one who will cause his demise. Pharoah is victimized by the series of plagues that climaxes in an ironic reversal of his plot to kill the sons of the Hebrews. It is Egyptian children who die as a result of Pharaoh's treachery. Finally Pharaoh and his best warriors are humiliated by the motley collection of slaves. In the final reversal the oppressor himself is crushed.

When we remember that Pharaoh was accorded divine status in Egypt, the ironic portrayal takes on deeper significance. This is more than the humiliation of a human despot; it is the deflation of the claim of divinity for the Egyptian king. The real contest dramatized in Exodus 1—18 is between the LORD and a pretender to divine power. The narrative and the victory song (Exodus 15) leave no doubt who is the victor.

> Sing to the LORD, for he has triumphed gloriously;
> the horse and rider he has thrown into the sea! (15:21)

Mighty Pharaoh is powerless in comparison with the true divine warrior and king. With his heart hardened by the LORD, he is little more than a helpless pawn in the drama.

Irony in Exodus 1—18 is not confined to the portrayal of Pharaoh. Moses is not exempt. His first decisive act of leadership of his people—killing an Egyptian who is beating one of the Hebrews (2:11–12)—is immediately undercut by suspicion of his motives by other Hebrews. Their reaction foreshadows the recurrent motif in the Torah narrative of the people complaining to Moses about his leadership. Another example of irony is the strange incident that occurs as Moses returns to Egypt to carry out the LORD's commission. With no explanation, we are told, "At a lodging place on the way the LORD met him [Moses] and sought to kill him" (Ex. 4:24). Why would the LORD try to kill the one he has just chosen to lead his people from slavery? The irony of this incident serves to add a touch of mystery to the story. Just when it seems the LORD's ways are clear and intelligible, the narrative shocks us into realizing they are not.

These observations must serve as one of the few hints we will be able to provide of the rich irony pervading biblical literature. The general effect of irony is to enliven the literature with humor, surprise, and mystery.

The Historical World: The Exodus in History

Israelite folk memory recalled the Exodus and the manifestation of the LORD at Mount Sinai (Exodus 19—20 and following) as a single complex of events. Indeed, these events became the charter of Israel's national existence, and the reference point for understanding the meaning of her life and her relationship with God.

Some literary historians (notably G. von Rad) have argued that not all circles in Israel shared this full complex of traditions. When we examine the establishment of Israel in the land of Canaan in the next chapter, it will become clear why something of the sort might well be the case. At this stage we need only observe that the group that experienced the Exodus became the bearer of Israel's national traditions. These traditions became the common property of all those who came to think of themselves as Israelites, whether or not they had a real ancestor who had followed Moses in the wilderness. Thus, in rabbinic practice, converts to Judaism immersed themselves as a part of their ritual of induction, re-creating the experience of passing through the waters of the sea. Similarly, all the events surrounding American independence are the property of every American citizen, whether native or naturalized.

Looking beneath the recognizably stylized aspects of the narrative concerning the Exodus, a plausible sequence of events can be seen. Perhaps

---

FIGURE 4-1

Political Situations in the Ancient Near East During the Period of the Exodus and Occupation of Israel

Date (B.C.E.)	Egypt	Canaan (Palestine)	Mesopotamia
1300	New Kingdom continues; Egyptian Revival, Seti 1 (ca. 1305–1290)	(Israelite Exodus)	Assyrian dominance continues until ca. 1197
	Rameses II ca. 1290–1224 Battle of Kadesh with Hittites (ca. 1286)	(Wilderness wandering)	
	Merneptah (ca. 1224–1211) War with Sea Peoples (ca. 1220–1175)	Israelite occupation	
1200	Rameses III (ca. 1183–1152)	Invasion of Sea Peoples (Philistines and others)	Assyrian decline
	Egyptian decline	Period of the Judges (ca. 1200–1020)	Brief Assyrian revival (ca. 1116–1078)
1100		Philistine pressure on Israelite tribes Samuel	

abetted by natural misfortunes, a group of Hebrew slaves won manumission from their imperial master. Led by their advocate, Moses, a Hebrew with knowledge of Egyptian ways, they began their journey northeastward out of Egypt. But a contingent of Egyptian frontier guards, whether on orders of a central government that had changed its mind, or on their own initiative, pursued the escapees. A fortuitous thunderstorm prevented immediate capture. Then, at a crucial moment, the lightly shod Hebrews escaped through a body of water shallowed by the wind. The Egyptian chariots foolishly pursued for the kill, but the wind changed, the tidal flow shifted, and, in a moment of panic, the chariots turned into the resurgent flood.

All discussions of the Exodus are obliged to recognize that the topography of Suez-Sinai has been modified by the digging of the Suez Canal. Several candidates have been advanced as the possible location of the Exodus. One is Lake Timsah in the central Suez. Another is the nearby Great Bitter Lake, now incorporated like Timsah, in the Suez Canal. Another possibility is a "northern" route. The southern arm of Lake Menzaleh is one prominent northern candidate; Lake Sirbonis offers another. Other propos-

MAP 3 Possible routes of the Exodus

als have included the northernmost neck of the Gulf of Suez, where wind and tidal behavior (before dredging for the Suez Canal) permitted crossings. It is said that during his Egyptian campaign, Napoleon tried a crossing at Suez, only to barely escape the fate of Pharaoh's chariots when the wind and tide turned. The northern neck of the Gulf of Elath has also been proposed. However, this gulf is almost certainly too distant from Egypt.

If we could pinpoint the location of the sacred mountain, the location of the Exodus might be easier. But for the ancient Israelites, the mountain of God was movable. When Solomon built the Temple in Jerusalem, the holy mountain moved from the wilderness to Jerusalem. Israelite folk memory is vague on Mount Sinai's original location. Most interpreters are inclined to accept the traditional location in southern Sinai (for which there is no plausible pre-Christian evidence) or a more modest peak near Kadesh Barnea in north central Sinai.

We must admit that a consistent and plausible case can be made for the northern, the central, or the southern Exodus routes, and the biblical account of the stages of Israel's journey to the mountain of God squares with one of the two principal Sinai identifications. The popular view of modern biblical scholars that the name for the body of water that was crossed means in Hebrew "Sea of Reeds" supports the notion that a relatively shallow reed-grown lake or bay was involved. However, this language may be pressed too vigorously by scholars looking hard for evidence to support their reconstructions, for the term has been understood throughout history to mean Red Sea. Certainly, a shallow point in the sea is probable. The southern location on the Gulf of Suez (an arm of the Red Sea) may have the most historical probability.

There still seems to be a fairly strong consensus among knowledgeable historians as to the date of the Exodus, though it is not as widely held as it once was. It rests upon reasoning out the most probable conclusion from both biblical tradition and archaeology. Genesis 15:12–16 and 1 Kgs. 6:1 appear to presuppose an exodus in the fifteenth century B.C.E.; and Gen. 15:13 a lengthy enslavement in Egypt. But, upon careful reading, the Genesis passages are less clear. It is only with the rise of the Israelite monarchy that the chronological references in the Tanak can be correlated with the modern calendar to any degree of precision.

It was noted earlier that some scholars wish to put the Israelite descent into Egypt in the Hyksos period as the most likely time for an Asiatic, Joseph, to rise in the service of Pharaoh. However, foreigners were in important Egyptian governmental positions at other periods. Some would associate the Pharaoh who did not remember Joseph, and hence enslaved the Israelites (Ex. 1:8), with the expulsion of the Hyksos. Others associate the Exodus itself with the Hyksos expulsion.

But the Hyksos episode does not exhaust the sort of upheavals that could bring "new people" to the fore or dash down others in radical changes of government and policy in middle to late Bronze Age Egypt. Amenhotep IV (Akhnaton) of the dynasty XVIII, who lived from 1364 to 1346, presided over a great cultural revolution in Egypt (including an experiment in monotheistic religion) called the *Amarna Age*, after his new capital city. Discovery of the archives of the ruined palace at Tell el-Amarna have revealed a diplomatic correspondence from supposed vassal kings in Canaan. These *Amarna Letters* portray a region in turmoil. It was each against all, all against each, all after Egyptian foreign aid, and the Habiru on the prowl. Some have conjectured that the Israelite invasion under Joshua belongs at this time, but data do not support this view. A counterrevolution late in the reign of Akhnaton, or at the accession of the famed Tutankhamun, ended the Amarna experiment and achieved a temporary accommodation between old and new, while rebuilding the military and shoring up the empire. Tutankhamun was succeeded by his loyal vizier, the elderly Ay. A scheme to marry King Tut's young widow to a Hittite prince to solidify the dynasty and make peace with the northern empire failed. General Horemheb, who despised Tut and Ay, usurped the throne but failed to establish a dynasty. Then dynasty XIX under Seti I appeared. Many could rise and fall in such times.

The biblical narratives require a time for the Exodus when there were extensive building activities in the Nile delta, because that is where the Israelites were supposed to have been when the Exodus began. They also require that the Egyptian court be located nearby, because Moses and Aaron seemed to get back and forth handily between the Hebrew labor camps and Pharaoh's court. The early thirteenth century B.C.E. meets this requirement, because during the XIXth dynasty there was an infrastructure for imperial campaigns in Asia headquartered in the delta region. At the other end, the third ruler of dynasty XIX, Merneptah, claimed in a victory hymn to have inflicted grief on "Israel" during an Asiatic campaign. The inscription dates to about 1230 B.C.E., indicating that by this time somebody called Israel was on the loose in Canaan.

The biblical traditions say that Moses led the Exodus group in the wilderness for forty years, the conventional Hebrew figure for a generation. Then he yielded to Joshua, who led the second generation of the Exodus company across the Jordan River into the land of Canaan. Clear-cut destruction layers dating to the mid-to-late thirteenth century have been found at some of the towns said to have been captured by Joshua. Other sites not mentioned in the Joshua narrative suffered a similar fate at about the same time. The rebuilding of these sites tended to be cruder and more modest. New villages sprang up in previously unpopulated areas. This, along with distinct changes in pottery types, suggests that a different, culturally less sophisticated group was responsible for the destructions and for the new villages. Archaeological surveys of occupation patterns in the Transjordan seem to accord with a thirteenth-century date. According to the Book of Numbers, Moses and his band encountered armed resistance as they moved through the Transjordan on their way to Canaan. Although currently under scrutiny, archaeological surveys of this area seem to indicate that this type of opposition would have been more likely in the thirteenth century than one or two centuries earlier, because of relative population densities in the Transjordan.

Exodus 13:17 says that Moses did not lead the Israelites "by way of the land of the Philistines...for God said, 'Lest the people repent when they see war, and return to Egypt.' " That is, Moses avoided the more direct and heavily traveled coastal route to Canaan, for at the Egyptian end it would have been well supplied with checkpoints and fortifications, and further along (assuming a thirteenth-century date) there would have been the chance of encountering Egyptian-Hittite friction and the first ripples of the incursion of the Sea Peoples (including the Philistines).

These data constitute a strong if not compelling case for an early thirteenth-century B.C.E. date for the Exodus. Plausible hypotheses locating the Exodus a century or two earlier can be argued. But no alternative hypothesis can muster such a large body of converging and cumulative data in its favor.

YOU SHALL BE MY PEOPLE, AND I SHALL BE YOUR GOD (Exodus 19—50, Leviticus, Numbers)

The Literary World: Covenant and Law

The Sinai Covenant. The term *covenant* has already appeared in the biblical narrative with reference to God's promise to Noah and all flesh (Gen. 6:18; 9:9, 11–17), to Abraham (15:18; 17:2,4, 7–11, 13, 19, 21), and to the patriarchs in general (Ex. 2:24; 6:4–5). It has also been used to describe human, reciprocal relationships, in which both parties assume responsibilities (Gen. 21:27, 32; 26:28; 31:44). In the account of the agreement between the LORD and the people at Mount Sinai, a new meaning for *covenant* appears.

As the people camp near the holy mountain, Moses ascends and encounters the LORD. He is told to remind the people how the LORD delivered them from the Egyptians and brought them to this place, then to say "Now therefore, if you will obey my voice and keep my covenant, you shall be my own possession among all peoples; for all the earth is mine, and you shall be to me a kingdom of priests and a holy nation" (Ex. 19:5–6).

This is the heart of what became known as the *Sinai Covenant*. Unlike the earlier covenants, it is not an unconditional promise by God to the people. It is a conditional agreement, dependent on allegiance to the LORD and faithfulness to the covenant. The Sinai Covenant introduces the way to fulfillment of the third element of the patriarchal promise: blessing. Through obedience to this covenant, the descendants of Abraham will be blessed and through them others will be blessed. It should not be difficult to understand why observance of the stipulations of the Sinai Covenant became so central to the self-understanding of the nation Israel (and later, to Judaism). These commandments were considered Torah (the instruction or law delivered by God as the basis for the ordering of human life). They were thought to be the heart of the Books of Moses (the Pentateuch) and of the entire Tanak.

In the final form of the Pentateuch the stipulations of the covenant given through Moses at Mount Sinai continue (with one narrative interruption in which the covenant is broken and reaffirmed—Exodus 32—34) from Exodus 20 through the entire book of Leviticus and until Numbers 10. For a variety of reasons it is dubious that *all* this legislation was given to Moses at this time. Much of the law has the ring of later institutions and practices (such as extensive legislation concerning the priesthood and elaborate worship); it is probably grouped here for the sake of validating its authority.

Types of Laws.   To analyze the legislation from a literary point of view, let us first focus on the form of particular laws. There are two basic types of laws in the Sinai legislation. One is an unconditional command or prohibition (called absolute, or *apodictic law*). It is legislation. "You shall have no other gods before me" (Ex. 20:3) and "Honor your father and mother" (20:12) are examples. The other basic form is conditional law (called case, or *casuistic*). It is "common law." It includes an "if..." or "when..." (describing a situation) with the required or prohibited action. For example, "if you lend money to any of my people with you who is poor, you shall not be to him as a creditor, and you shall not exact interest from him" (Ex. 22:25).

The first type of law demarcates categories of actions to do or avoid in order to maintain the type of social order God desires. The second type identifies specific situations that can threaten social harmony, and it identifies what to do or not do in these situations in order to maintain or restore balance. Often the action mandated in conditional law is to "pay back" an injured party (see, for example, Ex. 22:14). If the reparation is the same as the action, the law is called a *talion*, stated, for example, in general terms in Ex. 21:23–24. Still another legal form is the curse (and its counterpart, the blessing), in which a general punishment (or state of well-being) is invoked for specific types of action.

The specific law is often elaborated when given, either to make it more specific or to provide a motive for obeying it. For example, after prohibiting "graven images" (Ex. 20:4), the law makes the prohibition more specific ("You shall not bow down to them or serve them"), then explains the motive ("For I the LORD your God am a jealous God..."). Frequently, the motive is based on assumptions about who God is and what he has done (e.g., Ex. 20:11). Other motives appeal to general principles of respect for human life and the minimal conditions of living.

Law Codes. Individual laws are combined in the Pentateuch as legal collections or codes with their own particular orientations. Grouped together in the Sinai setting, they are given equal authority as stipulations of the covenant, regardless of when they may have been composed.

Most basic is the *Decalogue (Ten Commandments)*, which appears first in Ex. 20:1–17. Its fundamental significance is underlined by its being placed first and by its subsequent repetition in Dt. 5:1–21. In these ten apodictic laws are found the essence of what it meant for ancient Israel to keep the covenant. The ten laws are divided into four that establish the parameters of the people's relationship with the LORD and six that set forth the boundaries of human relationships. Although seemingly negative ("Thou shalt not..."), they are actually "permissive." They establish the broad area within which Israel may find a harmonious life, establishing respect for the LORD and respect for human life, within and outside the family, as that framework.

The first appearance of the Decalogue is followed immediately by a collection of mostly casuistic laws, known as the *Covenant Code* or *Book of the Covenant* (Ex. 20:23–23:33). These laws seem to make more specific some of the Ten Commandments. Exodus 20:23–26, for example, specifies in what ways the LORD is to be worshiped if there are to be no graven images, and 21:15 and 17 indicate what should happen to those who do not respect their parents. The code establishes the rights of slaves (21:1–11); specifies how violence shall be controlled (21:12–32); states how property shall be respected (21:33—22:17); establishes a ritual calendar around a weekly sabbath, a sabbath year every seven, and three yearly festivals—Unleavened Bread in the spring (note that Passover is expressly not mentioned), First Fruits of the wheat harvest in the summer (the same as Pentecost or the Feast of Weeks), and Ingathering in the fall (the Feast of Booths) (23:10–19). This collection assumes a settled, agrarian style of life, which the Israelites did not begin until they entered the land of Canaan. And some of the laws (e.g., against nakedness at the altar) seem to be reactions against worship practices of the resident Canaanites.

After the Covenant Code is given, a ceremony is held to seal the covenant (24:1–18). The blood of a sacrificial animal is thrown by Moses on the altar and the people, and Moses reads the *Book of the Covenant* to them.

Another early code, usually called the *Ritual Decalogue*, is found in Ex. 32:10–26. Except for the Ritual Decalogue the next collection of laws continues, with one narrative interruption, from Exodus 25 until Numbers 10. Because of the dominant concern with matters of worship and the priesthood, this lengthy corpus has been called by interpreters the *Priestly Code*. However, to consider this long block of material a unity obscures the variety within it. For example, Leviticus 17—26 can be considered a separate collection of laws that revises much of the Covenant Code. Because of a basic concern with the "holiness" of the people (e.g., Lev. 19:2) Leviticus 17—26 is called the *Holiness Code*.

When Moses ascends the mountain again after the ratification ceremony, he receives an elaborate set of instructions on the building of an ark (container) for the tablets of the covenant. The Ark of the Covenant was also considered a symbolic throne for the LORD. In addition, an elaborate lampstand, an altar table, and a "tabernacle" to house them are mandated, with instruction for the priests who will conduct worship there. The priests will come from the family of Aaron. It stretches the most fertile imagination to see all of this happening in the Sinai Desert, and much of the description seems to be of the later Temple of Solomon in Jerusalem. Again, having this legislation (Exodus 25—31) in the Sinai setting gives it special authority.

The other major collection of law in the Tanak is delivered by Moses as part of his speech in Deuteronomy 12—26 and is called the *Deuteronomic Code*.

The Historical World: Law in the Ancient Near East

Common understanding concerning rules of behavior, notions of how to deal with rule breakers, and techniques for solving tensions caused by extreme forms of misbehavior (especially homicide, which can lead to acts of vengeance and feuds) are characteristic of almost all human social groups. Such systems have often been administered by family heads, tribal notables, a shaman or other cultic figure, or a special sort of arbitrator. Law in this simple sense is probably as old as living in communities. The formal codification of law and certainly the development of legal institutions and means for enforcing law and order accompany the emergence of social stratification and governmental organization.

Law codes are some of the earliest documents to survive from the ancient Near East. The code of the famous early Babylonian emperor, Hammurabi (1728–1686 B.C.E.), was the first to come to the attention of modern scholars and remains the best known. But it is predated by the Sumerian code of Ur-Nammu (ca. 2050), the code of King Bilalama of the city of Eshnunna (ca. 1920), and that of Lipit-Ishtar of Isin (ca. 1875?), all from Mesopotamia. These codes are compilations of laws and, hence, stand within a long process of development. Hammurabi's code reflects the background of a rigidly stratified society. The laws recognize degrees of social standing. The severity of the penalty for various transgressions (including medical malpractice!) increases with the status of the victims of the transgressions.

Not all legal documents were law codes. Contracts, including adoption contracts and slave acquisitions, have survived, as well as deeds and records of lawsuits. Various parts of the Tanak preserve a similar variety of legal documents and practices. Micah 6:1–8 reflects the literary form of a lawsuit. Job 31 is an oath of clearance of the sort a person would take to establish innocence before a court. Jeremiah 32:6–15 provides a great deal of information about property transfers and deeds. Ruth 4:7–12 portrays a transfer of the levirate marriage obligation (cf. Dt. 25:5–10).

Our literary analysis has shown that several major codes are embodied in the Torah, all of which seem to be compilations of material that grew up over a period of time. Actually, it is a bit misleading to speak of these compilations as *law codes*. They do contain what we today would regard as legal material. But they also contain religious rubrics, medical and public health protocols, rules for maintaining ritual purity (or resolving ritual pollution), obscure taboos (like the prohibition against weaving linsey-woolsey fabric [Dt. 22:11]), and many other items. Ancient law codes may not have been intended to be exhaustive bodies of law like the codes of modern states. Rather, they may have been handbooks for judges, giving them a variety of models on the basis of which they could deal with the more extensive range of issues that would ultimately come before them.

Law was administered in premonarchic Israel by tribal elders, village elders, or both, and by specialists whose particular skills or special charisma were widely recognized. The forensic activities of some of the judges and of the holy man Samuel are reminiscent of the anthropological description with which we began this section. As Israelite culture became more organized, important cultic centers and the gate courts of fortified towns and cities became the sitting places of sacerdotal and lay courts, respectively. Another legal judicial layer was created by the monarchy. But no royal decrees have survived, to our knowledge. Deuteronomy suggests a possible appellate court system with a high court in Jerusalem for the most difficult cases.

The monotheism of the Israelite Torah tradition and its inclusion of relatively rare (for that age) absolute law do not constitute its sole distinctions. Also notable is its persistent commitment to egalitarianism. This can be explained by its roots in the relatively egalitarian tribal culture of the premonarchic period. But all of Israel's great Torah compilations were "published" after the Israelites had developed a more stratified society and a state-level (monarchic) political organization. This aspect of the Torah tradition was not in the interests of the more prestigious circles in later Israelite society. Still, its survival and the persistence of prophetic condemnations of Torah infidelity point to the enduring influence of loyalty to the LORD's Torah in Israel's life.

A LOOK BACK, A LOOK AHEAD (Deuteronomy)

The Literary World:
The Farewell Address of Moses

Throughout history many great leaders have given farewell addresses in which they sum up what has happened during their term of service, give advice for the future, and symbolically pass the mantle of leadership to a successor. In its final literary form, the first thirty chapters of Deuteronomy are structured as the farewell speech of Moses to the people of Israel as they stand ready to cross over the Jordan River and enter the land of Canaan. This speech includes the three elements of historical review, advice for the future, and concern for succession. To the speech are added two poems (Deuteronomy 32—33) and a historical conclusion (Deuteronomy 31, 34), which links the entire Pentateuch to the subsequent narrative. The speech is divided by three separate introductions (1:1–5; 5:1; 29:1).

There are a number of theories concerning the literary structure behind the speech format. We will mention only two. It is possible to see most of Deuteronomy as a reflection and "updating" of much of the Book of Exodus:

Exodus	*Deuteronomy*
1—18 = Egypt to Sinai	1:1–4:43 = Sinai to Moab
19:1–20:21 = Covenant and Ten Commandments	4:44—5:22 = Covenant and Ten Commandments
20:22—23:33 = Book of the Covenant	12—26 = Deuteronomic Code
24 = Concluding Ceremony	27—28 = Concluding Ceremony

In addition, similarities have been noted between the structure of Deuteronomy and the form of a treaty between a dominant nation and its vassal states (called the *suzerainty treaty*) common in the ancient Near East from about 1500 through 700 B.C.E. In these treaties the suzerain (principal nation) agrees to protect the vassal, provided the conditions of the treaty are met. The treaties generally included the following elements:

1. Preamble identifying the suzerain and vassals
2. Historical prologue noting the suzerain's protection of the vassal
3. General principles
4. Detailed obligations imposed on the vassal
5. Directions as to the deposit of the treaty and future public reading
6. Lists of witnesses (gods)

7. Curses that would result from disobedience and blessings that would accrue if the treaty obligations were followed.

Deuteronomy can be interpreted as an adaptation of this form to the covenant between the LORD (the suzerain) and Israel (the vassal).

1. Preamble and historical prologue (Dt. 1—4).
2. General principles (Dt. 5—11).
3. Detailed obligations (Dt. 12—26).
4. Curses and blessings (Dt. 27—30).
5. Provision for deposit and public reading (Dt. 31—34).

Because the LORD is the only God, according to Deuteronomy, there can be no other divine witnesses, so that element is not present.

The language of Deuteronomy is markedly different from any we have so far encountered. It has the ceremonial style encountered today in many sermons and political speeches. The sentences are more involved than those to which we have grown accustomed. Formulas (such as "Hear, O Israel...") are repeated, and a few central points are emphasized again and again. Deuteronomy seems to be framed in the splendid rhetorical prose of Judah's professional scribes of the eighth to seventh centuries B.C.E.

The Historical World: The Lawbook in the Temple

According to 2 Kings 22, in the eighteenth year of King Josiah of Judah (621 B.C.E.), Hilkiah, the chief priest, found the "book of the law" in the Temple during repairs and gave it to the royal secretary. When the king heard what this scroll said, he was distraught. If this was indeed the Torah, the express teaching of God, both he and his people were potentially in a great deal of trouble. Neither they nor their immediate ancestors had observed its teachings. Its authenticity had to be ascertained at once. A very high level delegation was dispatched to consult the person who must have been the most highly regarded prophetic figure in the realm, Huldah, the prophetess. Much of the news was bad. She informed the royal commission that the scroll was indeed authentic, and Judah was doomed for transgressing its teaching. The doom was mitigated on Josiah's behalf. Because of his piety, the doom would strike only after his death.

Josiah's response was decisive. Perhaps in an effort to head off the threatened doom of his people, his own death notwithstanding, he launched an extensive and radical religious reformation. The local sacrificial shrines throughout Israel were closed, and prominent ones like the royal shrine at Bethel were deliberately and grossly desecrated. All sacrificial worship was centralized in the Jerusalem Temple, from which every trace of pagan religious influence was expunged.

Since the early nineteenth century, biblical scholars have argued whether the "book of the law" found in the Temple was the Book of Deuteronomy or a portion of it. The reasons, still considered compelling by most interpreters, are that the major interests of Deuteronomy (centralization of worship, the removal of pagan elements from the temple, and the incorporation of the provincial priesthood in the central shrine) were the key elements in Josiah's reform. Indeed, the remark of 2 Kgs. 23:9, that the provincial priests did not repair to Jerusalem, is one of those offhand asides that catches the historian's notice. They were, according to Deuteronomy 18:6–7, expected.

That something like Josiah's reform was in fact executed is now witnessed by archaeology. For example, excavations at Arad in Judah have shown that during the time of Josiah a wall was constructed through the middle of the nave of the Solomonic shrine at Arad, rendering any sort of worship there impossible (the altar had been closed earlier by Hezekiah). This accords with the biblical tradition that Manasseh repealed many of his father Hezekiah's reforms, setting the stage for his grandson Josiah's more radical actions.

Josiah was a Davidic zealot like his greatgrandfather, Hezekiah, dedicated to restoring the independent Davidic kingdom from Dan to Beersheba. It is not surprising that both these kings were religious reformers as well. Political and religious revitalization movements frequently go hand in hand. It is equally unsurprising that the Deuteronomic reform foundered after Josiah's death. A pro-Egyptian cabal gained sway in the Jerusalem court, creating an atmosphere hostile to revitalization and independence.

SUMMARY

The books of the Torah after Genesis (Exodus, Leviticus, Numbers, and Deuteronomy) form a narrative of the deliverance (exodus) of the heirs of the patriarchal promise from slavery in Egypt, their wandering in the wilderness of Sinai, and the making of a covenant with the LORD. The narrative includes much law concerning how the people of the covenant are to conduct themselves and climaxes in a long farewell address by their leader, Moses.

In Chapter 4 we highlighted the role of the literary device of irony in Exodus 1—18, the literary shape of the Sinai covenant and the laws of the Pentateuch, and the structure of Deuteronomy. We also advanced hypotheses on some of the principal historical issues arising from the narrative: the nature and date of the exodus from Egypt, the ancient near Eastern context for the laws of the Pentateuch, and the relationship between the Book of

Deuteronomy and a "book of the law" reputedly found in the Temple of Jerusalem in 621 B.C.E.

Exodus and Covenant are not only constituitive themes in the Bible. They have also played important roles in the self-understanding of Jewish and Christian people through the centuries. The following questions will focus discussion and reflection on the continuing impact of these and other themes from this section of the Tanak.

THE CONTEMPORARY WORLD:
QUESTIONS FOR DISCUSSION AND REFLECTION

1. Many American leaders from the period of the American Revolution to modern times have described America as a "New Israel," the "people of God." Like ancient Israel, the new American "Israel" has a divinely given mission in the world, according to this view. How has this attitude affected the policies of the United States? What have been the positive and negative impacts of this attitude? Is this a legitimate use of the Bible?

2. Some contemporary interpreters of the Bible feel that the LORD's act of deliverance of ancient Israel from slavery in Egypt shows that God is on the side of the oppressed people of the world today. Is this a legitimate use of the Bible?

3. What impact have the Ten Commandments (and other legislation in the Tanak) had on American society? Has the impact been positive or negative? What is the present impact of biblical law on American society?

4. Although ancient Israelite law codes reflect practical legislation and judicial application rather than general principles of law, certain broad principles can be seen to underlie them (such as the principle of liability, which holds that persons are responsible for the consequences of their actions, even when unintended). What other general principles do you think may be derived from biblical law? How do they compare with principles of modern law?

5. The Code of Deuteronomy (Deuteronomy 12—26) is usually considered a humanitarian law code. It established a limited welfare state that benefited aliens as well as citizens, limited royal prerogatives, and extended greater protection to women. Survey the code and see what evidence you can find for and against this humanitarianism.

6. How does the historical observation that the "miracles" described in Exodus (such as the splitting of the sea) may have natural explanations affect their contemporary significance?

CHAPTER 5

The Nation Israel: Joshua, Judges, First and Second Samuel, First and Second Kings (The Former Prophets)

Courtesy of the British Museum

The Siege of Lachish (701 B.C.E.). The Assyrian emperor Sennacherib was quite proud of his capture of the great Judean citadel of Lachish during his war against King Hezekiah (2 Kgs. 18:13—19:27). A stone relief depicting the battle and its aftermath in collapsed spatiotemporal perspective surrounded the throne room of his palace in Nineveh. The visage of the emperor on the relief was defaced, apparently during the coup in which he was assassinated and the palace was burned.

INTRODUCTION

The Pentateuch ends with the promise to the patriarchs unfulfilled. The descendants of Abraham have become numerous, but they are a wandering band, not a great nation. The people have been blessed by the LORD, who has delivered them from Egyptian slavery and entered into a covenant relationship with them, but their name is not yet great, nor have they become a source of blessing for other nations. And, at the end of the Pentateuch, they are still at the border of the promised land. It is not yet theirs.

The next section of the Tanak, the Former Prophets, continues the narrative that began in Genesis 12, telling the story of the people of Israel from their entry into the land promised to the patriarchs to their exile from that land.

The books of the Former Prophets hold to the position that obedience to the LORD leads to blessing and disobedience leads to disaster for the nation and for individuals. Because this point of view is presented so forcefully and so clearly in Deuteronomy, many modern interpreters feel that the Former Prophets and Deuteronomy form what they call the *Deuteronomistic History*. That is, the history of this period was edited by a school or editor who took a deuteronomic perspective on events. Although this theory has come under criticism, it is still the dominant one among literary historians who study this material.

We cannot attempt a thorough analysis of the literary and historical worlds of the Former Prophets. Rather, we will present overviews, then focus on particular literary units as examples of the whole and on specific historical questions such as, How did the tribes of Israel occupy the land of Canaan? How did Israel develop from a group of tribes to a state-level society? What was the "empire" of David and Solomon like? How and why did the United Kingdom divide? How and why did Israel (the Northern Kingdom) and Judah (the Southern Kingdom) fall victim to outside aggression?

THE OCCUPATION OF CANAAN (Joshua and Judges)

The Literary World:
Balance in Joshua 1—12 and Judges 1—2

The Books of Joshua and Judges tell an overlapping and sometimes conflicting story of the occupation of the land of Canaan by the tribes descended from the sons of Jacob, and of the situation that followed among the tribes. Our emphasis in this section will be to show how these two books balance one another. What may seem to a modern reader to be contradictions between Joshua and Judges may instead reflect complementary narrative

MAP 4 Traditional locations of the tribes of Israel

patterning of history, a technique we have already observed in Genesis 1—2 (see chap. 3).

In the Book of Joshua all Israel, led by Joshua in strict obedience to the LORD, conquers the entire land of Canaan (Joshua 1—12). Then the land is distributed among the tribes, in accord with the assignments made by Moses in Numbers (Joshua 13—21), and the men of the tribes who had settled in the Transjordan leave the army and go home (Joshua 22). Joshua, like Moses before him, gives a farewell address in which he reiterates the warning that success for the people depends on allegiance to the LORD and His command-ments (Joshua 23). Finally, Joshua gathers all the tribes together at Shechem for a covenant renewal ceremony (Joshua 24). According to the Book of Joshua, the occupation of the land of Canaan is the story of an obedient people led by a faithful leader.

Although the Book of Judges begins with the harmonizing note "After the death of Joshua..." (1:1), it is soon obvious that 1:1—2:5 is another account of some of the same events covered in Joshua, but from a much different perspective. In 2:7, Joshua is still alive, so 1:1 must on internal grounds be considered an editorial attempt to link Judges with Joshua. Whereas Joshua 1—12 portrays "all Israel" rumbling through the whole land like Sherman's army through Georgia, the first two chapters of Judges speak of individual tribes (focusing on Judah in the south and Joseph in the north) taking different areas and having great difficulty dislodging the inhabitants. In fact, the account lists those areas not conquered alongside the cities taken. In some cases the very same city that Joshua identifies as having been conquered by "all Israel" is linked to a tribe or clan in Judges (e.g., Hebron in Jos. 10:36–37 and Jg. 1:9–10).

These conflicting accounts create a historical problem to which we will soon turn: How *did* the tribes occupy the land? However, from a literary point of view, the two contrasting accounts function much like the two creation accounts in Genesis. Just as the first creation account describes creation as the carefully orchestrated carrying out of the divine plan, Joshua is an account of the occupation of the land as God intended. And just as this account of a perfect creation is balanced by the more haphazard, spontaneous version of the second account, Joshua's version of the occupation is balanced by the more chaotic version of Judges. Joshua 1—12 is a carefully orchestrated description of the taking of the land just as God intended; Jg. 1:1—2:5 is a less idealized, less ordered account. As the conclusion to the Judges account suggests, it was the disobedience of the people that led to a chaotic situation (Jg. 2:2), just as it was the rebellion in Eden that was ultimately responsible for the disruption of the created order.

The Historical World:
How Did the Israelites Occupy Canaan?

Three major hypotheses have been posited by modern biblical historians to account for the Israelite occupation of Canaan. The great American archaeologist W.F. Albright and his followers offered a sort of *blitzkrieg* model that followed the schematic history of the book of Joshua and was supported by some archaeological evidence. The great German scholar, Albrecht Alt, developed a *peaceful infiltration* hypothesis that accords more closely with the narrative in Judges and that also comports with a substantial amount of archaeological evidence. Another prominent American scholar, George Mendenhall, first tentatively proposed a *peasant revolt* hypothesis, though in the context of a more elaborate view. Another American, Norman K. Gottwald, developed straight out the notion that Israel originated in a revolt of Canaanite peasants against their aristocratic Canaanite overlords. There is little direct literary evidence for this hypothesis, and some archaeological data seems to tell against it.

We take the position that the origin of Israel as portrayed in the biblical traditions was an involved historical process and therefore unlikely to be explained by a single simple model. Our approach to the question of the Israelite occupation of Canaan is to work out a synthesis of the complex biblical traditions, then to test this picture with the "control" provided by archaeological evidence.

Beneath the stylized, "all-Israel" account in Joshua there is an indication that more than a ritualistic blitzkrieg was involved. The inhabitants of Gibeon tricked Joshua into a treaty of amity (Joshua 9), and no fighting is recorded in the neighborhood of Shechem, where Joshua conducted his great covenant renewal ceremony (Jos. 8:30–35; cf. Joshua 24). In the ceremony itself, "sojourner" as well as "homeborn" Israelites are mentioned (8:33, 35). The Book of Joshua also recognizes that not all possible territory was conquered (13:1–7; 23:4–6). Judges notes that others besides Joshua (e.g., Caleb in the south) were involved as leaders. Judges 1:19—2:5 lists unconquered Canaanite centers. In the rest of the Book of Judges the struggles described with the Canaanites are on a tribal level, though some "judges" led coalitions of tribes. Judges 1:16 records the settlement of Moses' in-laws the Kenites (Midianites) among the Judeans, and 4:11, 17 and 5:24 locate one Kenite family much further north. But not all the information is in the Former Prophets. Numbers 14:39–45 describes an abortive assault on Canaan from the south, set in the lifetime of Moses. Exodus 12:38 mentions a "mixed multitude" that accompanied the Exodus group out of Egypt. These data from the biblical text itself, more examples of *narrative honesty*, make it clear that a facile reading of the text does not do it justice.

We begin our hypothesis by proposing that the Exodus group must have been relatively modest in size. Exodus 1:15 assumes that two midwives could see after the women's needs at the time of Moses' birth. The population could hardly have skyrocketed in the subsequent generations, particularly as one was spent on migrating. This band probably included elements of the Joseph tribes (eventually split into Ephraim and Manasseh), the tribe of Levi, and possibly others. But it also had acquired additional adherents (a mixed multitude) who were not biological descendants of Jacob-Israel.

The Exodus group, led by Joshua, entered the lands west of the Jordan near Jericho in the middle of the thirteenth century B.C.E. They brought with them the traditions of the Exodus and the Sinai Covenant. They met a varied reception as they migrated toward the central highlands. Some settled on unoccupied marginal land. In some instances they were obliged to fight indigenous people. In others, local inhabitants entered into treaty relationships with them. In yet other instances, they seemed to move in peacefully among the indigenous population, as at Shechem (Jos. 8:30–35). In the process, additional peoples became parties to the Sinai Covenant. Some might have been members of the traditional twelve tribes who had not sojourned into Egypt but had remained in Canaan. Some might have otherwise claimed kinship (see Gen. 25:1–6) or some sort of special relationship from the past (as suggested by the various treaties and covenants made by the patriarchs). Others were previously unrelated Canaanite groups (Gibeon in Jos. 9:3–27) or *habiru* (the sojourners of Jos. 8:33, 25?), making common cause with a group that seemed to be on a roll. All adopted fidelity to the LORD as patron of their covenant relationship, whatever their previous allegiance may have been.

The activities of Joshua and other leaders during the thirteenth and twelfth centuries gave the expanding group of YHWHistic tribes a firm footing in the land of Canaan, but Canaan was hardly yet Israel. As the book of Judges shows, the Israelites were at times dominated by the Canaanites. At times they were independent. *But never did they decisively dominate the Canaanites.* We should recognize in reading these accounts that *no judge was a national leader.* Most led a single tribe or a coalition of neighboring tribes. The song of Deborah (Jg. 5:14–17) condemns some nearby tribes as slackers while praising those who supported Deborah and Barak; but more distant tribes, including the great southern tribe of Judah, are not even mentioned.

The indigenous population continued to control most of the great walled cities, which meant that they also controlled most of the lowlands constituting the agricultural hinterland of these cities. Although Jg. 1:8 claims a Judean conquest of Jerusalem, the city was still a Jebusite stronghold when David captured it. The Israelites were settled mostly in the hills and mountains (or in the semiarid Judean Negev), lands suited to subsistence farming, vine culture, and the husbandry of ruminants but not to the extensive feudal agricultural practices of the Canaanite city-states. The situation could hardly be described as one of symbiosis, but it was one that permitted peaceful coexistence. Friction probably arose when some Canaanite ruler (or Midianite raider) looked at the Israelites in their unfortified villages with their tribal form of social organization as sheep to be sheared. Except in these circumstances neither the Israelites nor the Canaanites particularly needed or wanted what the other had. The Israelites were strong enough, when properly aroused and led, to convince greedy neighbors that the return on taxing or raiding them was not worth the cost. The Canaanite armies were suited to fighting one another or, in conjunction with the forces of an imperial overlord (Egypt), against other empires (the Hittites). They were not designed to hunt guerrillas in the hills. This balance persisted until about 1100 B.C.E., when burgeoning Philistine power upset the balance once and for all (see pp. 99–100).

How does this account, framed so far on the basis of literary evidence, square with archaeological data? We noted in Chapter 4 that some sites in traditional Israelite territory seem to have been violently destroyed in the mid-to-late thirteenth century B.C.E., the most congenial time for the Exodus-Wilderness-Occupation series of events. These sites, and others vacant since the early Bronze Age, were occupied by people who utilized both a different pottery tradition and a different architectural tradition, a cruder one than their predecessors in both instances. The Book of Joshua says that Hazor was the only city that stood on a mound that Joshua burned (i.e., the only major fortress city), though lesser fortified towns are claimed for his bag. The excavation of Hazor has revealed evidence of a massive destruction in the thirteenth century. The Book of Joshua also says Joshua took Lachish (10:31–32). The thirteenth century Canaanite city of Lachish had no wall, as recent excavations have shown.

Jericho remains the most celebrated of Joshua's victories. But from the standpoint of archaeological evidence, Jericho is one of the most problematic sites for reconstruction of the first stages of the Israelite occupation. There is no evidence that the city was occupied during the thirteenth century.

Less dramatic than war, burning, and destruction, but certainly at least as important for our historical understanding, is archaeological evidence that a substantial part of the Israelite settlement was a peaceful infiltration into vacant land rather than an armed invasion. Both in the hill country and in the Judean Negev, a substantial portion of the "new people," as identified by their pottery and architecture, settled on land that had for some time been unoccupied.

Finally, how does our reconstruction fit with anthropological observations? The Book of Judges concludes with the observation, "In those days there was no king in Israel; every man did what was right in his own eyes" (21:25). The Israelites are pictured as living in villages, with a tribal social organization and no major intertribal institutions. The most that one might expect is some sort of tribal league, although it would have been a very loose one, based on claims of kinship and common loyalty to the LORD. Such an association usually functions only when there is a common interest at stake, and only to that extent. This is what one sees in the Book of Judges. Such an association does not function very efficiently. These observations are illustrated in Judges 19—21, the story of the sin of Gibeah.

Also typical of a tribal culture is charismatic leadership, persons "anointed" with natural leadership gifts. The judges are nothing if not charismatic leaders. This type of leadership functions most effectively when people are galvanized by the coincidence of a crisis and a leader. However, no one fades more quickly than a charismatic leader who cannot maintain success.

The military behavior of the Israelites is also consistent with what we would expect from anthropological models. The fighting force was essentially the able-bodied men mustered by families and clans. Such an army cannot maintain itself long in the field and lacks the equipment to conduct sustained operations. The judges usually went for a quick and decisive action, often involving surprise or ambush.

Tribal society is also generally egalitarian. There is no elaborate or rigid status system. Many of the most fundamental traditions of the Israelite Torah were laid down in this period, and they are reflected in the law codes and oracles of the later prophets. Much of the ideological tension in later Israelite society would grow out of conflict between the egalitarian tradition of its formative tribal culture, hallowed in the Sinai Covenant teachings, and the pretensions of the higher orders generated by the emergence of a more complex, stratified society. Archaeology joins literature in giving evidence of this tension. Monumental architecture appeared in Israel with the monarchy, but residential housing remained basically egalitarian down to the ninth or eighth centuries B.C.E.

FROM TRIBES TO STATE (Judges, Samuel)

The Literary World:
A Cycle of Legends about Heroes

After its version of the occupation of Israel (1:1—2:5), most of the rest of Judges (2:6—16:31) is a collection of legends about heroes among the tribes who demonstrated their leadership by delivering people from oppression at times of crisis. We would call them *charismatic heroes*. But it is the stereotypical phrase that connects the legends that gave them their "title." Typically, after telling of the exploit, the text says that the hero "judged Israel——years." So they are called *judges*, although, except for Deborah, none seemed to exercise a judicial or administrative function. A few judges are simply named, without being identified with any act of deliverance (10:1–5; 12:8–15), giving rise to the label *minor judges* to distinguish them from the more prominent *major judges*, and to fanciful theories about their role among the tribes. The remainder of the Book of Judges is not about judges at all, but instead relates incidents explaining why the tribe of Dan migrated from south to north and why a punishment was inflicted on the tribe of Benjamin in a tribal civil war (Judges 17—21).

As an example of one of the legends about the charismatic heroes called judges, let us analyze the story of Ehud in Jg. 3:12–30. Ehud was a member of the tribe of Benjamin (which means literally "son of the right"), whose warriors were renowned for their military prowess. Ehud was left-handed. He arose as a hero at a time of oppression at the hands of the nation Moab, just across the Dead Sea from Benjaminite territory. Under the obese King Eglon (a term suggesting the Hebrew word for calf), Moab had taken Jericho and had stationed an occupying army of at least 10,000[1] men in Israel. Ehud was to deliver Israel by "killing the fatted calf" and leading a massacre of the Moabite occupation force as they tried to flee for home after hearing about the death of their leader. The story of how Ehud accomplished all this is full of sarcasm and lowbrow humor directed against Eglon and the Moabites, which would have undoubtedly delighted an Israelite audience listening to it.

The clever Ehud prepares for his dastardly act by making a small two-edged sword, which he puts on his right thigh under his cloak, aware that a quick motion with his left hand toward his right side would not alarm his unsuspecting victim. Ehud is careful not to arouse suspicion. He goes to Eglon to deliver tribute and starts for home. All alone, without any Israelite soldiers, he turns around at the stones near Gilgal (symbol of Israel's claim by divine right to the land, see Jos. 4:20) and goes back with a "secret message" for the king. Because the Hebrew word for *message* also means *thing*, there is a clever double entendre. The gullible king falls for the trick and sends his attendants away. There may be sexual nuances intended in the expression "came to" the king, for this is an idiom frequently used to indicate sexual contact. This may explain why Eglon so foolishly and excitedly sends his attendants away and why they are so reluctant to disturb him. Eglon is so eager for his "secret message" that he either misses or ignores the insult Ehud pays him by addressing him as "King" rather than with the address protocol would indicate—"My lord."

Alone in Eglon's private roof chamber, Ehud repeats the play on message-thing, this time identifying the source as God. Out of reverence for the one from whom the message comes, or out of excitement, the fat king stands up to receive it. In a flash Ehud delivers the message-thing, and the king's rolls of fat close over the sword. In his death throes the king's anal

[1]Or, "ten brigades," or "ten musters."

sphincter muscle relaxes and the "dirt came out." The scatological humor climaxes as Ehud makes his escape while the king's attendants, seeing the locked door and probably smelling the odor, decided the king is relieving himself and should not be disturbed.

In the subsequent battle the Moabites are portrayed as mirroring their king. They too are fools, for they rush toward home through the fords of the Jordan that provide the Israelites excellent opportunities for ambush. In a sarcastic play on words, the story says that the 10,000 Moabites killed were all "strong, able-bodied men." In Hebrew the word *strong* also means *fat*. The fat Moabites were subdued (literally, "laid low"), just like their corpulent king.[2]

Although the other legends of the judges are not so raucous in their humor, they are nonetheless all popular folktales about memorable people: Deborah ("Honey Bee") and Barak ("Lightning") in Judges 4—5, Gideon (Judges 6—8), Jephthah (Judges 11—12), and Samson (Judges 13—16).

All of these stories are woven together as a cycle, with a clearly stated theme introducing them (2:11—3:6). The theme is a pattern that is repeated in the stories.

1. The people turned from the LORD and served other gods.
2. The LORD became angry and allowed them to be oppressed.
3. The LORD raised up judges to deliver them.
4. When the judge died the people turned again to evil, and the cycle began again.

This pattern is illustrated in the otherwise vague story of Othniel (3:7–11), then used as a framework for the other tales. We have already observed a cyclical pattern in the shaping of legends, as in the Prehistory of Genesis 1—11.

First Samuel begins with the story of another hero who is associated with judging: Samuel (1 Samuel 1—12). Samuel's judging, however, seems to involve administration of justice (7:13–20), and he is not portrayed as a war hero like most of the judges in Judges. Samuel is a transitional figure between the loosely organized situation of Judges and the emergence of Israel as a state under a king. However, he too is a charismatic hero who plays a role in the deliverance of the people from a threat.

The next focal character, Saul, is also a charismatic hero and a transitional figure. He is a Benjaminite who emerges, like the judges, as a deliverer at a time of oppression. As a result, he is named king by the people (1 Sam. 11:1–15). However, this story is balanced against other traditions concerning

[2]Based on Robert Alter, *The Art of Biblical Narrative* (New York: Basic Books, 1981), pp. 37–41.

Saul's rise to power that suggest a certain ambiguity in Israel's remembrance of him. In one of these, Samuel anoints Saul not as king, but as "prince" (1 Sam. 9:1—10:16). Another pictures a reluctant Saul being chosen king by lots (1 Sam. 10:17–27). These accounts reflect a balanced attitude toward kingship. Just who wanted a king and why is obscured in these accounts of the first king of Israel, and that is presumably a purposeful clouding of the issue. The narrative portrays Saul in tragic terms. He is rejected by God for a seemingly minor sin (1 Sam. 13:7–15). He is quickly overshadowed and driven to depression by the more charismatic David. He is called "king" but without the support or administration to govern effectively. He was a victim of his times.

The Historical World

The equilibrium between Israel and her Canaanite neighbors was upset by the activities of the Philistines, who appeared in Canaan during the twelfth century B.C.E. or perhaps earlier. They were part of the "Sea Peoples" from the Aegean region. Although defeated by the Egyptians when they attempted to enter the Nile Delta, the Philistines became rulers of the "Philistine plain," probably with Egyptian sanction. They also ruled Bethshan, which controlled traffic around the southern end of the Sea of Galilee into the Jezreel valley.

The Philistines rapidly assimilated the culture of Canaan, probably because they were not very numerous. They were a warrior aristocracy, replacing the previous Canaanite warrior aristocracy. Their serfs probably could not tell the difference, but their neighbors soon could. Although they did not *introduce* iron to the Near East, they did have an advanced metals technology that allowed them to make superior weapons. The Philistines also had a more adaptive political system than the Canaanite city-states, organizing themselves under a national council, "the Lords of the Philistines." And they made astute use of heavy infantry, well-armed and protected foot soldiers who, in man-to-man combat, were invincible.

All this was bad for the Israelites. Concentrated as they were in the less productive hill country, they were relatively out of reach of the chariot-based armies of the principal Canaanite cities. But the Philistine infantry could march anyplace an Israelite could walk, and the Israelite citizen-soldier was neither trained nor equipped to confront such formidable adversaries. The Philistines probably did not want to take the Israelites' lands, but only to milk them for tribute and tolls. The Samson tales (Judges 13—16) show Israel's low estate. Poor Samson had no success trying to raise an army against the Philistines; the fearful Judahites even bound him and turned him over to the enemy. The Philistines were the probable cause of the migration of Dan northward (Judges 18). Even the Holy Ark of the Covenant could not give the Israelites victory over the Philistines (1 Samuel 4). First Samuel 7 credits Samuel with great success against the Philistines. He could win a guerrilla assault, but he could not drive them home. When Saul became king there was a Philistine garrison and custom station at Geba, in the heart of the Benjaminite hill country (1 Sam. 13:3).

Anthropologists observe that states tend to rise when an area becomes *circumscribed* or impacted. This can happen in two ways. Either the population grows to the point that the habitable environment is pressed to the limits of its carrying capacity, or social developments have the effect of closing people in.[3] At the time the Israelites arrived in Canaan, the indigenous population was organized into city-states, with no good reason to try to incorporate the Israelites. There was plenty of land in the hill country and the Negev for the Israelites to practice subsistence agriculture; they had no need for a state-level organization. However, the more aggressive Philistines did attempt to annex Israelite holdings, and they had the means to do it. Thus Philistine activity created *social circumscription*. The choice for the Israelites was: Submit or organize to resist. The latter required more than the guerrilla warfare of the Israelite tribal militias; a trained standing army was needed to fight the Philistines.

To raise a standing army requires a reorganization of society, with the emergence of social stratification, the warrior class on top, in league with bureaucrats and priests who organize the social system. That is, it requires a system of centralized control. States emerge in stages. That is what happened in Israel. In anthropological terms, Saul's kingdom appears to have been more like a *chiefdom*, an intermediate development, than a state-level monarchy. Abner, his uncle, was the only cabinet minister, and the ministry of war was the only government department. There is no evidence that Saul was able to institute a tax system. He depended on tribute not collected by force (1 Sam. 10:27) and expropriated Canaanite property (1 Sam. 22:7). If the fortress-palace excavated at the site of ancient Gibeah was in fact Saul's, its limited size accords with the literary data. Nevertheless, Saul took the essential first step on the road to statehood and created the catalyst for further advance. He recruited a standing army, organized into three battalions. Despite his inner turmoil, Saul carried on his duties, as he understood them, with fortitude. He secured the central heartland of Benjamin and Ephraim against Philistine exploitation and brought the great southern tribe of Judah more fully into a total Israelite structure than it had ever been before. Overextended in the field, he fell before the Philistines at Mount Gilboa (1 Samuel 31). But his achievements survived his death and the demise of his kingdom-chiefdom. They were part of his legacy to David, a fact that should not be overshadowed by David's rather more monumental accomplishments.

[3]Robert Carneiro, "A Theory of the Rise of the State," *Science,* 169, 1970, pp. 733–38.

FROM STATE TO EMPIRE: THE UNITED KINGDOM
(Second Samuel, First Kings 1—11)

The Literary World: David and Solomon

The Book of Second Samuel focuses on the rule of David, first as king of the southern half of the territory of Israel (1—4), then as king over the United Kingdom of Judah and Israel (5—24). The narrative weaves together a record of the achievements of David and a behind-the-scenes look at the intrigue of his court, particularly in chapters 9—20.

First Kings begins with the death of David and the ascendancy of Solomon (1 Kings 1—2). It then portrays the reign of Solomon, renowned for his wisdom (1 Kings 3); his administration (1 Kings 4); his building projects, including the Temple (1 Kings 5—9); and his wealth and success in trade (1 Kings 10), but with a fatal flaw (1 Kings 11).

One section of this narrative (2 Samuel 9—20; 1 Kings 1—2) is often considered a single literary unit because of its unity of style and theme. It is called the *Succession Narrative* (SN) (because the underlying question is "Who will succeed David as king?") or simply the *Court History of David*. Whether or not it was ever a single literary unit, it is one of the most polished sections of the Tanak's narrative and well worth our careful attention.

The narrative begins against the background of 2 Samuel 7, the promise of the LORD to David, delivered by the prophet Nathan that, "your house and your kingdom shall be made sure for ever before me; your throne shall be established for ever" (7:16). In broader perspective, this *Davidic Covenant*, based on the unconditional promise of the LORD that there will always be a Davidic king, introduces a new tension. With the patriarchal promises of people, land, and blessing having been at least partially realized, the promise to David replaces them as the "goal" toward which the biblical narrative is moving. It is a concern of both the Hebrew Bible and the New Testament, and it is a recurrent interest in the literature that arose after the Tanak but before the New Testament. How will the promise of a Davidic king be kept, especially after the destruction of Jerusalem and the exile of the house of David? The full scope of this promise leads to the hope for a messiah (anointed one) who will arise from the line of David as a new king and restore Israel to Davidic glory. More immediately, the promise raises the question of how the Davidic dynasty will begin. Which of the sons of David will inaugurate his father's everlasting kingdom?

The Succession Narrative itself opens in chapter 9 with a scene highlighting the ambiguity of David's character. David takes into his home Meribbaal,[4] the crippled son of Jonathan, the only remaining heir of

---

[4]This was probably his real name. It means "Baal is my lord" (cf. the genealogy of 1 Chr. 8:34). Hostility toward Canaanite Baal worship is reflected by the change of the name from Meribbaal to Mephibosheth ("he who [spreads] shame" in 2 Samuel (4:4; 9:1–13, *et passim*).

Jonathan's father, King Saul. The motives are obviously mixed. David's compassion for his friend's son may be genuine, but so is his desire to keep tabs on the only survivor of a rival dynasty.

The stage is then set for the most famous incident of the SN—David's affair with the beautiful Bathsheba. We see from this story that the most important events in the court of the king are not always the most public. At the level of public affairs, this is a time of war against a neighboring nation, Ammon. A description of the war (10; 12:26–31) serves as the frame for the private events that overshadow the public in their long-term significance.

The scene opens innocently enough. Confined to Jerusalem while his commander Joab leads the war against the Ammonites, a restless king is strolling on the roof of the palace. His eye catches a beautiful woman, whom he does not know, bathing on a nearby roof. The narrative then moves quickly, as though the events flow together spontaneously. When David learns that the woman is Bathsheba, wife of one of his mercenaries, Uriah the Hittite, who is fighting in the war, David acts. He orders Bathsheba brought to him, they go to bed, and she becomes pregnant. The deed has the marks of a spontaneous act of passion. It could have ended there. But the act has consequences that begin the unraveling of David's rule. Whether out of concern for Bathsheba, fear of blackmail, or both, David now acts to cover up the sin. He brings Uriah home from the front and instructs him to go home, obviously so that he will have intercourse with Bathsheba and cover up the king's act. Ironically, Uriah, a foreigner, shows himself more faithful to the law of the LORD, than David, whom the LORD has chosen to be king. Uriah refuses to violate the taboo against intercourse by soldiers consecrated for war (see 1 Sam. 21:4–5), and he refuses to sleep in his own bed while his comrades are sleeping in the field. Even when David gets him drunk, Uriah's integrity does not waver!

Now the tragic consequences of David's violation of the Torah begin to play themselves out. Greater sin follows upon lesser. In desperation, David orders Joab, his commander, to place Uriah in the hardest of the fighting, where he will surely be killed. Joab enthusiastically obeys, sacrificing elite troops to accomplish the murder of Uriah. When the news of Uriah's death reaches him, David says "the sword devours now one and now another..." (2 Sam. 11:25), as though Uriah's death were mere chance. It is difficult to imagine a more cynical statement.

The cover-up is complete when David marries Bathsheba. A son is born, and that seems the end of it. It appears that a king can use his great power any way he pleases, even in violation of the law he has sworn to protect. But this is not the end. We are told that the LORD sent the prophet Nathan to David. Interestingly, David's compassion and sense of justice are used to condemn him. When told a parable of a rich man who arrogantly takes a poor man's only ewe lamb, David renders judgment without hesitation. He deserves to die! He *shall* pay! David has unwittingly determined his own fate. *"You* are that man," says Nathan. With hindsight on the tragedies that were to befall David and his family, the narrative offers a theological explanation. It is David's sin that is at the root of the tragic events that now unfold.

As a result of his sin, David's first son by Bathsheba dies. The last scene in this story is the obverse of the first. A once proud and cynical king is now a humbled mourner, lying on the ground helpless beside his dying son. Yet David is not broken. When the boy dies he ends his fast and returns to the palace to resume his responsibilities. He bears the burden of his guilt, but he is able to lay it to rest and continue on. The last word is that even out of tragedies such as this, good can come. A second son is born, Solomon, successor to David, who brings the nation Israel to the pinnacle of its glory.

The remainder of the SN weaves a tangled web of intrigue, passion, and power plays. Solomon slips into the background as the tragedy of David's kingship unfolds in a series of devastating blows. David's son Amnon mirrors the sin of his father, raping his half-sister Tamar. When an indecisive David refuses to respond, Tamar's brother Absalom takes vengeance himself, killing Amnon. This sparks hostility, which leads to a rebellion by Absalom, the flight of David, and, ultimately, the death of Absalom at the hands of Joab. The cry of David when he learns of his son's death is a tragic reversal of his cynical response to the death of Uriah. Now he feels the pain deeply, crying "O my son Absalom, my son, my son Absalom! Would I had died instead of you, O Absalom, my son, my son!" (2 Sam. 18:33).

Finally, Solomon reenters the drama. With a cold political acumen that is in tension with his earlier moral earnestness, Nathan manipulates Solomon's rise to power. Neither king nor prophet can claim total righteousness! Given the right circumstances, anyone can fall victim to arrogance and deceit. A now feeble and impotent David, ironically warmed by a young virgin whose status does not change while she serves the king, confused by the wiles of Nathan in collaboration with Bathsheba, fulfills an oath he had never made to name Solomon his successor. His final words to his successor are an ironic combination of advice to follow the law of Moses and requests for ruthless retribution against Joab and others. To the end David is fully human—vain, sensitive, manipulative, arrogant, forgiving, humble, repenting.

In contrast with earlier narratives, the SN portrays a diminished public role for the deity. Never does the LORD directly intercede with miracles or with direct revelation to principal characters. Here the LORD speaks only through the parables of prophets and acts indirectly or not at all. Only two asides in the story suggest divine involvement (2 Sam. 12:24–25 and 17:14).

In this sense the story is a *secular tale*. The complex flow of events is a result of human decision and actions. There is an observable skein of causes and effects that are set in motion by David's affair with Bathsheba. Humans are clearly free to decide, but they are also held accountable for their actions by a moral law of cause and effect not unlike the law of karma in Indian philosophy. For David, Amnon, Absalom, Joab, and others, violence begets violence. Although the role of the LORD is muted, this is not to say the deity has been written out altogether. The narrative reflects a more subtle view of divine involvement. In a way not comprehensible to human minds, through events calculated by human arrogance to thwart the divine law, the plan of the LORD for the blessing of his people is at work nonetheless. At the end, the promise to David is intact. It is the LORD who has the last word. These points, of course, are not made abstractly. That is not the style of the Hebrew narrative. Yet for the careful reader, they are there to discern.

The Historical World

There is more literary evidence in the Bible for the reigns of David and Solomon than for virtually any other period of biblical history. Therefore, a historical analysis of this period is essentially a review of the history of the United Kingdom in Samuel and Kings, supplemented by additional material from the two Books of Chronicles and observations from archaeological and anthropological research. Following the death of Saul, a combination of appropriate circumstances and Davidic military and political skill made Israel a power to be reckoned with, not a pawn in the games of empires. The achievements of David were consolidated under Solomon, so that this period was the "glory age" for Israel as a nation-state, even a mini-empire.

David. Son of a notable Judean family, David appeared in Saul's court as a talented young soldier with great popular appeal who became commander of the royal bodyguard, closest friend of crown prince Jonathan, and son-in-law of the king through his daughter Michal. David was to some degree the victim of his own success. Whether or not Saul ever heard of the stories that Samuel had anointed David in boyhood to be king, replacing him, he began to suspect that David had designs on his crown. Worse yet, Jonathan seemed quite content to see it happen, and Michal connived to save David from her father's hand.

The narrative, with an obvious pro-Davidic slant, portrays David as loyal to a fault but finally obliged to flee for his life. After a brief refuge in Philistia, where he feigned madness to save his life, David became a fugitive in the hills of his native Judah. Some of his own kinsmen and an assorted company of fugitives and malcontents rallied to his standard and constituted the nucleus of the legendary "Mighty Men," the professional heavy infantry that proved the instrument of David's triumphs.

Saul perceived David with an armed company as an even greater threat to security than before and came after him with his professional army. David eluded pursuit and, according to the traditions, eschewed several golden opportunities to kill Saul. Meanwhile, he used his outlaw band to defend his Judean kinsmen from the Philistines and other assorted enemies.

David at length withdrew into Philistine territory to escape Saul's tenacious pursuit and took his troops into the service of Achish, king of Gath, who in return gave David the border town of Ziklag as his personal hold. David used the opportunity to play a double game. He exterminated Judah's enemies on his raids and told Achish he was raiding against Judah.

The news of Saul's death led David to bestir himself from his Philistine exile. Each step reflected his native political genius. He had exercised great care all along to ingratiate himself with his Judean kinsmen by defending them against predatory incursions, by sharing the booty of his own raids with Judah's elders, and by sparing them the embarrassment of choosing between Saul and him. Except for his appearance at the Aphek muster (1 Sam. 28:1–2; 29:1–11), he had carefully avoided assuming the role of an active rebel and visibly eschewed regicide. When an Amalekite adventurer appeared to claim credit for Saul's death, David dealt him an assassin's proper desserts. With similar effect, David congratulated the men of Jabesh Gilead for rescuing Saul's desecrated corpse from the walls of Bethshan. A total cynic could attribute David's actions to opportunism. But he was a complex person with complex motives.

Prompted by a favorable oracle, David marched his 600 professional warriors from Ziklag up to Hebron, the principal town of Judah (Israel, as yet, had no proper cities). The elders of Judah, not surprisingly, acclaimed him king over their tribe. The stage was now set for internecine conflict. David's long-range intention to be king over all Israel was by this time obvious to most observers. The upshot was a dynastic war between the house of Saul and the house of David, with the balance turning in David's favor. Joab's murder of Saul's commander Abner and Saul's son Ishbaal's murder by two of his own henchmen threatened to derail David's plans. But he absolved himself in a way that actually advanced his interests (2 Sam. 3:6—4:12). In due course, the elders of the northern Israelite tribes showed up in Hebron to acclaim David and anoint him king over the rest of Saul's former dominions.

David acted quickly to solidify his kingdom. Hebron was too far south and too closely identified with Judah to be a proper capital for all Israel. Nor was a northern location wise. Instead he seized the formidable Jebusite stronghold of Jerusalem, astride the watershed highway between Judah and Benjamin and a neutral site in relation to tribal rivalries.

Since the Battle of Gilboa, seven years earlier, the Philistines had been strangely silent. But David's capture of Jerusalem jarred them into action. They sent a force against Jerusalem, but David escaped. Assuming that he was still in Jerusalem, they twice laid siege to the city, permitting David on both occasions to hit them from an unexpected quarter. He pressed his second pursuit into Philistia itself and exacted a toll that probably insured his ultimate victory.

David made a generous peace with Philistia. Their territory was limited to the lands surrounding their pentapolis on the southern coastal plain, but they retained their own governments under treaty alliances with David. He also proceeded to recruit mercenary battalions for his own army from among the recently defeated Philistines.

The lowland city-states and their rich farmlands and orchards, whether ruled by native Canaanites or by Philistines, fell into David's lap with the defeat of Philistia. Under David, the land of Canaan finally became the land of Israel. He completed the conquest begun by Joshua. No one in the west was disposed to challenge his Mighty Men, the professional heavy infantry battalion, or perhaps by this time battalions, that had brought down the proud might of Philistia. To the northwest, in Phoenicia, Hiram of Tyre entered friendly and mutually beneficial treaty relationships with David.

Things were not, however, so tranquil east of the Jordan valley. Warfare somehow erupted between Israel and Moab. Moabite provocation can be suspected because David uncharacteristically inflicted a vicious atrocity on the defeated enemy, executing two-thirds of his prisoners. With the Moabite war David stumbled onto the slippery path of empire, subjecting the territory of another people. In the process, he reaped a harvest of suspicion among the other peoples of Transjordan, leading to wars against Ammon, Aramea (Syria), and Edom, and to additional conquests.

Under David the religion of the LORD became a state religion, centered in the royal capital of Jerusalem. As noted, anthropologists have shown that national religious institutions develop only when a state-level organization that both needs and supports them has arisen. It was not until the time of David that such a situation was obtained in Israel. David was a modest monarch. He did not saddle his kingdom with the costs of ambitious building projects. His standing army was not very large, centering around the relatively inexpensive heavy infantry. His strategic approach did not require large fortified cities. The royal bureaucracy, though larger than Saul's, still lay within very limited bounds. The flow of war booty through the first half of his reign would have spared Israel and Judah the burden of heavy taxation. Still, unlike Saul, David was capable of extracting taxes when they were needed and perhaps of conscripting the militia with unrivaled thoroughness. He put conquered peoples to forced labor, but it is not clear whether he instituted forced labor for his own people, as Solomon later did.

In spite of the relatively light burden that David's administration constituted, the later years of his reign were troubled by revolutions led by his own sons. The narrative attributes this unrest to the sin of David. Historians must look for proximate causes. Tribal rivalries from the past persisted. The northern tribes never embraced the Davidic dynasty the way Judah did. Absalom's campaign to gain popular support suggests that David's administration, able in war, was inept in peace. Finally, Jerusalem and the former Canaanite enclaves were the personal holdings of the conquering monarch. Monarchy had come into being in Israel as a response to the Philistine menace. It might seem a dispensable luxury in a stabilized situation.

Solomon. Tradition remembers Solomon for two things, his wisdom and the building of the Jerusalem Temple. The wisdom for which Solomon was remembered was the ancient counterpart of a university education in Business and Public Administration. Royal bureaucrats in the ancient Near East were schooled in such wisdom. Indeed, Solomon gave Israel a modern executive organization, including reorganization of the kingdom into tax districts that cut across traditional tribal boundaries and were capable of raising the revenue and the forced labor to support a splendid royal superstructure. On the second item, Solomon spent twice as long constructing his own palace as he did the LORD's house, though the subsequent importance of the Temple defies estimate. Solomon did not stop with the Jerusalem building projects: the palace, the Temple (his court chapel), an armory, and others. Modern archaeology has revealed impressive Solomonic fortifications and splendid administrative structures, including palaces for the local governors and extensive storage magazines, at such important centers as Hazor, Megiddo, and Gezer. Small frontier outposts like Arad, overlooking the marches to Edom, received proportional attention. Where comparison with earlier, modest Davidic installations are possible, as at Megiddo, the contrast is tremendous.

Militarily, Solomon opted for a more traditional imperial establishment than the small, highly mobile professional field army of David. This required an extensive system of fixed fortifications, a large chariot force based in the lowland fortress cities, and an infantry. All this was costly to sustain.

Solomon also launched a state-owned trading enterprise, which took advantage of Israel's strategic location on the main overland arteries between Africa and Asia. He entered into a merchant marine venture with Hiram of Tyre, which seemed to concentrate on luxury trade. Whether successful or not, Solomon's policies were undoubtedly costly. Despite tribute from foreign territories, Israel itself was obliged to support the imperial establishment with taxes, including forced labor. Some Canaanite inhabitants were reduced to permanent slavery.

On the one hand, Solomon's reign was a time of peace and prosperity, a golden era for those in a position to enjoy it. Only one large-scale military operation is recorded (2 Chr. 8:3–4). The story of the visit of the Queen of Sheba suggests an international reputation for wisdom and splendor. However, there were signs of trouble. Outside Israel Solomon seemed unable to maintain David's control of empire. Further, the rise of the aggressive Sheshonk to power in Egypt spelled trouble. After Solomon's death Sheshonk took advantage of the revolt led by his former guest, Jeroboam, and mounted a campaign that ravaged the land.

Internally, important factions were seriously disaffected before the end of Solomon's long reign. Tribal rivalries were worsened by Solomon's apparent policy of giving his native Judah a tax advantage. The heavy burden of taxation and forced labor alienated the elders and people of the northern tribes. Solomon's taste for splendor miffed the Levitical priesthood (Dt. 17:14–20), and both they and the emergent prophetic party (see chap. 6) were disenchanted with Solomon's practice of making diplomatic marriages and then permitting his foreign brides to practice their religions in Jerusalem. The king was suspected of not only condoning but also participating in the abominable practices. Surely Solomon in all his wisdom could not have realized how his actions were robbing his court of two of its most important sources of support! The prophets had helped create the monarchy and exalt the house of David. The zealously YHWHistic Levitical priests had been David's instrument for unifying his kingdom through propagation of a royal cult. Had Solomon left an heir as astute as he himself was supposed to be, the situation might have been salvaged. But such was not to be the case.

FROM EMPIRE TO EXILE: THE DIVIDED KINGDOM
(First Kings 12—22, Second Kings)

The Literary World:
The Patterning of History in Kings

The Books of Kings might best be called a historical overview of the period from the end of the reign of David in 961 B.C.E. through the destruction of the Southern Kingdom of Judah in 587 B.C.E., with a brief postscript concerning the release of the exiled King Jehoiachin from prison in Babylon some years later.

The narrative assumes that readers have access to the chronicles on which this sketch of history is based, such as the Book of Acts of Solomon (1 Kgs. 11:41), the Book of the Chronicles of the Kings of Israel (1 Kgs. 14:19), and the Book of the Chronicles of the Kings of Judah (1 Kgs. 14:29). The purpose is not a detailed account of events but a survey that reveals the pattern evident in the story of this period and highlights crucial moments.

Because the aforementioned sources are now lost, historians are frustrated by the lack of data about the kings who followed Solomon. From a literary point of view, the schematic presentation gives us a fairly clear view of the patterning of history.

One important internal indication of the patterning in Kings is the repeated use of a formula that summarizes and assesses the reigns of the kings. It first appears in 1 Kgs. 11:41–43, applied to Solomon. The formula includes a reference to another historical source, a statement about the length of the subject's reign, and the naming of his successor. This is preceded by an identification of the "fatal flaw" in Solomon's reign, which was the cause of the rupture of the United Kingdom, according to the narrative. Solomon forsook the LORD and worshipped other gods. He failed to obey the LORD "as David his father did" (1 Kgs. 11:31–40).

Each subsequent king of the Southern Kingdom (Judah) and the Northern Kingdom (Israel) also receives a report card followed by a summarizing formula. Jeroboam, the first king of the north after the split, had been promised "a sure house (dynasty), as I built for David" if he was obedient to the LORD, but he too fell victim to idolatry and "unlike David" was not faithful to the covenant (1 Kgs. 14:7–11). Because of the sins of Jeroboam, the promise of a dynasty is invalid and the Northern Kingdom will eventually be destroyed, the narrative announces (14:15–16). Under Rehoboam, Solomon's successor in Judah, idolatry continued, we are told. A note about royal and Temple treasures that Rehoboam handed over to Pharaoh Sheshonk of Egypt to spare Jerusalem is juxtaposed, suggesting again the outcome when the people are not obedient to the LORD.

Every king of the north is given a negative assessment, generally with the note that he followed in the sins of Jeroboam. Most kings of Judah are chastised, like Solomon and Rehoboam, with comments to the effect that "his heart was not true to the LORD his god, as the heart of David his father." Only two southern kings, Hezekiah (2 Kgs. 18:3–7) and Josiah (2 Kgs. 22:2), are given high marks. Both, we should note, championed reforms aimed at removing idolatry from the Temple in Jerusalem and keeping the commandments of the LORD. Their positive evaluation is stated in terms of their walking in the way of David. Other kings of the south—Asa, Jehoash, Azariah, and Jotham—are given qualified approval. They did what was right except they did not remove the high places (shrines outside Jerusalem).

The twin concern in the narrative's evaluation of kings is restriction of worship outside Jerusalem and obedience to the "statutes and commandments of the LORD." Because these same concerns are so dominant in Deuteronomy, this is often taken as evidence of a "deuteronomic" historian's hand. However, as there is no such identification in the text, this theory goes beyond strict literary analysis and is the proper concern of literary history.

FIGURE 5-1

Political Situations in the Ancient Near East During the Period of the Monarchy in Israel

Date (B.C.E.)	Egypt	Israel		Mesopotamia/Syria
1000	Weakness continues	United Kingdom (ca. 1020–922) Samuel Saul (ca. 1021–1000) David (ca. 1000–961) Solomon (ca. 961–922)		Assyrian decline continues in Mesopotamia
		Southern Kingdom (Judah)	**Northern Kingdom** (Israel)	Assyrian resurgence begins (ca. 935)
900	Revival (935–725)	Rehoboam (922–915)	Jeroboam I (922–901)	
	Sheshonk I (ca. 935–914)	Abijah (915–913)	Baasha (900–877)	Benhadad I (Syria) (ca. 880–842)
	Invasion of Judah (ca. 918)	Asa (913–873)	Omri (876–869)	Battle of Qarqar (853)
		Jehoshaphat (873–849)	Ahab 869–850)	Hazael (Syria) (ca. 842–806)
	Decline			
		Joash (837–800)	Jehu (842–815)	Shalmaneser III (Assyria) receives
800		Amaziah (800–783)	Jehoahaz (815–801)	tribute from Jehu (841)
		Uzziah-Azariah (783–742)	Jehoash (801–786)	Assyrian Decline
			Jeroboam II (786–746)	(800–750)
750				Assyrian Expansion begins (ca. 750)
		Jotham (742–735)	Menahem (745–738)	
		Ahaz (735–715)	Hoshea (732–724)	Syro-Israelite alliance (735) Syria falls to Assyria (732)

FIGURE 5–1 *(cont.)*

Political Situations in the Ancient Near East During the Period of the Monarchy in Israel

	Samaria falls to Assyria (722)	
		Assyrian kings: Tiglath-pileser III (745–727) Shalmaneser V (727–722)
	Hezekiah (715–687)	Sargon II (722–705) Sennacherib (704–681)
700 Thebes falls to Assyria (663)	Lachish falls (701) Manasseh (687–642)	Invades Judah (701)
	Josiah (640–609)	Rise of Neo-Babylonian Empire begins (ca. 627)
	Jehoiakim (609–598)	Fall of Assyria (610)
	Jehoiachin (598–597) First deportation (597) Zedekiah (597–587) Fall of Jerusalem (587) Second deportation (587)	Battle of Carchemish (605) Nebuchadnezzar of Babylon (605–562)

Another indication of the patterning of history in Kings is the role of prophets. We have already witnessed the crucial part played by the prophet Nathan in the story of David. In the sections of Solomon and Jeroboam, another prophet—Ahijah—figures prominently (1 Kgs. 11:29–39; 14:1–16), first announcing judgment on Solomon for his sins, then on Jeroboam for his. Another prophet is mentioned in passing in a similar role—Jehu (1 Kgs. 16:1–7). Then the overview of the reigns of the kings is interrupted by an extended narrative on the prophet Elijah (1 Kgs. 16:29—19:21; 21), who was active in Israel. The king at the time, Ahab, becomes the secondary character in the story. In the chapter not concerned with Elijah, another unnamed prophet dominates the action (1 Kings 20).

In First Kings 22 the prophet Micaiah is the focus of a fascinating story. The basic plot is a conflict among a true prophet who says one thing, false prophets who say something else, and a king who ignores the advice of the true prophet and pays the price.

After the Micaiah interlude, Elijah reappears and is succeeded by Elisha (2 Kings 1—2; 4—13), with overviews of the kings interspersed. Also in Second Kings, the role of the prophet Isaiah of Jerusalem is highlighted (2 Kings 19). So crucial are the prophets to the narrative that, beginning with Ahijah's announcement of the division of Israel and Judah (1 Kgs. 12:15), every significant act of destruction in the narrative is foretold by a prophet before it occurs, creating a pattern of prophecy and fulfillment. In this way all disasters, including the greatest—the Babylonian Exile—are linked to covenantal disobedience, with the people warned by the LORD via prophets of the consequences of their actions. The Word of the LORD is the implicit source of the pattern the narrative is relating.[5]

The ending of Kings gives us still another indication of the patterning of history. Both Israel and Judah have been conquered by foreign nations. The Temple has been destroyed. For failure to be obedient to the law of the LORD, a terrible price has been paid. Yet the narrative does not end without a glimmer of hope. The postscript says that the Davidic king has been freed from prison and is being treated well in Babylonian exile. The promise to the house of David is in jeopardy but not lost.

The patriarchal promise is in similar straits. By the end of Kings, many of the people are separated from the land. Israel-Judah is no longer a great nation, and the people are not blessed by the LORD. The reason, the narrative wants us to understand, is clearly discernible. Moses warned that disobedience would lead to destruction and exile, to curse rather than to blessing. It did. Yet there is still hope. The promise to the Davidic house is still alive. And the Sinai Covenant has not been invalidated.

The Historical World

The institution of kingship was only a century old when Solomon died. Some living adults could remember a time before Solomon's efficient redistributive system began its exactions. Empires ordinarily solve their economic problems by forcing the provinces to pay for their mistakes. The empire had begun to creak even in Solomon's lifetime, and a substantial proportion of his revenues had had to be raised from domestic sources. But Israel was not

---

[5]Leonard L. Thompson, *Introducing Biblical Literature: A More Fantastic Country* (Englewood Cliffs, N.J.: Prentice-Hall, 1978), pp. 124–27.

a wealthy nation to begin with. Production cannot be intensified beyond a certain point, no matter how efficient the tax system.

Solomon's death about 922 B.C.E. found Jerusalem, a personal hold of the royal house, and Judah, the royal tribe, ready to acknowledge the dynastic principle. They accepted the middle-aged crown prince, Rehoboam, as king. But Rehoboam still had to be confirmed by an assembly of tribal elders at Shechem before he could be recognized as king of all Israel. Jeroboam, son of Nebat, who had heard of Solomon's death while in exile in Egypt, showed up at the Shechem meeting armed with the prior warrant of prophetic support. Rehoboam was confronted by a restive assembly, protesting Solomon's exploitative policies and demanding a less rigorous order. Rehoboam listened to the wrong advisors. He pledged his reign to harsher, not milder, policies. Restive tribesmen thus became active rebels. Solomon's great fortress cities availed little for counterinsurgency. His chariots proved an ineffective weapon for keeping order in the hill country.

Rehoboam, in desperation, mustered the militias of Judah and Benjamin, which alone remained loyal, in hopes of suppressing the revolt. The prophet Shemaiah warned against fratricidal warfare, and the militia went home. The Shechem assembly anointed Jeroboam king over the northern tribes, now the kingdom of Israel, and Rehoboam was left to rule over a Southern Kingdom, which included the tribes of Judah and Benjamin. This period of chaos opened the door for a campaign by Pharaoh Sheshonk. Archaeological evidence shows that Sheshonk directed more of his destruction against the kingdom of his former guest, Jeroboam, not surprisingly, as it was larger and stronger than Judah. His purpose was to eliminate the Israelites as a check on his Asiatic policy. The Davidic empire was no more. Where once a sturdy and more or less unified kingdom had stood, two smaller kingdoms weakened by foreign invasion and border skirmishes now surveyed one another across hostile frontiers.

The Northern Kingdom was the larger, stronger, and more populous. It had the best agricultural land. The most important strategic points and fortress cities lay within its borders (such as Hazor, Megiddo, and Gezer) along the main transport route, the inland extension of the Way of the Sea. Shechem, later overshadowed by Samaria, was an important city in the central hill country.

The Northern Kingdom really had no fixed capital in its early decades. The royal residence was most often at Tirzah. Israel gained a permanent capital and royal citadel when Omri built the new city of Samaria, a fortress so formidable that the Assyrian army, mightiest in the ancient world, required three years to capture it. Archaeologists have discovered not only massive fortifications but also evidence of the opulent life-style of the Israelite court.

Dynastic instability was characteristic of the Northern Kingdom. The existence of a professional army with ambitious generals was a destabilizing element. The usual course of things was for a strong king to die in bed or in battle. Soon thereafter, his dynastic heir would be assassinated by a senior military officer who would make himself king. The process would be repeated, unless the usurper himself fell to another conspirator first. Only two northern ruling houses, those of Omri and Jehu, extended through four reigns. Omri and Ahab were probably the strongest and most able of the northern monarchs. Assyrian records referred to Israel as "the house of Omri" in the century following the demise of his dynasty. Jeroboam II's reign was the most tranquil, largely because Egypt and Assyria were minding their own business for a change.

The more exposed and strategic situation of the Northern Kingdom probably meant that it could not avoid entanglement in international power politics, with the shifting fortunes and ultimate doom involved. Judah, though smaller and poorer, might have avoided that ruinous game in her mountain terrain and played the role of an ancient Switzerland. But her best kings could not resist the temptation to try to restore the Davidic kingdom and in the process run afoul of the games empires play. And her worst kings seemed to be addictive, inept players of those games. Even so, Judah survived her stronger northern sister by a century and a half.

Royal stability characterized Judah. The Davidic dynasty ruled nearly uninterrupted to the end of the kingdom, even beyond. Jerusalem was Judah's capital throughout, to the fall of the kingdom, and it has remained so in fact or in ideal for the Jewish people.

Three periods of international crisis punctuated the history narrated in the Former Prophets: the Aramean wars of the mid-ninth century, the Assyrian conquests of the mid-eighth through the mid-seventh centuries, and the Babylonian conquests of the late seventh to early sixth centuries.

Israel and the Aramean kingdom of Damascus (Aramean is often translated "Syrian") were the prime adversaries of the ninth-century wars. David had beaten the Arameans to the punch in the tenth century, but a century later they came into their own. Omri was the architect of such success as Israel enjoyed during the Aramean wars, nurturing an alliance with Judah in which the Judeans became de facto vassals and cementing an alliance with the great Phoenician city of Tyre through a diplomatic marriage between his son Ahab and Jezebel, princess of Tyre. One example of Israel's strength comes from an inscription of the Assyrian emperor Shalmaneser III. When the resurgent Assyrians came adventuring southward, the little Levantine states buried the hatchet temporarily. An alliance of kings met the Assyrian army at Qarqar (853 B.C.E.) in northern Syria and fought it to a standstill. By Shalmaneser's estimates, Ahab of Israel supplied a bit over half of the allied chariots.

One of the most interesting archaeological documents relating to the Hebrew Scriptures comes from this period. It is an inscription from Mesha, king of Moab, that recounts the events narrated in 2 Kgs. 3:4–27 from the Moabite perspective. Neither of the divided kingdoms ever bid fair to restore the Davidic empire, though Israel sometimes dominated Moab, and Judah ruled Edom.

The rebellion of Jehu, instigated by a prophetic faction, brought down the Omride dynasty and made a shambles of Omri's diplomatic achievements. Not only did the mad chariot general Jehu exterminate the Omride line, but he also massacred the king of Judah and his brothers when they crossed his path, accomplished the murder of Jezebel, and slaughtered worshipers of the Tyrian god Baal in Samaria. Bereft of allies, Jehu is shown on the "Black Obelisk" of Shalmaneser III, bowed to the ground and offering tribute to the same Shalmaneser against whom Ahab had launched 2,000 chariots.

The baleful effects of Jehu's folly were mitigated for Israel by external forces. Assyria greatly weakened Damascus, then obligingly went into a period of quiescence. This paved the way for the long, peaceful, and prosperous reign of Jeroboam II in Israel and its counterpart in Judah under Uzziah (or Azariah). The reigns of these two kings constituted a sort of golden age, and their deaths marked its end, for within a decade the resurgent Assyrians were embarked on a century of unprecedented conquest.

Much of the remaining history narrated in the Former Prophets will be examined (though not chronologically) in our account of the Latter Prophets. We will thus conclude our treatment here with a sequential summary, referring the reader to the next chapter for more details.

Israel and Aramea (Syria) tried to organize a coalition to oppose Assyrian expansion, as Ahab and his allies had done a century earlier. They went to the extent of war against Judah (the Syro-Ephraimitic War of 735 B.C.E., Ephraim being another name for the Northern Kingdom) to compel cooperation. But the scheme misfired. Damascus fell to the Assyrian Tiglath-pileser III's legions in 732, and Samaria to Sargon II, in 722, after a three-year siege.

Judah enjoyed a brief renaissance under the nationalist reformer, Hezekiah, who actually reconstituted the Davidic kingdom under the nose of Assyria. He overreached himself and paid a dreadful price. Assyria pressed on in the next century to do what no Asiatic group, dynasty, or nation had done in the millennium since the Hyksos—conquer and rule Egypt. The long reign of Manasseh in Judah, the abject and obedient vassal of Assyria and Judah's worst king in the eyes of the editors of the Former Prophets, filled the middle years of the seventh century.

The beginning of Assyria's sudden collapse, precipitated by the Medo-Babylonian alliance, coincided roughly with the coming of age of the former boy-king, Josiah, in Judah. Probably an active ally of Babylon himself, Josiah was another Hezekiah, a reforming nationalist whose writ ran from Dan to

Beersheva. He died in 609 B.C.E. at Megiddo, possibly by treachery, in a futile attempt to prevent Pharaoh Necho II's equally futile expedition to shore up the last remnants of Assyria.

The Judean monarchy itself became an imperial pawn following Josiah's death. The Egyptians deposed Josiah's acclaimed heir Jehoahaz and installed Jehoiakim. He maladroitly offended Babylonian interests and died just in time to avoid Nebuchadnezzar II's invasion of his realm in 597. His heir, Jehoiachin, reigned only long enough to effect a prudent surrender and go away to lifetime exile in Babylon, initially as a prisoner, accompanied by many prominent Judeans. Nebuchadnezzar elevated Jehoiachin's uncle, Zedekiah, to king, but that worthy allowed himself to be swayed by pro-Egyptian interests and rebelled against Babylon, to his own ruin and that of his kingdom (587).

Our literary analysis has already recounted the hopeful note on which the Former Prophets and Jehoiachin had been elevated to a place in the court of the Babylonian emperor, Evil Merodach, about 561. But Jerusalem was still in ruins, and the other prominent Judeans exiled during the Babylonian campaigns remained in exile.

SUMMARY

The Former Prophets (the Books of Joshua, Judges, First and Second Samuel, First and Second Kings) form a connected narrative recounting the creation and destruction of the nation Israel. The perspective from which the story is told stresses that obedience to the LORD results in blessing, whereas disobedience leads to tragedy. Because this is the theme of the Book of Deuteronomy, many interpreters call the narrative the *Deuteronomic History*.

Our literary discussion of the Former Prophets described the balance between Joshua 1—12 and Judges 1—2, complementary accounts of the occupation of the land of Canaan by the Israelites. We then observed closely one of the hero legends in the Book of Judges, the exploits of Ehud in Jg. 3:12–20. We also noticed the pattern that weaves the tales of the judges together. We next examined one of the most refined literary units in the Tanak—the story of the transition from King David to his son Solomon. Finally, we identified the patterning of history in the Books of Kings through repeated formulae and the recurrent role of prophets.

These books are a rich resource for the historian seeking to reconstruct key periods in the history of ancient Israel. In this chapter we defended the hypothesis that the occupation of Canaan by the Israelites was a complex process that included elements of violent destruction and peaceful occupation and assimilation. We also discussed the evidence concerning the rise of a state-level society in Israel and the reigns of the only two monarchs of the

United Kingdom—David and Solomon. We then described the division of Israel into a Northern Kingdom (Israel) and a Southern Kingdom (Judah), and the defeat of Israel by the Assyrians and the vanquishing of Judah by the Babylonians. With many leaders in exile in Babylon, Israel's independent status was ended, but for the Hasmonean interlude in the second through first centuries B.C.E. (see chap. 10).

We turn now to questions of contemporary significance arising from our analysis of the Former Prophets.

THE CONTEMPORARY WORLD: QUESTIONS FOR DISCUSSION AND REFLECTION

1. The Former Prophets describe the history of the nation Israel from the occupation of the land of Canaan to the fall of the Northern and Southern Kingdoms from the perspective that when there was obedience to the LORD the nation prospered, but when there was disobedience, the nation suffered. Should this perspective be applied to modern nations? Why or why not?

2. In the nuclear age, when human civilization could be destroyed, how should we view the attitude toward war shown in the Former Prophets? For example, does the "romantic" view of war in Joshua pose a danger in our time?

3. The prophet Nathan was able to confront King David with the king's wrongdoing without being punished. Does anyone play that role with leaders today?

4. Does the story of David's affair with Bathsheba and the subsequent cover-up teach any lessons about human nature that are as meaningful today as when the story was written?

5. The situation portrayed in this chapter, down to the reemergence of Assyrian power, represents what political scientists today call a *power vacuum*. Do you see any ways in which this historical experience has application in the modern world?

6. A group of prophets instigated the revolt of Jehu in the Northern Kingdom, apparently for moral reasons. However, the revolt turned into a vicious bloodbath. Why do such things happen? Do they still happen?

CHAPTER 6

Covenant Advocates: The Prophets of Ancient Israel (The Latter Prophets)

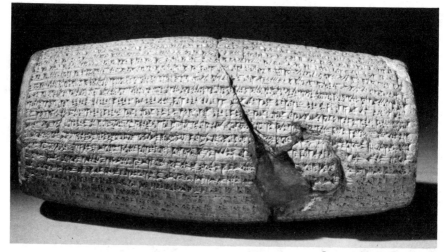

Courtesy of the British Museum

The Cyrus Cylinder. The inscription on this clay cylinder is an early example of political propaganda. It claims that Cyrus's conquest of Babylon was instigated by Marduk, the chief god of Babylon, to liberate the country from an unworthy tyrant and to restore right religious practices. Cyrus is pictured as the true friend of the gods and people of Babylon. He figures prominently in the postexilic history of the people of Israel.

INTRODUCTION

In modern parlance a *prophet* is someone who predicts future events before they occur, and *to prophesy* is simply to predict. The first step in understanding the prophets of ancient Israel and the *prophetic books* is to set aside this definition. For although biblical prophets often spoke of the future, their concern was not prediction per se. The prophets were not so much *foretellers* as *forthtellers* who spoke the word of the LORD to people of their own time. The Hebrew word for prophet (*nabi*), which appears over 300 times in the Hebrew Bible, probably means "one who announces" or perhaps "one who is called."

PROPHECY AS A SOCIAL PHENOMENON

Every human culture has had techniques for establishing contact with holiness, that is, with the realm of reality beyond the ordinary, everyday world of time and space. Anthropologists call this realm the *spirit world*. Human attempts to communicate with the spirit world usually fall into two categories. On the one hand, there are persons who seem to have an inborn talent or gift for moving between the world of normal wakefulness and the world of the spirits, gods, and ancestors. Anthropologists call such persons *shamans*. On the other hand, there are all the manipulative techniques, the professional skills that give access to the spirit realm and its wisdom. Here one would place the medicine man or woman, who can use spells, drugs, and other means to go where the shaman moves naturally, and all the methods utilized by priests, soothsayers, fortune-tellers, spirit mediums, and augurs.

Ancient Near Eastern cultures witnessed both phenomena. Indeed, archaeologists have found model livers (similar to those used in modern biology classes) used to instruct fledgling augurs. There is also ample documentation for the more charismatic sort of seer, whose contact with the spiritual was more spontaneous.

Many passages in the biblical prophetic books refer to the hand or spirit of the LORD being upon the prophet, in a form of shamanlike possession. The Hebrew phrase often translated "oracle of the LORD" literally means "burden of the LORD." Other important prophetic passages suggest that the prophets found themselves in the court of the LORD, surrounded by the heavenly council (e.g., 1 Kings 22).

These data suggest that the prophets of ancient Israel should be associated with the spontaneous, charismatic side of religious behavior. This may be troublesome for modern interpreters, who might prefer biblical personages to be more staid and conventional. It seemed already to be a problem in the biblical period, for association with prophets and prophetic behavior was sometimes deemed inappropriate for persons from "nice" families (1 Sam. 10:11–12; 19:24).

Precisely *what* the form of Israelite prophetic behavior was is less clear. As we have seen, the Hebrew term for prophet, *nabi*, seems to support the notion that prophets were speakers who carried messages from the divine realm to the earthly. The forms of behavior recognized as appropriate to the reception and delivery of prophetic oracles probably differed from time to time and from place to place.

Prophets were perceived as useful persons to have about. Other means of consulting the spirit realm had serious limitations. Lots could generally say only yes, no, and maybe. Omens and auguries were notoriously vague, and oracles were ambiguous. A prophet in direct communication with the spirit realm could elicit a discursive response. In addition, given the common folk belief in the effective power of world formulas (as in blessings and curses), the prophet could also be a dangerous person to have around. The word spoken by the prophet was the Word of the LORD. It was a causal force. Not surprisingly, prophets were themselves considered holy. Even when they were hated, they were not often killed. Deuteronomy does decree death for the prophet who seduces Israel to follow strange gods (13:1–5; 18:20). It appears that the "presumptuous" prophet who speaks words not commanded by God may be safely ignored (18:18–22). But the criterion of a true word is that it comes true! In most cases, the issue would be moot by the time the evidence was in. Deuteronomy's efforts illustrate the difficulty of dealing rationally and bureaucratically with charismatic phenomena (cf. Jeremiah 23:18–22).

Some prophets were associated with shrines and the Temple, and these are called *cultic prophets*. Others were members of the court—*royal prophets*. Some belonged to guilds or bands. Both Samuel and Elisha headed such bands, and Isaiah of Jerusalem had disciples. The term "sons of the prophets" usually designated these prophetic bands. Some prophets apparently went "on the road," showing up at important local festivals (as did Samuel). Some seemed to be in private practice. Some, like Amos, were not professionals. Prophecy was an avocation they did not choose. Some prophets, like Jeremiah and Amos, claimed an explicit call from God to a prophetic mission.

The word "spoken forth" by the prophet might be as commonplace as Samuel's information to Saul about the fate of his father's herd of lost asses, and it was frequently a response to everyday inquiries. But Samuel also anointed and denounced kings, and Elijah, Elisha, and Nathan felt themselves commissioned to make and unmake monarchs. Nathan, Gad, Isaiah, and Jeremiah advised kings. A number of prophets announced oracles bearing upon matters of high policy.

The prophets mentioned in the Bible were a minority, perhaps a maverick minority, of the prophets who flourished in ancient Israel. The biblical prophets understood themselves not merely as having access to the spirit world, but as ambassadors of the divine court to the earthly seats of power. It is in this role that they can be seen as advocates of the Mosaic covenant, the holy treaty that formalized the special relationship between the LORD and Israel. Of course, diplomacy is a two-way street. Like good ambassadors, prophets also interpreted the case of the government to which they were accredited to the chancery of the Sovereign. Thus, prophets made intercession to God on behalf of Israel, and they were believed to have special powers in this regard.

Each of the prophets had particular points of interest and emphasis, to judge from the surviving materials. Still, as covenant advocates, they all shared in common an uncompromising demand for justice and righteousness, that is, for the creation on earth among God's people of those conditions representing the divine intentions as made explicit in the Torah—a religiously faithful people living under a decent government that sought to create a just and humane social order.

Given their source of authority, it is not surprising that the biblical prophets vigorously denounced the veneration of other gods, whether it was for political purposes (as when the king agreed to place objects associated with other gods in the Temple to cement diplomatic ties with another government) or devotional ends (as when individual Israelites turned to other gods to try to ensure an abundant harvest). Baal was the object of the greatest prophetic ire. The term *Baal* is both a name and a title (meaning "lord") associated with a number of Canaanite deities. They were all fertility gods associated with myths reflecting the yearly cycle of agriculture. The fact that some of the Canaanite religious festivals involved both orgiastic drinking and sexual license put the Baal cult at cross-purposes with the Torah's demands for both covenant loyalty and moral behavior. The concern of Torah and prophet was not so much proper belief as right practice.

Prophets concerned themselves with the future, in an ambassadorial sense. They brought messages warning what would happen if covenant abuse continued. That is, their predictions were addressed to immediate circumstances. For example, when Isaiah spoke the oracle to King Ahaz about the birth of a child named Immanuel ("God with us"), which is preserved in Is. 7:14, he was addressing the situation of the time. The theological use of this text by the New Testament to see a prediction of the coming of Jesus lies outside the bounds of historical method to judge. All interpretations that claim to see in prophetic texts specific predictions of a far future age fall into the same category. They may be legitimate readings from a theological or devotional perspective, but they are outside the purview of historical analysis.

There is one major exception to the rule of immediacy in prophetic prediction. Some oracles forecast an age when the divine promises to Israel will be realized. Some foretell blessings for all nations (e.g., Is. 2:1–4 and Mic. 4:1–4). Before the Babylonian Exile, which marked the practical end of the Davidic dynasty, prophets in Judah might speak of an ideal king of David's line, unlike the less than ideal monarchs they had to deal with. Isaiah 9:2–7, 11:1–10, and 32:1–8 may be concerned with such an ideal Davidic king. After the Babylonian Exile, prophets associated the hope of a messiah ("anointed one") with the expectation of a restored Davidic kingdom and a new age of peace and prosperity.

After the Exile there was no court and thus no need for ambassadors. Later rabbinic interpretation held that prophetic inspiration ceased in the time of Ezra. Regardless, the role of prophecy diminished with changes in circumstance, and, over the long haul, prophecy itself faded. But for popular religion, the spirit of prophecy was maintained, especially in the hope of a restored age of glory, which would be announced by the return of Elijah (Mal. 3:1; 4:5–6).

THE PROPHETS AND THEIR TIMES

The Origins of Prophecy

When did prophecy arise in Israel? In one sense, prophecy was always present, for the charismatic aspect of religion has been shown to be as old as religion itself. The evidence for prophecy as a distinct, recognized phenomenon begins to appear in materials associated with the Philistine oppression that led to the rise of the Israelite state and its monarchy. Given the nature of the evidence, the question of whether later generations would have recognized as prophets earlier heroic figures (such as Abraham, Moses, and Deborah) so designated in the Tanak must be left open.

Samuel is the first individual figure portrayed in the Bible who exhibited the characteristics of what was later deemed prophecy. He headed, and sometimes was accompanied by, a band of "sons of the prophets," a prophetic guild of which he was the head, or "father." Samuel anointed kings, delivered divine oracles, and conversed with God concerning the destiny of Israel, all prophetic functions.

The "historical" books (the Former Prophets and Chronicles) contain a variety of traditions bearing upon a number of other prophets. Together with the Levitical priests, these prophets are portrayed as the great zealots of Mosaic religion.

Saul had no developed bureaucracy, but two prophets are associated with David's entourage. Gad the Seer was a part of David's wilderness company (1 Sam. 22:5) and served as the intermediary during the Jerusalem years, when a plague following David's census was interpreted as evidence of divine wrath (2 Sam. 24:1–25). The other, Nathan, appeared to be a central figure in the Jerusalem court. He is shown first approving, then forbidding, David's project to build a temple for the LORD in Jerusalem. He is credited with the great oracle that was the foundation of the messianic hope (2 Sam. 7:1–19). The story of Nathan's condemnation of David for his sin against Uriah the Hittite (2 Sam. 11:1–12:26) is a classic confrontation between the prophet as covenant advocate and the king. Nathan was the key figure in the palace coup that quashed Adonijah's attempt to take the throne and that led to Solomon's accession (1 Kgs. 1:1–53). According to Chronicles, Nathan wrote an important source document on the reigns of David (1 Chr. 29:29) and Solomon (2 Chr. 9:29).

Prophetic activity was also associated with the disruption of the Israelite kingdom. Ahijah planted seeds of sedition in the mind of the young bureaucrat Jeroboam with a graphic, enacted oracle (1 Kgs. 11:26–40). Shemaiah persuaded Rehoboam not to launch a fratricidal war at the time of Jeroboam's revolt (1 Kgs. 12:21–25).

Elijah and Elisha

The Aramean wars of the ninth century were the occasion for another upsurge of prophetic activity. The prophets played an ambivalent role in these events. On the one hand, they appear as Israelite patriots, helping Ahab and his sons against their external enemies. On the other, they condemn the entire house of Ahab, apparently for policies that were the handiwork of Ahab's queen, Jezebel, princess of Tyre.

The two principal prophets associated with this period in the narrative are Elijah, called the Tishbite (ordinarily associated with the region of Gilead), and his follower and successor, Elisha, son of Shaphat, from the tribe of Issachar. Micaiah ben Imlah is the central figure in a single, fairly long narrative unit in 1 Kings 22, which is packed with information about the prophetic phenomenon, and which may reveal the deuteronomic (Levitical) historians' attitude toward some aspects of prophecy.

Elijah is portrayed as a person of remarkable strength and energy, whose rude and unusual costume (2 Kgs. 1:8) may symbolize a rejection of settled agrarian life, above all, urban life. Elijah appears as the adversary of King Ahab, but his real target was the patronage of the Baal cult by Queen Jezebel. The Elijah cycle (1 Kings 17—21; 2 Kings 1:1—2:18) ends with his being taken up to heaven by a whirlwind, while horses and chariots of fire interpose between Elijah and his chosen successor, Elisha. That Elijah (like

FIGURE 6-1

The Prophets of Ancient Israel Beginning with Elijah

Prophet/Location	Approximate Dates	Ruler(s)
Elijah/Israel (1 Kings, 17—19 2 Kings 1—2)	850	Ahab of Israel (869–850)
Micaiah/Israel (1 Kings 22)	850	Ahab of Israel (869–850)
Elisha/Israel (2 Kings 2—10)	825	
Amos/Israel	750	Jeroboam II of Israel (786–746)
Hosea/Israel	740-730	Jeroboam II of Israel and others
Isaiah of Jerusalem (Isaiah 1—39)	742-695	Jotham of Judah (742–735) Ahaz of Judah (735–715)
Micah/Judah	730-701	Hezekiah (715–687) Manasseh (687–642)
Zephaniah/Judah	630-622	Josiah of Judah (640–609)
Jeremiah/Judah	627-580	Josiah, Jehoahaz (609) Jehoiakim (609–598)
Habbakuk/Judah	605-600	Jehoiachin (598–597) Zedekiah (597–587)
Ezekiel/Babylon	593-570	Nebuchadnezzar of Babylon (605–562)
Second Isaiah/Babylon (Isaiah 40—55)	540	Nabonidus of Babylonia (556–539) Cyrus of Persia (550–530)
Haggai/Jerusalem	520	Zerubbabel of Judea (520–518) Darius I of Persia (522–486)
Zechariah/Jerusalem	520-515	
Third Isaiah/Jerusalem (Isaiah 56—66)	515 (?)	
Joel/Jerusalem	400-350 (?)	
Obadiah	?	

Enoch, see Gen. 5:21–24) was supposed not to have experienced death like ordinary people sets the foundation for the growing role he was to play in later Jewish lore. The earliest evidence of the growth of an Elijah tradition is Mal. 4:5–6, where he is to be the herald of the day of the LORD. Thus he became the forerunner of the Messiah. The tradition continued to develop in the New Testament. The gospels portray John the Baptizer as Elijah to Jesus' David. In the Jewish Passover celebration a cup set out for Elijah stands as a powerful symbol of the hope of a coming messianic age.

Unlike the prophets of the Latter Prophets, Elijah and Elisha were portrayed as wonder-workers. Both performed feeding miracles Both resuscitated dead children. Elisha headed a band of sons of the prophets, and, because Elijah was addressed as "father," he may have preceded in the position.

The final recorded act of Elisha marks a turning point in Israelite prophecy. After executing Elijah's revolutionary commission in Damascus by instigating the murder of the sick King Benhadad by his servant Hazael, Elisha sent one of his disciples to anoint General Jehu king in place of Joram (Jehoram), a son of Ahab. In the event, Jehu went berserk, making common cause with the Rechabites, the most radical religious element in Israel, and launching an unprecedented bloodbath that almost led to the extermination of the Davidic line in Jerusalem and the prophets' Samaritan adversaries (see chap. 5). Elisha's reaction to the excesses of his former client is not recorded. A later response is. The eighth-century prophet Hosea condemned the Jezreel bloodbath in unconditional terms (Hos. 1:4–5).

Prior to these events, Israelite prophets appeared as revolutionary activists. Samuel made Saul king, then tried to break him in favor of David. Prophets played a role in the division of the kingdom on both sides of the border. Elijah slaughtered prophets of Baal, and Elisha brought down dynasties. But after Jehu's bloodbath, the prophets seemed to recoil from such direct revolutionary action. By the time the cycles of tradition in the earliest section of the Latter Prophets emerged, the prophets seem to have settled into a less violent diplomatic role, serving as advocates rather than activists.

The Latter Prophets

The next period from which a substantial body of prophetic material survives marks yet another major change in Israelite prophetic traditions. The earliest collections of substantial prophetic oracles, many in poetic form, have been preserved in the scrolls of the Latter Prophets and issue from the mid-to-late eighth century B.C.E. This period witnessed the decline of the "tarnished" (in the eyes of the prophets) golden age of Jeroboam II in Israel and Uzziah (Azariah) in Judah and the rise of Assyria to regional dominance. The last prophet to receive substantial attention in the Former Prophets is Isaiah, whose name also appears in one of the major scrolls of the Latter Prophets. A number of prophets, other than those discussed here, are referred to in the Former Prophets and the Chronicler's History. A number of the references are anonymous. Only a few refer to prophets known from the Latter Prophets (Isaiah, Jeremiah, Jonah).

PROPHETIC SPEECH
AND PROPHETIC LITERATURE

Unlike many other biblical books, where a pattern of organization is evident, if not to the casual reader then to the careful student, the prophetic books seem to have no ordering to them in most cases. So the most secure starting point in a literary overview of the prophetic books is the individual literary units, the prophetic sayings and narratives.

Let us first examine the narratives found in prophetic books. One type of story found in several of these works is the *call narrative* (Isaiah 6; Jeremiah 1; Ezekiel 1—3; Amos 7). The subject is the initial encounter of the prophet with the LORD, presumably as a form of validating the prophet's credentials as someone designated by the LORD as a messenger. The story in Isaiah 6 is an especially vivid, first-person description of a vision of the LORD seated on his heavenly throne, surrounded by an entourage of angelic beings who are proclaiming his holiness (6:3). Their threefold repetition (Holy, Holy, Holy) is the Hebrew way of saying that the LORD is *the* holiest. The prophet then describes how he was overwhelmed by a feeling of unworthiness at being in the presence of the LORD, but one of the angelic beings symbolically cleansed him and the voice of the LORD commissioned him with a message for the people of Israel. In the call narratives a basic pattern is observable.

> The LORD appears or speaks
>
> Prophet expresses unworthiness
>
> Prophet is reassured
>
> The LORD commissions prophet

Other types of narratives include reports of visions received by prophets (e.g., Am. 7:1–9; 8:1–3; 9:1–4; Ezekiel 8—11; 37; 40—48). Probably the most famous prophetic vision narrative is Ezekiel's account of seeing a valley of dry bones come to life when he prophesies to them (Ezek. 37:1–14). The visions are frequently symbolic messages rather than clairvoyant pictures of specific happenings. Ezekiel's vision symbolizes what will happen to the house of Israel. Although they are languishing in exile ("dead bones"), with no hope for a new life, the LORD will give them hope and a new life, restoring them to their own land (37:11–14). It is a secondary application of the vision narrative to say that it predicts resurrection after death for individuals.

Another form of prophetic narrative relates *symbolic actions* performed by the prophet as a visual statement to the people of the divine will. For example, when the prophet Jeremiah bought land at Anathoth near Jerusalem, it was a symbol of his confidence in the LORD's promise to restore Judah after the Exile (Jer. 32:1–44). Other examples of symbolic actions by prophets are found in Isaiah 20; Jeremiah 35; Ezekiel 4—5; 12; and Hosea 1; 3:1–5. In all cases, the prophet is directed by the LORD to carry out an action that seems strange, in order to draw attention to himself and thereby be heard.

Also in the prophetic books are narratives describing *dramatic encounters with kings,* similar to those we have already seen in the Former Prophets. Directed by the LORD, the prophet goes to the monarch or is summoned to the court for consultation. He delivers to the king a message either directly or through a symbol. For example, during the Syro-Ephraimitic wars, the LORD sent Isaiah to King Ahaz to reassure him, first directly, then, when the king apparently ignored him, with a sign: the birth of a child named Immanuel (Isaiah 6—8). Other encounters between prophet and king are related in Isaiah 36—39 (paralleled in 2 Kgs. 18:13—20:19) and in Jeremiah.

Still another type of prophetic narrative is the account of the *persecution of the prophet* by opponents who have been unsettled by his announcement of judgment (e.g., Jer. 20:1–6; 26:1–4; 36—45).

The narrative sections of the prophetic books amount to only about 20 percent of the content. Most of the prophetic literature is poetry, ranging from very brief utterances, such as the saying of Amos:

> Hear this word that the LORD has spoken against
> you, O people of Israel, against the
> whole family which I brought up out of the
> land of Egypt:
> "You only have I known
> of all the families of the earth;
> therefore I will punish you
> for all your iniquities." (3:1–2)

to quite lengthy prayers, songs, and poems (such as those found in Isaiah 40—55). Some of these poetic forms are unique to the prophetic books; others are adapted from other settings.

For the most part, the prophetic books are collections of *prophetic oracles;* that is, sayings in which the prophet announces a message of the LORD. Frequently the oracle is introduced by a formula: "Thus says the LORD," or "Hear the word of the LORD." However, the message that follows might be one of a variety of types. Most common is the *oracle of judgment.* It might be a denunciation in a situation of present faithlessness. Or it could be an announcement of a future punishment. Usually a present indictment is combined with the announcement of coming results. For example, the Book of Amos begins with a series of oracles of this type (1:3—2:8).

Other prophetic sayings are *admonitions to repentance,* such as the straightforward oracle in Jer. 3:12: " 'Return, faithless Israel,' says the LORD." Some exhortations add a warning of what will happen if they are ignored (e.g., Jer. 4:3–4).

Another basic type of prophetic saying announces a *future deliverance* of the people, sometimes juxtaposed with an oracle of judgment (for example, Is. 1:26 added to 1:24–25).

Some prophetic sayings reflect the influence of wisdom literature. For example, the oracles in Am. 1:3—2:8 adapt the numerical saying form of wisdom teaching (cf. Prov. 30:15–31) to a prophetic context. In Jer. 17:5–11 we find a group of proverbs adapted to a prophetic setting.

Besides these basic types of prophetic oracles, prophetic books include more developed sayings. One of these is the *woe oracle*, which generally has three elements, as illustrated in Hab. 2:6–8:

Announcement of distress (2:6)

Reason for distress (2:7)

Announcement of doom (2:8).

Other examples of woe oracles can be found in Mic. 2:1–5 and Zeph. 2:5–7.

Another developed prophetic saying is the *covenant lawsuit*, in which the LORD is portrayed as bringing Israel to court, accusing the nation or its leaders of violation of the stipulations of the Sinai Covenant, stating the evidence, and announcing the punishment. The prophet plays the role of prosecuting attorney. Hosea 4 provides a good example of this form of prophetic speech:

Summons (4:1a)	To the people of Israel
Charge (4:1b–2)	A general accusation of covenant dereliction, followed in this case by a specific allegation of violations amounting to the breaking of specific commandments of the Decalogue
Evidence (4:3–6a)	The upheaval in nature caused by the covenant violation followed by the specific behavior of priests and prophets
Verdict (4:6b–10)	Priests, prophets, and people to be punished.

Other covenant lawsuits can be found in Mic. 6:1–8 and Is. 3:13–26.

In addition to sayings, prophetic literature includes other poetic forms, adapted from other types of literature. For example, Is. 5:1–7 adapts the popular form of a harvest song into an allegory about the LORD's relationship to Israel and Judah. Ezekiel 19:2–14 is a dirge or funeral song. The laments and hymns common in the Psalms (see chap. 7) are also found in prophetic literature. Jeremiah especially utilizes the *lament of the individual* in his "confessions," cries of anguish to the LORD (11:18—12:6; 15:10–21; 17:14–18;

18:18–23; 20:7–13; 20:14–18). Amos 4:13, 5:8–9, and 9:5–6 are short hymns in praise of the LORD (called *doxologies*) that stand out amid the oracles of doom dominating the book. In Isaiah 40—55 the hymnic form predominates. These chapters include the longest, and probably the most sophisticated, poems in the prophetic literature. For example, 40:12–31 is a carefully crafted hymn utilizing rhetorical questions to elicit praise of the LORD as the all-powerful creator of the universe, leading to an affirmation of the LORD as the source of strength for those who wait on him.

Prophetic poetry, like other poetry of the Tanak, is rich in imagery, which unfortunately loses some of its force for modern readers unaware of its meaning. For example, we find imagery drawn from myths that would have been familiar to ancient Israelites but that are foreign to modern readers. When Is. 51:9 asks the LORD

> Was it not thou that didst cut Rahab in pieces,
>   that didst pierce the dragon?

the imagery is that of a mythic battle between the divine king and the forces of chaos, which results in order and fertility. The statement is directed to the LORD as an appeal for him to conquer current enemies as he had once vanquished these cosmic agents of chaos. Rahab and Tannin ("Dragon" or "Sea Monster") are two of the numerous names by which the divine foes are known in Semitic mythology.

Prophetic poetry is also rich in the use of such devices as alliteration, assonance, and paronomasia, which are lost to students unfamiliar with Hebrew. Isaiah 5:7, for example, loses its poetic force when the reader is not made aware of the paronomasia (word play) present:

> And he the LORD looked for justice [*mishpat*],
>   but behold bloodshed [*mispah*];
> for righteousness [*sedaga*],
>   but behold, a cry [*seaga*]!

Good commentaries will clarify such difficult imagery and point out poetic devices that depend on a knowledge of Hebrew.

However, much of the poetic imagery is accessible in translation. Careful attention to it will reward the sensitive reader. There is nothing esoteric about the metaphors the prophet Amos uses to condemn the social injustice of his day. You do not need to know that Bashan was a fertile area well-adapted to raising cattle or understand the meaning of Harmon (no one in fact does!) to grasp the force of the imagery Amos used to indict the women of Samaria in 4:1–3. Nor does the reader need to know a great deal about ancient Near Eastern religions to feel the satirical irony in the poem about idols in Is. 44:9–20.

In addition to an orientation to the forms of prophetic discourse, an introduction to prophetic literature should at least attempt to sort out some of the basic themes recurrent in the prophetic books. Any such summary risks oversimplification, but it can also be a helpful framework within which to consider each particular prophet.

PROPHETIC THEMES: COVENANT, JUDGMENT, REDEMPTION

All of the prophets assume the special relationship between the LORD and Israel expressed in the Sinai Covenant. They frequently base their indictment of the people and leaders of the nation on violations of the covenant. The prophets are *covenant advocates* or *covenant mediators*, who remind the nation of its responsibilities because of its relationship with the LORD (see Am. 3:2).

Because the LORD has chosen Israel and entered into a covenant with this nation, the divine expectations for Israel are more rigid. On the other hand, because of this special covenantal relationship, the LORD is more reluctant to destroy the nation. Thus, the covenant creates a tension reflected in the movement in prophetic literature between the announcement of judgment on Israel for covenant abuse and the announcement of restoration of the nation or some part of it. The intimate relationship between the LORD and Israel is expressed in a number of images: parent-child (Hosea 11), owner-vineyard (Isaiah 5), shepherd-flock (Is. 40:11), potter-clay (Jeremiah 18), and, frequently, husband-wife (Jer. 2:1–7). The term often used to describe the LORD's basic attitude toward Israel, and what he expects from them as his covenant partners, is *hesed*, translated into English as "steadfast love" (RSV), "mercy," "compassion," "faithfulness," "devotion," or "grace." It is because of his *hesed* that the LORD cannot let Israel go (see, for example, Hos. 2:16–20; Jer. 3:12; Is. 54:7–8).

The basic prophetic tension is heightened by the rebellion of Israel (and other nations), which leads inevitably to punishment. One of the most graphic images of Israel's rebellion is Jeremiah's portrayal of Israel as a camel or wild ass in heat (2:23–25). More common is the image of Israel as prostitute (e.g., Ezek. 16:8, 15). For virtually every prophet, this rebellion is the subject, with inevitable punishment, often described as total (e.g., Is. 30:12–14; Jer. 5:1–17). The inevitability of judgment does not stop the prophets from calling for repentance. Even Amos, a prophet of doom, admonishes the people to turn from their evil ways (5:14–15). Even if punishment is inevitable, perhaps a few of God's chosen people—a remnant—who remain faithful to him will be saved (see Is. 3:12–13; 4:2–6; 7:3: 10:20–22; 11:10–16; 28:5; 37:32; Zeph. 3:13; Hag. 1:12–14; Zech. 8:6; 11—12).

The prophets also look beyond the time of judgment to a time of restoration or new beginning. After announcing the inevitable destruction of Israel, the Book of Amos draws on the promise to David to envision a restoration (9:11–15). Isaiah 40—55 is the most sustained section developing the theme of restoration. Sometimes the restoration includes a picture of an age of universal peace, as in the vivid picture of the nations coming to Jerusalem to learn the ways of the LORD and inaugurate a time when swords will be beaten into plowshares and spears into pruning hooks (Is. 2:2–4 and Mic. 4:1–3). Other vivid images of universal redemption can be found in Is. 11:6–9, Hos. 2:18–23, and Is. 49:6.

THE PROPHETIC BOOKS

Our survey of the Latter Prophets will examine each book in the canonical order: Isaiah, Jeremiah, Ezekiel, and the Scroll of the Twelve. There are two reasons for this nonchronological approach. First, it is less complicated for readers who are trying hard to integrate their reading of this account with a reading of the Bible. Second, the Book of Isaiah, which is first in the canonical order of the Latter Prophets, is an anthology of the work of a school of prophecy descending from the great eighth-century prophet, Isaiah of Jerusalem. In working through the contents of the scroll of Isaiah, one receives a survey introduction to almost the entire age of the Latter Prophets.

The Isaiah Anthology

The evidence within the Book of Isaiah makes it plain that the material it contains cannot all have issued from a single eighth-century prophet, Isaiah of Jerusalem. Isaiah himself mentioned a circle of disciples who would treasure his teaching in an unfavorable era (Is. 8:16). Apparently they did more. The continuity of themes through the scroll, despite evidence that various parts of it could not have come from the eighth-century master, is most readily explained by the hypothesis that the school of disciples persisted for more than 300 years, not only treasuring up the words of Isaiah, but also adding their own prophetic insights from generation to generation, in Jerusalem, in Babylonian exile, and again in Jerusalem.

Biblical scholars conveniently refer to the principal blocks of material in the sixty-six chapters of Isaiah as First Isaiah, Second Isaiah, and Third Isaiah. To be sure, no Hebrew manuscript is so divided. This division is a theory that will stand only so long as none better comes along to explain the data. The following outline is one way the parts of the book can be associated with the three different levels.

Isaiah 1—12; 20; 22; 28—33——First Isaiah, material issuing from Isaiah of Jerusalem in the eighth century.

Isaiah 36—39——First Isaiah, historical appendix (a slightly edited recapitulation of 2 Kgs. 18:13—20:19, from the eighth to the sixth centuries).

Isaiah 35; 40—55——Second Isaiah, material issuing from the "Isaiah" of Babylon, an anonymous prophet of the Isaiah school (sixth century).

Isaiah 34; 56—66——Third Isaiah, a collection of oracles from various postexilic members of the Isaiah school (sixth to fifth centuries).

Isaiah 13—23——Oracles against foreign nations, probably issuing from a broad spectrum of history. Except for Isaiah 20 and 22, all are probably later than First Isaiah.

Isaiah 24—27——A visionary section, called the *Isaiah Apocalypse* because of some colorful apocalyptic imagery. It is considered by many to be the latest section of the book (a fourth Isaiah?), but by others to be earlier.

First Isaiah. The earliest datable material in the Book of Isaiah is the Temple vision of chapter 6, which supplies a date in the year of Uzziah's death 742 B.C.E. This vision underscores a basic theme of First Isaiah that became a trademark of the entire school: the holiness of the LORD. (The vision is treated on p. 126).

The decree Isaiah was to carry as ambassador of the divine court was one of condemnation, but the LORD would not strike without warning. Most of the first five chapters of Isaiah (except 1:1–9 and 2:1–5) belong to the next few years, before the human agency of doom was clearly visible. Isaiah probably seemed as odd in these years as Jeremiah did a century later, proclaiming a doom that never seemed to materialize. Isaiah singled out the greedy and the proud for special condemnation: absentee landlords (5:8–10), the Jerusalem debutante cotillion (3:16—4:1), and self-indulgent, self-deceived leaders (5:11–30). Like other great prophets, Isaiah insisted that justice, righteousness, and compassion, especially toward the poor and weak, were essential aspects of communal life. And obedience to the Torah was indissolubly connected with religious fidelity to the LORD as the only appropriate repository of trust.

Crisis arose about 735 B.C.E., with a new king, Ahaz, on the throne of Judah. Assyrian expansion was the problem. King Pekah of Israel and King Rezon of Syria decided to try to repeat the strategy of the previous century, when the Levantine coalition, including Ahab, had held Assyria at bay. When Ahaz held back, the Samaria-Damascus alliance schemed to depose Ahaz and install a puppet. Isaiah found King Ahaz inspecting the Jerusalem defenses. Isaiah 7—8 narrates the prophet's response to the crisis (the Syro-Ephraimite war). At first Isaiah offered hope based on trust in the LORD, but

Ahaz, in a mock show of piety, declined Isaiah's sign. The prophet gave it anyway: the sign of a child, Immanuel (God with us). By the time the child attained the age of responsibility, Pekah and Rezon would long since be in history's ash heap, and Judah would be enjoying Edenlike prosperity (7:10–17).

In 735 Isaiah had a son old enough to accompany him on a royal interview. The prophet gave him a symbolic name, Shearjashub, which means "A remnant shall repent (or return)." Thus, Isaiah already had developed at this early period the notion of a *remnant* that became another of the central ideas of the Isaiah school.

Ahaz had already sent messengers to the Assyrian king Tiglath-pileser III, begging aid. So Judah became Assyria's voluntary vassal, and Ahaz dutifully introduced Assyrian religious objects into the Temple of the LORD in Jerusalem. With the addition of a single phrase to the Immanuel oracle—"the King of Assyria" (7:17)—its thrust was changed from hope to doom.

Isaiah withdrew from public life after Ahaz's treachery (8:16–17), but returned about 715 B.C.E. to advise a new king, Hezekiah, in a new crisis. There was widespread rebellion against Assyria, but Isaiah warned against it. He made the point symbolically by walking around Jerusalem dressed as a war slave (Isaiah 20). Apparently Hezekiah listened.

The materials in Isaiah 36—39 (cf. 2 Kgs. 18:13—20:19) are almost certainly not in strict chronological order. The embassy of the Babylonian king to Hezekiah certainly precedes the war with Assyria. Fortunately, we are aided by the records of the Assyrian King Sennacherib in understanding what happened. Hezekiah joined a rebellion, fomented in part by the Babylonians. Sennacherib dealt with the rebels in a series of ruthless campaigns. It was Judah's turn in 701 B.C.E. Every fortified city of Judah was destroyed. Sennacherib was so proud of his conquest of the great Judean fortress city of Lachish that he made the siege of that city the subject of the stone relief decorating the throne room of his palace in Nineveh. Jerusalem seemed doomed. In desperation, King Hezekiah turned to Isaiah. Isaiah's message was consistent: Trust in the LORD. Miraculously, the Assyrian army withdrew. Judah was ruined, but Jerusalem was spared, its walls intact. Why did Sennacherib let Hezekiah off so lightly with a payment of tribute and a promise of good behavior, as both 2 Kgs. 18:14–16 and the Assyrian records record? Assyrian records are mute. The biblical accounts mention sickness in his army, but from their perspective, the power of the LORD was the real answer.

The remaining materials associated with First Isaiah (chap. 28—33) probably issue from the years surrounding the crisis of 701, and they underscore the basic themes of faithfulness and trust in the LORD and scorn for all false sources of confidence. The very first words of the scroll (1:1–9) portray the conditions of those sad days after Assyria's withdrawal.

Second Isaiah. The historical notes in Isaiah 40—55 seem to set this block of the scroll off from the earlier chapters (except for chap. 35). Jerusalem is in ruins (44:26–28). The Judeans are suffering at Babylonian hands, some as exiles, but Babylon herself is on the verge of doom (47:1–15). Cyrus of Persia is named as the deliverer (indeed, he is called the Messiah of the LORD in 44:28—45:7). The sufferings of war and exile have paid for the guilt that stood under judgment in First Isaiah (40:2). This evidence suggests that Second Isaiah speaks near the end of the Babylonian Exile (539–538 B.C.E.).

The historical evidence accords with the literary data. The style of Isaiah 40—55 is distinctive. These chapters contain long, complex poems, unlike the short prophetic sayings typical of earlier chapters. The theme of hope and redemption has replaced the mood of doom. In 40:1–11 the prophet, hearing the decrees of the heavenly court like his master, receives a commission to announce a message of hope and redemption.

Still, these materials share more with First Isaiah than the same scroll. Second Isaiah continues the theme of the holiness of the LORD (using the Holy One as a name for God). Perhaps influenced by Babylonian creation mythology, Second Isaiah places the great event of the LORD's redemption of Israel, the Exodus, on a par with his creation of the cosmos. Second Isaiah speaks of a "new exodus" through which the LORD will bring the exiles out from bondage in Babylon (40:3; 41:17–20; 42:16; 43:16–19).

Second Isaiah also develops the theme of holiness into a theoretical assertion of monotheism. Earlier prophets had been *practical monotheists* who did not explicitly say that only the LORD existed as god. For Second Isaiah, the LORD is the only deity. The LORD is god of all peoples. Second Isaiah combines this with the old patriarchal motif of the LORD's blessing being extended to all nations. It declares that Israel will be "light to the nations," carrying the truth of the LORD to all peoples. Second Isaiah can be cutting in its satire on idolatry (44:9–29; 46:1–13). More positively, the poet can meditate beautifully on the nature and power of the Word of the LORD (chap. 55).

The mission of Israel is portrayed in a series of *servant songs* (42:1–9; 49:1–7; 50:4–9; 52:13—53:12). Elsewhere Israel is clearly the servant of the LORD (42:18–25; 44:1–5), and traditional Jewish interpretation has always held that the prophet is personifying the nation in the figure of the servant. Some interpreters think the servant must be an individual, perhaps the prophet, especially in 52:13—53:12. In any event, Second Isaiah introduced a motif that became important both for the development of the thought of the Tanak on the matter of suffering, and of later Christian thought (see chap. 11). The servant vicariously bears in his suffering the sins of the nations.

Third Isaiah. Isaiah 56—66 does not exhibit the same consistencies of theme and style as First and Second Isaiah. Rather, it is unified by a common historical setting, the situation of Jerusalem after some of the exiles have returned. Third Isaiah is probably an anthology within an anthology, a collection of prophecies of the Isaiah School produced after about 515 B.C.E. The Temple has been rebuilt (56:5–7; 60:7; 66:6), and sacrifice has resumed (66:3). The Second Isaiah-like oracles in 60:1–3 and 61:1–4 contrast with the vindictive song directed against Edom in 63:1–6. But most of the material is of a classical prophetic style. The exception is the concluding oracle in 66:22–23. It envisions a "new heaven and new earth," exhibiting apocalyptic flavor similar to Isaiah 24—27.

Oracles Against Foreign Nations. Archaeologists have unearthed numerous texts from ancient Near Eastern cult sites in which curses are leveled against foreign enemies. Thus, it is not surprising that Israelite prophets sometimes proclaimed the wrath of the LORD upon Israel's foes. Of the oracles in Isaiah 13—23, which are drawn from a range of historical settings, one is of particular interest. It is a taunt song over a dead Babylonian king (14:4–20). It gives us one of our more graphic biblical descriptions of the underworld (Sheol) where the dead dwell, and it includes one of the few biblical allusions to the motif of a fallen god-angel.

The Isaiah Apocalypse. Isaiah 24—27 seems more attuned to apocalyptic than prophetic literature (resurrection, universal judgment, a cosmic battle between the LORD and mythic foes, and a banquet heralding a new age of peace). Because other apocalyptic motifs are missing (such as visions and symbolic numbers; see chap. 9), this section is sometimes called *protoapocalyptic* and is used as an example of a transitional form between prophetic and apocalyptic writing.

Jeremiah

The Book of Jeremiah transmits more information about the prophet who stands at the head of its tradition than any other. There is descriptive data about the activities of the prophet and subjective information from the prophet himself. This gives us insight into the activities and attitudes of at least one, if not all, prophets. With the note (Jeremiah 36) that Jeremiah's secretary Baruch wrote down a collection of Jeremiah's oracles, we have a bit of evidence about the development of prophetic books.

Jeremiah's activities spanned the most calamitous decades of Judean history prior to the Christian era. The years from 620 through 609 B.C.E. had been years of nationalism, reform, expansion, and prosperity under Josiah (see chap. 5). But from Josiah's death in 609, disaster piled upon disaster, culminating in the destruction of Jerusalem and its Temple by the Babylonian army in 587–586 B.C.E.

Scholars have long debated the role Jeremiah may have played in the deuteronomic reform. The earliest datable oracle in Jeremiah (22:10–12) issues from 609, the year of Josiah's death and the effective end of the reform. If Jeremiah was active in the reform, we have no concrete evidence.

Unlike Isaiah of Jerusalem, Jeremiah was an unwilling prophet. He protested his youth at the time of his call (1:1–10). Later in his career he tried, but failed, to quit prophesying. His reluctance is understandable, for his prophetic activity made him the target of an assassination plot (involving members of his own family). A priest, he was barred from the Temple. He was without friends and alone much of the time, and he was forbidden by the LORD to marry. He was put in stocks, beaten, left in a muddy cistern to die, and imprisoned through much of the Babylonian siege. To keep at his prophetic mission under these circumstances suggests rather remarkable courage.

The early oracles of Jeremiah spoke of doom and made him the butt of mockery when, as in Isaiah's time, the catastrophe was slow to materialize. From a secular viewpoint, Jeremiah was a lackey of the pro-Babylonian party at court, opposing the pro-Egyptian party. From a prophetic viewpoint, the LORD had commissioned him to announce that the Babylonian yoke was divine judgment on the sins of the nation, especially her unworthy rulers. The burden was to be borne with patience until the LORD lifted it, as Jeremiah dramatically illustrated (Jeremiah 28). Other prophets expressed contrary views, which Jeremiah roundly condemned (23:9–40). He accused his prophetic adversaries of being phonies who had never stood in the LORD's court.

The "Confessions of Jeremiah," mentioned earlier, are unique in prophetic literature. These utterances not only mourn the prophet's fate but they also challenge the LORD, accusing him of deception and unfair use of his greater power. Then they swing to the realization that the LORD is the prophet's only source of hope. There are no specific divine answers to these laments, only the LORD's promise that if Jeremiah is steadfast, God will not allow the prophet to be totally overwhelmed.

When the doom of which Jeremiah had spoken arrived, a new side of the prophet emerged. Like Second Isaiah, he turned from the time of judgment to envision hope for Israel. It was not the naive hope he had condemned other prophets for voicing. It was a long-range hope grounded in a deep faith in the love and fidelity of the LORD. Three examples of this side of Jeremiah must suffice.

(1) Jeremiah wrote the exiles of the 597 deportation, warning them against superficial hopes of an early restoration, but with the promise that the LORD would ultimately restore Jerusalem (Jeremiah 29).

(2) While he languished in prison during the Babylonian siege, Jeremiah took the seemingly illogical step of buying property in his hometown, Anathoth, near Jerusalem (see p. 126). Appropriately, Jeremiah was redeeming family property, as he expected God to redeem Judah.

(3) Finally, the "new covenant" passage (Jer. 31:31–34) promises a renewal of the LORD's relationship with Israel and Judah based on a covenant inscribed upon the heart (that is, upon the consciousness and will) of people. The passage had great influence on later Jewish groups, including the Dead Sea community and the early Christians.

Jeremiah survived the fall of Jerusalem. He declined a Babylonian sinecure to share the lot of his people in a ravaged Judah, joining the court of Gedaliah, the Jewish governor appointed by King Nebuchadnezzar of Babylon. Gedaliah was murdered, and a group of fearful refugees forced Jeremiah to go with them to Egypt. He is last seen continuing his courageous prophetic work, an exile in a foreign land (Jeremiah 40—43).

A note of concern for individual responsibility emerged in Jeremiah's oracles. Everything cannot be blamed on the sins of the fathers. People will reap the benefits and misfortunes of their own behavior. The buck cannot be passed to others (Jer. 31:29–30; cf. Ezek. 18:1–4).

Ezekiel

The autobiographical introduction to the Book of Ezekiel presents him as a priest among the exiles of the first Babylonian deportation (597 B.C.E.). His prophetic activity he dated from the fifth year of Jehoiachin's exile (592 B.C.E.). His datable oracles extend to the late 570s.

The rabbis of the late first century C.E. debated whether Ezekiel really was canonical. The "problem" with Ezekiel was apparently twofold:

(1) Ezekiel's vision of the Chariot of the LORD (1:4–28; cf. 9:3—10:22) was a source of mystical speculation. As with other objects of mystical speculation, many authorities felt the use of Ezekiel should be restricted.

(2) Ezekiel's envisioned plan for the reconstruction of the Temple in chapters 40—48 differed from the rules for the Tabernacle-Temple in Leviticus.

Ezekiel's own reported trance states have been a source of controversy among modern students. However, his reported levitations, transports, visions, trances, catalepsy, and other phenomena are all well documented in the literature of anthropology. One need not propose elaborate editorial theories for the book or consider the prophet psychologically unstable.

The Book of Ezekiel locates the prophet's primary activity among the exiles in Babylon. But he claimed access to Jerusalem by vision and levitation and seemed well informed about the situation there. The contents of the book are topically arranged into four blocks. Chapters 1—24 are mostly oracles denouncing the sins of Israel and Judah (even though the Northern Kingdom had been gone for over a century). Chapters 25—32 contain oracles against foreign nations, and chapters 33—39 mainly oracles of hope. The latter section concludes with the elaborate Gog-Magog oracle, possibly pro-toapocalyptic (Ezekiel 38—39). Chapters 40—48 contain a highly idealized plan for the reconstruction of the Temple, and of the national life of Israel, on lines more congenial to the priesthood than to the secular nobility.

Ezekiel exhibits more colorful symbolic actions than any other prophet. He ate a scroll (2:9—3.3; cf. Rev. 10:8–11). Chapter 4 recounts his lying first on one side, then on the other for long periods, drawing war comics on a brick, and subsisting on the foul diet of a siege victim or war slave. He shaved his head and beard and did some strange things with the hair (Ezekiel 5). He dramatized the fate of Zedekiah, perhaps bemusing his neighbors in the process (12:1–16). He cooked meat in a rusty pot (24:1–14). At the death of his wife, he did not mourn (24:15–27). These actions are, in context, graphic prophetic messages.

The career of Ezekiel, like that of Jeremiah, may well have reached a turning point with the fall of Jerusalem. When judgment struck, the prophet of doom became the prophet of hope.

Again like Jeremiah, Ezekiel denounced those he considered false prophets, saying they plastered and whitewashed a faulty defensive wall (13:1–16). He stands in the classical prophetic tradition with his condemna-tion of ethical transgressions, violence, corruption, and bloodshed (see Ezekiel 22). But idolatry and religious infidelity were the most serious sins to this priestly prophet, for they beget all other transgressions (Ezekiel 8, 14, 16). Like Jeremiah, Ezekiel emphasized the idea of personal responsibility (Ezekiel 18). He also applied the idea of responsibility to the work of the prophet, "the watchman," (3:16–21; 33:1–20).

Two other themes in Ezekiel deserve our attention. The term *son of man* is God's favorite title for the prophet. It means *human being*. The clear meaning of this phrase here cannot be ignored when considering its meaning in other biblical documents. Finally, Ezekiel's life-giving stream, which issues from the restored Temple in his reconstruction, not only had roots in Gen. 2:10 and other Near Eastern lore, but it is also the probable source of the similar image in Rev. 22:1–2.

The Scroll of the Twelve

This section of the canon is known to modern Christians as the books of the *minor prophets*. They should be considered minor only in terms of length. They are united, because all twelve together roughly equal the length of one of the three major prophets, thus bringing the Latter Prophets up to four scrolls, balancing the four scrolls of the Former Prophets (Joshua, Judges, Samuel, and Kings).

There is no clearly discernible scheme underlying the arrangement of materials within the Scroll of the Twelve. Certainly the twelve sections do not stand in chronological sequence (see Figure 6–1).

Hosea. The evidence within the Book of Hosea suggests that this prophet witnessed the disintegration of the era of prosperity in the Northern Kingdom under Jeroboam II and in the south under Uzziah as well as the Syro-Ephraimite war that followed. The most likely dates for Hosea's prophetic career are 745–725 B.C.E. He is unique among the Latter Prophets as a native of the north.

Extremes of wealth and poverty were abhorrent to the egalitarian values of the Torah tradition. Thus Hosea vigorously denounced oppression and exploitation of the poor, especially through the perversion of the courts by the wealthy and powerful. Hosea also shared the prophetic repugnance at religious apostasy, including cultic aspects of foreign diplomatic alliances. Hosea equated such with adultery, an apt image given the fertility overtones of most pagan ritual at the time and the religious aspect of the Sinai Covenant (cf. chap. 4; Hos. 4:11–14). Hosea also denounced unworthy priests, some of whom he accused of brigandage (6:8–10).

Hosea's private life was intertwined with his prophetic message. At the LORD's instruction he married a common prostitute (as opposed to a cultic prostitute who participated in pagan ritual). She left him, which became a metaphor for the LORD's relationship with Israel. Like Hosea's Gomer, Israel had gone "whoring" after other husbands (in Hebrew, *baals*). And just as Hosea continued to love his wayward spouse, the LORD continued to love Israel, and, in the long run, wanted to win her back and purify her. There are many questions about how to untangle the events alluded to in chapters 1—3, but this is the substance of the action and its symbolism.

Hosea was not preoccupied with only a single metaphor. He also used the picture of a stubborn domestic animal (4:16) and a rebellious child (11:1–9) to speak of the LORD's deep love for his wayward people. The key to Hosea's understanding of the LORD is the Hebrew term *hesed*, which, as noted, means "steadfast love," "faithfulness," "fidelity," among others. It describes the covenant relationship between the LORD and Israel, portraying both the LORD's intention toward Israel and his expectation for the people (6:6). Hosea apparently thought of the sufferings of war and exile as the path to penitence. The saving purpose of the LORD's love for his people would not be thwarted.

Joel. Internal evidence from the Book of Joel suggests a postexilic date (fifth or fourth centuries B.C.E.) for Joel's prophecy. The sacrificial practices mentioned seem to reflect the priestly code (see 1:9; 13; 2:14; cf. Ex. 29:38–42 and Num. 28:3–8). The dispersion of Jews seems to be a fact of life (3:1–3).

The Temple stands with a functioning priesthood (which means after 515 B.C.E.). Joel seemed to know the prophetic tradition. Joel 3:10, for example, contains a parody of Is. 2:4 and Mic. 4:3. The influence of Amos may elsewhere be discerned. The most likely time for the Book of Joel is about 400—350 B.C.E.

The prophecy begins with an account of a severe locust plague accompanied by drought. The prophet suddenly realizes that the disaster may be a harbinger of cosmic catastrophe, the dreaded Day of the LORD. The LORD himself interrupts the litany of doom. He commands a fast, one undergirded by genuine penitence. The lament of priest and people is answered by an oracle of assurance. The Day of the LORD has become a day of fulfillment for Israel. Israel's enemies will suffer, but Israelite exiles will return home and Judah will become both fertile and secure, with the LORD in the midst of Zion (2:28—3:21).

In fuller canonical context we could examine the citation of Jl. 2:28–32 in the Pentecost sermon of Peter in Acts 2:17–21. Form criticism has pointed to the Book of Joel for the "setting in life" of the laments so common in the Psalms. Theologians point to Joel's expression of true repentance: "rend your hearts and not your garments" (2:13).

Amos.   The Book of Amos contains the earliest collection of oracles in the Scroll of the Twelve. Like Hosea, he lived in the time of Jeroboam II and Uzziah (1:1). Amos can be placed at about 750 B.C.E.; he does not reflect the chaos of the 730s.

The superscription introduces the collection as the words that Amos *saw*. More typically, the word of the LORD is described as *coming* to a prophet. Some of Amos's visions are narrated: a locust plague, a drought so severe that the cosmic deep was consumed, and a wall (Israel) hopelessly out of plumb. Amos interceded after the first two visions, and the LORD "repented." Amos was silent after the third, and the LORD proclaimed irrevocable doom (7:1–9). Later, doom was portrayed as a basket of summer fruit (a pun in Hebrew; Am. 8:1–2). Amos's visions, like those of Jeremiah (see Jer. 1:11–14), may reflect the perception of profound significance in ordinary sights rather than mystical experiences.

Amos's first set of oracles (1:2—2:16) reflects the rhetorical skill of the prophet (or the compiler). He used the 3 + 1 formula of wisdom teaching ("for three transgressions, and for four..."; cf. the three visions of Am. 7:1–9). Amos played upon the prejudices of his Israelite audience by denouncing the surrounding nations, culminating in an oracle against his own Judean homeland (he was from Tekoa, south of Jerusalem). Then, with the audience in the palm of his hand, the prophet swatted, pronouncing a detailed condemnation of Israel's Torah violations.

In his condemnation of foreign nations, Amos appealed to a sense of common morality. In his denunciation of Israel and Judah, he held them accountable to the Mosaic covenant. Repression and exploitation of the poor and the perversion of justice called forth wrath. He excoriated the religious hypocrisy that substituted ritual for ethical behavior (4:4–5; 5:21–27). Amos the radical went so far as to suggest that the sacrificial cult was a human innovation, not a Mosaic institution!

Amos was not a professional prophet, as his encounter with Amaziah the priest makes clear (7:10–17). He was minding his own business when God sent him north to denounce covenant dereliction. Amos did not hold out hope for his audience. Although repentance could bring redemption (5:4–6, 14–15), he did not expect it to happen.

The prophecy of restoration in 9:11–15 has the marks of a later addition. The booth of David (Jerusalem) had not yet fallen in Amos's day (9:11).

Obadiah.   The Book of Obadiah is only one chapter long. It belongs to the *oracles against foreign nations* category of prophetic sayings. Obadiah's wrath was directed against Edom (Esau). Prior to the Babylonian wars, the Israelites apparently looked upon Edom as cloddish kinsmen, fit butts for ethnic humor (Gen. 25:27–34; 27:1—28:9). However, Edom took advantage of Judah's prostrate condition after 587 to loot, pillage, and annex territory in the Negev. Thereafter, Edom became the object of the wrath reflected by Obadiah (and Third Isaiah in Isaiah 34 and 63:1–6). A date during the Exile or the early postexilic period is generally accepted. The vision (1:1) may have been offered on a cultic occasion.

Jonah.   There *was* a prophet named Jonah of the eighth century B.C.E. (2 Kgs. 14:25–27). But the book called Jonah is quite unlike any other block of tradition in the Latter Prophets. It is not a collection of oracles with narrative interludes; it is a narrative with only one oracle (3:4). It is more like the short stories of the Tanak (see chap. 9) than the other books of the Latter Prophets.

It is hard to miss the satire and irony in this delightful tale. The prophet, who knows better than God, is drawn with broad and absurd strokes. Everything he does is inappropriate, and his only correct action occurs under duress. Even his pious psalm from the belly of the great fish (Jonah 2) is more appropriate for a near-drowning victim. Everyone in the story turns out to be more devout than the self-righteous prophet: the pagan sailors, the king and people of Nineveh, even the domestic animals. The story illustrates how a comic art form can be a powerful vehicle for religious meaning. Jonah is the archetype of the hypocritical person who would reserve God's love for himself and his own and consign his enemies to God's wrath.

A precise date for this work is nearly impossible to defend. The popular notion that it was propaganda against the "exclusivism" of Ezra and Nehemiah distorts their policies (cf. chap. 9). The sympathetic and ahistoric view of Assyria strongly suggests a postexilic date.

Micah. Micah is the only canonical prophet quoted by name in another section of the Latter Prophets (cf. Mic. 3:12 and Jer. 26:18). His career fits between the Assyrian campaign against Samaria (mid-720s) and Sennacherib's siege of Jerusalem (701 B.C.E.). Micah was from a rural village (Moresheth-Gath) southwest of Jerusalem, and may have been a member of Isaiah's school. The most direct evidence is the Zion oracle common to Mic. 4:1–4 and Is. 2:2–4. A number of other oracles seem similar (such as Mic. 1:10–16 and Is. 10:27–34, and Mic. 2:1–3 and Is. 5:5–30).

Like Isaiah, Micah denounced the exploitation of the rural poor (2:1–5; 3:1–3) and saw the cities as repositories of evil (1:5; 13). He had little use for mercenary prophets (3:5–8), and he felt that many of his contemporaries would rather hear a windy temperance preacher than a true prophet of justice (2:6–11).

The most famous passage in Micah (6:6–8) takes the form of a covenant lawsuit. Its conclusion as to what the LORD requires of people is sometimes taken as a summary statement of eighth-century prophetic themes: Do justice (Amos), love mercy (Hosea), and walk humbly with God (Isaiah).

Nahum. Nothing is known of Nahum of Elkoah, whose vision stands next in the Twelve. Its superscription even lacks the usual association with a king. Nahum's prophecy is concerned solely with the fall of Nineveh, the Assyrian capital, to the Medo-Babylonian coalition in 612 B.C.E. His words have the character of a taunt song over a defeated foe rather than an oracle against a foreign nation. Nahum's prophecy may have been part of a liturgical re-creation of Nineveh's downfall, the end of the "bloody city" that had visited such grief on so many.

Habakkuk. The setting for this work is suggested by the reference to the Chaldeans, the aristocracy of the Neo-Babylonian empire (Hab. 1:6). The Babylonian armies are active, but Jerusalem has not yet fallen, suggesting a period between 605 and 600 B.C.E.

Like his contemporary, Jeremiah, Habakkuk dared to question the LORD about the moral operations of the world (1:2–4). The LORD responded that he was raising up the wrath of the Chaldeans (1:5–11). Habakkuk quickly concluded that the cure was worse than the disease (1:12—17). Here, the prophet literally challenged God to give him the answer he had been seeking. He took his stand in the watchtower until the answer came (2:1).

Habakkuk did not have to wait long. The LORD instructed him to write the answer so plainly that it could be read on the run. The answer itself was, "He whose soul is not upright in him shall fail, but the righteous shall live by his faith" (2:4). In a canonical and theological context, Paul's use of this verse in Gal. 3:11 and Rom. 1:17, and Martin Luther's use of Paul, make this one of the more influential prophetic utterances.

Habakkuk 3 is a lament with indications of liturgical use. The poem draws on the mythic imagery of the cosmic combat between the LORD and sea monsters (3:8). It offers another response to Habakkuk's question from the watchtower. The LORD, Creator, is the master of all chaotic powers (3:17–19).

Zephaniah. The superscription of this book locates the prophet in the reign of Josiah (640–609 B.C.E.). He stands in the classical prophetic tradition, denouncing religious apostasy (1:4–6), social syncretism (1:8), religious indifference (1:12–13), violence and oppression (3:1–2), official corruption (3:3–7), and pride and lying (3:11–13). Most notable is his awesome account of the approaching Day of the LORD, which eclipses even the visions of Amos and Joel (1:12–18). It appears that everything on the face of the earth will be swept away. The medieval hymn, *Dies Irae* ("A Day of Wrath") was inspired by this oracle.

But the Zephaniah tradition is not totally bereft of hope, despite the radical language. A few of the humble and lowly will be spared (2:1–3); 3:11–13). Zephaniah does not use the term *remnant*, but the concept is present.

Haggai. Ezra 5:1–2 reports that Haggai prophesied at the time that Zerubbabel, the governor, and Joshua, the High Priest, began to reconstruct the Jerusalem Temple. His work is dated to the second year of Darius I, 520 B.C.E., which accords with Ezra's reference.

Haggai's prophecies offered strong support for the Temple program. He promised that the restored house would exceed the glory of its predecessor, despite current appearances. The wealth of nations would flow into Jerusalem (2:1–9; 20—22). He also promised Zerubbabel (a Davidic descendant), nothing less than the throne of David (2:23; cf. Jer. 22:24). Soon thereafter Zerubbabel disappeared from the records.

Haggai has been criticized for his practicality. But his prophecy is a counterweight to romantic idealism. As any anthropologist or sociologist can testify, no human idea, however worthy or spiritual, will long survive without embodiment in some sort of institution.

Zechariah. Although Haggai and Zechariah made no mention of one another, they were contemporaries. Zechariah shared Haggai's zeal for a rebuilt Temple and a purified community, and he held out the hope of divine intervention to create an ideal age.

Zechariah 1—8 records a series of *night visions* (1:7—6:8), followed by a description of the crowning of Joshua as messianic leader (there were originally two crowns, one for the missing Zerubbabel; 6:9–15). Zechariah 7—8 offers classical prophetic oracles. Satan makes his only appearance in the Tanak (other than in Job 1—2) in 3:1–10. As in the Book of Job, Satan is the heavenly prosecutor, failing to make a case against Joshua (3:1–10). Satan as leader of a heavenly rebellion against God is a later tradition.

Zechariah 9—14 seems to be later than 1—8. Chapters 9—11 are called "an oracle," and they announce the restoration of Israel, with the messianic king entering Jerusalem on a colt (9:9–10; cf. Mt. 21:4–5). Chapters 12—14, also called simply "an oracle," announce the coming Day of the LORD, when Jerusalem will be purified, the covenant will be renewed, and there will be a universal kingdom centered in Jerusalem. There seem to be links between this material and apocalyptic literature.

Malachi. The name Malachi may actually be a title, "my messenger," drawn from Mal. 3:1. Reflections of religious customs in the book suggest that Ezra's work still lay in the future. However, the fervor stirred up by the Temple rebuilders had cooled, and Malachi devotes much of 1:6—2:9 and 3:6–11 to attacking religious indifference. Among the oracles of judgment in chapters 3 and 4 we find a reference to a coming messenger who will prepare the way for the LORD. Elijah is named as the forerunner of the Day of the LORD, performing the remarkable task of reconciling the generations. These oracles have deeply influenced Jewish and Christian eschatology.

Malachi's penultimate words constitute an apt point on which to conclude a consideration of the prophets of Israel. Every one of them would have echoed his call to Torah fidelity.

> Remember the law of my servant Moses, the statutes and ordinances that I commanded him at Horeb for all Israel. (4:4)

SUMMARY

The books of the Latter Prophets are mostly collections of the utterances of charismatic figures who lived between the eighth and sixth centuries B.C.E. They are divided into so-called major prophets (Isaiah, Jeremiah, and Ezekiel) and minor prophets or the Scroll of the Twelve. These prophets were not so much predictors of the future as ambassadors of the divine King, bringing messages of judgment and hope to the covenant people and other nations. In addition to the writing or classical prophets, the subject of the Latter Prophets, other prophets such as Nathan and Elijah are prominent figures in the Former Prophets.

In our treatment of the prophets in this chapter, we discussed prophecy as a social phenomenon, stressing its spontaneous, charismatic character. We also traced the history of prophecy from its origins in premonarchic Israel. Our literary analysis highlighted the form of individual prophetic sayings and narratives and the recurrent themes of covenant, judgment, and redemption.

Following the canonical rather than chronological order, we then examined each prophetic book to try to reconstruct its most likely original context and to emphasize its most important themes.

Although the period of classical prophecy ended and the prophetic canon closed before the New Testament era, the phenomenon continued, as we shall later see. For that matter, contemporary voices, speaking words of judgment and hope, claim to speak with divine authority, like prophets of old. Many choose to call such charismatic figures modern prophets. One way to evaluate these contemporary prophets is to measure their messages against the standard established by the classical prophets of ancient Israel.

THE CONTEMPORARY WORLD: QUESTIONS FOR DISCUSSION AND REFLECTION

1. The Israelite prophets offered strong political and diplomatic advice to the governments of their time. They did so quite avowedly on religious grounds, speaking as God's representatives. Would the prophets have been more effective if they had practiced practical diplomacy rather than speaking so absolutely? Who are the modern "prophets"? Subject their approaches to influencing policy to the same critique. Are they, or should they be, more practical and less "preachy" in their approach to leaders and to the public?

2. Among contemporary prophets you can think of, how does their message compare with those of the biblical prophets?

3. Which of the ancient Israelite prophets spoke "messages from God" that relate to modern American society? Which are the most important?

4. According to the New Testament, "a prophet is without honor in his own country." Was that true in ancient Israel? Is it true today?

5. Israelite prophets were charismatic, in the sense that they practiced spirit-endowed behavior. Modern technological society is skeptical of such behavior. Yet sociologists and journalists continue to describe contemporary forms of "charismatic behavior" and note its powerful effect on people. In ancient Israel appropriate and inappropriate forms of prophetic behavior were acknowledged. If there are contemporary forms of charismatic behavior, which are appropriate and which are inappropriate? How can a person tell the difference?

CHAPTER 7

Israel's Sacred Songs: Psalms, Song of Songs, and Lamentations (The Writings I)

This view of the Old City of Jerusalem looks from west to east across the city and the Temple Mount, identified by the prominent Muslim Dome of the Rock (Haram es Sharif). Mount Scopus rises on the horizon to the left, and the Mount of Olives runs from the center to the right. Jerusalem is frequently mentioned in the Psalms as Zion. The destruction of Jerusalem by the Babylonians in the sixth century B.C.E. inspired the Book of Lamentations.

INTRODUCTION

The third section of the Hebrew canon is the Writings (*kethuvim* in Hebrew). It was the final section of the Tanak to be incorporated into the canon. Inclusion of some of the books (especially Esther, the Song of Songs, and Ecclesiastes) was the subject of serious discussions within the Jewish community. Several types of literature are found in the writings: songs, wisdom literature, short stories, historical narrative, and apocalyptic literature. Except for the historical narratives (Ezra, Nehemiah, and the Chronicles), the rest are types of literature that we have not yet encountered in the biblical books. We will organize our discussion of this section of the canon around these different literary forms.

The Book of Psalms, the Song of Songs, and Lamentations represent different types of songs of ancient Israel. The Psalms is a collection of songs, most of which were sung in the context of worship. The Song of Songs is an anthology of love poetry from ancient Israel. And Lamentations is a group of songs of anguish that were all motivated by the destruction of Jerusalem in 587 B.C.E. They are all poetry, with no narrative introductions (except for the brief titles on many Psalms).

A PEOPLE'S POETRY: THE BOOK OF PSALMS

Introduction

The Book of Psalms (also called the Psalter) is a collection of 150 poems, most addressed to God. The twentieth-century Catholic mystic Thomas Merton called the Psalms "the most significant and influential collection of religious poems ever written."[1] They are the substance of daily worship in Jewish and Christian practices to this day, a staple of Sabbath or Lord's Day celebrations in nearly all Jewish and Christian communities, and a source for private devotion and reflection for millions. People who know nothing else about the Bible are familiar with quotations from the Psalms. In short, it may be the most influential single book of the Bible and, therefore, deserves our careful attention.

To orient you to the Psalms as literature we will examine (1) the types of poems found in the Psalter, (2) the Psalms as unique poems, and (3) the relational world of the Psalms. To introduce the historical world of the Psalms, we will discuss their original setting in the worship of ancient Israel.

---

[1]Thomas Merton, *Bread in the Wilderness* (London: Hollis and Carter, 1953), p. xi.

Courtesy of the Israel Museum, Jerusalem

Dead Sea Psalms Scroll from Cave 11. Among the Dead Sea Scrolls was a selection of Psalms concluding with a Hebrew text of Psalm 151, which appears in the Greek (Septuagint) Psalter, but not the masoretic Hebrew.

The Literary World: The Psalms as Poems

The Types of Psalms. Although the Psalms are not organized in the Psalter according to literary types, twentieth-century interpreters have recognized several different literary categories, based on the psalms' form and content. We will briefly describe the major types of psalms, discuss an example of each, and list the psalms that probably should be considered part of each category.

The most frequent type of psalm is the *lament*—a prayer to God that describes a situation of distress (the lament proper), cries out to him in anguish, and calls upon him to act to relieve the situation (the petition). Laments usually express confidence in the LORD's mercy and promise to praise him for the anticipated deliverance. However, some laments do not have such expressions. Frequently, the psalm includes reasons intended to motivate God to intervene.

Approximately one-third of the psalms are *personal laments* describing the situation of a single person, although in such a general way that it is difficult to identify the specifics of the distress or the personal identity of the one in anguish. Some apparently personal laments may in fact be prayers of a personified community. Psalm 13 is a brief example of an individual lament. Its structure illustrates the typical threefold focus of the description of distress: God (v. 1), "me" (v. 2a), and enemy (v. 2b). In this psalm the petitioner's appeal to God is combined with the motives for action (vv. 3–6).

In addition to Psalm 13, the following psalms and a few other scattered psalms can be considered individual laments: 3, 4, 5, 6, 7, 10, 11, 12, 14, 22, 25, 26, 27, 28, 35, 36, 38, 39, 40, 51, 52, 53, 54, 55, 56, 57, 58, 59, 61, 62, 63, 64, 140, 141, 142, 143. Outside the Psalter there are examples of this type of poem in Lamentations 3, Jeremiah (the "Confessions"), and Job (especially chap. 3).

There are a few *communal laments* in the Psalter that focus on the plight of a sometimes ambiguous "us." They have a similar structure and also use stereotyped language to address God and describe the plight of the people. Psalm 79 is an example of this type. The situation is described in terms of enemies (vv. 1–3), "us" (v. 4), and God (v. 5). A petition (vv. 6–12) is followed by a promise of praise (v. 13).

One element of the individual laments not found in the communal laments is a clear-cut expression of confidence. Instead, there are reminders to God of his gracious acts in the past (e.g., Ps. 44:2–3; 74:12–17; 80:8–11). Other examples of communal laments in the Psalter include Psalms 44, 74, 80, 83. Outside the Psalter communal laments are found in Lamentations.

The next most common type of psalm is the *song of praise*, a poem that acknowledges and affirms God, either in terms of who God is or what God has done. Some psalms of this type give thanks to God for specific deeds of deliverance and could be called *songs of thanksgiving*. Others praise God in general. This type of psalm is usually called a *hymn*.

Among the songs of thanksgiving, the most frequent is that voiced by an "I" and relating to a personal situation, exemplified by Psalm 138. Other examples are 9; 18; 22:22–31; 31; 32; 34; 40; 66; 92; 116; and, perhaps, 107. Outside the Psalter this type of psalm can be found in Jonah 2 and Lam. 3:52–57. Most of the psalms found among the Dead Sea Scrolls are of this type. There are only a few communal songs of thanksgiving in the Psalter, among them Psalms 124, 129, and 66:8–12.

The *hymns* are all communal. They include some of the most beautiful poems in the Psalter. A good example of the simple and straightforward hymnic form is found in Psalm 113, in which a call to praise (vv. 1, 9b) surrounds descriptive praise of the LORD's majesty and mercy (vv. 2–9a). Characteristic of hymns is praise of the majesty of God, evidenced in nature, and of the goodness of God, manifested in his treatment of the poor and needy. Other hymns in the Psalter include 8; 19; 29; 33; 57:7–11; 65; 66; 89:5–18; 93; 95; 96; 97; 98; 99; 100; 103; 104; 111; 113; 117; 134—136; 139; 145—150. Outside the Psalms, hymns are found in Isaiah 40—55, the Book of Job, and Chronicles.

Beyond laments and songs of praise, attempts at classification of the psalms become more problematic. Scholars have not developed a generally accepted set of types. There is disagreement over which psalms fit which type. As we have noted, some psalms do not address God at all, in praise or lament. Some of them are didactic, designed to instruct (e.g., 34:11–22; 37; 112; 128), while others reflect on human mortality (90), the suffering of the righteous (73), or both (39, 49). Because of the similarity between these psalms and the wisdom books (Job, Ecclesiastes, Proverbs), they are some- times grouped together as *wisdom psalms*. Still other psalms seem to have in common a concern with the king and are called *royal songs* (2, 18, 20, 21, 45, 72, 89, 101, 110, 132, 144). However, they are diverse poetically and could, using different criteria, as easily be placed with other types. Similar observations could be made about the so-called *liturgical psalms,* which give indication of some specific use in public worship (e.g., 15, 24, 107, 122), the *Zion Psalms,* which focus on Jerusalem (46, 48, 76, 84, 87, 132), or psalms of divine kingship (47, 93, 95, 96, 97, 98, 99).

The assignment of one psalm to various categories should alert us to the limits of literary classification. It is helpful to realize there are different kinds of psalms, but merely "typing" a psalm does not tell us what it means. We must also consider the Psalms as unique poems.

The Psalms as Unique Poems. Thomas Merton also wrote in his meditative study of the Psalms, "A good poem...stands by itself, graced with an individuality that marks it off from every other work of art."[2] Although the Psalms do reflect typical patterns, they should also be appreciated as individual poems that create worlds of their own. The best way to make this point is to explore the unique world of one of the Psalms.

Psalm 8 is classified as a hymn, for it is a psalm praising the LORD as creator. However, merely to classify it does not do justice to its richness. That is apparent when we treat it not as a hymn but as a unique poetic utterance. This psalm, which uses a poetic meditation on the creation of mankind as a basis for praising the LORD, is structured to communicate a sense of order that is in harmony with its theme. The frame of the meditation on the place of humanity is the ascription of praise in verses 1 and 9. This sense of symmetry underlies the theme of a divinely created order, and it frames the expression of awe at the majesty of humankind within the context of the sovereignty of the LORD. Within the body of the poem (vv. 2–8) there is a balance between the heavenly bodies ordered by God (v. 3) and the creatures of earth, sky, and sea for which humankind has responsibility (vv. 6–8). In the center of this symmetrical pattern is the pivot, the question and answer in verses 4 and 5. At the center of the psalm is verse 5, making the point that the glory and honor of humanity derive from the majesty and splendor of the Creator. The distinct sense of movement in the psalm includes a flow from acclamation of God's majesty to the seeming insignificance of human-kind measured against God and his Creation; a pivot at the affirmation of the centrality of humankind in God's plan; a movement back through creation, now focusing on that for which humankind is responsible; and a return to the beginning and the acclamation of God's sovereignty.

The imagery of the psalm is built on a series of contrasts. The basic contrast is between the majesty of God and the insignificance of humankind, mediated by the glory bestowed upon humanity by the Creator. In verses 1–2 the praising of God "above the heavens" is contrasted with that which comes from the mouths of babes and infants. It is an image of God being praised from the mightiest to the weakest of creatures, but with an ironic

[2]Merton, *Bread,* p. 45.

twist. For it is from babes and infants that the power to still the forces of chaos comes. At the heart of the psalm is an even more ironic twist. The Divine King, who has all hostile powers under his control, who needs no "help" managing the cosmos, assigns to mere humanity a royal status (the "glory" attributed to the LORD is shared with humankind, vv. 1, 5). It is this paradox at which the psalm marvels. Its pivotal verse goes so far as to place humanity in the company of the *elohim* (the divine beings who serve and praise the LORD in the heavenly court).

Like other Hebrew poems, the psalms utilize *parallelism* as the basic poetic technique. For example, Ps. 8:3 is a good example of *synonymous parallelism*. The second half of the verse balances the thought of the first half, element for element. However, it is not enough merely to note the type of balancing used. The question is: How does it function in the poem? In Ps. 8:3 we note that, despite the synonymous parallelism, the second line drops the *I* after contrasting the human *I* with the divine *your*. By not repeating the *I*, the second half of the verse sharpens the sense of human insignificance toward which the poem is building. This is a subtle nuance contributing to the effect of the psalm as a whole. Another good example of the function of parallelism in a psalm is Ps. 29:1–2. Here, *stairlike parallelism*, in which an element is repeated and the thought is extended, serves to build a crescendo, climaxing in the voice of the LORD upon the waters (v. 3), like a thunder-roll leading to the thunderclap that follows.

These examples must suffice to support the point that the student who desires a full appreciation of the poetry of the Psalms must treat each psalm as a unique poem.

The Relational World of the Psalms. Although each psalm is unique, all of them come from a poetic tradition with a common stock of imagery. That imagery reflects a basic view of life that we might call the *relational world of the Psalms.* Each psalm focuses on one of the following basic relationships: God and I, God and other divine beings, God and Israel, and God and nature.

God and I.[3] Most of the psalms are written from a first-person perspective, speaking to God. Usually the identity of *I* is ambiguous, so that it might be an individual, a representative of the people (priest or king, for example), or a symbolic expression for everyone (an everyman). The situations described are so general that we can identify only two basic patterns: dislocation and reorientation.

In many psalms (especially the laments), *I* articulates a situation of dislocation. Often vivid, but general, images of physical distress are present (e.g., Ps. 22:14–15). Either directly, as in this psalm, or indirectly, the infirmity

[3]See Lawrence Thompson, *Introducing Biblical Literature: A More Fantastic Country* (Englewood Cliffs, N.J.: Prentice-Hall, 1978), pp. 53–66.

is linked to God; thus the physical distress becomes a relational problem, a situation of dislocation or disorientation in the relationship between God and *I*. This creates a tension that only divine action can resolve.

Sometimes the disorientation is linked to the moral failure of *I* (e.g., Ps. 25:11 or Ps. 51), and often it is linked to the persecution of "foes" whose identity is always ambiguous, allowing the psalm to be adapted to a variety of situations (e.g., Psalm 3). Invariably, *I* portrays the situation as hopeless without divine intervention. The imagery is often that of life and death. Unless there is action by God, *I* is, in effect, as good as "dead." In ancient Near Eastern mythology, the dead were thought to go to an underworld (in Hebrew, as mentioned, called *Sheol*, "the Pit") where they continued a minimal shadow existence cut off from the relationships that give meaning to life. In particular, it is a place where people no longer have a relationship with the divine, and from which they are unable to praise God. Thus, the *I* of the psalms uses the image of death and Sheol to speak of the complete dislocation from the deity toward which *I* feels "myself" moving (e.g., Ps. 88:3–7). Another image of separation from God is the waters, symbolic of the chaos God has not yet ordered (e.g., 69:2), which is saying that "my world has collapsed and the forces of chaos are overwhelming me."

Balancing dislocation imagery, often within the same psalm, is reorientation imagery. Although rarely described within psalms, an act of divine deliverance is assumed, which has restored the *I* to harmony with God, reversing the previous disorientation (e.g., Ps. 30:1–3). The result of the reorientation is often expressed in terms of the reidentification of the individual *I* with the larger worshiping community. For example, in Psalm 22 the *I* moves from a situation of isolation and persecution by enemies to an anticipated reorientation expressed in terms of participation in the worshiping community (22:22–31).

Many psalms give a spatial identification to reorientation, using the Temple in Jerusalem as a symbol of harmony with God. In the Temple the community gathers for worship, and the individual feels a sense of orientation. In distress *I* is alienated from the Temple (e.g., Ps. 28:2). The joy of feeling oriented and in harmony is expressed in imagery of either going up to or being in the Temple (e.g., Ps. 122:1–2). The ascent imagery of going up to the mountain of God reflects the fact that in ancient Near Eastern mythology the dwelling of the divine king is always symbolized as a mountain (in the imagery of the Hebrew Bible, first Mount Sinai [Horeb], then Mount Zion in Jerusalem). In contrast is the descent imagery of going down into Sheol.

For most *I* psalms, the tension and movement, then, is within these poles. Some psalms (like the famous Psalm 23) are fully on the side of orientation, although a past disorientation is almost always acknowledged, and some (like Psalm 10) are almost totally focused on disharmony, though there is virtually always some anticipation of restored harmony.

God and other divine beings. Often confusing to modern readers of the Psalms are references to other divine beings besides the LORD. Although many English translations mute this mythological imagery, it is important to understand it if the relational world of the Psalms is to be fully appreciated. As we have noted in our discussion of prophetic literature, the LORD is sometimes portrayed as the king of a divine court, surrounded by a heavenly entourage of other beings (e.g., 1 Kings 22, Isaiah 6). This same imagery is present in the Psalms. For example, Psalm 82 opens with a picture of God in the role of administrator of cosmic justice, addressing the divine court (vv. 1–2). Psalm 29 begins in the heavenly court with a call for the "sons of God" to praise the LORD. Other examples of divine beings surrounding the LORD as servants appear in Ps. 89:5–8 and Ps. 103:21.

In addition, the Psalms draw on the imagery of a primeval battle between the divine warrior-king and his cosmic foes (e.g., Ps. 89:9–10; 104:5–8; 74:13–14). Invariably, the imagery serves to herald the might and power of the LORD, sometimes as the basis of an appeal for the divine warrior to engage contemporary, historical foes as he did the primeval, mythic ones. Imagery such as this raises the question of the attitude of the Psalms and other biblical literature toward the mythology of the cultures surrounding Israel. It is apparent that biblical writers could both attack the other gods who were the actors in these myths, such as the Canaanite Baal, even denying they existed, and also adapt the myths of other cultures to their view of the LORD and his interactions. This conflict might bother us, but it was apparently not a problem for those who originally wrote or read the Bible. Although the LORD, unlike other ancient Near Eastern deities, was portrayed as a god who made himself known through historical events (such as the Exodus), this did not stop biblical writers from using the imagery of the nature myths of surrounding cultures to speak of him. Sometimes (as in Ps. 74:13–14 and Exodus 15) the imagery of what was an ahistorical fertility myth is used to suggest the cosmic significance of one of the LORD's deeds within history.

God and Israel. The Psalms stand within the same covenantal tradition as the Prophets and Torah, alluding to the special relationship of the LORD with the nation Israel, manifest in acts of deliverance in fulfillment of the patriarchal promises, the covenant at Sinai, and the promise to David of an everlasting dynasty. Within the Psalms there are sometimes general references to the "deeds thou didst perform in...the days of old" (e.g., 44:1–3), which calls forth the imagery of patriarchs, exodus, wilderness, and conquest. In several psalms (66, 78, 105, 106, 135, 136), these deeds are recited in detail not only so that they may not be forgotten, but also so that they may be made present (see, for example, 66:1–7, especially v. 5), just as Deuteronomy places a later generation at the Exodus.

God and nature. In a number of psalms the "earth" in general is admonished to praise the LORD (e.g., 66:1; 96:1; 97:1), and various elements of nature are called to join in exultation of the kingship of the LORD (e.g., 96:11–13). When God appears, nature convulses (e.g., 68:7; 29:5–8; 114). In the world of the Psalms nature is not inanimate matter, but alive, a dynamic part of the web of relationships to be taken seriously. Thus, Psalm 104 lauds God's provision not only for humankind but for all of nature.

The Historical World:
The Psalms in Israel's Worship

There can be no doubt that many, if not all, of the psalms were associated with acts of worship in ancient Israel, in the Temple at Jerusalem and perhaps at other shrines before worship was centralized. Some of the titles added to the psalms give instructions for their use in worship (e.g., Psalms 4 and 5). The repetition of the word *Selah* probably is a notation

Photograph by Arthur C. Young

Model of the Second Temple, Jerusalem. The Jerusalem Temple, first built by Solomon in the tenth century B.C.E., was rebuilt on its original site after being destroyed by the Babylonians in the sixth century B.C.E. A reconstruction project, originated by Herod the Great in the first century B.C.E., continued into the first century C.E. This model of "Herod's Temple" at the Holy Land Hotel in Jerusalem is based on both literary and archaeological evidence. The rabbinic literature preserves memories of the use of biblical Psalms in the worship of the Second Temple.

concerning performance of the psalm, although its precise meaning, as noted, is a mystery. There is also evidence in the Bible outside the Psalms of their use in Temple worship (e.g., 1 Chr. 16:7–36). Moreover, some psalms seem to reflect a specific liturgical event. Psalm 24, for example, was probably used in association with a procession of the Ark of the Covenant into the Temple. These hints of the cultic use of the psalms have sparked a great deal of speculation on the types of services or festivals with which various psalms may have been associated. Rabbinic literature records the liturgical use of a number of psalms in the worship of the Second Temple. For example, Mishnah Pesahim 5:7 notes that the *hallelujah psalms* (Psalms 113 to 118) were chanted by the Levitical choir while the Passover lambs were being sacrificed (see chap. 10, on rabbinic literature).

Because many psalms acclaim the Lord as king (e.g., Ps. 96:10), and there is evidence in the culture surrounding Israel of yearly festivals in which a god was enthroned as king, many interpreters believe that these psalms reflect an *enthronement festival* in Israel. At this festival, associated with the beginning of the new agricultural year in the autumn, the LORD's enthronement as Divine King would have been reenacted in the Temple, the earthly representation of the heavenly palace. Unfortunately, there is no evidence within or outside the Bible of any such festival in ancient Israel, so it must be considered only a hypothetical possibility. A modification of this hypothesis holds that, in association with the enthronement of the Divine King, there was a yearly Royal Zion festival in which the earthly, Davidic king was also enthroned. But these psalms may be equally well understood as proclamations of the LORD's continuing kingship.

Because of the importance of the remembering-reenacting of the LORD's mighty deeds of deliverance for Israel, and of the evidence of covenant renewal festivals in ancient Israel (e.g., Joshua 24), some interpreters theorize that many psalms were originally associated with an annual *covenant renewal festival*.

It is also possible to conceive of worship events that might have been the context for the individual and communal laments. In many laments there is, as we noted, a transition from the situation of distress and petition for help to an expression of confidence. Perhaps this transition reflects the giving of an oracle of assurance by a priest or other religious leader (see, for example, 1 Samuel 1:17). There is also some evidence in the Bible of communal fasts at times of crisis such as crop failure, pestilence, or attack from enemies (e.g., 1 Kgs. 21:9; Am. 5:16; Is. 22:12; Jer. 14:2). Thus, it is possible that communal laments originated as songs used at times such as these. The prophetic book of Joel illustrates at least one cultic situation in which communal laments might have been used, a fast day proclaimed in the light of some great disaster (Jl. 1:13—2:29). Indeed, Jl. 2:17 contains a highly condensed lament using very typical language. The ninth day of the month

Ab, when the Babylonians destroyed the Temple, and anniversaries of other such great tragedies probably were occasions of annual fasts. Because the Romans destroyed the Temple a second time on the ninth of Ab, in 70 C.E., this is one of the saddest days on the Jewish liturgical calendar.

Interpreters have also associated the Songs of Ascent (Psalms 120—134) with the journeys to Jerusalem that would have been a part of the pilgrimage festivals identified in the Torah. Whether or not any of these particular festivals might have been occasions for enthronement or covenant renewal festivals has also been the source of much speculation.

Although there is little clear evidence as to particulars, we can assume that most psalms originated as songs associated with corporate worship. In that sense they were the product of the life of the community as much as the work of individual poets. However, some psalms may well have originated as religious poems by individuals, apart from a liturgical setting. For example, the psalms that are reflections on the importance of the Torah of the LORD (1; 19:7–14; 119) might not imply a background of worship. The so-called *wisdom psalms* (such as 36, 37, 49, 73, 112, 127, 128, 133) have no obvious connection with worship.

The many attempts to date particular psalms have proven largely futile because of the lack of external evidence and the ambiguity of their imagery. Even when a psalm pictures a specific situation (such as the destruction of the Temple in Psalms 74 or 79), too few details are given to link the psalm with a concrete historical event. Although King David may have composed some of the seventy-three psalms attributed to him in the titles added to the psalms, the traditional assumption that David is the author of all the Psalms is inconsistent with the editorial superscriptions of many psalms, let alone with the internal evidence of the Psalter. Some psalms are attributed to other famous persons such as Moses (90) and Solomon (72, 127). Psalm 72:20 indicates that the Davidic collection has concluded. Moreover, the phrase translated into English "of David" in the titles of the Psalms does not necessarily imply authorship. The relation of David to the Psalter is probably like that of Moses to the Pentateuch and Solomon to Proverbs and the other works attributed to him: original inspiration but not necessarily authorship of the books. It is likely that psalms were composed throughout the biblical period, certainly from the time of David and Solomon onward. The present collection comes from the postexilic period, although individual psalms may have been composed much earlier.

THE MEGILLOTH

Five of the short works among the Writings are grouped together as the Five Megilloth, the Five (festival) Scrolls. They are Ruth, Song of Songs, Ecclesiastes, Lamentations, and Esther. The custom developed of reading one of these scrolls on each of five important festivals or days of religious observance through the year. The connection of Esther with Purim is obvious, because it explains the origin of the feast. Similarly, Lamentations, which bemoans the Babylonian destruction of Jerusalem and its Temple, fits well the fast of the ninth of Ab, the anniversary of that tragedy. The connection of Song of Songs with Passover may reflect the influence of the allegorical reading noted in a later discussion here. However, the association of Ruth with Shavuot (The Feast of Weeks) and Ecclesiastes with Sukkot (The Feast of Tabernacles, or Booths) appears more arbitrary.

THE SONG OF SONGS

The Song of Songs (also known as the Song of Solomon, or Canticles) is a collection of erotic love poetry. Quotations from this work, which frankly celebrates physical passion, have inspired incredulous responses like "Is *that* in the bible?" It is not surprising that many have interpreted the poems allegorically since rabbinic times. For Jewish interpreters, the Song was taken as an allegory of the LORD's relationship with his "bride," Israel. Christian commentators saw in the imagery a symbol of Christ's love for the Church. From our perspective, these interpretations are part of the historical world of the Book. However, as we shall see, they are not especially helpful in leading us into the literary world of the Song.

The Literary World: An Anthology of Love Poems

In its final form the Song of Songs is an anthology of between eighteen and thirty-one separate poems, depending on how they are divided by the reader (they are not distinguished in the text).[4] Despite their common interest in erotic love, they are in fact quite diverse in subject matter, tone, and situation. The poems are *lyric* in the sense that they are subjective expressions of the feelings of a speaker addressed to a particular listener. Several types of poems can be distinguished. In *love monologues* an *I* (male or female) speaks either to or about his or her beloved, for example,

> My beloved is mine and I am his
>   he pastures his flock among the
>   lilies.
> Until the day breathes
>   and the shadows flee,
>   turn, my beloved, be like a gazelle,
>   or a young stag upon rugged
>   mountains. (2:16–17)

---

[4]We are indebted in our literary analysis to Marcia Falk, *Love Lyrics from the Bible: A Translation and Literary Study of the Song of Songs* (Sheffield, England: The Almond Press, 1982).

Other love monologues are 1:1; 1:9–11; 2:4–7; 2:14; 3:1–5; 4:1–7; 4:8; 4:9–11; 6:4–10; 6:11; 8:1–4; 8:5b; 8:6–7. Another type is a *love dialogue*, in which there is conversation between two lovers, for example,

> Behold, you are beautiful, my love;
>   behold, you are beautiful;
>   your eyes are doves.
> Behold, you are beautiful, my
>   beloved,
>   truly lovely.
> Our couch is green;
>   the beams of our house are cedar,
>   our rafters are pine. (1:15–17)

Others of this type are 1:7–8; 2:1–3; 2:8–13; 4:12—5:1; 8:13–14. In addition, there are monologues by an *I* in a love relationship with an audience outside the relationship (1:5–6 and 8:11–12); monologues by a group to an unspecified audience about love (2:15; 3:6–11; 8:5a); dialogues between an *I* and a group about erotic matters (7:1–6 and 8:8–10); and one composite poem (5:2—6:3).

Several of the poems are *wasfs* (from the Arabic word for "description"). A *wasf* is a poem or section of a poem that describes the parts of the human body through a series of metaphors. In ancient Hebrew literature these are unique to the Song of Songs. Song 4:1–5 is a partial *wasf*, describing a woman from her eyes down to her breasts. Each part is described with an agricultural image. In 5:11–16 a female speaker describes her beloved, from his head down, with various images. In 7:1–6 there is another complete *wasf* describing a female body.

Despite ingenious efforts to find an organic structure uniting these poems, it is very likely that the Song of Songs is simply a group of love songs gathered together without any overarching pattern of organization.

In these poems male and female speakers voice freely their affection and desire for one another in passionate, but never lurid, expressions of erotic love. As a whole, then, the poems are a celebration of the love a man feels for a woman and the love a woman feels for a man. This is quite in keeping with the understanding of sexuality in both the creation accounts in Genesis and elsewhere in Scripture. In the dramatized relationship there is no sense of one of the lovers being possessed or dominated by the other. The physical expression of love is portrayed with a mutuality and caring often missing in erotic literature. The mood of the Songs can perhaps best be expressed in an utterance by one of the females, speaking to an audience of the "daughters of Jerusalem": "This is my beloved and this is my friend,..." (5:16b).

The Historical World:
Authorship and Original Function

Although the first verse identifies the work as Solomon's, and Solomon is remembered for his proverbs and songs (1 Kgs. 4:32), it is unlikely that Solomon is the author of these poems. Some of the poems do refer to him. In 1:5 a woman compares her dark beauty to the "curtains of Solomon." The poem in 3:6–11 speaks of Solomon on the day of his wedding, and 8:11–12 refers to the vineyards of Solomon (his harem) in contrast with the speaker's own vineyard (his beloved). These third-person references are internal evidence that Solomon did not author these poems. The maiden, the Shulammite (6:13), has been associated with Abishag the Shunammite, David's virgin bedfellow (1 Kgs. 1:3–4). Because Solomon did not give her to Adonijah (1 Kgs. 2:13–17), the presumption is that he kept her for himself. But Shulammite and Shunammite look no more or less alike in Hebrew than they do in English. It is most likely that the attribution of the Song to Solomon was added to lend authority to it by linking it to the king renowned for his wisdom and his many loves. Given the variegated nature of the anthology, it may be more appropriate to speak of an editor or collector who gathered a variety of love poems together.

There have been numerous attempts to reconstruct the original setting of the Song, some of them highly imaginative but none of them very convincing. As mentioned, early interpreters viewed it allegorically. Unfortunately, unlike Isaiah 5, an allegorized love song, there is no evidence within the text for this interpretation. Modern commentators have suggested a dramatic interpretation with two or three main characters, such as Solomon and one or two lovers. But there is absolutely no hint of a plot or a setting, and a drama can be detected only by a very imaginative reading. Other theories hold that the Song has been adapted from an ancient fertility ritual involving a god and goddess or that it is a cycle of wedding songs used at marriage ceremonies in ancient Israel (with the bride, groom, and guests as speakers). However, none of these theories has won a consensus of scholarly opinion, suggesting that they are all attempts at forcing the Song into a mold it does not fit. Until there is further evidence supporting these or some other as yet unforeseen view of the Song's original function, we should probably hold our imaginations in check and take the song for what it is—an anthology of sensuous love poetry celebrating human love.

As a whole the Song echoes the view of human sexuality that Genesis presents as the way God intended it to be (Gen. 1:27–28; 2:24–25) before the rebellion of man and woman led to the embarrassment and manipulation that still plague the expression of physical love today.

LAMENTATIONS

The Book of Lamentations is a collection of five poems mourning the destruction of the city of Jerusalem (see 2 Kgs. 25:8–12). Originally composed after Jerusalem was sacked and the Temple destroyed by the Babylonians in 587 B.C.E., the poems became a part of the yearly remembrance of this terrible event in the Jewish liturgical calendar. In the Writings it is the only one of the five festival scrolls associated with the yearly fast on the ninth of Ab. Although tradition assigns it to Jeremiah (see 2 Chr. 35:25), and this is the title and location of the book in Christian Bibles (following the LXX), it was probably an anthology of poems by several poets.

The Literary World: An Anthology of Laments

The first four poems (Lamentations 1—4) are *acrostics;* that is, each stanza begins with a subsequent letter of the Hebrew alphabet. Because there are twenty-two letters in the Hebrew alphabet, there are twenty-two stanzas. The final poem in chapter 5 also has twenty-two stanzas but does not follow the acrostic form. This acrostic pattern is fairly common in the Hebrew Bible (for example, Nahum 1, Psalm 119, Proverbs 31), and it was most likely a device to assist memorization when the poems were circulated orally. The acrostic form also creates a sense of thoroughness; everything from A to Z is covered in them. This artifice might seem to limit the spontaneity of feeling in the poems; however, reading Lamentations gives no such sense of artificiality. The poem in chapter 2 gives a vivid, first-person (some think eyewitness) description of the anguish of the residents of Jerusalem under siege (2:11–12; cf. 4:2–10). The poems in chapters 1, 2, and 4 utilize the rhythm associated with funeral dirges, in which the first line receives three beats and the second two. This is one of the few clear-cut examples in biblical poetry of this *qinah* meter, as it is called. Even in translation we can sense the difference in length and accentuation of the lines in these chapters. Reading them aloud gives a sense of rhythm.

The poems are not only vivid descriptions of the horrors of the total destruction of Jerusalem by the Babylonians, but they also step back and reflect on the meaning of the event. Jerusalem was not merely the capital of the nation, it was Mount Zion, the symbol of the LORD's presence with his people. In the symbolic universe of ancient Israel, Jerusalem was the center.

As modern studies have shown, the first step in facing the loss of someone or something essential to life is often to express the volatile emotions aroused by the loss. The poems in Lamentations first of all verbalize the feelings of the community and individuals who have seen their loved ones killed and the symbols at the center of their existence destroyed. But grieving also involves trying to place the loss in some framework that makes sense out of it. Lamentations finds that context in the belief that Jerusalem and her inhabitants were being punished by the LORD for their disobedience. The LORD allowed the Babylonians to destroy his Temple and his people because of his indignation (see, for example, 2:17). The poems give voice to this explanation, but they do not simply accept it meekly. Speakers also urge the survivors to cry out in anguish to the LORD for allowing this to happen (e.g., 2:18–22), and the collection ends with an impassioned plea to the LORD to "remember."

At the center of the anthology (Lamentations 3), the tone abruptly changes. The speaker expresses a hope based on his trust in the unceasing, steadfast love (*hesed*) of the LORD (3:22–51). The basic tension of the collection is apparent here. It is between the experience of the presumed anger of the LORD and a stubborn faith that he is merciful. This hope is anchored in neither the covenantal nor the creation traditions; it is based on a fundamental perception of the divine character, that both good and evil come from God (3:38) and "though he cause grief, he will have compassion according to the abundance of his steadfast love" (3:32). Despite this general hope, there is no anticipation that circumstances will soon change, as in many of the laments of the Psalms. Our attention is also drawn to chapter 3 by the form. Not only does every stanza begin with a subsequent letter of the alphabet, but also every verse in each stanza begins with the same letter.

The Historical World: Original Setting

There is biblical evidence of acts of lamentation carried out soon after the destruction of Jerusalem in 587 B.C.E. (Jer. 41:5). Zechariah 7:3–5, written about 518 B.C.E., suggests that a fast had been held during the fifth month (Ab) ever since the city fell. On the basis of this data, we can legitimately argue that the poems of Lamentations were used liturgically in the exilic period. This practice was probably the reason for making Lamentations one of the festival scrolls, associated with the annual fast on the ninth of Ab in the Jewish liturgical calendar.[5]

Although there is a change of speakers (from the first-person singular to the first-person plural), there is no substantial evidence of any dramatic setting for the collection. This has not stopped some interpreters from trying to reconstruct one.

SUMMARY

The songs included in the Tanak range from the impassioned love poetry of the Song of Songs to the anguished laments of the Psalter and the Book of

---

[5]The apparent contradiction in language here goes back to ancient rabbinic usage. Fasts were treated along with feasts in one section of the Mishnah, which bore the title *Moed* ("feasts").

Lamentations. In this chapter we considered the literary character and most likely original historical settings of the songs of ancient Israel.

The 150 poems of the Book of Psalms are a rich anthology of the best of ancient Israelite religious poetry, most of it associated with worship in the Jerusalem Temple. In treating the psalms as literature, we surveyed the types of psalms and offered a reading of Psalm 8 to illustrate the importance of recognizing the unique as well as typical features of the psalms. We then described the basic relationships with the psalmic world. Our historical analysis identified the various acts of worship with which the psalms may have originally been associated.

Although most traditional interpreters read the Song of Songs allegorically, we chose to present this anthology of love poems in terms of their implicit speakers and audiences. We assessed the mood of the Song as a frank and sensitive celebration of the physical expression of human love.

Lamentation is an anthology of five poems inspired by the destruction of Jerusalem traditionally associated with the prophet Jeremiah. We found these poems not only moving evocations of the horror associated with the annihilation of a city but carefully crafted meditations on the significance of the event. The laments almost certainly appeared in the liturgies of cultic events marking this pivotal event in Israel's history.

Poetry is the literary medium by which we express our deepest emotions. Although the style and imagery of many of these songs may make them seem impenetrable to the modern reader, they reward any who allow themselves to feel the moods they evoke.

THE CONTEMPORARY WORLD:
QUESTIONS FOR DISCUSSION AND REFLECTION

1. Think of the Psalms as if they were the popular songs of ancient Israel. They gave expression to a wide range of human emotions—joy, anger, pride, inferiority, fear, hope, despair, and so on. Do contemporary popular songs fulfill a similar need? Do the Psalms still fulfill this need? Compare some popular songs with the Psalms.

2. Many Psalms were used in worship in ancient Israel. They are still used in worship by Jewish and Christian communities. In your experience, are Psalms effectively used in contemporary worship? How might Psalms be used in worship in new and creative ways? Take Psalm 24 or Psalm 8 as examples.

3. The Book of Psalms, especially in the Miles Cloverdale and the King James translations, has had a strong influence on English and American poetry and language generally. Which of these influences are you aware of, if any?

4. A law student had begun to date a very religious young lady. He asked a friend who was a graduate student in biblical studies to recommend a biblical passage about love that he could read to his friend to impress her. His friend replied, without reflection, "Oh, the Song of Songs is a love poem. Read her that." The law student did, and the relationship ended on the spot. What is the significance of this incident in terms of the contemporary impact of the Song of Songs?

5. How does the view of sexuality in the Song of Songs compare with attitudes prevalent today? How might the view of sex in the Song of Songs positively (or negatively) affect male-female relationships today?

6. Does the Book of Lamentations have a message or messages for persons living under the threat of nuclear war? If so, what is it, or what are they?

CHAPTER 8

The Way of Wisdom: Proverbs, Job, Ecclesiastes (The Writings II)

Courtesy of The Pierpont Morgan Library, New York

Illustration of a scene from the Book of Job. The imaginative English poet, artist, and mystic William Blake (1757–1827) created a set of woodcut illustrations for the Book of Job. He insightfully caught the mythological symbolism in the background of the Behemoth and Leviathan passages (Job 40:15—41:34) and here renders these beasts as marvelous, but relatively benign, creatures.

INTRODUCTION

Although the Books of Proverbs, Ecclesiastes, and Job are not a distinct subgroup within the Writings, they are the Tanak's example of a type of literature common in the ancient Near East (and throughout history)—*wisdom literature*. They are distinct from the rest of the Bible (except for isolated examples, particularly among the Psalms) in their style and their view of the world. Stylistically, these works are dominated by short observations and instructions about life and how to live (Proverbs, Ecclesiastes), poetic dialogue (Job), and poems focusing on the nature and meaning of life (Ecclesiastes, Job).

In these books the themes that recur in the rest of the Tanak are missing—exodus, covenant, Torah, and the rest. The concern is not the LORD's involvement in history with Israel and other nations and the hope of fulfillment of God's promises. Instead the wisdom writings treat the human search for and maintenance of order. This is a practical search for happiness through living with propriety and decorum, that is, in accord with the natural and social order. But the search goes on at a deeper, more speculative level too, for these works (especially Job and Ecclesiastes) reflect the quest for an underlying order in the world and the answers to such basic questions as Why do the innocent suffer? Is there justice in the world? If we all die, what is the meaning of life? As a whole the Bible tells the story of God's involvement with people in history. These works must be bracketed off from the major story line. They stand on their own as a set of writings whose concerns are always contemporary. For that reason they are probably the most widely read books in the Tanak.

As mentioned, the wisdom books are unique in the Hebrew Scriptures, but they stand squarely within a literary and intellectual tradition pervasive throughout history. Every culture produces proverbs that gain authority through usage (such as, "an early bird gets the worm") and literary works that reflect on basic human questions. Wisdom works are found in the Apocrypha (Ben Sirach, the Wisdom of Solomon; cf. chap. 10) and the New Testament (James and many of the sayings of Jesus within the gospels). They are also present among Egyptian and Mesopotamian works unearthed by archaeologists. Our introduction to these writings will be divided into a literary analysis of each book and a historical discussion of the wisdom tradition in Israel and the ancient Near East.

THE LITERARY WORLD

Proverbs: The Blessings of Wisdom

The Book of Proverbs is divided into a series of collections of short sentences and admonitions, with a few longer poems interspersed.[1] The short sayings are usually in poetic form as well. Most of the collections have titles:

1. Chapters 1—9. The Proverbs of Solomon, son of David, King of Israel
2. Chapters 10:1—22:16. The Proverbs of Solomon
3. Chapters 22:17—24:22. The sayings of the wise
4. Chapter 24:23–34. More sayings of the wise
5. Chapters 25—29. More proverbs of Solomon transcribed by the men of Hezekiah, King of Judah
6. Chapter 30:1–9. Sayings of Agur, son of Jakeh from Massah
7. Chapter 30:10–33. Numerical proverbs (no title)
8. Chapter 31:1–9. Sayings of Lemuel, King of Massah, that his mother taught him
9. Chapter 31:10–31. An acrostic poem in praise of a "good wife" (no title).

Therefore, as a whole the book is an anthology of sayings and poems, in the same way as the Song of Songs is an anthology of love poems, Lamentations of laments, and Psalms of sacred songs.

The first collection is much different from the others, which are sets of individual, loosely connected sayings (except for the final poem). In chapters 1—9 we find sayings, but they are linked together into short "essays" on various themes such as the dangers of association with the wicked (1:8–19) and the blessings associated with wise living (3:1–18). They are presented in the form of a father speaking to "my son." Also included are poems in which a personified Wisdom speaks to indict the fools who ignore her instruction (1:20–33) and to proclaim her worth, authority, and place in the creative process (8:1–36). In contrast, Folly is personified uttering her enticements to the foolish (9:13–18). This collection begins with a preface, probably intended for the book as a whole, suggesting the variety of audiences and levels of meaning to be derived from the work (1:2–6) and stating its basic theme (1:7a): "The fear of the LORD is the beginning of knowledge." This might be paraphrased as "Reverence for the LORD is the starting point and essence of knowledge."

---

[1]Our interpretation of the literary world of Proverbs is indebted to James Crenshaw, *Old Testament Wisdom: An Introduction* (Atlanta: John Knox, 1981), pp. 66–99.

The second collection gathers together 375 sayings covering a wide range of observations and maxims on everyday life, each of them two lines in length (except for 19:7). There is no evident thematic unity in the collection. In the first half (10:1—15:33), the second line generally contrasts the first, suggesting a stylistic principle of organization. Of the two basic types of proverbs (sayings that make observations on the way things are in life and instructions that give advice or admonish), the first is dominant.

> God scorns the wicked,
>   but the upright enjoy his favor. (14:9)

> A man of crooked mind does not
>   prosper,
>   and one with a perverse tongue
>   falls into calamity. (17:20)

> When a man's folly brings his way
>   to ruin,
>   his heart rages against the LORD. (19:3)

The third collection, part of which is nearly identical with an ancient Egyptian collection of proverbs (discussed later), has one brief essay on the plight of drunkards (23:29–35), along with such admonitions as

> Do not toil to acquire wealth;
>   be wise enough to desist. (23:4)

The fourth collection is a brief set of exhortations and admonitions and includes a short essay on laziness (24:30–34), concluding with the observation

> A little sleep, a little slumber,
>   a little folding of the hands to rest,
> and poverty will come upon you
>   like a robber,
>   and want like an armed man. (24:33–34)

The fifth collection is marked by the frequency of comparative statements such as

> Better is open rebuke
>   than hidden love. (27:5)

> Better is a poor man who walks in
>   his integrity
>   than a rich man who is perverse
>   in his ways. (28:6)

It also includes a proverb quoted by the Apostle Paul in Rom. 12:20 (Pr. 25:21–22) and the proverb that has given many children throughout history tender posteriors, wounded egos, and in some cases, much worse (29:15).

The sixth collection is a dialogue between a skeptic and an unquestioning believer in God and a poem asking that the speaker be kept from these two extremes.

The seventh section is a miscellaneous set of numerical sayings, using a form similar to the opening chapters of the Book of Amos, prefaced by an admonition and a list of types of sinners.

The eighth section is advice given by the Queen Mother to her son, King Lemuel, concerning proper behavior for a king.

The last section is an acrostic poem (see chap. 7) extolling the virtues of a good wife—hard work, good business sense, strength, compassion for the poor, constancy in trouble, a sense of humor, kindness. This is the kind of woman who is to be praised because she "fears the LORD" (31:30).

In general, proverbs that make observations on the way life is and how to succeed dominate in sections 2, 4, and 5; and the proverbs that are instructional, giving advice or admonishing, are more prevalent in 1, 3, and 8.

The Book of Proverbs contains both practical wisdom, some of which is secular and some religious, and theoretical or speculative wisdom. The practical wisdom can perhaps best be understood in terms of several pairs of opposites that recur. One contrast is between life and death. Especially in the first section, the father admonishes his son

> My son, keep sound wisdom
>   and discretion;
>   let them not escape from your
>   sight,
> and they will be life for your soul
>   and adornment for your neck. (3:21–22)

The life that is promised is not life after death, but a long and fulfilling life on earth (3:15–18). Those who ignore wisdom and pursue wickedness will find themselves "dead," in the sense of lost, confused, and hopeless (1:18, 4:19).

Another image is the "way" or "path." The way of wisdom (that leads to life) is contrasted with the way of folly (that leads to death). The assumption is that wisdom is like a map that will assure that one keeps to the path of life and avoids the path of death (see, for example, 4:18–19).

A related pair of opposites is the wise person and the fool. In the Book of Proverbs's view of the world, everyone falls into one of these two groups. Likewise, there is a dualism between good and evil. The world of Proverbs is quite black and white, with a clear choice between life and death, good and evil, wisdom and folly. The individual proverbs are nearly all concerned with discriminating between these opposites and laying forth the consequences of behavior related to them. The instructions are designed to encourage behavior that is good, wise, and leading to life and discourage actions that are foolish, evil, and leading to death.

Many of the observations and much of the advice in Proverbs makes no mention of God. It claims nothing more than the authority of experience. Much of the material can be considered textbook lore for the ancient counterpart of a school of business and public administration, training the scribes who would be the clerks, managers, executives, and ranking officials of government and cult. The prudence counseled is not unlike the conventional wisdom that has guided organization men and women through much of history. However, many proverbs are tied to belief in God as the power who desires and rewards good behavior and abhors and punishes evil actions, for example,

> He who oppresses a poor man
> insults his Maker,
> but he who is kind to the needy
> honors him. (14:31)

Basic to the life-or-death orientation of Proverbs is the claim that "fear (reverence) of the LORD is rewarded with "life," while disdain for the LORD leads to "death." Without this basic attitude, the final edition of Proverbs assumes, no one can be truly wise.

In addition to grounding its practical teachings in reverence for the LORD, Proverbs also asserts an authority for wisdom rooted in creation itself. Wisdom is personified as a principle associated with the creative process, present with God from the beginning (3:19–20 and 8:22–31). Wisdom is here heralded as the life-giving principle of cosmic order. This gives a theoretical foundation to the claim that wisdom is the order for everyday living. The personification of Wisdom in Proverbs introduces us to a type of speculation that we will encounter again in Job, the wisdom literature of the Apocrypha (see chap. 10), and the New Testament.

In sum, the Book of Proverbs presents wisdom in practical terms, contrasting the rewards of wise living with the perils of foolish behavior. It assumes that God rewards goodness and punishes evil. The book also speculates on the source of authority of wisdom, claiming that wisdom is the life-giving principle apparent in the very process of creation. These are assumptions the Book of Job challenges.

Job: The Limits of Wisdom

At a conference several years ago, the authors had the opportunity to study with a teacher, who, in 1944 as a boy of fifteen, was taken to the Nazi death camp at Auschwitz, Poland. There his entire family died in the gas chambers, part of the Nazis' "final solution of the Jewish problem." He alone survived. After class one day, someone asked our teacher how he could retain his faith in God after what he had experienced at Auschwitz. His response was simply, "Have you read the Book of Job?"

Besides being widely considered the literary masterpiece of the Bible, the Book of Job speaks to some of the most profound questions of the contemporary world. Its meaning, perhaps more than any other book in the Bible, transcends the time in which it was written. Like other great literary works, it defies simple interpretation. This reading of the book should be considered only an invitation to enter the world of Job and marvel at its mysteries, not a final resolution of them.

The Book of Job, like so many other literary units we have examined in the Bible, has what might be called an *envelope structure*. It is a poetic drama (3:1—42:6) framed by the opening and closing scenes of a folktale about Job (1:1—2:13 and 42:7–17). Many interpreters treat the two entirely separately. However, because in the final form they are bound together, we must ask how they are related to one another.

The legend about Job (probably linked to the patriarchal figure Job named in Ezek. 14:14, 20) is a tale about a righteous, blameless man tested by God at the urging of the member of the divine court who was charged with earthly intelligence work—the Satan. The scenes in the story move back and forth between earth and heaven. In the first, we are introduced to Job as a non-Israelite, Transjordanian sheikh who practices the advice of Proverbs. He reveres God and shuns evil. His ten children and plenteous herds are a sure sign that, from the perspective of Proverbs, he is being blessed with "life" because of his following the path of wisdom. Job is so righteous that he even tries to intercede for his sons, lest they sin and be punished. Meanwhile, at the heavenly court, on the day when divine beings are received by the Divine King, the Satan (here the term is a title, not a proper name, meaning "accuser," that is, "prosecuting attorney") appears. Apparently the LORD is proud of Job, for he asks the Satan if he has observed this righteous man. The Satan responds with a question of his own, showing that he is clever, "What do you expect; you have given him everything?" He challenges the LORD to take it all away and then see what happens. Without comment, the LORD takes the wager and allows the Satan to remove the "hedge" around Job's faithfulness but not to touch Job himself. This establishes the basic theme of the story: Is there disinterested piety (righteousness), or do people revere God only because it pays? Job is to be the guinea pig in a divine experiment. There is no vendetta against him. Ironically, there is nothing personal in his suffering.

Having established the basic theme, we can move quickly through the rest of the story. Job's servants, flocks, and children are all killed, but he remains faithful. Even when the screws are tightened, and Job himself is afflicted, he refuses to give in to his wife's advice to "Curse God and die," calling her (in good wisdom style) "a foolish woman." Job is willing to accept both good and evil from the LORD without question. Three friends come to comfort him and sit in silence. When the story resumes, after the long poetic interruption, the righteous Job has his fortunes restored, receiving twice as much as before his ordeal. In other words, after Job has proven he will remain faithful even when everything is taken away from him, and the LORD has won the divine bet, Job is rewarded. Implied in the story are at least two answers to the questions of undeserved suffering: (1) if you keep your faith throughout a time of suffering, you will ultimately be rewarded and (2) suffering may be a test of one's faith and fidelity. The story has given rise to the idea of the "patience of Job," the image assumed in the New Testament Book of James (5:11).

However, when we turn to the poetic section of the work, the sufferer is hardly patient. As his friends sit silently, Job speaks, in chapter 3. His words astonish his companions, for they are totally out of character. Job utters not trust in God, but a bitter lament. He comes perilously close to cursing God by deprecating the day of his birth and the night of his conception. Included in the lament is the first of a number of mythic images. In calling for darkness to replace the light of his birth, the sufferer appeals for the arousal of two of the monsters of chaos who opposed the Divine King in primordial combat, Yamm (Sea)[2] and Leviathan (3:8).

Job's curse arouses his friends, who take it upon themselves to go beyond merely comforting him. It is obvious to them that he needs instruction, which they feel qualified to give. Three "cycles" of speeches follow, with Job responding each time a friend speaks. In fact, each utterance is more a monologue than part of a dialogue, for both the friends and Job talk right past one another. Although there are various subtleties to the friends' arguments, their general approach is a defense of the doctrine of retribution, found both in Proverbs and in the Sinai Covenant tradition. According to this teaching, God rewards the righteous and punishes the wicked. That is the moral law he has established and that he guarantees. The friends seem to reason that, because sin causes suffering, all sufferers must be sinners. From this perspective, Job must be suffering because of sin. He is being punished or disciplined. He is obviously the problem. Assuming this view of Job's predicament, the friends first gently, then with increasing vigor and venom, argue that Job must have sinned, because he simply would not be suffering if he had not. Their remedy is for Job to repent, even if he is unaware of what he has done. Eliphaz, the first friend, sets the tone when he argues that

---

[2]The Hebrew word translated "day" (3:8) in many translations, could, with different Hebrew vowels, read "sea" and be an allusion to Prince Yamm, who, like Leviathan, is one of the gods of chaos in Semitic mythology.

> For affliction does not come from the
>   dust,
>   nor does trouble sprout from the
>   ground;
> but man is born to trouble
>   as the sparks fly upward. (5:6–7)

All three friends assure Job that God will be merciful and deliver him, if only he will acknowledge his wrongdoing. They grow increasingly angry as Job steadfastly refuses to accept their advice.

Job's replies are hardly responses to the friends. He rejects out of hand their arguments, maintaining that he is innocent, and, at the very least, his sufferings are completely out of proportion to any minor sin he may have committed (6:1–7). His friends have ceased to be friends, and they thus show that *they* are the ones who do not revere God (6:14). Job challenges them to show him his sin, but as the replies progress, he increasingly turns his attention away from the friends and toward the one whom he accuses of unjustly causing his anguish—God. Again, using mythic imagery, Job accuses God of treating him, a mere mortal, like one of the monsters of chaos (7:12). He bitterly parodies the question at the heart of Psalm 8 (8:4), asking

> What is man, that thou dost make so
>   much of him?
> and that thou dost set thy mind upon him,
> dost visit him every morning,
>   and test him every moment? (7:17–18)

On the one hand, Job longs for vindication and clings to the hope that a vindicator will arise to intercede for him (9:33–35; 16:18–22; 19:25–27). However, on the other hand, he recognizes that he is powerless before the might of the one who created everything and vanquished the forces of chaos (9; 12:7–25; 26). He reluctantly recognizes that

> It is all one; therefore I say,
>   he destroys both the blameless and
>   the wicked. (9:22)

Only if God stops his arbitrary punishment will Job be able to speak with him. Still, Job stubbornly maintains his innocence and his anger at God's unjustified treatment of him. He sarcastically points out that while he, an innocent and righteous man, suffers, the wicked go unpunished while they spurn God. The problem is that God is not living up to his own moral law! Job remains bold in his belief that, if he could somehow get a fair hearing, he could prove his innocence.

After the cycle of speeches, a poem on the inaccessibility of wisdom (28) appears without introduction. The poem is built around the refrain

But where shall wisdom be found?
And where is the place of understanding? (28:12)

The answer is that despite the marvelous achievements of human ability, wisdom is beyond mankind's reach. Only God knows its place. The poem ends with the familiar motto from Proverbs, "the fear of the LORD, that is wisdom" (28:28). In its current context the poem functions as an interlude.

When Job speaks again it is to bring the matter to a head. If God will not grant him a hearing, Job will force the issue. This he does by offering an "oath of clearance" (31), a legal device in which an accused person lists the crimes he is alleged to have committed and invokes a curse on himself if he is guilty of them. Because no charges have been filed against him, Job makes his own list of possible offenses, ranging from lust to failure to help the poor. In a final, dramatic flourish, he signs the oath, saying that if he had an indictment from his adversary, he would wear it like a crown and come before him like a prince (31:35–37).

Before the climax of the poem, there is another interlude (Job 32—37). A new speaker enters the stage, the arrogant young Elihu. (Elihu is a variant of Elijah, the one who "prepares the way for the coming of the LORD"). Elihu is angry with both Job and the three friends. Although younger, he claims that he speaks with authority because the Spirit of God is upon him. Like the friends, he defends God's ways, accusing Job of speaking without knowledge. It is not really clear whether Elihu really adds anything to the defense of God or simply repeats the arguments of the friends. He does stress one line of argument only touched on by the others, that God uses suffering to strengthen people's character. In any event, the speeches of Elihu heighten the tension, for when Elihu moves off stage, there is another voice that booms from behind the scenes.

The voice is the LORD, speaking from a storm. Interestingly, the special name for the deity appears only in the legend framing the poem and in the divine speeches. (The Hebrew *eloah,* a form of the same noun that appears more frequently in the Tanak as *el* or *elohim,* is the most typical term for God in the poetic section.) There are actually two speeches of the LORD from the tempest (38:1—40:1 and 40:6—41:34), each followed by a statement from Job. Although the introductions say the LORD "answered" Job, the divine speeches are questions rather than answers. Nowhere does the deity respond to Job's impassioned plea for a justification of his suffering. Instead, the speeches put the sufferer on the defensive. In the first, the LORD challenges Job to explain the mysteries of the natural world. He wastes no time making the point about the limits of Job's understanding.

Where were you when I laid the
    foundation of the earth?
Tell me if you have understanding. (38:4)

The implication, of course, is "How can Job demand answers from God, when he cannot even understand the world God has created?" In his description of the creation and control of the cosmos, there is, interestingly, no mention of humanity! The universe is quite complete without humankind! As Job had feared, when God speaks he overwhelms a mere mortal with his power. In response, Job can only admit that there is nothing more for him to say (40:2–5).

But this does not stop the LORD from blasting Job once more. This time he accuses Job of attacking Him in order to justify himself (40:8–9). The LORD asks Job if he is able to control wickedness in the world. Then he refers to two creatures—Behemoth and Leviathan—which are described ambiguously as a hippopotamus and a crocodile, but, especially in the case of Leviathan, with the characteristics of mythic dragonlike beasts. Job is unable to control these creatures that the LORD has made. How then can he try to challenge their creator?

In his final words (42:1–6), Job admits that the LORD is right. The divine purposes are beyond his understanding. He has spoken without knowledge about things beyond his ken. He has made assumptions about God based on what he had been told; now, having seen the LORD, he "melts into nothing" and "repents in dust and ashes."

The last phrase indicates that, in one sense, Job is back where he started—a sufferer sitting in dust and ashes, unaware of why he is afflicted. However, the story resumes immediately. The friends are condemned because they have "not spoken of me what is right, as my servant Job has" (42:7,8). Job intercedes for them, and his fortunes are restored—in double.

The question that bedevils interpreters who wrestle with this book is "What is the meaning of the Book of Job?" Can we make sense out of this highly complex, ambiguous book, or is it hopelessly confusing? Of course, as with all great literary works, there is not just one meaning but many levels of meaning. What follows should be seen as an attempt to understand the book at one level.[3]

The basic issue raised by the poem is the question of divine justice; in particular, if God is just and powerful, why does he cause innocent people to suffer? Philosophically, this is the question of theodicy—how can evil (such as the suffering of an innocent person) exist in a world under the control of a just and powerful God? Interpreters have wrestled with the problem of whether the poem answers this question. Some have suggested that there is no answer, because Job is as confused at the end of the poem as he is at the beginning. He is simply overwhelmed by God's power and wisdom. According to this view, the poem is an "anthology of doubts" that are expressed but not resolved. Others have argued that the answer is

---

[3]We are indebted here to the perceptive reading of Job by Matitiahu Tsevat, "The Meaning of the Book of Job," *Hebrew Union College Annual* 37 (1966), 73–106.

indirect. The LORD's questioning implies that he has the cosmos under control. By analogy, we are to assume that God will take care of human affairs. Simply by speaking to Job, the LORD shows his compassion for humanity. In the end, each person will get a just reward. The epilogue would seem to confirm that. Humankind must learn to accept what seems like temporary injustice, secure in the knowledge that there is divine justice that will ultimately prevail. Another approach is to say that even though the question is not answered, Job learns through the appearance of the LORD to trust in a God he cannot understand. It would be well for readers to evaluate each of these possibilities and think of others before continuing.

Another possible answer emerges when we consider the poem in the context of the story that frames it. In the story we are clearly told that Job's suffering is not a matter of divine justice; it has nothing to do with punishment of Job. His suffering is merely a test of the issue of disinterested piety, conducted to settle a heavenly wager. Of course, unlike the reader, Job and his friends are unaware of this bet. The friends assume that Job is in error by stubbornly maintaining his innocence; Job assumes that God is in the wrong. Both take for granted the doctrine of retribution.

God's response indicates that both are wrong, because of their assumptions about his ways. To assume that God's involvement with the universe revolves around the issue of retributive justice for humans is to place humankind at the center of the cosmic stage. Morality is a human problem, not a divine one. God's first speech implies that there is no guarantee of retribution in the cosmic order. The rain, often portrayed as an instrument of justice, falls in the desert where there is no human (38:25–27). When properly translated, 38:12–15 suggests that the sun shines not only on the righteous, but also on the wicked. The universe does not revolve around humanity; therefore, retribution is not a part of the cosmic order. Job is chastized for making erroneous assumptions about God's ways based on a too narrow viewpoint.

There is another dimension to the divine speeches, when we consider the basic arguments Job tries to raise.[4] He has tried to hold God to the doctrine of retribution, and is told that this is not a part of God's ways. Job has also appealed to the mythic view of the deity as a divine warrior who establishes his control of the universe in combat with cosmic foes. Job has even suggested that God is treating him like a monster of chaos (7:12). The implication is that God is not discharging his cosmic responsibilities. He is not controlling evil in the world. Instead of restraining the forces of chaos, God is venting his rage on hapless Job, a mere mortal. The LORD's speeches blast this mythic assumption. In the first one, he speaks of Sea (Yamm) not as his cosmic foe, but as a huge baby whom he has delivered and wrapped

[4]See William A. Young, "Leviathan in the Book of Job and *Moby Dick*," *Soundings: An Interdisciplinary Journal* 65 (1982), 388–401.

in swaddling bands (38:8–9). In the second speech, he suggests that Behemoth and Leviathan are not the cosmic monsters Job has implied (see 3:8). They are a part of God's creation, of no threat to Him. Only humanity confronts them as powerful enemies. In effect, the LORD deflates the mythic explanations Job has attempted to use, even as he shows up the moral argument.

According to this interpretation, the "answer" in the Book of Job is a redefinition of the questions. If God does not guarantee the moral order and retributive justice for humankind, then the question of justice is thrown back into the lap of humanity. Will humans find ways to control evil and to promote goodness? That is your problem, the LORD is saying in the Book of Job. And will people be able to believe in God without myths that assume he has control of chaos in the world? What if the truth is, as Job reluctantly realized, "It is all one; therefore I say, he destroys both the blameless and the wicked" (9:22). Indeed, if morality is a human concern, then the truth of this statement is not an indictment of God. That is where Job erred. Unlike the friends, he spoke rightly of God (even though he did not realize it himself until after the divine speeches). The friends, on the other hand, spoke wrongly, because they presumed to speak for God in defense of his ways, which they distorted.

By dealing with the question of justice in this way, we are led back to the underlying question—Can there be disinterested piety? Will a person really maintain faith in God after realizing that there is no automatic reward for righteous behavior or punishment for evil deeds? The legend gives a simple answer. Of course, Job remained firm in his faith despite his suffering. The poem moves to a deeper level. The journey to disinterested piety is not so easy for the Job of the poem. He wrestles with the problem and comes perilously close to rejecting God. He expresses a bitterness toward God that becomes quite ugly. It takes a theophany (appearance of God) for Job to learn the lesson taken for granted in the story, that he must revere God even though he does not understand why he is suffering. Job has poured out the depth of his anguished soul to God, and God has responded, but on his own, not Job's, terms. The Job of the poem clings by a very thin thread to his faith in the God who seems to be his enemy. But in the end the thread holds.

So, in the final analysis, the Book of Job dramatizes two quite different roads to the basic truth that faith in God cannot be a conditioned response to the expectation of reward or the fear of punishment. God is not a behavioralist, who practices operant conditioning on humankind.

Ecclesiastes: The Futility of Wisdom

Like the Book of Job, Ecclesiastes reflects a search for meaning amid a world in which evil flourishes and good goes unrewarded. However, the style and tone of the book are much different. Whereas Job is a poetic dialogue surrounded by a story, Ecclesiastes is an anthology of the reflections of an old sage. The Joban poem reverberates with the cries of an anguished sufferer and the blast of the divine voice from the storm. It is immediate and impassioned. Ecclesiastes is detached and philosophical. It looks back over life and shares the findings of someone who has "seen it all." In Job we come hard against the limits of wisdom; in Ecclesiastes we feel the futility of wisdom. That is not the end of this book, but the beginning.

Despite the ingenious attempts of interpreters to find structural unity in Ecclesiastes, it is most likely simply a collection of proverbs, brief essays, and poems, which can be grouped as follows:

1:2–11	Poem: The futility of life
1:12—2:26	The search for meaning
3:1–15	Poem: The pattern of life
3:16—4:3	The problem of evil
4:4–16	The folly of fame and fortune
5:1–7	The folly of religiosity
5:8—6:9	The folly of wealth
6:10—7:12	The futility of trying to change life
7:13–21	The way of moderation
7:23—8:1	The futility of seeking wisdom
8:2–9	Obedience to the king
8:10—9:12	The failure of retribution
9:13—10:20	Observations on life and wisdom
11:1–6	Action in spite of uncertainty
11:7–10	Relishing youth
12:1–8	Poem: The allegory of old age
12:9–14	Editorial footnotes.

A few structural observations can be made. The work begins and ends (before the editorial epilogue) with poems. In 1:14—6:9 the refrains "emptiness (vanity)" and "striving after wind" dominate, while in 6:10—11:10, the refrains are "cannot find out," "do not know," or "no knowledge."[5] In addition, the work weaves throughout these collections the recurrent motif that "there is nothing better for a man than that he should eat and drink, and find enjoyment in his toil" (2:24; cf. 3:12–13; 5:18; 9:9–10).

---

[5]Crenshaw, *Old Testament Wisdom*, p. 145.

The anthology begins and ends (1:2 and 12:8) with a statement of the underlying conclusion the old sage has come to about life.

> Vanity of vanities, says the
>   Preacher,
>   vanity of vanities! All is vanity.

"Preacher" is one way to translate the Hebrew term *Qoheleth* (in Greek, *Ecclesiastes*, the name or title the author uses for himself). It literally means "one who gathers together," and it could also mean a teacher. The Hebrew term translated "vanity" literally means "without substance, empty," like a puff of air, present only for an instant, then gone without a trace. According to Qoheleth, life is empty, there for a moment, then gone forever.

The first poem states the thesis, then produces evidence from human life and nature to support it. Everything moves in cycles but is never complete. "The more things change, the more they remain the same" is a modern proverb with the same point. Moreover, whatever is done is soon forgotten.

Next Ecclesiastes puts himself temporarily in the position of King Solomon (to whom the title attributes the collection). As First Kings describes him, Solomon was heralded for his wealth, luxurious life-style, and wisdom. Yet, as Ecclesiastes portrays him, Solomon discovered that the search for wisdom leads to the conclusion that all is emptiness. Likewise, he found that pursuit of pleasure, accumulation of possessions, and devotion to work all are the same—empty. The wise man and the fool have the same fate: They die and are forgotten. This led "Solomon" to despair but also to the conclusion that it is best to find enjoyment in life day by day rather than to try to find some overarching purpose.

The well-known "catalogue of the seasons" in 3:1–9 suggests a predetermined pattern of life that is beyond human ability to understand or to alter. This too leads to the conclusion that there is nothing better than to enjoy life moment by moment.

Like Job, Ecclesiastes challenges the doctrine that the righteous are rewarded and the wicked are punished found in Proverbs and other traditional wisdom teaching. Here we find the fatalistic attitude that humans are like any other animals, with no advantage, for all die. This too leads to the conclusion that the best we can hope for is the enjoyment of daily work.

As the outline suggests, Ecclesiastes sees folly and futility in those things often put forward as the answers to life's frustrations: fame and fortune, religiosity, changing one's life, and seeking wisdom. Time and again, his "answer" is to seek satisfaction and fulfillment in the daily activities of work, eating, and family life. The fullest expression of this sentiment is found in 9:7–9.

Go, eat your bread with enjoyment, and drink your wine with a merry heart; for God has already approved what you do. Let your garments be always white; let not oil be lacking on your head. Enjoy life with the wife whom you love, all the days of your vain life which he has given you under the sun, because that is your portion in life and in your toil at which you toil under the sun.

This sounds similar to the popular philosophy to which many have turned over the centuries: eat, drink, and be merry, for tomorrow you may die. Or, to quote a modern commercial: "Grab all the gusto you can; you only go around once in life." However, Ecclesiastes is not counseling the pursuit of pleasure for pleasure's sake, or gluttony. That too is vanity. Rather, moderation is the key (7:13–22). Despite the similar fate for the wise man and the fool, there is still a difference between wisdom and folly (10:12–20). Even though everything, including the pursuit of wisdom, is futile, that is no reason to give up. Go ahead and do your best, the old sage advises (11:1–6). Enjoy your youth (for the time will come when you cannot find such enjoyment). That is what life (and God) has to offer.

As should be obvious by now, the Book of Ecclesiastes is iconoclastic. It refuses to accept the traditional verities such as, "If you work hard, you will be rewarded." One technique used to question traditional teachings is to quote a popular proverb, then immediately refute it with a second (see 4:5–6). At the speculative level, Ecclesiastes challenges the assumption traditional wisdom takes for granted—that there is an order to life that humans can understand and follow (e.g., 1:15; 3:11).

Apparently, the intended audience for Ecclesiastes was young people (11:9). The old sage is trying to spare youth the bitterness and disillusionment that he passed through as he tried to find the meaning of life. The search is futile; better to face the meaninglessness of it all and find joy day by day. It is often said that Ecclesiastes is a pessimistic and skeptical book. It might be better to say that it tries to face life realistically, so that life can really be enjoyed *for what it is*. Nor is Ecclesiastes an antireligious work. It does caution against hollow religiosity (5:1–7), but throughout it maintains belief in the God who is the Creator and Judge of mankind. Like Job, however, Ecclesiastes claims that the ways of God are beyond human understanding and that humans must not assume justice is guaranteed by God. Unlike Job, Ecclesiastes has no direct encounter with God. Qoheleth's God is probably closer to the Force of Star Wars fame than to any description of the deity in Scripture. However, Ecclesiastes edges back from such an impersonal understanding of the divine when he says that God's "gift" is to enjoy life. Nevertheless, Qoheleth's understanding of God is considerably different from the God of compassion, mercy, and justice who intervenes in history, which most of the rest of the Bible portrays.

The anthology ends as it begins, with the theme of "emptiness." However, two editorial footnotes are appended. The first (12:9–12) describes Ecclesiastes in the third person. This note interprets the sayings as "goads" (that is, provocations) and "pegs" to hang things on. That is to say, their limitations should be recognized. They are *not* the whole story. The second note says in effect that the last word is "Revere God and keep his commandments, for he is the ultimate judge." That brings the collection back within the circle of traditional wisdom, and, for that reason, is almost certainly the addition of an orthodox editor intending to qualify the fatalism of the book.

To sum up, the theme of Ecclesiastes, an anthology of proverbs, poems, and brief essays of an old teacher that is intended primarily for young people, is that there is no great meaning or purpose to life. The truth is that we live for a while, die, and are forgotten. Whatever humans do to try to accomplish or discover meaning leads only to frustration. God is in control of life, but his purpose is beyond human comprehension, despite our deep yearning to know it. The best we can hope for is enjoyment of the daily routine of life, shared with others. For Ecclesiastes, that is all there is, but, as the gift of God to humankind, it is enough.

THE WISDOM MOVEMENT IN ISRAEL AND THE ANCIENT NEAR EAST

In a verse that apparently speaks of the situation in the sixth century B.C.E., the prophet Jeremiah quotes his opponents as saying, "Come, let us make plots against Jeremiah, for the law shall not perish from the priest, nor counsel from the wise, nor the word from the prophet" (18:18). This revealing statement recognizes three learned professions in ancient Israel—priests, who had charge of the law (Torah); prophets, who spontaneously spoke messages from the LORD; and sages, who gave advice based on their observations of the way things were. In order to place the wisdom writings in their original historical context, let us try to reconstruct briefly the role of the wise in ancient Israelite society, and in the wider ancient world.

In Israel there were probably three separate settings for wisdom teaching: the clan, the court of the king, and the school.[6] In the clan the father was the sage, teaching his children how to behave in society and how to look at the world. Remnants of this type of teaching are found, as noted, in Proverb's references to the instruction of a father to "my son." Proverbs also gives evidence of maternal wisdom in the counsel to heed the mother's teaching as well as the father's (7:8, 5:20) and in the poems of chapter 31. Typically,

---

[6]Crenshaw, *Old Testament Wisdom*, pp. 42–65.

these teachings are oriented toward the practical—how to succeed in work, whom to seek out and whom to avoid, how to be ready for life's pitfalls, and how to recognize the basic morality by which all should seek to live.

There is evidence of the place of wisdom in the court of the king in the historical narratives. Solomon, especially, took note of the importance of wise counsel and of searching for wisdom himself, but other kings are associated with sages who advised them (see 2 Sam. 16:23; 20:14–22). Women as well as men are portrayed as sages consulted by monarchs (e.g., 2 Sam. 14:1–20). Second Sam. 20:16–22 records an instance when a wise woman saved her town from great harm.

Later wisdom writings give evidence of a house of learning, that is, a school setting in which sages instructed the young (Sirach 51:23). As noted, it is likely that Ecclesiastes emerged from the setting of school instruction.

In all its contexts, wisdom teaching tended to be conservative, cautiously accumulating observations of the ways of nature and society. The teaching of wisdom was a way to foster commitment to the perceived order at various levels of society. In traditions such as wisdom, which tend to justify the status quo, change tends to come spasmodically. Pressures build up until a new idea breaks the hardened shell of accepted teaching. It is fascinating that, of the three wisdom writings in the Tanak, two come from the "rebels" who challenged the assumptions of their traditions.

Israelite wisdom was part of a much wider movement that directly influenced the wisdom literature of the Bible and that manifests similar, but also different, forms of wisdom writing and thought. We can only give a hint of this huge corpus of literature here.

In Egypt there are a number of examples of instructional literature, in which a father addresses a son or a teacher or a pupil, with advice on behavior in various settings, frequently the court. One of these, the instruction of a minor official of the New Kingdom (thirteenth to twelfth centuries B.C.E.) named Amenemopet, was probably the source for Pr. 22:17—23:14. Also present in Egyptian wisdom were *onomastica*, lists of the names of various natural phenomena such as flora and fauna. This example of early science is similar to the divine naming of phenomena in Job 38—39. There are also examples in Egyptian wisdom literature of speculative literature with a pessimistic bent, most from the chaotic Twelfth Dynasty. There are also several fables and debates.

In Mesopotamia we also encounter instructional literature. One piece, the so-called *Book of Ahikar*, may have inspired Pr. 23:13–14 and 27:3. Unlike in Egypt, but similar to the custom in Israel, sages collected proverbs, which were published for the benefit of students. Like the Book of Job, several Mesopotamian compositions wrestle with the problem of the suffering of the righteous. There are also a number of fables and debates and one example of a skeptical and pessimistic dialogue.

Attempts to determine authorship and times of origin for wisdom writings have yielded only limited results. Although there is no reason to doubt that some of the sayings collected in Proverbs stem from the time of Solomon, the book probably continued to develop well into the exilic period. Some scholars think they have found stages of development in which secular collections within Proverbs have been given a religious bent. The Book of Job includes both a narrative frame that is probably based on ancient traditions of a righteous patriarchal figure named Job and a poem so sophisticated in style and so dependent on other poetic forms that it is generally assumed to have come from the exilic or perhaps postexilic period. The author of Job was one of history's finest writers. Unfortunately, we do not have a trace of reliable evidence to determine who that person was.

There is a somewhat firmer basis for dating Ecclesiastes. The language of the book is late, probably from the fourth to the third centuries B.C.E. Although the title links the work to Solomon, and Solomon's experience is used in the first two chapters, this is a literary device that is soon dropped. The book later refers to the king in the third person. The author of Ecclesiastes was probably a scribe or teacher who lived in Jerusalem. Some of the teachings might mirror such Greek views as Stoicism (the sense of fatalism), suggesting that the book was written sometime after the beginning of the Hellenistic period. However, such ideas also occur in much earlier Mesopotamian wisdom lore.

SUMMARY

The wisdom books of the Tanak (Proverbs, Job, and Ecclesiastes) are examples of a corpus of literature found throughout the cultures of the ancient Near East. Unlike other books of the Hebrew Bible, the wisdom writings do not center on the history of the people of Israel and the LORD's involvement with the covenant people. Instead, these writings raise timeless questions, both practical and speculative, about the conduct and meaning of life in the world.

The Book of Proverbs is largely an anthology of collections of short sayings and admonitions on the way life is and should be. Interspersed we find several longer, more speculative poems. In Proverbs wisdom orders life and is accessible to those who have reverence for the LORD. Proverbs assumes that the LORD rewards goodness and punishes evil.

The Books of Job and Ecclesiastes balance this understanding of wisdom by questioning whether life always follows the pattern of retribution Proverbs assumes. In our reading of Job we emphasized that the book challenges the assumptions that God necessarily guarantees justice for humans and that God's ways can be explained in human terms. The collection of proverbs, poems, and short essays attributed to a sage called Ecclesiastes (in Hebrew, *Qoheleth*) suggests that life is vanity and challenges readers to find joy in spite of life's emptiness and futility.

The evidence for understanding the original historical context of the wisdom books comes from hints in the Tanak about the role of wisdom in the clan, court, and school as well as a rich collection of practical and speculative wisdom writings from ancient Egypt and Mesopotamia.

Many modern readers find the wisdom books of the Tanak the most interesting and accessible books in the Tanak. They identify with the practical wisdom of Proverbs and find the questioning, skeptical spirit of Job and Ecclesiastes an attitude easy to affirm in the latter decades of the twentieth century.

THE CONTEMPORARY WORLD: QUESTIONS FOR DISCUSSION AND REFLECTION

1. List a few modern proverbs. How do they compare with the sayings in the Book of Proverbs?

2. The Book of Proverbs might well have been a textbook for the ancient counterpart of a school of business and public administration. How does its advice compare with the education offered in parallel contemporary textbooks and schools? Is there any religious component in contemporary teaching on "how to succeed in business"? If so, what is it? If not, should there be?

3. If wisdom is the search for, and teaching about, how to live according to the way things are in the world and the reflection about order in life, where is wisdom to be found today?

4. With which biblical wisdom book—Proverbs, Job, or Ecclesiastes—do you most closely identify? Why?

5. Suppose Job had been a prisoner during World War II in one of the Nazi death camps like Auschwitz. How do you think he would have responded?

6. Do you know of situations of innocent suffering like Job's? Does the Book of Job provide any help in reflecting on these situations?

7. Do Job and Ecclesiastes belong in a canon of "sacred scripture"? How can we reconcile the fact that their teachings sometimes seem to contradict those of other parts of the Bible?

8. Some interpreters call Ecclesiastes the most modern book in the Bible. Why do you think they say that? Do you agree?

9. Ecclesiastes was a "believing skeptic" who questioned the assumptions many people had about God and religion and yet still believed in God. Is there a place for religious skepticism today?

CHAPTER 9

The Rest of the Writings: Chronicles, Ezra, Nehemiah, Ruth, Esther, and Daniel

Courtesy of the Israel Government Tourist Office

Reading from the Torah scroll. The "Book of the Law of Moses," which Ezra read to the people in Jerusalem (Neh. 8:1–12) was probably part or all of the Torah. Today the reading from the Torah scroll is an important part of the Sabbath morning service in Jewish synagogues. These worshippers are assembled at the Western Wall ("Wailing Wall") of the Temple Mount in Jerusalem. The masonry of the wall, part of Herod the Great's reconstruction of the Temple in the first century B.C.E., is visible in the background.

INTRODUCTION

The remaining books of the third section of the Hebrew canon, the Writings, represent three different types of literature: historical narrative (Chronicles, Ezra, and Nehemiah), short story (Ruth and Esther), and apocalypse (Daniel). The historical narrative is another version of events from the time of Saul through the Babylonian Exile, with a genealogical introduction that links the story to the beginning of time (Chronicles) and a narration concerning life after the return from the Exile in 538 B.C.E. (Ezra and Nehemiah). We will confine our historical discussion here to the postexilic period. We will then analyze Chronicles, Ezra, and Nehemiah as literature. Ruth and Esther provide us with an opportunity to examine two Hebrew short stories, both of which focus on a courageous woman. Daniel introduces us to apocalyptic literature and invites historical reflection on apocalyptic movements and apocalyptic thought.

THE HISTORICAL WORLD: AFTER THE EXILE

Cyrus and the Fall of Babylon

When we interrupted our historical discussion to examine the poetic sections of the Writings, the Babylonian Exile was the topic. That is where the historical narrative of the Former Prophets (paralleled in Chronicles) leaves the people of Israel. The leaders of Judah have been taken to Babylon, leaving behind a Jerusalem in ruins and a disheartened populace. The Exile was interpreted by theological historians and prophets alike as judgment for national sins. But prophets like Second Isaiah (Isaiah 40—55), Jeremiah, and Ezekiel held out hope for a restoration.

Internal dissension played a role in Babylon's sudden decline. Nabonidus, who seized the throne in 556 B.C.E., became embroiled in a program to reduce the power of the Marduk priesthood in Babylon. When he withdrew to Tema on the caravan route to Arabia, apparently to police against menacing raiders, administration in Babylon was left to his son, Belshazzar. The rise of Cyrus the Great counted for a great deal more than the decline of Babylonian power. Cyrus began his royal career as king of the small kingdom of Anshan in Persia. About 550 B.C.E. he began his advances, which ultimately produced the Persian Empire. Classical writers like Herodotus tended to idealize Cyrus, but his reputation was not undeserved. Apparently Cyrus was the first great master of propaganda, and he preferred intrigues like bribery to pitched battles. He was able to march into Babylon "without firing a shot" and take the throne. The Cyrus Cylinder (see p. 118) acquaints us with some of his propaganda. He claimed that Marduk had called him to come and rescue Babylon from the evil clutches of irreligious usurpers.

FIGURE 9–1

Political Situations in the Ancient Near East
After the Fall of Judah

Date (B.C.E.)	Egypt	Judah/Palestine	Babylonia	Persia
600		Fall of Jerusalem (587) Third deportation (582)	Nebuchadnezzar (605–562)	
			Nabonidus (556–539) Fall of Babylon to Persia (539)	Cyrus (550–530) Empire begins (550)
	Falls to Persia (525) Persian Rule (525–401)	Edict of Cyrus (538) and return to Judah Zerubbabel (520–515) Temple rebuilt		Darius I (522–486)
500		Ezra (458?) Nehemiah (445–?)		Xerxes (486–465) Artaxerxes I (465–424) Darius II (423–404)
400	Independence (401)	Ezra(398?)		Artaxerxes II (404–358)
	Reconquered by Persia (334) Falls to Alexander (332)	Falls to Alexander (333)	Falls to Alexander (Battle of Gaugamela, 331) Seleucids Rule (312–63)	
300	Ptolemy Rule (323–116)	Ptolemy Rule (301–198)	Parthian (neo-Persian) Empire (250 B.C.E.–225 C.E.)	
200		Seleucid Rule (198–167) Maccabean Revolt (167–164)	Antiochus IV (Epiphanes) (175–163)	

FIGURE 9–1 *(cont.)*

**Political Situations in the Ancient Near East
After the Fall of Judah**

	Maccabean Rule/Hasmon- aean Dynasty (167–63)	
		Parthians establish a frontier on the Euphrates (155 B.C.E.) Syria Falls to Rome (63)
100	Falls to Rome (63)	Abortive Roman campaigns against Parthia (53 and 36)
Falls to Rome (30)		

Cyrus was a tolerant overlord, patronizing the Babylonian worship of Marduk. We have already seen the positive reception given to Cyrus in Second Isaiah 45:1, where he is called the messiah (anointed one) of the LORD. Indeed, Cyrus allowed foreign exiles in Babylon (including the Judeans) to return to their homes and to take with them their images and religious objects, which had been seized by the Babylonians as war prizes. The Judeans had no images, of course, but the sacred vessels of the Jerusalem Temple were returned to them.

The Return

Many exiles from various places elected to remain in Babylon, where they had made homes. For the Jewish exiles, return home meant an arduous journey, much of it across desert, to a land still in ruins. As a consequence, the successive companies of Jewish returnees from about 539 B.C.E. onward tended to be high-status persons coming to assume leadership roles or to be the more deeply religious exiles. Some fell into both categories. This should not be taken as a slight to those who remained. Babylon became the center of some of the most important Jewish religious scholarship over the next thousand years and more. The Babylonian community flourished under the titular headship of the exilarch, a descendant of King Jehoiachin.

The land of Judah had been ravaged, but it had not been depopulated. The Book of Jeremiah, which seemed to have access to the best data, put the total number of deportees at 4,600 (52:28–30). Jerusalem was a ruin without a defensive wall. But it is again Jeremiah who informs us that even northern Israelites still made pilgrimage to Jerusalem to present offerings on the

Temple site (41:4–5). The Babylonians had deported the people considered most likely to make trouble or the most useful for their purposes. These included members of the royal family, prominent priests, other aristocrats, soldiers, and skilled craftsmen. Those survivors left behind were largely of the lower orders. The society that emerged from the ruins of Judah probably resembled the village-tribal culture of the premonarchic period. Archaeology shows that the Babylonians did take over some Judean royal estates and operate them for their own imperial profit. But for the most part, small farmers and husbandmen probably appreciated the absence of royal revenue agents and the collection of tithes by the established priesthood. Some of the frictions experienced by the postexilic prophets and Ezra and Nehemiah are probably rooted in this time.

The reconstruction of Jewish life in the homeland under the leadership of exilic repatriates may be conveniently viewed in three stages. First, the Temple was rebuilt, then the walls of Jerusalem. Finally, the Mosaic Torah, either the Priestly Code or perhaps even the completed Pentateuch, was embraced as the national constitution of the Jewish people. Each of these was, in its own way, essential to the survival and integrity of the community.

The Temple

A foundation for the Temple was laid almost immediately after the first group of returnees arrived in Jerusalem. Then the project languished until taken up again in 520 B.C.E. by the Jewish prince and Persian governor, Zerubbabel; the high priest Joshua; and the prophets Haggai and Zechariah.

It is not surprising that a leadership group composed of a substantial proportion of priests regarded the reconstruction of the Temple as the top priority. Judaism had not yet become, though it was becoming, "the religion of the Book." At this time the Temple still constituted the common focus of Jewish loyalty. That continued until the Roman period. It was only when the Temple was destroyed in 70 C.E. that Jews discovered it could be *replaced* by Torah piety centering in the synagogue and the house of study.

Historians conveniently refer to the building raised on the site of Solomon's Temple between 520 and 515, and its successors, as the *second temple*, despite the fact that there were several extensive renovations and a total reconstruction by Herod the Great.

Nehemiah: The Wall

The reconstruction of the Temple provided a center for the reorganization of life in Judah and Jerusalem. But so long as Jerusalem remained defenseless, it was at the mercy of all comers. The jeopardy was enhanced by the rebuilt Temple, the growing wealth of which tended to attract covetous eyes.

This need was taken up by Nehemiah, a Jewish civil servant who had risen high in Persian service. Becoming aware of the situation in his homeland, he requested and received from the emperor a warrant to serve as royal governor in Jerusalem and to rebuild (refortify) the city. Back in Jerusalem he organized the task of rebuilding. But his project was opposed, particularly by the neighboring peoples, and above all, by Sanballat, the governor of Samaria. The danger was such that laborers were armed, but the project was carried through to completion. It appears that Nehemiah served two terms as governor, or took a leave during his term of service, as the case may be. On his return, he instituted religious reforms and expelled Sanballat's ally, Tobiah, from an apartment in the Temple complex.

The Torah

Ezra, an Aaronid priest and a "scribe skilled in the Torah of Moses" (Ezra 7:6), was the central figure of the third major aspect of the restoration of Jewish life in the homeland. He went to Jerusalem armed with royal warrants to revivify the worship of the Jerusalem Temple. Ezra carried out a series of social and ritual reforms. He did not hesitate to use the coercive power at his disposal. The high point of Ezra's work was a great ceremony of covenant renewal, narrated in Nehemiah 8—10. Ezra read the Torah, his Levitical associates interpreted it for the congregation, and the assembled citizens of Judah and Benjamin affirmed it. It is probable that Ezra had a complete Torah, or at least the priestly section, whether he read every word of it or not. Ezra's activity marked a significant step on the road toward Torah-centered piety as it emerged in the second century B.C.E. and later. Israel was a province of the Persian Empire, not an independent nation. But the threefold reconstruction of Temple, city, and Torah provided the means to maintain identity and integrity.

Nehemiah, Ezra, and prophets like Malachi were vexed by Israelite marriages to foreign women. The two reformers obliged citizens of Jerusalem to rid themselves of foreign wives. This policy was not racist. The women who troubled the reformers were those who *remained* pagan and foreign. Women who converted to Judaism were no longer foreigners. Before the Exile, Israel, as a flourishing independent state, could permit marriages to foreigners. But in the postexilic period, the Judean community was small and threatened. They could not afford losses. The seeming harsh marriage policy was motivated by a realistic concern for survival.

We have not yet attempted to date Ezra and Nehemiah. Taking the dating notations of the books at face value, Ezra came to Jerusalem in 458 and Nehemiah in 444. But on closer reading, we see that Ezra found the wall rebuilt (Ezra 9:9), and the two influential leaders never seem to have interacted. Further, they dealt with different high priests. The standard solution among historians is to move Ezra to 398–397, by placing him in the reign of

Artaxerxes II rather than Artaxerxes I. Because the biblical text does not differentiate monarchs by Roman numerals, this is a convenient resolution of the conflict. However, it has been challenged by other historians. It must suffice for us simply to say there is a dating problem.

After the Exile the Jewish High Priest began to fill the functions of both chief magistrate and chief priest. Government by the major religious leader in a city or small province represents a situation fairly widespread in the Persian Empire. The Persian period is the "Dark Age" of biblical history. From the end of the time covered by the Books of Ezra and Nehemiah to the early years of the second century B.C.E., there is almost no documentary evidence on the affairs of the restored Jerusalem community. The recently discovered *Samaritan Papyri* (found in a cave in the Jordan Valley below Samaria) are largely commercial and legal documents that do not fill the narrative gap. There is a legend that when Alexander the Great marched through Israel on his way to Egypt in the fourth century B.C.E., he was greeted by the Jewish High Priest in full regalia and, being much impressed, showed kindness to the Jews. The legend cannot be confirmed.

The Hellenistic Age

Alexander's meteoric imperial career, from the assassination of his father, Philip II of Macedon, in 336 B.C.E. to his own death at age thirty-three in 323 B.C.E., was fraught with consequences for the Jewish community. During that brief period, Alexander marched his army from Europe into Asia, swept southward into Egypt and Libya, turned back north to gain Babylon, and then invaded Persia proper. He fought his way eastward to the Indus, before a reluctant turn homeward. If he wept, it was not because there were no more worlds to conquer, but because his trusted soldiers would go no further.

After Alexander's untimely death his empire was divided among four feuding generals. The two who loom largest in biblical history were Ptolemy, who established a dynasty in Egypt, and Seleucus, who established a dynasty in Babylon and Syria. The land of Israel first fell to Ptolemy, but, following battles at Gaza and Paneas (200–199 B.C.E.), the Seleucids gained control.

On the surface, things seemed not to change much when first Alexander, then the Ptolemys, then the Seleucids took control. In Jerusalem the hereditary high priesthood stayed within the Aaronic Zadokite family. Taxation was left to a local aristocratic house, the Tobiads. But change was under way. Alexander was an evangelist for Greek language and (Hellenistic) culture, as were his successors. They built their cities in the Greek fashion, with Greek temples, theaters, gymnasia, stadia, libraries, and Greek-style dwellings. When Alexander established Alexandria in Egypt, the most splendid city to bear his name, and one destined soon to eclipse

Athens as the intellectual capital of the Greek-speaking world, he invited Jews to settle there under favorable conditions. The Alexandrian community became (with the Babylonian) one of the two most brilliant and prosperous Jewish diaspora communities. The Greek-speaking Jews of Alexandria spawned both the Septuagint (LXX) translation of the Scripture and Philo, one of the most creative philosophers and biblical interpreters of antiquity.

Greek culture also infiltrated Jewish life in the homeland. By early in the second century B.C.E., some prominent Jewish priests were beginning to use Greek names. There was a theater, a stadium, and a gymnasium in Jerusalem. In due course this Hellenizing tendency came into bruising contact with traditional Jewish belief and practice, and this collision coincided with tumultuous political developments (see chap. 10). A glance ahead at the discussion of these developments will make the impending study of Daniel clearer.

THE LITERARY WORLD: THE CHRONICLER'S HISTORY (Chronicles, Ezra, and Nehemiah)

In the Tanak, the Books of Ezra and Nehemiah are considered one work, as are First and Second Chronicles. Although in the Hebrew canon Chronicles is placed after Ezra-Nehemiah as the last book in the Bible, there is internal evidence to support the theory that Chronicles originally preceded Ezra-Nehemiah. Ezra begins precisely where Chronicles ends, with a note about the decree of Cyrus that allowed the restoration to Jerusalem and the rebuilding of the Temple. Considered together, Chronicles and Ezra-Nehemiah tell a story that begins at creation and ends with the establishment of the Jewish province of Judea under priestly leadership. Because of stylistic similarities, many contemporary biblical scholars view this block as the work of a single author (or school), the "Chronicler." In any event, we can speak of Chronicles and Ezra-Nehemiah conveniently as the *Chronicler's History.*

The Chronicler's History portrays the rise and fall of the nation Israel and its limited resurgence after the Exile. Beginning with creation, but skipping quickly to David, the Books of Chronicles show how the nation prospered when there were rulers who were concerned with the proper worship of the LORD in the Temple in Jerusalem, who supported the priesthood, and who lived piously. When this high level of devotion to the LORD faltered, the nation weakened, until disaster struck and the Temple was destroyed. Ezra-Nehemiah portrays the restoration, not only of a people to their land, but also of the level of devotion to the LORD reminiscent of the time of David. Against considerable opposition, the Temple was rebuilt, the priesthood was allowed to function again, and devotion to the Torah of the LORD was renewed. Now, under a hierarchy, there was new hope for Israel.

TWO SHORT STORIES: RUTH AND ESTHER

The Book of Ruth: A Woman of Valor

In the Hebrew canon the Book of Ruth is one of the festival scrolls (megilloth) read annually at Pentecost (Shavuot, the Feast of Weeks). In the Christian canon it appears in its presumed chronological setting (Ru. 1:1), after the Book of Judges.

The first verse and the last verses (4:17–20) give the book a historical context. Set during the period of the judges, it is the story of the foreign woman who was the great grandmother of King David. Between these historical notes, however, the story moves from the history of the nation to a smaller stage. Between its beginning and its ending, Ruth is a story of the struggle and triumph of two women in a male-dominated society. Before trying to place the Book of Ruth in its historical context, let us seek to enter the world of Ruth and her mother-in-law, Naomi, as it is created in one of the short stories of ancient Israel.

The Literary World.   On two levels Ruth is a story of redemption. On the one hand, it is the story of how two courageous women succeed in winning the legal right of redemption. Under the so-called *levirate law* (or law of redemption) of ancient Israel (see Dt. 25:5–10), if a man died without any sons, it became the responsibility of the nearest male relative to marry his widow and sire a son, so that the deceased man's heritage could continue and his immortality be assured. How far this responsibility extended, when the dead man had no brothers, is not clear. Apparently, sometimes a relative had to be convinced to exercise his role as "redeemer." This is what Naomi and Ruth did, cleverly creating the circumstances that caused Boaz to recognize and to fulfill his kinship responsibility.

However, at another level, another kind of redemption takes place in Ruth. At this level the Book of Ruth is the deeply moving tale of the selfless love of Ruth, who "redeems" a broken and bitter Naomi. There was no law requiring Ruth to stay by Naomi's side. In fact, prudence dictated that when her husband, Naomi's son (who was an alien sojourner in her homeland of Moab), died she should return to her father's home. Because of her stubborn devotion to Naomi, Ruth violated custom and common sense to comfort her mother-in-law during her time of grief and restore hope when all seemed lost.

The story moves quickly, as is the style in Hebrew narrative, with only the most essential details and few indications of the inner thoughts and feelings of the characters. Through what the characters say and do we catch glimpses of the inner drama. The story is structured in four scenes (conveniently reflecting the four chapters). In the first scene the central dilemma is identified; in the second and third the tension increases as solutions are sought; and in the final scene resolution occurs.

The Historical World. The Book of Ruth not only highlights the devotion and faith of a foreign woman, but it also makes the remarkable claim that the great King David descended from a Moabite great grand-mother. When might such a story have been written and why? Many modern scholars feel that the Book of Ruth was written to attack the postexilic policy in the restored community of Judah against marriages with foreign women (Ezra 10:1–5; Neh. 13:23–27). Ruth is generally set alongside Jonah as fifth or fourth century B.C.E. reactions against the narrow nationalism and exclusiv-ism that some have attributed to this era. There can be no doubt that Ruth is a critique of such attitudes.

The question being raised by some recent interpreters is whether exclusivism and responses to it were characteristic of only the postexilic period. The fact that Ruth accepted Naomi's God, the God of Israel, places her in the role of a proselyte, a convert to Judaism. As we have already noted, it was only wives who remained pagan foreigners that the reformers of the restoration regarded as dangerous. So in fact, Ruth may be construed as propaganda in favor of the Ezra-Nehemiah policies. In any case, the evidence for dating Ruth to the postexilic age is somewhat less than convincing. The clean narrative Hebrew prose could well be preexilic. Some have even suggested that the tradition of David's alien female ancestor is in fact anti-Davidic propaganda, of a piece with the tale of Judah and Tamar in Genesis and the seamier parts of the Succession Narrative. This case might be made stronger if it could be shown that Ruth is written in a northern dialect. But no general agreement exists on this issue. Here, as at other points in the study of the Tanak, the final conclusion must be that the evidence does not warrant final conclusions.

The Book of Esther: A Dream Fulfilled

There are a number of similarities between the Books of Ruth and Esther. Besides being among the festival scrolls in the Hebrew canon, both are found among the historical books in the Christian canon (Esther is after Ezra and Nehemiah). Both are short stories about courageous women whose actions have far-reaching consequences for their people. Both are set rather loosely in historical contexts (Esther in the Persian period). In both books God is not an onstage character. However, unlike in Ruth, in the Book of Esther the name of God is not even mentioned (unless the additions found in the Apocrypha are included). It is not surprising that the canonical status of Esther was debated in both Jewish and Christian circles.

The Literary World. Whereas the Book of Ruth is a sensitive portrayal of women in a time of crisis, Esther is a potboiler, a tale full of intrigue, violence, and dramatic action. There are several major themes in the book—the gaining of power by Jews in a situation of powerlessness, the importance of loyalty to the Jewish community over fidelity to unjust civil powers, and the underlying pattern beyond the level of human intrigue. Throughout the story, reversal and irony are used to develop these themes. The following observations are based on the recent literary analysis of Esther by Sandra Beth Berg.[1]

A story that begins with a feast showing the power of the Persian king ends with a feast celebrating the power of the Jewish people over their enemies. Jews in a situation of powerlessness have attained power. The reason for this dramatic change is Jews showing loyalty to the community over loyalty to those in power. At first this seems foolish and costly. Mordecai's disobedience in refusing to honor Haman precipitates the planning of the annihilation of the Jews. This crisis causes Esther to take a risk she might otherwise have avoided. It is her disobedience that initiates the series of actions that lead to deliverance for the Jews and victory over their enemies. Both Mordecai and Esther are motivated by their identity as Jews to disobey civil authority (3:4; 4:13–16). Yet their disobedience jars with their typical concern to be loyal to those in power. In disobedience they are willing to accept the consequences of their actions (4:16), and when the crisis is past, they are again obedient to their king.

The story is full of reversals and ironies supporting these themes. For example, Queen Vashti is punished for refusing to appear before the king when he has requested her presence. Queen Esther is rewarded for appearing without being asked. Haman, thinking he is honoring himself, chooses and bestows honors on his archenemy. Haman's plot to kill Mordecai backfires. Instead, Haman is hanged on the gallows built for Mordecai, and Mordecai received Haman's office and Esther his house. The planned destruction of the Jews is reversed, and their enemies pay a price in blood.

The Book of Esther is full of "coincidences," such as the king's just happening to be reading the report of Mordecai's loyalty when Haman is plotting to kill him. These coincidences suggest an underlying pattern to events that will lead to the deliverance of the Jews, raising the question of whether a subtle hint of divine providence is present. The unexpected reversals that permeate the story are just too overwhelming to be a matter of chance. Even though God is never mentioned in Esther, the story could still be pointing toward the divine patterning of events, with the purpose of

---

[1]Sandra Beth Berg, *The Book of Esther: Motifs, Themes and Structure* (Missoula, Mont.: Scholars Press, 1979).

release and fulfillment for the people of God. The precedents of the Joseph story, the Succession Narrative, and Ruth can be cited in this connection.

The Historical World. Interpreters disagree on the question of whether the events described in Esther actually took place. Some feel that the wealth of details about Persian court life and Ahasuerus (Xerxes I) make the story credible. Others argue that there are too many historical improbabilities and inconsistencies for the story to be considered historical. Most importantly, there is no extrabiblical record of a Jewish queen at the Persian court. When Esther was supposed to have been queen, the Greek historian Herodotus names another. Still others take a middle ground, suggesting that there is a historical kernal in the story that has been embellished with nonhistorical legends.

Many interpreters who question the historical nature of the Book of Esther suggest that it arose as an explanation for the origin of the feast of Purim, originally a non-Jewish festival that was adapted for use in the Jewish community. The names Mordecai and Esther might be adaptations of the names of two central Mesopotamian deities—Marduk and Ishtar—and might hint at a myth behind the story. Because of indications such as this, speculation abounds about the possible mythical background of the story. However, there is little concrete evidence in support of any of the imaginative hypotheses about the type of myth involved.

THE HORIZON OF HISTORY: THE BIRTH OF APOCALYPTIC (Daniel)

Introduction: Apocalyptic Literature and Movements

In the Book of Daniel we encounter a new type of literature—*apocalyptic* (from the Greek word for "a revealing"). Apocalypses are unveilings of things to come, revelations of the pattern of events that will lead to the end of the present historical epoch (*aeon*) and the beginning of a new age. Because of the use of highly symbolic language, apocalyptic literature is both difficult to understand and susceptible to manipulation by interpreters who feel they have discovered *the* key to unlock its mysteries. Although Daniel is the only apocalyptic book in the Tanak, there are apocalyptic-like sections in some of the prophetic books, for example, Isaiah 24—27, Ezekiel 38—48, Zechariah 9—14, and Joel 3. In the New Testament there is also one apocalyptic book, the Revelation to John, and there are apocalyptic passages in the gospels (Mark 13, Matthew 24—25, Luke 21) and the letters (First Corinthians 15,

First and Second Thessalonians, Jude, and Second Peter). There are also a number of apocalyptic works in the literature after the Tanak.

As literature, apocalyptic has a number of characteristics, not all of which are necessarily present in every apocalyptic writing. Apocalyptic literature reports visions from God concerning events that will climax in the vanquishing of the forces of evil and the establishment of a new age of righteousness. This is similar to the theme noted in the prophets of a time of judgment (the Day of the LORD), to be followed, according to some prophets, by the establishment of the LORD's universal rule and a new age of peace. However, apocalyptic moves beyond this view of an ending and new beginning in several respects. Most importantly, apocalyptic works portray the end of the present *aeon* and the dawn of a new *aeon*, as a radically new beginning beyond history as currently experienced. The present age is perceived to be under the dominion of evil, whether human or demonic in origin. This renders God's saints helpless pending His intervention to set things right. The new age is sometimes called the Kingdom of God in apocalyptic writings. Apocalyptic visions typically reveal a series of cataclysmic events leading to a final climax in which God acts directly to end the old age and begin the new.

There are a number of paired opposites in apocalyptic literature—between this age and the next, between the forces of good and evil, and between heaven and earth. The visions are of the heavenly events that will determine the course of history at the earthly level. They are full of highly symbolic, mythic imagery of angels, God himself, and dragons and other animals representing the forces of chaos. This imagery constitutes a secret code that, when deciphered, reveals to the faithful the truth about the end and the events leading to it. This veiled language also serves to conceal the truth from the reprobate, whether they are foreign enemies or native quislings. When the recipients of these visions are named, they are invariably heroes of the faith who have demonstrated their righteousness (like Daniel). They receive the visions, usually in a trance state, often with interpretations by an angel. They are usually instructed to seal them up until the time of the end. Sometimes the visions are "raptures," as the seer is transported into the heavens to see what will transpire. Apocalyptic writing focuses on reporting these visions recorded by the seer, and sometimes it establishes the "credentials" of the seer through stories demonstrating his faithfulness (as in Daniel 1—6).

Two other characteristics of apocalyptic literature should be mentioned. Apocalyptic writings often speak of life beyond death, ensuring that the righteous who die before the end of the present age will not be denied their place in the Kingdom (e.g., Dan. 12:2–3) and that the wicked will receive their just punishment. There is also in apocalyptic literature mention of the agent or agents will rule in the new age for God (as in Dan. 7:13–15). In some apocalyptic writings this figure is harmonized with the messianic expectation of a new King David who will restore the fortunes of Israel. Sometimes the figure is the "son of man," with no apparent link to the messianic hope.

Apocalyptic movements (and literature) developed in Judaism at times of persecution and crisis, when hope seemed lost. Usually, alienated from traditional religious teachings and institutions, apocalyptic movements took refuge in the alternative, symbolic universe of the visions they believed predicted an imminent deliverance and a new age. Invariably, the apocalyptic movement interprets its own time as the age just before the end. For example, the Qumran community of the Dead Sea Scrolls was part of an apocalyptic movement that withdrew from society to purify itself in preparation for the final battle between the "sons of light" and the "sons of darkness" and the new age to follow. Some early Christian communities were apocalyptic groups, believing that Jesus would return soon to inaugurate God's kingdom. Some apocalyptic communities did not resist those persecuting them with force, believing instead that God would act to vanquish these foes himself. Victory was predetermined, so resistance was unnecessary. Others, like the Qumran sect, were simply awaiting the signal to launch a holy war.

The relationship of the Zealot movement of the first century C.E. and the messianic claims of Simeon bar Cocheba in the second century C.E. to apocalyptic thought have not yet been clarified by scholarship. Because of their rejection of tradition and their esoteric teachings, apocalyptic movements were looked on with suspicion by most religious authorities. Apocalyptic movements within Judaism were rejected by rabbinic leaders who feared the consequences of militant enthusiasm.

Apocalyptic literature and movements have arisen throughout history at times of crisis and persecution. In the current age the threat of nuclear annihilation and the confrontation of the two major superpowers has elicited an apocalyptic response in many religious communities. Christian apocalyptic groups often strongly believe that the canonical apocalypses (Daniel and Revelation) point to the present era as the end time. The so-called *cargo cults* of the South Pacific represent the transmission of Christian apocalypticism to folk cultures victimized first by European colonialism and later by indigenous state-level organizations.

The Book of Daniel

The Literary World. Although placed among the prophets in the Greek canon (the order adopted by the Christian churches), its placement among the Writings in the Hebrew canon indicates that Daniel was recognized as a different type of literature and completed after the prophetic canon was closed, a point made explicit in rabbinic sources.

The Book of Daniel has two easily distinguished sections. The first six chapters form a collection of legends about Daniel and three friends, who are presented as deportees to Babylon after an otherwise undocumented Babylonian siege of Jerusalem in the third year of King Jehoiakim (606 B.C.E.).

The elements of the story should have a familiar ring. Daniel, like Joseph, is a handsome young man who demonstrates his allegiance to God when tested and rises to influence in a foreign court because of his skill as an interpreter of dreams. Like Esther and Mordecai, Daniel and his friends are victims of court intrigue. Like these tales, the legends of Daniel 1—6 are instructive, giving a model of persons in situations of crisis displaying exemplary behavior. The message is that if you maintain loyalty in the face of persecution, everything will work out in the end. Not only will you survive, but you will also triumph.

The second half of Daniel (7—12) is a collection of four apocalyptic visions, with interpretations by angels, received and written down by Daniel. At the conclusion Daniel is told that "the words are shut up and sealed until the time of the end" (12:9), when those who are wise will understand, but the wicked will not. The visions are graphic symbols of the unfolding of history from the time of Daniel until the end, when an everlasting kingdom will be established. The visions are rich in the mythic imagery that we have encountered before. For example, the description of "one like a son of man" coming on the clouds of heaven to the throne of the Ancient of Days (7:13–14) is rooted in Canaanite imagery of the god Baal (rider of the clouds) coming before the high god El. This imagery is elsewhere applied to the LORD himself in the Tanak (e.g., Ps. 104:3). One of the classic problems of interpretation is the meaning of "one like a son of man." Although this phrase sounds like the description of an individual, later in the same chapter it is the saints (the community of the righteous) who seem to be in the situation attributed to the "son of man" (7:18, 22, 27). So "son of man" may be a corporate symbol here for the community of the faithful.

In another vision (Daniel 9), Daniel learns from the angel Gabriel that the "true" meaning of Jeremiah's prophecy of seventy years of exile (Jer. 25:11,12; 29:10) is seventy weeks of years. This type of commentary on Scripture, which looks for a deeper meaning, is a typical apocalyptic technique, based on the assumption that hidden in Scripture are the keys that, when properly understood, will reveal the secrets of the end time. In chapter 12, Daniel is reassured by Gabriel that when the present age draws to a close, Michael (Israel's guardian angel) will arise, and the righteous will be victorious. The dead will be raised—some to everlasting life and others to everlasting contempt. But for now Daniel is to seal the visions until the time of the end and "rest" until the time of resurrection. To this are added two separate attempts to determine when the end will come (12:5–13).

The Historical World. The second half of Daniel is dated by many modern interpreters more precisely than any other section of the Bible, on the basis of both external and internal evidence. Externally, the book is not among the Prophets in the Hebrew canon, so it is most likely post-fourth century B.C.E. It is first mentioned in a work that dates about 140 B.C.E. It is not mentioned in Ben Sirach (ca. 190–180 B.C.E.), where one might expect to find it. Internally, the visions lead step by step to the year 165 B.C.E., but not to 164 B.C.E. Especially in chapters 10 and 11, the detailed vision points to the profanation of the Jerusalem Temple by the Seleucid ruler Antiochus Epiphanes, which took place in December 167 B.C.E. (11:31). There is an allusion to the subsequent revolt of the Maccabees (the "little help" in 11:34), but the vision is somewhat misleading concerning the death of Antiochus and stops short of the rededication of the Temple in 164 B.C.E. This evidence leads to the conclusion that Dan. 7—12 emerged in 164 B.C.E. (see chap. 10).

This method of dating reflects the modern view that apocalypses are frequently pseudonymous works, that is, attributed to one source but actually coming from another. In the case of Daniel, this means that the visions are a literary creation, written during the Antiochian persecution to inspire hope, using the device of visions received long before and sealed up until the present time. The visions are, according to this view, predictions after the fact. They have been combined with legends about the righteous Daniel and his friends, the models of piety in the face of persecution. The Prayer of Nabonidus, a document found among the Dead Sea Scrolls, confirms that the narratives in Daniel have a complex tradition history.

If this view of the origin of Daniel is accepted, what can be said of the apocalyptic movement of the second century B.C.E. with which the work was associated? By this time there was an identifiable group within Judaism known as the *hasidim* (faithful ones). They were dedicated to maintaining traditional practices (such as dietary laws) when many Jews, including religious leaders, were falling under the influence of Hellenistic (Greek) culture. When Antiochus enforced Hellenistic ways and outlawed Jewish practices, the *hasidim* practiced passive resistance. They felt that faithfulness to the LORD, rather than armed struggle, was the best course. Thus, they were unlike the Maccabees, who led a revolution against Antiochus. The *hasidim* believed that if anyone died refusing to compromise the faith, then that person was assured of resurrection when God brought victory and his Kingdom to earth. The consensus of modern historians is that the *hasidim* were the apocalyptic community for which Daniel was written.

SUMMARY

In this chapter we resumed our discussion of the history of Israel (see chap. 5), picking up the story at the time of the Babylonian Exile. When the Edict of Cyrus in 539 allowed those exiled to return from Babylon to Judah, some did. They rebuilt the Temple in Jerusalem, constructed a new wall around the city, and embraced the Mosaic Torah as a basis of a renewed Jewish community. Unfortunately, historians of the postexilic period face a lack of solid evidence upon which to construct as complete a narrative as they would like.

The Chronicler's History (First and Second Chronicles, Ezra, and Nehemiah) offers a different perspective on Israel's history than that found in the Torah and Former Prophets. Chronicles focuses on the rule of David, and the other two works highlight two prominent leaders of the postexilic community. The ongoing debate on how to date Ezra and Nehemiah reflects our historical uncertainty.

In this chapter we also analyzed the literary and historical worlds of two short stories—Ruth and Esther. Both works portray strong, heroic women who take the initiative to redeem others.

The Book of Daniel is a highly symbolic work, the only fully apocalyptic book in the Tanak. We provided in this chapter background information on the characteristics of apocalyptic literature and movements. We presented an interpretation of Daniel, reflecting the broad consensus of modern scholars that the book is a pseudonymous work written in 164 B.C.E.

The issues raised by the books of Ruth, Esther, and Daniel range from the role of women in societies dominated by men to the end of history as we know it. Discussion of them, guided by the following questions, should prove to be fascinating and perhaps somewhat intense.

THE CONTEMPORARY WORLD:
QUESTIONS FOR DISCUSSION AND REFLECTION

1. Ruth and Esther are stories about courageous women who stood up for themselves and their people in male-dominated societies. Do they offer any examples for people in contemporary society?

2. What is your opinion of modern interpretations of the Book of Daniel that contend that the real meaning of the visions is that they predict contemporary events and show that we are living in the end time now?

3. Do we live in an apocalyptic age today because of the threat of nuclear annihilation? Are there apocalyptic movements, communities, and literature today?

4. Ezra and Nehemiah portray the Jews of Judea as a marginal, threatened group clinging to their land, their treasured traditions, and life itself in the face of threatening neighbors and powerful empires. Think about the situation of small, threatened populations today and about minorities in modern industrial societies. Do Ezra and Nehemiah (and perhaps Ruth and Esther) help you understand them? Do these works offer people in such circumstances any guidance?

5. Compare the different treatment of King David in Chronicles and Samuel-Kings. Which is the more "modern" approach? What is the role of heroes in modern society? Should their weaknesses be ignored or emphasized?

CHAPTER 10

Jewish Life and Literature (200 B.C.E.–100 C.E.)

Cave 4, Qumran. This is the most famous of the caves near the Dead Sea in which the Dead Sea Scrolls were found. In this cave, carved out of the marl terrace between the rocky Dead Sea beach and the limestone cliffs in which the other caves were located, were found fragments of most biblical books, the apocryphal and pseudepigraphical works, and the sectarian documents of the Qumran community.

INTRODUCTION

The period between 200 B.C.E. and 100 C.E., and even beyond, was one of the most vital and creative periods in the history of Judaism, or any other religion for that matter. From a historical perspective this period witnessed the flowering of a number of movements within Judaism, one of which became the form of Judaism that continues to flourish to this day (the movement associated with the Pharisees), another of which became a new and influential religion in its own right (the movement associated with Jesus of Nazareth).

From a literary point of view, this period witnessed the creation of a number of works that, despite their failure to achieve canonical status in the Tanak, are worthy of our consideration. We will survey some of the variety of literature from this period. This chapter is one of the most important in this book because it supplies the framework essential to a full grasp of the wider historical and literary contexts of the Tanak and the New Testament.

THE HISTORICAL WORLD:
VARIETIES OF CLASSICAL JUDAISM

The Maccabean Period

The apocryphal Book of Sirach (Ecclesiasticus) ends its famous passage in praise of the great heroes of Israel (44:1—50:29) with a reference to a contemporary of the author Joshua-Jesus, the High Priest Simon II. According to tradition, Simon had one foot in an old order that was passing away and one in a new, emerging order. He was the last of the great Zadokite high priests and rulers of the principality of Jerusalem. In the eyes of rabbinic tradition he was also the patron of an emerging pietism that bore Judaism's ultimate future.

Early in the second century B.C.E. the Seleucids were still the overlords of Judea. Their loss to Rome at the Battle of Magnesia in 190 meant that they owed the Romans tribute, which they exacted from subject peoples. This probably explains an abortive attempt to loot the Temple treasury during the reign of Simon's successor, Onias. With the coming of Antiochus Epiphanes to the Seleucid throne in 175 B.C.E., the situation of the Jewish community deteriorated. According to some sources, Antiochus was very ambitious, highly eccentric, and possibly a bit mad. *Epiphanes* means "God (Zeus) manifest", and he may have believed his own label. He was approached by Onias's brother, Joshua (who took a Greek name, Jason) and bribed into deposing Onias and installing Jason as High Priest. The tables were turned on Jason by the unscrupulous Menelaus (another Jew with a

MAP 5 Roman world of the first century

MAP 6

Greek name), who offered Antiochus a bigger tribe. This intrigue upset the customary inheritance of the high priesthood through the Zadokite line.

The process of Hellenization had been going on for at least a century by this time, as discussed in Chapter 9. However, it was not until the 170s and 160s that a strong reaction to Hellenization emerged. Then a variety of factors combined to produce polarization, persecution, and ultimately, rebellion. Hellenistic culture came from a brilliant and attractive civilization. It was "where the action was" for young sophisticates throughout the Mediterranean world, including Judea. Ultimately, Rome conquered the Greek east, but Hellenistic culture conquered Rome. The polytheism and pluralism of Rome could better accommodate Greek customs than could Judaism. Greek gods could be given Roman names and absorbed (e.g., Zeus became Jupiter). That does not work in Jewish monotheism. Nor could one dress like a Greek and fulfill the customs of the Mosaic Torah, especially the requirement of the *zizith* (fringed robe). The Dead Sea Scrolls and rabbinic traditions alike suggest that there was an upsurge of Jewish pietism among both priests and laity in the early second century B.C.E. Perhaps this renewal of commitment to the Torah was motivated at least in part by reaction against Hellenization. In any event, this new pietism was a strong center of resistance to the inroads of offensive Greek customs.

After Rome thwarted an unsuccessful attempt to add Egypt to Antiochus Epiphanes' empire, he salved his ego by entering Jerusalem on the Sabbath, slaughtering innocent people, and looting the Temple, with the full cooperation of Menelaus. The Temple was converted to pagan worship, and by 167 B.C.E. customary Jewish practices were outlawed. The *hasidim* practiced passive resistance, suffering torture and death as a consequence.

A radical turning point came in the village of Modein, northwest of Jerusalem, on a day when an apostate Jew, supported by Seleucid troops, sought to compel a pagan sacrifice. An old priest of Modein, Mattathias, led his neighbors in sacrificing the interlopers instead. Mattathias did not survive to lead the resistance movement inspired by his act. Rather, the struggle was led by three of his sons: first Judas, called *the Maccabee* ("hammerer"), then Jonathan, and finally Simon.

Judas was a brilliant guerrilla fighter who, in December (Chislev) 164, liberated the Temple (although he failed to dislodge the Seleucid garrison in Jerusalem). The Temple was cleansed and rededicated, an action that is celebrated in the Jewish calendar through the annual Feast of Lights, or Dedication, Hanukkah.

The war was punctuated by truces, negotiations, and diplomatic exploration. Sparta and Rome pledged moral support for the rebels but gave no tangible aid. Judas fell in battle. Jonathan and Simon were capable warriors, but they were even more adept as masters of politics in an age when Machiavelli's *Prince* would have sounded tame. Both died as victims of treachery. But before Simon's death (135 B.C.E.), total political independence had been won, and he had taken the titles of High Priest and king. He began the Hasmonaean Dynasty, named for the family patronymic, ben-Hashmon.

Simon had two strong successors, John Hyrcanus and Alexander Jannaeus. Thereafter, the dynasty weakened through squabbles over succession. In 63 B.C.E. the Roman general Pompey entered Jerusalem, and the Jewish homeland was thereafter subordinate to Rome either directly or indirectly.

The Hasmonaean family had given Israel nearly a century of political and religious independence. Most information suggests that they were generally popular with the masses. But more dedicated pietists were reserved or hostile toward the Hasmonaean line. From the second generation onward, the Hasmonaeans took Greek names. Though not Davidic, they claimed the throne, and, though not Zadokites, they assumed the high priesthood. Thus they were usurpers on two counts for Jews who valued tradition. Their military activities also exposed them to corpse impurity, an outrageous ritual violation for an officiating priest.

Rome was not the only power to exercise its influence in the traditional sphere of biblical history during the last few centuries B.C.E. As early as the mid-third century B.C.E., a Parthian dynasty had begun the process of restoring Persian independence. Mithridates I, perhaps the greatest Parthian emperor, pushed the Parthian boundary to the Euphrates about 155 B.C.E. When Rome terminated the Seleucid empire in 63, the Romans became the masters of Syria and began to view the Parthians across their common frontier with suspicion and hostility.

Rome had been drawn to the east by instability in the Greek-speaking world, and by her own deep-vested interest in the eastern Mediterranean grain trade, particularly the Egyptian, to feed agriculturally deficient Italy. Both Crassus (53 B.C.E.), who died in the process, and Mark Antony (36) conducted abortive campaigns against Parthia, and the Parthians reciprocated with an invasion of the Levant (44 B.C.E.) that included an attempt to restore the Hasmonaean dynasty to a position of effective authority. The Parthians lent encouragement and aided Jewish resistance to Rome, particularly during the two Jewish revolts (discussed later). Indeed, the Neo-Persian Empire remained Rome's greatest adversary in the east until the Muslim invasions created a new international situation.

The wily Edomite adventurer Antipater had wormed his way into Hasmonaean affairs. He quickly made himself useful to the Romans when they appeared. As a consequence, his son Herod was named Rome's client-king of the Jews, though he was to a substantial degree left to his own devices to make the claim stick. Antony and Cleopatra lent him aid against the resurgent Hasmonaeans. When the famous lovers fell into disfavor with Augustus, Herod indulged in some fancy footwork to retain Roman favor and, as a consequence, enjoyed a long reign (40–4 B.C.E.).

Herod was an able ruler and an ambitious builder. His splendid reconstruction of the Jerusalem Temple was his most famous achievement, though his founding of Caesarea as the capital and main seaport of his kingdom and the rebuilding of Samaria under the name Sebaste rank close behind. Both names, the first Latin, the second Greek, honored Augustus. But Herod was also a paranoid who brought about the deaths of his own sons and of his wife Mariamne (a Hasmonaean), among others. Some writers attribute Jewish contempt for Herod to his being a "half-breed" with an Idumean (Edomite) father. To the contrary, because his mother was Jewish, Herod would be considered a Jew under developing rabbinic custom. Jewish dislike for Herod was based on the fact that he was a bloody tyrant who patronized paganism in other places while he rebuilt the Jerusalem Temple. Through it all Herod remained the faithful servant of Rome.

Both Herod and his heirs were at least technically answerable to the Roman governor of Syria, though they fell into the category of the type of client-king to whom the Romans entrusted the security of many imperial frontiers. At Herod's death, his kingdom was divided among his surviving sons. The one entrusted with the southern portion of the kingdom, Archelaus, proved a disaster and was removed by Rome, with a procurator (Roman governor) assuming the reins of power. Thus, Jesus lived in a Galilee ruled by Herod Antipas. But when he came to Jerusalem, he was under the authority of the procurator, Pontius Pilate.

The emperor Caligula (best remembered for his madness) made Herod's grandson Herod Agrippa master of much of the original Herodian kingdom. But after Agrippa's death (44 C.E.), Roman procurators assumed full power. Poor judgment (or worse) on the part of some, the earlier threat by Caligula to install an image of himself as Zeus in the Jerusalem Temple,

Masada. The name means "stronghold." This natural citadel by the Dead Sea served Herod the Great well during his struggle to possess his crown. Later he turned it into one of several heavily fortified palaces, located in various parts of his realm. This view shows the steplike northern palace complex, the royal pleasure house, sited to benefit from the prevailing northwesterly breezes. Zealot warriors seized Masada during the first war with Rome and held out against the Romans until 73–74 C.E., when they committed suicide rather than be taken as slaves.

Courtesy of the Israel Government Tourist Office

and the unbalanced behavior of yet another mad emperor, Nero, probably hastened the outbreak of open rebellion.

The Zealot uprising that began in 66 C.E., against the better judgment of many priestly notables and pharisaic leaders, gained major popular support through the success of early guerrilla ambushes of Roman forces. But Rome's fear of Parthia and her disinclination to permit colonial escapes meant that maximum power would be used to crush the rebellion, and so it was. Jerusalem was captured and the Temple destroyed in 70, and the last Zealot holdouts perished at Masada in 73–74. The Jewish population would not fully recoup its numerical losses until modern times, and Jewish political independence in the traditional homeland was dead until 1948. But anti-Jewish measures under Trajan and Hadrian produced a second revolution (132–135), led by the messianic claimant, Simeon bar Cocheba. Again Rome brought its awesome power to bear, and Judea was ravaged. The center of Jewish life in the homeland shifted northward into Galilee, and Jerusalem was reconstructed under Hadrian as a pagan city.

The New Order

John Hyrcanus was friendly with the Pharisees until there was a falling out over his fitness to serve as High Priest. Thereafter, he patronized the Sadducees. The appearance of these two names is a clear-cut indication that the old order had passed and a new order was dawning. Neither group is mentioned in sources predating the Maccabean Wars. By the same sign, the prewar and wartime *hasidim* had disappeared from the record, as had the hereditary Zadokite high priesthood. Thus, this was a watershed time in Jewish history. The Hebrew Scriptures had now all been written and the threefold canon of Tanak was well along the way to completion. A flourishing array of competing viewpoints in Judaism was a fact of life. Still, Torah and Temple remained the central operative symbols for all forms of Judaism (including early Christianity, when it appeared).

A variety of terms has been used to designate these competing viewpoints in classical Judaism. The ancient Jewish historian Josephus used *parties* and *philosophies*, terms meaningful to the Greco-Roman audience to which he was writing. Others speak of *sects*, though this is not an appropriate term to apply to all of them from a sociological standpoint. We have decided to use the term *denominations* to describe these various groups. It is, of course, anachronistic, because the term *denominationalism* is strongly associated with American Protestant Christianity. However, American Protestantism offers a good analogy for understanding the varieties of early classical Judaism. In good denominational fashion, each and all thought of themselves as Jewish but were obliged to recognize the Jewishness of their rivals. To be sure, their own group were the truest Israelites. The harshness of their judgments on Jews outside their own group was a function of how sectarian they were in their outlook. We will confine our discussion to those groups that can be documented in some detail. Our account begins with the four groups described by Josephus and documented in other sources.

The Pharisees

The Pharisees were a pietist movement composed largely of laity. Their name comes from a Hebrew word meaning "the excluded" or "the separated." It was perhaps, like *Christian*, a slur that stuck as a public nickname and perhaps became a badge of honor to a group excluded from national counsels by Hyrcanus. Or it could refer to their self-separation in a quest for ritual purity. They did not use this name among themselves, preferring instead the title of the ancient wise men, the *hakamim*. Some would equate the Pharisees with the *hasidim*, but there is no firm evidence.

Ancient societies had no middle class in the modern sense. However, references to the occupations of pharisaic leaders suggest that they were recruited largely from the middle orders of society: tradesmen, craftsmen, merchants, farmers, and others, though a few were of lower rank. They could not claim many priestly adherents. They were led by a company of lay scholar-saints whose authority was their power to persuade through reason and example rather than hereditary office or charisma. The few wonder-workers who cropped up among them constituted a qualified embarrassment on occasion. Ideally, every Pharisee was a scholar, though in practice this would have been unlikely. Their origins probably go back to the lay scribes (religious scholars) who emerged in postexilic Israel. Ezra and his colleagues and successors, to whom the title *Men of the Great Academy (Synagogue)* was applied, loomed large in pharisaic tradition. But Moses was considered their founder and supreme teacher.

The Pharisees saw the necessity of adapting Jewish piety to the changed conditions of life in the Jewish homeland (and in Babylon where they had strong connections), to enable the ordinary Jew to be a good Jew and still live as a productive citizen in the modern world. They accomplished this adaptation through two radical devices. One was through free interpretation of Scripture by their scholarly leaders. As noted earlier, *halakah* (obligatory customs and observances) had to be derived from the Torah. But any part of the Tanak could yield *haggadah*, inspirational teaching. According to the Pharisees, all Scripture bore witness to Torah, and all sacred teaching embodied Torah in some sense. They may well have played an important role in the recognition of the threefold canon, the Tanak.

Alongside their free interpretation of Scripture, the Pharisees introduced the even more radical notion of *two Torahs,* one *written* and the other *oral.* The oral Torah was none other than the traditional teachings of the great pharisaic scholars. These two devices, free interpretation of the Bible and authoritative oral tradition, gave the Pharisees the means to adapt Jewish practice to a changed world and to keep pace with a changing world. No *Midrash* (biblical interpretation), *Mishnah* (oral Torah), or *Targum* (translation of the Bible into Aramaic) was permitted to be written down during this period. In this way, the Pharisees retained flexibility while showing deference to the written Scripture.

The Pharisees introduced a third device to hold their two radical ones in moderate check: *the principle of authority*. An interpretation of the biblical Torah or a purported oral teaching of halakah could be accepted *only* if it could be attributed to a recognized and authoritative leader.

Part of the pharisaic program seems to have been to permit pious Israelites in Jerusalem, in the villages of Judea and Galilee, and the Diaspora to participate in the high piety that the written Torah reserved for priests serving at the altar. They could not approach the altar, but they could maintain the purity called for in the Torah.

Phariseeism was centered in observance of the Torah. Actions and purposes were more important than words or doctrines. The Pharisees believed that God had given Israel the whole Torah (written and oral) as an express statement of his will for his people. The keeping of Torah therefore was *not* a legalistic quest for the favor of a coldly demanding God, but a response to the goodness of a loving Father. To keep a commandment, the Pharisees taught, was a joy, not a burden. Given the flexibility of determining commandments, the number multiplied. Multiplication occurred in part to "build a fence around the Torah," so that major commandments were "surrounded" with lesser ones to give them a "protective shield." Someone could bump up against the fence, so to speak, without violating a major commandment. The *principle of intention* was central to the Pharisees. Basically, it held that the purpose a person had in mind when doing a deed determined its validity. This tended to lighten the burden of religious observance for lay people.

There were two major schools among the Pharisees, the free constructionist school of Hillel and the strict constructionist school of Shammai, named for the two great masters whose careers spanned the turn of the eras. The terms *conservative* and *liberal* are sometimes used of the houses of Shammai and Hillel, respectively. But this can be done only advisedly. To oversimplify, the house of Shammai was inclined to stick up for the letter of the Torah, while the house of Hillel sought out its spirit. The outcome was that Hillelite usage tended to put people ahead of the letter of the law. At first, the Shammaites were dominant, but then the Hillelites gained the upper hand.

The Galilean Pharisees who disputed points of law with Jesus (as remembered in the gospels) tended toward the Shammaite view. The teachings of Jesus inclined more toward the Hillelite position. Jesus' disputes with the Pharisees were not unlike their arguments among themselves. However, after the time of Jesus, Jewish Christian leaders found themselves locked in dispute with pharisaic leaders for recognition in the community. This antagonism is reflected in the editing of the gospels, especially Matthew and John, as we will see in Chapter 12. Later gentile Christians tended to go even further and read into these "family arguments" a "we versus they" hostility. This antagonism has persisted through the centuries and has, regrettably, been the cause of Christian persecution of Jews in many periods.

During this period the Pharisees evolved what was to become the characteristic Jewish attitude toward civil authority. They were willing to put up with just about any government, so long as Jewish religious practices were not utterly repressed. Though they detested the Roman occupation, most Pharisees eschewed armed revolution. They shared the general expectation of a messianic age, which God would begin in his own good time. In the meantime, they believed their obligation was to create a congenial environment for King Messiah's coming by living a life of Torah-faithfulness.

After the destruction of Jerusalem and the Temple in 70 C.E., the Pharisees emerged with a form of piety and an institution, the synagogue (which they had not invented, but which was an ideal setting for their piety), adapted to carry on Jewish life and religion. The Romans recognized the principal pharisaic academy at Yavneh (Jamnia) as the Sanhedrin (highest court of the Jews). After 70 C.E., pharisaic Judaism became rabbinic Judaism. All forms of Judaism that exist today (except for the few Samaritans) descend from rabbinic Judaism.

The earliest references to what later generations would call *kabbalism,* the peculiarly Jewish and rabbinic form of mysticism, are associated with the students of Hillel around the turn of the eras. The earliest well-documented mystical traditions date from the post-70 C.E. academy of Yavneh.

Mysticism is a religious discipline that leads to direct encounters with the holy. In Judaism, two basic forms of mysticism developed. One was Chariot (or Palace) Mysticism, which was the most popular. The chariot was the Divine Chariot of the visions of Ezekiel (see chap. 6). The palaces were the wondrous structures beheld by the mystics as they moved through the seven levels of heaven. As will be noted in Chapter 14, the Apostle Paul may have been associated with this tradition. The other form of mysticism was Creation Mysticism, which made the light of the first day of creation (Gen. 1:3) the object of contemplation. The Johannine School (see chap. 12) may have been associated with this tradition.

Study of Torah was central to the discipline of both schools. The great masters would generally not admit novices to mystical training until they were already well grounded in Torah studies. And mystical discipline itself involved intensive, probably esoteric, inquiry into the text of the written Torah. It was said that birds so unlucky as to fly overhead when one gifted early mystic performed his meditation were incinerated.

The Sadducees

This group was composed of prominent priests and other aristocrats. The High Priest was ordinarily the titular head. Aristocratic religion is usually traditional and conservative, and this seems to have been true of the Sadducees. They insisted on a strict literal interpretation of the Mosaic Torah. They are said to have had books of such interpretations, but none has survived. They may even have restricted their biblical canon to the first five books, like the Samaritans (discussed later).

Josephus, the New Testament, the Dead Sea Scrolls, and the rabbinic literature all accuse the Sadducean leadership of violent and unprincipled behavior to attain their ends. These are all hostile witnesses, but there is probably enough smoke to suspect some sort of fire. The Pharisees had once been the political antagonists of the Sadducees, and they remained their religious adversaries. The Sadducees wanted the High Priest to envelop himself in a cloud of smoke from incense before entering the Holy of Holies in the Temple on the Day of Atonement, lest he see God and die. The Pharisees insisted he light it inside the Holy of Holies. The Pharisees affirmed belief in resurrection from the dead and in angels, while the Sadducees rejected such ideas. It is recorded that the Sadducees had to defer to the Pharisees' interpretation of ritualistic matters because of popular pressure.

The Temple was the power base and source of wealth for the Sadducean movement. Because the High Priest was among their ranks, and because the Romans placed him at the head of the Sanhedrin, there was undoubtedly close contact between the Sadducees and the Romans. They were obliged to collaborate with the Romans, or at least with their Herodian clients. The alternative was to give up their privileged position.

The Essenes (Covenanters)

A sectarian movement called the *Essenes* ("purified ones") is described by Josephus in his histories, by the philosopher Philo, and by the Roman naturalist Pliny the Elder. The Essenes were a sect in the sociological sense; that is, they withdrew from the "sinful world" to live their higher form of life uncontaminated. All three sources agree that the Essenes had a major sectarian center in the isolated wilderness of the Dead Sea area, near Jericho. Philo and Pliny emphasized their celibacy, but Josephus said some were married and some lived in villages. Celibacy would have been extremely unusual among Jews, given the commandment of Gen. 1:28.

The discovery of the Dead Sea Scrolls and the center of community life associated with them at Qumran caused many historians to conclude that the Covenanters of the scrolls were Essenes. The Qumranians called themselves *Covenanters*, the men of the New Covenant or the Covenant who remained faithful while Israel went astray. Their writings suggest that they represented the radical priestly wing of the pietist movement that had been patronized by Simon the Just in the early second century B.C.E. They were once led by a charismatic priest whom they called the Teacher of Righteousness. He received from God the ability to discern all the secrets of the prophets. They applied the words of Scripture to their own time in apocalyptic commentaries.

The community was rigidly hierarchical with the sons of Zadok, the faithful priests, at the head. Each member had an assigned rank within his respective order (priests, Levites, and laity), which was reviewed yearly. The rule for communal meals ordained that *even if* the Messiah be present, he and his lay entourage must defer in all things to the priests.

The Covenanters were radically separatist. They were the Sons of Light. Everyone outside the sect, Jew or Gentile, was a Son of Darkness, a man of Belial's lot (their favorite name for the Devil). The Jerusalem Sadducees were "wicked priests." The Pharisees were "seekers after smooth things" (they made religion too easy). The Romans (known as *Kittim* in the texts) were the great foreign enemy.

The Qumran sectarians believed a great apocalyptic war was about to erupt, in which the Sons of Light would be victorious. Then the Sons of

Photograph by the senior author

Common Room, Qumran. This hall in the sectarian complex at Qumran, which scholars believe was an Essene community, served as the refectory and meeting hall for the members. This view to the east looks across the Dead Sea toward the land of Moab, today part of the Kingdom of Jordan.

Zadok would be installed in the Jerusalem Temple, and Jewish life and institutions would be restored according to the sect's teaching. The Qumran compound and another related to it further south were built as fortresses in preparation for the war. There was a conflict, but it resulted in their being wiped out by Roman Legion X. Some Covenanters may have joined the resistance at Masada, but the sect did not survive the catastrophe of 70 C.E.

The Zealots

According to Josephus, the Zealots were a "fourth philosophy" among the Jews. He said that they agreed with the Pharisees on religious matters. What set them apart was their attitude toward Rome. Looking back to the success of the Maccabean revolt, the Zealots, perhaps spurred on by apocalyptic fervor, counseled armed resistance. The Zealots exhibited the sort of contentious factionalism that often characterizes revolutionary movements. They dealt harshly with those they considered inadequately enthusiastic about their campaign against Rome, which flared into a war by 66 C.E. And they fought among themselves. However, the heroic defense of Masada by a handful of Zealots who committed mass suicide rather than surrender to the Romans is justifiably legendary.

The Samaritans

Tension between Jerusalem and Samaria goes back to the foundation of Samaria as the capital of the Northern Kingdom. It was intensified during the postexilic reconstruction when the Samaritans sought, on one side, to gain a foothold in the Jerusalem cult, and on the other, to impede the refortification of Jerusalem and hence its independence. The final major event in the schism between the Samaritans and the established leadership was the destruction by John Hyrcanus of a "counter-Temple" the Samaritans had established on Mount Gerizim.

The Samaritans were a localized and generally conservative denomination led by hereditary priests. Their Scripture consisted of only the Pentateuch. Rabbinic practice treated the Samaritans as marginal and suspect keepers of the Torah. The Samaritans reciprocated by showing contempt for "the Jews" as they called them, meaning those Israelites who acknowledged Jerusalem's priestly and rabbinic leadership.

The Samaritans survived the debacles of the classical age, but their numbers were much reduced over the years by Christian and Muslim ill treatment, so that only a small group survives today.

The People of the Land

Rabbinic literature used the term "people of the land" to describe the less observant members of the Galilean and Judean communities. They probably stood outside identifiable denominational movements. Some were simply ignorant of the final points of Torah piety. Others were excluded by choice, chance, poverty, or occupation. *Publicans*, those who collected taxes for Rome and lined their own pockets in the process; prostitutes; and persons whose work made them ritually contaminated would have been included under the last heading. Taken in sum, this category probably constituted a substantial majority of the Jewish population of the traditional homeland. Ironically, although the Pharisees held them somewhat in disdain, their admiration gave the Pharisees much of their public influence. The gospel narratives suggest that Jesus aimed much of his energy at these "straying Israelite sheep."

Hellenistic Judaism

This is a catch basket phrase for a variety of forms of Judaism that developed after the time of Alexander. In general, it refers to those Jews who continued to consider themselves Jewish after they had become native Greek speakers and assimilated other aspects of Hellenistic culture. These Jews lived for the most part in centers of the Diaspora like Alexandria, but there was also a Greek-speaking synagogue in Jerusalem, in the very shadow of the Temple. Indeed, we should not overplay the valid distinction between Hebraic and Hellenistic Judaism. Much of Jewish life had become influenced by Hellenism to some extent. The real questions were, How much? Where did a person's heart lie? With Athens or Jerusalem?

Hellenistic Judaism did not survive the classical age. Some of it was assimilated into Christianity, some passed into the pagan world, and some accepted rabbinic norms. The works of the great first-century C.E. Alexandrian philosopher and mystic, Philo, are Hellenistic Judaism's finest surviving intellectual monument. Philo used Greek allegorical interpretation to show that the Mosaic revelation had anticipated and indeed excelled the truths later discovered by Greek philosophy. The historical writing of Josephus reflects the influence of Hellenistic historiography, as does Luke-Acts in the New Testament (see chap. 13).

The Septuagint (LXX) was Hellenistic Judaism's most influential legacy. The triumph of rabbinic Judaism meant that most of the LXX's influence would be upon Christianity, specifically the Greek-speaking gentile church. As early as the New Testament itself, biblical quotations were often from the LXX. Indeed, the LXX gave Greek-speaking Christians access to Scripture.

In the diaspora communities gentile converts to Judaism were not uncommon. To convert required instruction, followed by self-baptism, reenacting the Exodus deliverance at the Red Sea. Men had to be circumcised, which may explain why many men remained "God-fearers," who participated to varying degrees in things Jewish but did not take the full step of conversion. But if their wives were Jewish, either by birth or conversion, their children were Jews.

The Nazareans

No discussion of the variety of denominations in classical Judaism would be complete without mention of the small messianic community that arose in the first century C.E. and went on to become the world's largest religion. The rabbis of the time called this movement *Nazareans*. They called themselves, according to the New Testament, *The Way*. In Antioch they were called *Christians*, the name that stuck. Five of the six remaining chapters of this book are devoted to the literary and historical worlds of this movement, so no more need be said here.

Conclusion

This survey should suffice to demonstrate that the first three centuries of classical Judaism were an age of variety and creativity. It was an age that hinged on two great crises for the Jewish community. The first, culminating in the Maccabean Wars, saw an old order pass away and a new order, rich, varied, and dynamic, emerge. The emerging new order survived the fall of the Hasmonaeans and the arrival of Rome and, with Rome, the House of Herod. The second great crisis was the Zealot War of national liberation against Rome (66–73 C.E.), in which the fall of Jerusalem and destruction of the Temple in 70 was the pivotal point.

The events of 70 led to the winnowing of the new order. Rabbinic Judaism emerged from the maelstrom as the normative form of Judaism, and the process of estrangement between traditional Judaism and the increasingly gentile Christian movement was exacerbated. The Second Jewish War with Rome (132–135 C.E.) widened the gulf. However, recent archaeological research, and the critical resifting of other historical data, suggest that final estrangement lay in the future, on the whole in the early Byzantine period, even later in the special case of Galilee. But that is far beyond the purview of this book.

THE LITERARY WORLD

There is a variety of types of religious literature composed during the period between 200 B.C.E. and 100 C.E. that are not found in the Jewish canon or the New Testament. They can be divided into the following groupings:

1. The *Deuterocanon*, or *Apocrypha* ("Hidden Writings"), consists of material that did not stand in Tanak, but is found in most LXX manuscripts

and in most Greek and Latin copies of the Christian Old Testament. It is assumed that these materials were regarded as Scripture by substantial, perhaps largely Hellenistic, Jewish communities during the early classical period. Clearly, they were not part of the canon of Tanak. We shall consider the complete traditional collection, including material relegated to an appendix by the Council of Trent. See Figures 1–1 and 1–2, and the discussion of canon (chap. 1) for the variations in Christian and Jewish usage.

2. The *Larger Apocrypha* is the term we have selected to denote a number of Jewish religious writings from the early classical period that are not regarded as canonical by any substantial Jewish or Christian group today. The two major English translations of this body of writings entitle them *Pseuedpigrapha*. This is an unfortunate title on two accounts. First, a pseudepigraph is a work that is attributed to a false author, and only some of these works are such. Secondly, the title suggests that these works are some sort of coherent collection. But they are not. It is later scholarly activity that has brought them together. But students should nonetheless know and recognize the term *Pseudepigrapha*, for it is widely used.

3. The *Dead Sea Scrolls* are the writings found near the ruins of the Covenanters' community at Qumran. The Scrolls do include canonical and Deuterocanonical works but also a number of noncanonical writings appropriate for our consideration here.

4. *Rabbinic literature* refers to the body of traditions of pharisaic-rabbinic Judaism that were circulated orally during this period and later written down.

In this section we will briefly survey the writings included in each of these groups.

The Deuterocanon

The Deuterocanonical works, called "the Apocrypha" by some Protestant groups, include several different types of literature similar in form to the books of the Tanak, and, in one case, to a form that became popular in the New Testament.[1]

First Esdras and *First and Second Maccabees* are historical narratives. First Esdras (called Third Esdras in Roman Catholic Bibles) closely parallels sections of the Hebrew canon (Second Chronicles 35—36 and Nehemiah

---

[1] The Revised Standard Version translation of the Apocrypha, with introductions and notes for each of the books, is available in Bruce M. Metzger, ed., *The Oxford Annotated Apocrypha* (New York: Oxford University Press, 1965).

7:38—8:12). First Maccabees covers the period from 168 to 134 B.C.E., when the Maccabean revolt threw off Seleucid control. A straightforward narrative, it is almost the only record of this important period. Second Maccabees parallels First Maccabees 1—7, but it stresses miracles and divine appearances. It develops a theological interpretation of history that holds that the persecution of the Jews by Antiochus was a form of discipline.

Tobit, Judith, Susanna, and *Bel and the Dragon* are, like Ruth and Esther, short stories that teach moral lessons. Like Ruth, Tobit shows how the righteousness of ordinary people is rewarded. Like Esther, Judith is a historical romance in which the heroic action of a woman saves her people from an oppressor. The other two works are among the additions to the Book of Daniel in the Apocrypha.

The *Wisdom of Solomon* and *Ecclesiasticus (the Wisdom of Jesus, the Son of Sirach)* are, like Proverbs, Job, and Ecclesiastes in the Tanak, examples of wisdom literature. The Wisdom of Solomon (sometimes called simply the Book of Wisdom) purports to be an address by King Solomon to the rulers of the world, showing that the ethical and religious wisdom of the Tanak is superior to the wisdom of the Gentiles. In fact, the work is a creative synthesis of ideas drawn from canonical wisdom writings (such as reward of the righteous and punishment of the evil) and Greek concepts (such as immortality of the soul). As in Proverbs 8 and Job 28, Wisdom is personified as an independent agent. Ecclesiasticus, like Ecclesiastes, is an old teacher's collected wisdom. The work is an anthology of aphorisms, brief essays, hymns to Wisdom, reflections on existence, and advice on proper conduct. Its style and view of life are similar to that found in Proverbs.

The *Additions to the Book of Esther* give Esther an overtly religious dimension lacking in the Hebrew story. The other *Additions to Daniel (the Prayer of Azariah* and the *Song of the Three Young Men)* are devotional poems. The *Letter of Jeremiah* uses the letter form, which became popular in the New Testament. It purports to be a letter from the prophet Jeremiah to the leaders of Judah about to be deported to Babylon, warning them of the dangers of idolatry.

Second Esdras (called Fourth Esdras in Roman Catholic Bibles) is, like Daniel, an apocalyptic work, with visions giving symbols of the end of history. Included is an interesting explanation of the origin of the canon and the extracanonical works that claims that Ezra restored by inspiration the "twenty-four" books of Scripture and wrote seventy more reserved for the "wise."

Baruch is a composite work, including a confession of sins (linked to Jeremiah's secretary, Baruch), a poem linking Wisdom and Torah (cf. Sirach 24), and poems of hope and comfort.

The *Prayer of Manasseh* is a poem the wicked King Manasseh (2 Kings 21) ostensibly composed while in exile in Babylon, repenting of his sins. The Council of Trent removed it from the Deuterocanon and made it, along with first and Second Esdras (Third and Fourth Esdras), an appendix to the canon.

The Larger Apocrypha

Many extracanonical works from the early classical age survived and have been collected together by scholars under the title *Pseudepigrapha*, as noted. Some are in fact pseudepigraphs, claiming to be the work of such ancient worthies as Enoch, Noah, Moses, and Isaiah. Others are not. We will describe briefly some of the most important works in this extensive and varied body of literature.

The *Letter of Aristeas* includes the legend of the translation of the Septuagint. *Third Maccabees* is a legend that, like Esther, explains the origin of a Jewish festival. *Fourth Maccabees* is a philosophical essay on the question, Can reason rule the passions? The two works attributed to Enoch exploit the Tanak's mysterious note that Enoch was taken by God and walked with him (Gen. 5:24), to spell out what Enoch saw while on his heavenly stroll. *First Enoch* (called *Ethiopic Enoch* because it was preserved in an Ethiopian Christian community) is a complex anthology of apocalyptic visions, theological history, primitive science (astronomy), sayings about the Messiah, announcement of judgment by one called the Son of Man (interpreting Daniel 7), and an interpretation of Genesis. *Second Enoch* (*Slavonic Enoch*, so named because it survived only in a Slavonic translation) reveals the mysteries of creation seen by Enoch.

The *Sibylline Oracles* use the device of a sibyl (the Greek name for an inspired woman who utters predictions of imminent events) to continue the prophetic tradition of announcing judgment on idolatry and the climax of history. *The Greek Apocalypse of Baruch* (Third Baruch) is a description of Baruch's journey through five heavens, where he learns cosmic mysteries. *The Syriac Apocalypse of Baruch* (Second Baruch) is another report of visions, similar to Second Esdras and Revelation.

Jubilees is named after the division of world history into periods of forty-nine years or "jubilees" (see Leviticus 25). In form, it is a commentary on the first section of the Pentateuch. *The Psalms of Solomon* is a collection of eighteen sacred songs emphasizing Torah obedience and reflections similar to those in the Psalms found among the Dead Sea Scrolls. *The Testament of the Twelve Patriarchs* purports to be the last testaments of the sons of Jacob, with advice that seems influenced by Hellenistic moral philosophy and with several apocalyptic sections. *The Assumption of Moses* alludes to an ascension of Moses into heaven, but includes only exhortation ostensibly given to

Joshua (including several apocalyptic predictions). *The Martyrdom and Ascension of Isaiah* is a compilation of three short works; a commentary on Second Kings 21, a Christian prophecy, and a description of Isaiah's journey through the seven heavens. *The Life of Adam and Eve* is a tale that picks up the action after Adam and Eve have been expelled from Eden, coupled with an apocalypse attributed to Moses. A recent English translation of the Pseudepigrapha includes these with twenty other apocalyptic writings and thirty-one other miscellaneous works.[2]

The Dead Sea Scrolls

The scrolls found in caves around the sectarian compound at Qumran were the library of the Essenes (Covenanters), who made their headquarters there. Many of the scrolls were copies of books from the Tanak, the Apocrypha, and the Pseudepigrapha. Others were apocalyptic commentaries on biblical books, written from a sectarian viewpoint, and collections of biblical verses esteemed by the community. The biblical documents have been of great value for the study of the history of the text of Tanak. However, some scrolls were original sectarian compositions. These, along with the apocalyptic commentaries, supply historians with firsthand information about a group concerning which little was previously known.

The Community Rule and *The Damascus Covenant Document* were manuals of community organization and practice. The latter had been known since copies were found in a Cairo synagogue around the turn of the century. But fragments have also turned up at Qumran. *The War Scroll* describes the great final struggle between the Sons of Light and the Sons of Darkness that is to usher in God's Kingdom on earth. *The Temple Scroll* offers an idealized reconstruction of Jerusalem, especially the Temple, in the form of instructions from God to Moses. It may have been intended to be a sixth book of the Torah! A number of original sectarian *Thanksgiving Psalms*, reflecting intense piety, were found. *The Habakkuk Commentary* was the most complete of the apocalyptic commentaries that read Scripture like a current newspaper, an interpretative approach still used. This summary only scratches the surface of the total scroll inventory.[3]

Rabbinic Literature

The lore of pharisaic-rabbinic Judaism, beyond Tanak itself, began to be published in written form only around 200 C.E., though private written sources had existed earlier alongside oral tradition. Its literary history is so

---

[2]James H. Charlesworth, ed., *The Old Testament Pseudepigrapha* (New York: Doubleday, 1984).

[3]For an English translation of the sectarian scrolls, see Geza Vermes, *The Dead Sea Scrolls in English* (Baltimore: Penguin, 1975).

complex that, like the documents of Tanak and the New Testament, it cannot be used uncritically as historical data. Used with care, it provides a rich source for understanding the circles that created and preserved it and the historical world in which they lived.[4]

Rabbinic traditions, as noted, are divided into the two categories of authority, halakah and haggadah. Halakah (meaning "the way," "the path") lays down obligatory principles on the way people should order their personal and communal lives. Haggadah ("narration") is devotional, inspirational, edifying lore. It does not command, but it helps one understand God and the holy life. The literature itself can be sorted into three major categories: the talmudic, the midrashic, and the targumic.

The heart of the talmudic tradition is the *Mishnah*, which is simply the rabbinic oral Torah reduced to writing. Officially published about 200 C.E. by Rabbi Judah the Prince, its contents are not exclusively halakic, though halakah dominates. Eventually the later rabbinic discussions of Mishnah, anecdotes about the rabbis of the Mishnah and later, traditions about how mishnaic decisions were reached, and a great variety of other lore were added to the Mishnah. This elaboration was known as *Gemara* ("tradition"). The combination of Mishnah and Gemara is the Talmud, the great repository of rabbinic lore. There are two editions of the Talmud, one with a Gemara edited in the academies of Babylon and one with a Gemara edited in the academy of Tiberias, both dating from around 500 C.E. The former is the more authoritative.

Midrash, or biblical interpretation, is of two sorts. *Halakic midrash* may be made only on the legal sections of the biblical Torah. *Haggadic midrash* may be made on any part of Tanak. Indeed, there are haggadic passages in what are regarded as halakic midrashim. The largest collection of midrashic lore, *Midrash Rabbah* ("the Great Midrash") is haggadic and treats every book of Tanak.

Targum describes the ad hoc oral translations into Aramaic that synagogue readers made of the lessons from Hebrew Scripture after Aramaic became the common language of Israel and neighboring areas. Greater care was required in translating the Torah lesson than the second lesson, but both types tended to be expansive and interpretive. Eventually several written Targums on Tanak were published.

The Babylonian Talmud and the classical halakic midrashim remain authoritative for traditionally observant Jews.

---

[4]English translations of rabbinic literature include Herbert Danby, *The Mishnah* (London: Oxford, 1933); the multivolume *Soncino Talmud* and *Midrash Rabbah*, from Soncino Press, London; see also C. K. Barrett, *The New Testament Background* (New York: Harper & Row, Pub., Harper Torchbooks, 1961); Salo Baron and Joseph Blau, eds., *Judaism, The Postbiblical and Talmudic Period* (New York: Liberal Arts Press, 1954).

SUMMARY

This chapter highlighted the significant historical developments and movements and the Jewish literature of the period between 200 B.C.E. and 100 C.E. Our thesis was that this was one of the most vital and creative eras in religious history.

Our historical commentary described the Maccabean Revolt, climaxing in the liberation of the Temple in 164 B.C.E. and leading to a brief resurgence of Jewish independence in the homeland. Roman invasion and subjugation marked the end of this period.

In these tumultuous times, a number of new groups arose in Judaism. They included the Pharisees, a pietistic and scholarly lay party; Sadducees, aristocrats and priests who often opposed the Pharisees; Essene Covenanters of the apocalyptic community near the Dead Sea, from whom the famous Dead Sea Scrolls came; militaristic Zealots; the marginalized Samaritans; and the group called by rabbis the Nazareans. In this chapter we discussed these groups and the so-called people of the land. We also touched on the important influence of Hellenistic (Greek) culture on many Jews during this time.

Our literary analysis briefly surveyed the writings known to Christians as the Deuterocanon (or Apocrypha) and Pseudepigrapha (or, more appropriately, Larger Apocrypha). We also identified the sectarian documents of the Dead Sea Scrolls and the types of rabbinic literature from this important period.

The importance of this era for the development of an understanding of both Judaism and Christianity cannot be overemphasized. The writings of this period (except Daniel) did not attain canonical status in the Tanak. (The Deuterocanon is Scriptural for a substantial part of Christianity.) Even so, some of this literature and the groups for which it was written shaped Judaism as it is still known today and provided the principal milieu for the origin and early development of Christianity. Any serious student of the Bible will find the material introduced in this chapter a fertile field for further study.

THE CONTEMPORARY WORLD:
QUESTIONS FOR DISCUSSION AND REFLECTION

1. The crises described in this chapter led to the demise of the old order and the emergence of a new order in the Jewish world. Ultimately, the many denominations were winnowed down to a few. The two that came through in best shape were the rabbinic movement and the Nazareans (early Christians). Both emerged from the moderate center. Both made accommodations to the then modern world without aban-

doning their most treasured convictions. By contrast, the groups that held most doggedly to the old ways and those that went furthest in adopting Greco-Roman fashions perished. Is this a unique first-century phenomenon, or can it be illustrated at other points in history? How does it apply to religion, politics, or whatever, in our time?

2. Compare the variety in Judaism during this period with the variety in contemporary Judaism or Christianity. Is pluralism within a religion inevitable in any age? Is it a sign of strength or weakness?

3. The Judaism that developed in the time of Ezra is sometimes caricatured as cold, legalistic, and moribund, standing in terror of a distant and unloving God of law. How does the survey in this chapter modify that perception of Judaism in this period? How does it affect your view of modern Judaism and Jewish teaching?

4. Which of the books of the Apocrypha and Pseudepigrapha would you be willing to consider as part of your private canon of especially meaningful sacred writings?

CHAPTER 11

The Proclaimer:
Jesus of Nazareth

Sunset on the Sea of Galilee. Much of Jesus' ministry was conducted around the shores of this freshwater lake. His disciples Andrew, Peter, James, and John had earned their livings as fishermen on the lake, known in Hebrew as Chinnereth. Herod Antipas built the lovely town of Tiberias (noted for its hot springs) on the western shore to replace Sepphoris as his capital. The great rabbinic academy relocated in Tiberias after the savaging of Judah during the second war with Rome.

226

INTRODUCTION

Is it possible to write a life of Jesus? Many people would regard this as a silly question. The New Testament contains not one, but four, lives of Jesus. Every historical era since the first century has seen the production of lives of Jesus of *some* sort. The shelves of bookstores and libraries are full of them. Of course one can write a life of Jesus, several if one pleases and one has time.

But when we inspect the lives of Jesus that have been written, it turns out that there are several different sorts. We confine ourselves in this observation to serious attempts at history or biography. We can safely exclude from discussion fad works that try to connect Jesus with the latest trend in pop culture (such as several during the 1960s that tried to prove Jesus was the leader of a drug cult). We can also pass over devotional works portraying Jesus as the world's best salesman or using some other gimmick to attract readership.

Before the advent of critical historical writing, serious attempts to reconstruct the life of Jesus were essentially harmonized retellings of the gospels, often following John's implied chronology and perhaps elaborated from extracanonical sources, usually the authors' imaginations. Such "traditional" biographies continue to be written.

The introduction of critical historiographic techniques into the study of the New Testament has led to several different sorts of treatments of the life of Jesus. During the nineteenth century, critical scholars engaged in the so-called *quest for the historical Jesus* sought to disengage the "Jesus of history" from that "creation of superstition," "the Christ of faith." This effort was somewhat embarrassed by an increasing recognition that its selection of data seemed to be dictated by a particular theological agenda. Some New Testament specialists reacted by going to the opposite extreme and declaring that the "Jesus of history" (if there was one) is unknowable. It was impossible, they held, to get behind the interpretation of Jesus in the gospels to any actual events. However, some scholars who were suspected (or accused) of such views had not in fact quite thrown in the historical sponge. Rather, a more circumspect account of the life of Jesus resulted, in which the historians "said what could be said" without trying to write a full biography. The so-called new quest for the historical Jesus fell into this pattern. Though we do not subscribe fully to this approach, our work may be grouped with it in a general way.

If the question, Is it possible to write a life of Jesus? means, Can you prove (or disprove) the theological claims that the gospels (or the Apostle Paul, or later Christians) make about Jesus?, the answer must be no. Historical method cannot answer theological questions. It might clarify such questions. For instance, it can discover what such religious ideas as *messiah* or *son of God* could have meant to various groups of people in particular times and places. If some fraud or forgery had been committed in the formulation and transmission of traditions it might be found out. But whether or not Jesus was *really* the Messiah or the Son of God (*whatever* those titles mean) is beyond the power of history to show.

Historians can reconstruct the lineaments of the world in which Jesus was supposed to have lived, the world of the first century in the Roman Empire; more precisely, the world of Judaism in the Jewish homeland of Israel. This picture can be enlivened by the stock of well-documented events from that general time and place. They can also sift available materials that purport to bear upon things that Jesus said or did according to critical historical canons. Out of building blocks such as these, a picture can be constructed, rather as the bits of data laboriously radioed back by a spacecraft can be assembled by a computer into a recognizable image. And, just as a computer program can erase the static from a spacecraft picture and enhance its imagery, so techniques of literary and historical analysis and models borrowed from the social sciences can enhance the historical picture. But it will not be a complete biography.

EVIDENCE OUTSIDE THE GOSPELS

It is no secret that the gospels lodge certain religious claims about Jesus and appear to have been written precisely to advance those claims. This requires the historian to approach them with care as historic sources. Indeed, it has even led some to suggest that Jesus was a fictitious character invented by the ambitious leaders of the early church to promote their own fortunes. Because the prudent historian adopts a "worst possible case" mentality about his or her subject, it is advisable to approach the question of a life of Jesus independently of the gospels. That is, one can ask if there is information outside the gospels and, indeed, outside the New Testament, that documents Jesus as a historical person. If the answer is affirmative, one can then proceed to see what can be learned of Jesus from these sources. Otherwise one is thrown back on the canonical materials for whatever may be made of them.

There are relatively few extracanonical references to Jesus in near-contemporary classical sources, whether Jewish or pagan. This is hardly surprising. Jesus may have been supremely important among his circle of devotees, but they were few in number and not at all prominent in a world where wonder-workers, religious teachers, and martyrs to Roman authority were quite commonplace. However, for authentic history, the quality of sources is much more important than their number. Two of the early non-Christian references to Jesus stand out precisely because of their quality.

Josephus, who was mentioned in Chapter 10, was a young Jewish aristocrat who served the father-son team of generals and future Flavian emperors, Vespasian and Titus. He was captured during the first revolt against Rome; and after the war, he embarked on a literary career, patronized by the Flavian house. He sought to further understanding of his people and managed in his writings to be both pro-Roman and pro-Jewish. Josephus is generally regarded as a reliable reporter where his own reputation is not at stake. Indeed, his writings are treasured as the best source on the last few centuries of Jewish history prior to and during the first Jewish revolt against Rome.

Josephus's writings include several references to Jesus, as well as mention of John the Baptizer and James the brother of Jesus. The reference to the Baptizer in the *Antiquities* (18.116–119) does not connect John to Jesus in any way. It differs in matters of interpretation (including Herod's motives) from the gospel accounts of the Baptizer's arrest and execution at the hands of Herod Antipas. But it is of interest in confirming the historicity of an important figure in the gospels and the manner and agent of his death.

The direct references to Jesus are more important, but (not amazingly) more controversial. A succinct account in the eighteenth book of the *Antiquities* (18.63–64) notes Jesus' role as a religious teacher, his crucifixion under Pontius Pilate, the traditions of his resurrection, and the notion that the prophets had foretold a great deal about him. Much of the language in this passage would be fitting from Josephus' pen only if he had become a Christian, *which he had not*, even decades after the publication of *Antiquities*. Thus, the passage, if authentic in its core, must have been retouched by later pious Christian editors.

A similar but much stronger judgment adheres to a longer and more fulsome account in the Slavonic translation of *The Jewish War* (204:1–45). Whether the passage in question was even a part of the original Greek or Aramaic text of the *War* has been disputed. If it does include an authentic core, its adulatory language about Jesus strongly suggests heavy Christian editing.

The most important reference to Jesus occurs in a passage about his brother, James, in the twentieth book of the *Antiquities* (20.199–203). Like the reference to the Baptizer, it is interesting for its confirmation of yet another New Testament character, thus lending general authenticity to that body of tradition. But its reference to Jesus is even more interesting. Josephus identified James as "the brother of Jesus, the *alleged* Christ." When the fourth-century Christian historian Eusebius cited this passage, he inverted Josephus's Greek word order so that it read something more like "Jesus, who is called Christ," rather than "the alleged" or "so-called" Christ.

Unlike the passages noted previously in Josephus, this is precisely the sort of reference to Jesus we might expect from a Jewish writer who was not a Christian convert. It informs us that there was a person named Jesus whom Josephus regarded as a messianic pretender, that is, for whom messianic claims were made that Josephus did not credit, and that this Jesus had a brother named James. All of this squares with information in the gospels and other parts of the New Testament. It is particularly impressive to the historian because of the innocent and offhand manner of its presentation. Forgers and interpolators are generally much more ponderous, serious, and heavy-handed.

The other important classical treatment of Jesus is found in the *Annals* of the Roman historian Publius Cornelius Tacitus, a near-contemporary of Josephus. Tacitus narrated the great fire in Rome in the fifteenth book of the *Annals*, his last and greatest work. He noted that when Nero was unable to allay the widespread suspicion that the fire had been started on an imperial order, the emperor blamed it on the Christians and subjected them to vile and vicious treatment in public spectacles. As a good, conservative senatorial moralist, Tacitus held oriental religions in deep contempt and wasted few tears on the victims, though he recognized that Nero's wanton cruelty produced public sympathy for the Christians. But Tacitus was also a good historian and therefore felt obliged to explain who the pitiful, if detestable, victims were. They were named, he said, from Christus (using the Greek title as a proper name) "...who suffered the extreme penalty during the reign of Tiberius at the hands of one of our procurators, Pontius Pilate, and the pernicious superstition was checked for a moment, only to break out once more not merely in Judaea, the home of the disease, but in the capital itself, where all things horrible or shameful in the world collect and find a vogue." (*Annals* 15.44).[1]

Tacitus did not cite his source or sources of information. But he was not a credulous individual. Further, given his negative attitude toward things Eastern, he would probably have included anything less favorable about the Christians than their connection with an executed criminal, such as fraudulent origins, had he known such. Tacitus's Tiberian date for Jesus corresponds with the explicit statement of Lk. 3:1 and the implications of Luke 2 and Matthew 2 that Jesus was born during the reigns of Augustus and Herod the Great, near the time of Herod's death. It is also congruent with the observation of Lk. 3:23 that Jesus was about thirty at the onset of his public career.

A more detailed study would consider the less important pagan references to Jesus and early Christianity and the implications that can be drawn from references in rabbinic sources, themselves too late to be considered direct evidence. The two central references we have discussed should be adequate to establish that Jesus was in fact a historic personage. At any rate, they would be considered adequate for anyone other than Jesus. And they

---

[1]Tacitus, *The Annals, Loeb Classical Library*, trans. by John Jackson (Cambridge, Mass.: Harvard University Press, 1937), p. 283 (cf. pp. 270–85).

anchor several important data about Jesus that can be gathered from the New Testament. He lived during the reign of Tiberius. He was executed on orders of the Roman procurator, Pontius Pilate. Messianic claims were lodged on his behalf whether he made them or not. He had a brother named James, a pietist of some prominence who was killed in Jerusalem shortly before the outbreak of the first revolt.

THE GOSPELS AS SOURCES: WHERE DID JESUS "FIT"?

One must avoid the temptation to jump from this independent confirmation of New Testament material to a naive reliance on the gospels as historical sources. Form criticism and redaction criticism (see chap. 1) offer evidence that the traditions contained in the gospels were shaped to meet the needs, concerns, and interests of the developing church. Redaction criticism tries to demonstrate how the respective gospels crafted traditions to emphasize their particular insights. These matters will be explored in Chapter 12. But this preliminary note indicates why it would be irresponsible to take the gospels at face value as historic sources.

Some form critics seem to assume as an axiom that the church of the Hellenistic world not only was the place where the gospel traditions were shaped but also was their place of origin. If this were the case, the gospels would be quite useless as historical sources on Jesus. However, recent research has suggested that a substantial proportion of the tradition units in the gospels reflects a background in first-century "homeland Judaism." Further, some larger units (e.g., the Q cycle, discussed in chap. 12, and the Gospel of Matthew) might have been shaped against a background in or near the Jewish homeland.

We will not be able to demonstrate in this brief introductory text the critical sifting of each particular unit of tradition that might be used to reconstruct a portrait of Jesus. But we hope to raise the fundamental issue: Does the portrait of Jesus that emerges from a critical sifting of gospel lore present a person who fits into a background in first-century C.E. homeland Judaism? We have pictured that world in Chapter 10. That is the world in which Jesus would have found his place unless he was an utterly unique "flying-saucer" man, literally an alien to his environment. Such a person would have found it quite difficult to communicate with anyone and would have been much more seriously misunderstood than the gospels suggest Jesus actually was. His disciples are represented as getting the general idea right, but misinterpreting it; Peter knew he was the Messiah, but could not understand why the Messiah must suffer. We propose to ask whether the resultant critical portrait of Jesus fits *historically, ideologically,* and *sociologi-*

cally into the first-century Jewish world. Preference will be given to information from the Synoptic gospels, Matthew, Mark, and Luke, in this process. Although the Gospel of John probably had independent and authentic sources of information about Jesus, the purpose of the Fourth Gospel had moved much further into the interpretation of Jesus' significance than the other three. Thus, John will be utilized more as an occasional supplement to the Synoptics. Other more refined issues, such as apparent differences between the Synoptic and Johannine chronologies, need not concern us in this introductory discussion.

The Historical Fit

Is the picture of Jesus derived from the gospels *historically* credible? Does it coordinate with independent information about the history and topography of Israel in the first several decades of the first century? If, for instance, a gospel passage claimed that Jesus amazed and confounded Alexander the Great, a historian would be suspicious to say the least. Similarly, if Jerusalem were placed east of the Jordan, there would be grounds for skepticism. There are, to be sure, some minor issues of historical detail that cannot be totally resolved. For instance, if Jesus was born during the reign of Herod the Great, as Matthew and Luke assert (apparently on the basis of independent sources), could Quirinius have been governor of Syria, and did the tax census ordered during his tenure fall at the right time to account for Jesus' being born in Bethlehem? The independent data may be ambiguous, but even if Lk. 2:1–2 errs on this matter, it is an error within the historical ball park and does not impeach his general accuracy. Similarly, not all of the topographic references in the gospels are entirely clear and identifiable. But none of them raises glaring difficulties.

The gospel traditions seem to have things pretty much in order. This does not mean that the final authors of the gospel documents had to be fully conversant personally with the geography or the history in question. It is enough for historical purposes that such information is embedded in the traditions they utilized.

Jesus is identified with the village of Nazareth, a minor hamlet in those days, located in lower Galilee, just north of the Valley of Jezreel and a few miles southeast of the sometimes provincial capital of Sepphoris (which, like its successor, Tiberias, Jesus never visited, so far as we know). He was pictured during his public career circulating among various towns of the area, with Capernaum as his apparent headquarters. Mark's version of the story of the healing of the paralytic (2:1–12) seems to reflect accurate knowledge of first-century home construction. His various travels and the hometowns of other characters are authentic places plausibly located.

Jesus lived and died in a land incorporated in the Roman Empire, and the gospel narratives record that fact. We noted earlier in this chapter that

Courtesy of the Israel Government Tourist Office

The Synagogue, Capernaum. Archaeologists now believe that this handsome classical house of prayer and study was constructed in the fourth to fifth centuries C.E., rather than in the third century, as previously thought. The synagogue where Jesus taught probably stood on this same site. The traditional site of Simon Peter's house was nearby and was occupied early in Christian history by a "house church" and later by an octagonal Byzantine church. That such a fine synagogue could be built so near a church after Christianity became the established religion of the Roman Empire suggests harmonious relations between Jewish and gentile Christians and traditional Jews in Israel.

the match between gospel narrative and Jewish and Roman rulers was accurate. Jesus died by crucifixion, a Roman, rather than Jewish, mode of execution, condemned by a documented Roman procurator. And so on.

The gospels also reflect accurate knowledge of the organization of the Jewish community in the homeland during the first century. At least one of Jesus' Disciples can be identified as a Zealot (Lk. 6:15; the form of the name in Mk. 3:18 and Mt. 10:4 might be a transliteration of the Hebrew noun). The Pharisees appear as the most frequent opponents of Jesus in arguments. The Sadducees also appear, but less frequently, as would be expected, especially in Galilee. The Essenes are not mentioned. If they guarded their purity, as the Hellenistic writers say and the Dead Sea Scrolls imply, this is not surprising. The tradition is aware of the dispute between Pharisees and Sadducees over resurrection. The Sanhedrin is the highest authority in Israel, but subject to the Roman authorities. It is headed by the High Priest, but includes both Pharisees and Sadducees. The overall picture suggests sources well informed about the world of which they speak.

The Ideological Fit

We indicated earlier in this chapter that Jesus would not have received a responsive hearing had he been totally alien to his world. His teachings had to be close enough to the ideas current in his time to be comprehensible to his contemporaries. This would be true even if his repertory included some new ideas (which it probably did), and even if some of his teachings were misunderstood (which they almost certainly were). On a general level, he was familiar with the Hebrew Scripture and drew heavily upon it. Even though the Greek gospels frequently seem to assimilate his Scripture citations to the LXX, his usage reflects the Hebrew canon of Israel and Babylon, not the more extensive LXX canon. Jesus frequented the synagogue in his hometown and in other communities he visited. In Jerusalem he and his Disciples seemed comfortable around the Temple, and the Disciples continued to go there after the Crucifixion and the Resurrection.

But what were Jesus' ideological affinities? If he was not a flying-saucer prophet, was he yet perhaps a sort of religious Lone Ranger? Such notions appeal to romantic imagination. But too much of the gospels bears the mark of the Judaism of the day. Attempts have been made to connect Jesus with various groups in first-century Judaism. That both he and all of them were Jewish means that they should share more in common than with non-Jews. However, only if the evidence is used very selectively can Jesus be made to appear as an Essene-Covenanter, Zealot, or Jewish Gnostic. The closest relationship that can be shown is between Jesus and pharisaic-rabbinic Judaism. Such an observation might offend persons who wish to distance Jesus from his Jewish roots. But, in fact, no teaching attributed to Jesus in the Synoptic Gospels is without its parallel in the rabbinic literature. This fact should be tempered by the equally true fact that the history of gospel tradition (about thirty-five years for Mark, about sixty years for John) is much shorter than the 400 years for Mishnah, the additional 300 for Talmud, and a similar amount for parallel midrashic lore (see chap. 10). But then, 200 years of Mishnah's history preceded the birth of Jesus! So there are really no points to be scored on these data; there are only counsels of caution to serious scholars.

An objection that will almost certainly be raised against these data is, as noted earlier, that most of Jesus' disputes in the Synoptics are with the Pharisees. Three things must be noted at this point. First, detailed arguments are possible only between persons who share some common ground. Second, Jesus' disputes with the Pharisees were largely over questions of the correct understanding of Torah, a matter of mutual concern. The other main issue was his personal authority, because he seems to have ignored the rabbinic practice of citing sources. Finally, persons familiar with the rabbinic literature are aware that most of the disputes between Jesus and the Pharisees in the gospels are similar to disputes *among* rabbinic authorities in their nature, subject matter, and intensity. In other words, Jesus' arguments with his Pharisaic contemporaries were good Jewish family arguments and should be so understood. They are distorted when placed in the context of later Jewish-Gentile Christian or church-synagogue hostility. Incidentally, as noted in Chapter 10, rabbinic-pharisaic Judaism did not use the term *Pharisee* for self-identification. Sometimes it is used, in rabbinic lore as in the gospels, to criticize persons whose pretensions to piety outran their achievements.

We noted in Chapter 10 that pharisaism, at least prior to 70 C.E., could be divided into two wings: the strict constructionist house of Shammai and the freer constructionist house of Hillel. In those cases where distinction is possible, Jesus' Torah teaching almost invariably inclines toward the Hillelite. And most of his Galilean disputes seem to have been directed against the stricter Shammaite position. The denunciation of the cleansing of the outside of a vessel (Mt. 23:25–26) is directed against Shammaite interpretation. The rigid Sabbath rules that Jesus opposed were also Shammaite. It may be that the house of Shammai was stronger than the Hillelites in Galilee; some evidence points to that. There is a measure of irony in the fact that Jesus was challenged on the issue of divorce as he passed into Judea. The question was a "litmus paper" issue between the Shammaites and Hillelites, and for once Jesus came down on the strict constructionist side (Mk. 10:1–2; Mt. 19:1–9). The Hillelites were much more permissive. It has been noted that the few instances in which Jesus sided with the Shammaites were those in which strict constructionism served humanitarian ends. In this case it offered a greater security for women in a patriarchal society.

The title *Rabbi* is closely associated with pharisaic Judaism and its successor. Actually, the word became a formal title only after the time of Jesus. But its application to him is indicative.

Does this mean, then, that Jesus was a Pharisee, albeit one at odds with his contemporaries? A judicious answer on this score would be in the negative. Jesus' closest affinities were with pharisaism. If his contemporaries had been obliged to categorize him in terms of the major first-century denominations, they might have described him as a Pharisee or perhaps a crypto-Pharisee. But Jesus' Sabbath teaching was even more permissive than the Hillelites. Also, he was apparently skeptical about the oral Torah. He based his own teachings on midrash to a greater extent than seems to have been customary among Pharisees of his time. Finally, he apparently eschewed the principle of authority (see chap. 10). Instead, he stood for his own teachings, whether midrashic or ad hoc (Mk. 1:21–22; Mt. 7:28–29).

Despite the hostility of the Matthean circle toward the late-first-century rabbinic leadership at Yavneh, the Gospel of Matthew transmits Jesus' endorsement of pharisaic authority, even while it transmits his (and their own) reservations about the depth of some pharisaic piety (Mt. 23:1–36). If there is an irony here it is that Matthew is, at the same time, the most pharisaic of the gospels. Matthew seems, for example, to subscribe to the view of the near contemporary Akiva that there are no surplus words in Scripture, so that every single one must be interpreted. Thus Matthew suggests that Jesus must have ridden two animals in the triumphal entry story (Mt. 21:1–11; Zech. 9:9).

Jesus' affinity to contemporary Jewish centrism is further evidenced by his use of parables as a teaching device. He also typically utilized rabbinic forms of argument such as "if…how much more…" This is the *light-to-heavy* form common in rabbinic debates.

We may safely conclude, therefore, that Jesus stood in basic ideological harmony with the Pharisees. But he entertained enough differences with them to justify the view that he was not simply a slightly deviant Pharisee. His general ideological niche is established, but a more precise location in the world of first-century Judaism remains to be established.

The Sociological Fit

Was there a place in first-century Israelite society in which a figure like Jesus, as portrayed by the gospels, would fit? That is the sociological issue to which we now turn.

It has been observed that Jesus was accorded the title *Rabbi* by both his followers and others. Further, his relationship to his immediate circle of followers was organized on the model of a rabbi and his disciples. His appointment of a special company of twelve (Mk. 3:13–19; Mt. 10:2–4; Lk. 6:13–16) is probably of eschatological significance, relating to the twelve traditional tribes of Israel (Mt. 19:28). Matthew and Luke assimilate the twelve to the Company of the Apostles, though for the earlier Marcan tradition they are simply *The Twelve*. The existence of a smaller company of three, Peter, James, and John, could be connected with the organization of the Dead Sea Covenanters (see chap. 10). But it was also typical for a great rabbi to have an inner circle of especially dedicated and beloved students (a sort of graduate seminar) with whom he was most closely associated and to whom he communicated the most confidential teachings, including secret mystical lore.

These general sociological data tend to confirm the affinity between Jesus and pharisaic-rabbinic Judaism. But is a more precise definition possible? It has long been recognized that there was a particular class of holy men, or *hasidim*, around the turn of the eras in Israel. But recently, within this class of holy men, there has been identified a group of wonder-working saints whose religious expression can be described as *charismatic Judaism*.[2] The term *charismatic* is used here not in the popular sense associated with Pentecostal Christianity, but in Max Weber's sociological sense: empowered with a special spiritual gift.

One of the things that sets Jesus apart from the traditional rabbis is the material that ascribed to him extraordinary spiritual powers. Rabbinic authority was rational, based on learning and on purity of life. Some rabbinic tales have as their main point the inferiority of miraculous events compared to sound learning and pious life. Thus, no miracle, however wondrous, could impeach a majority vote in the academy.

However, Jesus may have been associated with a charismatic form of Judaism that seemed to be centered in Galilee. At least one of the Galilean charismatics, Hanina ben Dosa, made it into the rabbinic chain of tradition. Like Jesus, he was a healer, even over long distances. Like Jesus, he was proclaimed "son of God" by a *bath qol* (voice from heaven; literally "daughter of a voice," that is, an "echo of *the* voice [of God]"). And like Jesus, Hanina apparently caused some discomfort in conventional pharisaic ranks.

Unfriendly rabbinic propaganda following the schism between church and synagogue portrayed Jesus as a sorceror. Recently it has been speculated that he was a necromancer or magician. These were nontraditional ways of getting in touch with the spirit world. The data concerning charismatic saints in Galilee in the first century is therefore particularly valuable in assessing Jesus' place in a first-century Jewish context. It shows there was a place on the fringes of rabbinism at this time for a teacher who was also a healer and a wonder-worker. It also shows that one need not resort to only one model, portraying Jesus as a wonder-worker, *or* a rabbinic teacher, *or* a mystic, *or* an eschatological prophet exclusively and attributing other sorts of traditions about him to later editorial activity. Two or more roles could be, and were, combined in first-century Judaism in Israel.

This charismatic aspect of the ministry of Jesus—the healings, resuscitations, exorcisms, and the few nature miracles attributed to him—has created the greatest problems of credibility for modern readers. This has led some interpreters to try to explain the so-called *miracles* in scientific or philosophical terms, or else to simply explain them away. Of course, anthropologists know well that the holy men and women of most pretechnological societies were believed to work wonders. It would have been as difficult for members of that overwhelming majority of humanity to believe that someone who could not or did not work wonders was a holy person as it is for a modern skeptic to accept the wonders themselves. Ordinary folks have generally expected wonders of their holy people, and they have seldom been disappointed. This does not solve the problem of credibility for persons

[2]Geza Vermes, *Jesus the Jew: A Historian's Reading of the Gospels* (New York: Macmillan, 1973), pp. 58–82.

imbued with the modern technological outlook. But it does suggest that the issue is too fundamental to be swept away by a bit of theological legerdemain or a touch of modern scientific dogmatism. In any case, Jesus is not represented as lodging much confidence in wonders as religious persuaders. This seems to be the point of the tag line to the parable of the rich man and Lazarus. If people are not persuaded by the Torah and the prophets, they are unlikely to be convinced by a dead man (Lk. 16:19–31).

JESUS AND THE TITLES ATTRIBUTED TO HIM

Even when it has been shown that Jesus fits rather well into the first-century Jewish world, some persons may remain uncomfortable with the fact that the materials used by the historian are infused with a set of titles ascribed to Jesus that have been the substance of later Christian theology. It is not our purpose to question or to quarrel with the later theological understanding of these titles. Rather, we are obliged to raise the question of whether they were meaningful in classical Judaism, and if so, what they might have meant. Otherwise they must be sifted out of any historical account of Jesus, though they would remain significant in understanding the convictions of the developing church. The titles we shall examine are Messiah (Christ), Son of God, Son of Man, and LORD.

Messiah

The inscription Pilate had affixed to Jesus' cross, "Jesus of Nazareth, The King of the Jews," was supposed to inform passersby of the nature of the charge for which he was perishing in such agony. It reflects the datum found in both Josephus and Tacitus, that Jesus was regarded by some as the Messiah.

We have noted that the most common Jewish messianic notion was that God would restore the anointed Davidic line to the throne of Israel, and, in the process, restore the Israelite kingdom. In some schemes, the "days of the Messiah" were a period of preparation for the realization of the heavenly kingdom on earth, "the world to come." (The Christian apocalypse, the Revelation to John, shares this pattern, though the terminology is somewhat different.) And the usage of some documents is ambiguous, with "days of the Messiah" and "world to come" used interchangeably. We have seen that the Dead Sea sect was more interested in the restoration of the anointed high priesthood ("the Messiah of Aaron") than in the monarchy.

Other figures were associated with the messianic age. Elijah would return to announce it (Mal. 4:5; Mt. 11:14; cf. John the Baptizer's costume in Mk. 1:6; Mt. 3:4). A "prophet like [Moses]" (Dt. 18:15) might have played a part in some expectations. Some also looked for a Messiah of Joseph (i.e., the

Joseph tribes), who would help prepare the way for the Davidic messiah. A general restoration of prophecy could have been expected in some circles, but folk religion apparently ignored the pharisaic notion that it had ceased in the age of Ezra. But when "messiah" is mentioned without qualification in Jewish sources, it is the Davidic messiah who is meant. If Jesus claimed to be the Messiah, or his followers lodged the claim for him, this is the territory they were staking out and not some exotic other.

There can be no doubt that Jesus' followers proclaimed him the Messiah. His Greek title, *Christos* ("Christ"), is a literal translation of the Hebrew *meshiah* ("Messiah"). But did Jesus lodge such a claim on his own behalf? The gospels make Jesus appear at least a trifle cagey on the subject. Mark features the "messianic-secret" theme, in which those who recognize that Jesus is the Christ are told by him to keep it quiet. Jesus' answers to Pilate are (understandably) guarded. A case can be made that he never explicitly claimed the title messiah for himself, which would turn his execution into a tragic case of mistaken identity.

However, there are several points at which Jesus appears clearly to have asserted his messianic identity. His answer to the High Priest in the Gospel of Mark (14:62) is quite direct. Matthew 26:24 may appear more evasive, but in fact is not, as we shall presently see.

The clearest personal claim to messianic status lodged by Jesus is found in his actions in the triumphal entry and cleansings of the Temple stories, directly linked in Matthew and Luke and proximate in Mark (Mt. 21:1–17; Lk. 19:28–46; Mk. 11:1–19). The triumphal entry is presented as a deliberate dramatization (i.e., fulfillment) of the messianic prophecy of Zech. 9:9. It is probably significant that this passage portrays a peaceful Messiah, a theme to which we shall return. But the Temple-cleaning story is at least as direct a claim. The gospels do not present it as a vigilante assault by an outraged pietist. That Mark inserts a night in Bethany between the survey of 11:11 and the action itself particularly suggests a calculated move. But only two officers in traditional Jewish circles had the requisite authority to police the Temple; the king and the High Priest. No claim that Jesus was of the house of Aaron was made before patristic times.

Finally, the Transfiguration vision (Mk. 9:2–8; Mt. 17:1–8; Lk. 9:28–36) is understood by all three Synoptics as a messianic confirmation experience. Mystical masters in rabbinic Judaism generally did not give their students direct answers to the more profound issues. Rather, they fed them clues, obliging the students to work their own way through to a personal discovery. (Perhaps all teachers could profit from their example!) If Jesus, like many of the rabbis, gave mystical as well as legal (halakic) and inspirational (haggadic) instruction to his Disciples, the Transfiguration could be showing that Peter, James, and John passed their examinations. The Synoptics link the Transfiguration Narrative rather closely with the story of Peter's declaration of Jesus' messianic identity at Caesarea Philippi (Mk. 8:27–33; Mt. 16:13–23; Lk. 9:18–22). The Disciples had worked their way through to a divine illumination that gave them the correct answer concerning Jesus' identity. They were rewarded with a confirming vision.

The question then becomes, How did Jesus plan to activate his royal prerogatives? Pilate's actions against him reveal the typical reaction of a colonial governor to a native pretender to power. The Gospel of John suggests, in a passage highly colored by John's theological concerns (which yet could contain an authentic reminiscence), that the High Priest did not so much fear Jesus as a rival for power as he feared his capacity to stir up a public uproar that would lead to vicious Roman reprisals (Jn. 11:45–53). Some historians believe that Jesus' Galilean homeland was the hotbed and headquarters of a great deal of Zealot activity, creating a revolutionary tinderbox where the slightest messianic spark might touch off a conflagration. Again, John, the least historical of the gospels, could contain a valuable reminiscence. John's narrative of the feeding miracle, the only miracle story recounted in all four gospels (Jn. 6:1–15; Mk. 6:45–51; Mt. 14:13–21; Lk. 9:10–17), concludes with the note that Jesus withdrew to avoid being acclaimed king against his will. Some within his own circle were already squabbling over cabinet appointments (Mk. 9:33–37).

Anthropologist Marvin Harris has used the happy phrase "the peaceful Messiah" to describe the gospel picture of Jesus.[3] Indeed, the gospel traditions are so imbued with this theme that it is plausible to assume that is was organic to them. An overlaid matrix of militant messianism is quite lacking. Illustration of the theme should begin with the Triumphal Entry, Jesus' most public messianic self-proclamation. He did not come as a triumphant warrior king in a chariot or on horseback, but on the mount of peace, a donkey, dramatizing a pacific prophetic oracle (Zech. 9:9). His explicitly anti-Zealot saying in Mt. 26:52 exemplifies the antimilitaristic flavor of his teaching. The Synoptic Apocalypse is, among other things, a warning against war with Rome (Mk. 13:5–37; Mt. 24:4–36; Lk. 21:8–36).

Is it possible to ground a peaceful messianism in the first-century world of homeland Judaism? There was a notion abroad in rabbinic Judaism that the coming of the Messiah and the realization of the messianic kingdom could be advanced by devotion to Torah. (Paul entertained a related notion, as will be noted in chap. 14). This theory grew in popularity over the years, becoming especially strong in mystical circles. Jesus directed his ministry toward "the lost sheep of the house of Israel" (Mt. 10:26; cf. 9:36), which could tell in favor of his endorsing this idea. His remark about the sick rather than the well needing a physician has sometimes been read as an ironic condemnation of his critics (Mk. 2:16–17; Mt. 9:11–13; Lk. 5:30–32). It was probably

[3]Marvin Harris, *Cows, Pigs, Wars and Witches: The Riddles of Culture* (New York: Random House, Vintage Books, 1975), pp. 179–203.

a very straightforward observation. The Torah keepers did not have to be recalled to Torah for the kingdom to be realized. The sinners did. The point is, the return of the lost would catalyze the dawn of the kingdom. Finally, the fact that Jesus chided both his Disciples and others for their dullness in not grasping what he was about suggests that in his own mind he was not confronting them with something absolutely strange and radical, but with something they should have been able to understand.

However, Jesus almost certainly added at least one new theme to the repertory of Jewish messianic ideas—the notion of the Messiah as suffering servant. The servant songs of Isaiah 40—55 (see chap. 6) had been interpreted collectively, the servant being understood as Israel personified. But Jesus apparently annexed the notion of the servant of the LORD whose suffering and unjust death achieved vicarious good to his own messianic understanding. The king in most ancient cultures (including Israel) embodied the nation, in a sense, so that his actions were crucial to national fortunes. Thus, the Messiah was, of all persons, best qualified to execute such a responsibility. Some have proposed that the interpretation was a product of the developing church, another piece of the program to rationalize its own understanding of Jesus. But it appears so early in the traditions that it is at least as plausible to attribute the insight to Jesus.

The resurrection of the dead was a feature of pharisaic and apocalyptic theories of the messianic age. But the death and resurrection of only one person, the Messiah himself, was not. That a dying and resurrected Messiah was an unprecedented notion in Judaism is the best evidence that the disciples of Jesus in fact had the Resurrection experiences they reported. For the first Christians themselves, their experiences of the resurrected Jesus were God's irrefutable endorsement of his messianic status and the earnest of his return to establish the Kingdom of God once and for all.

Son of God

The Egyptian pharaoh was extolled as the son of Amun-Re, the sun god. He embodied the god, and, at death, his *ka* ("soul") was reunited with his divine parent. Greek culture (and Roman after it) allowed not only that humans might be elevated to the status of gods and demigods, but that humans could even have a god as a biological parent. Alexander had permitted such a report about himself to circulate, if he did not actually encourage it.

Persons in the pagan environment of the Roman Empire were therefore probably disposed to so understand the ascription of the title *Son of God* to Jesus. This sort of literalism ultimately caused (and still causes) Christianity a great deal of vexation. An elaborate body of philosophical explanation (for which the doctrines of the Trinity and the Two Natures of Christ are a shorthand summary) has been devised over the centuries in an effort to preserve both Judeo-Christian monotheism and the unique status of Jesus in Christian faith.

Jesus' Jewish contemporaries, at least those who were not extensively assimilated into Greco-Roman culture, would have had no such problem. The notion of a human becoming a God or having a *literal* divine parent would have struck reasonably sophisticated Jews as being somewhere between trivial and absurd. Among the Semitic peoples of the Bronze and Iron Ages, the best a king could hope for was to be the *adopted* son of a god. Some of the other Semitic peoples got over this compunction in later times. Not so the Jews. The LORD was God, man was man, and that was that.

Still the term *Son of God* could be meaningfully used in first-century Jewish discourse, and was. We have already alluded to one use. The Davidic king was proclaimed God's son in the Scripture (see Ps. 2; 89; 2 Sam. 7:4–17). Thus, *Son of God* could have been meaningfully ascribed to Jesus in his own historical setting in relationship to the messianic claim.

The second documented usage of the term was to designate a particularly saintly person. The son of God is the one who behaves in a godly fashion, who does God's work in this world. The title was ascribed to several holy men in the rabbinic literature, including the Galilean charismatic mentioned earlier, Hanina ben Dosa. The ascription was made in several cases by a bath qol, a heavenly voice (cf. p. 237). This second sense of *Son of God* could also have been meaningfully applied to Jesus by his homeland contemporaries. It can be observed that on two notable occasions, a bath qol proclaimed Jesus the son of God. The first was at his baptism (Mk. 1:9–11; Mt. 3:13–17; Lk. 3:21–22). On that occasion, the second usage would perhaps have been most fitting, especially if the reservations expressed by the Baptizer are historic. God endorses Jesus' act; he is indeed a saintly one. It can be noted that the term in this sense is also applied to faithful Christians by both Paul and John (Rom. 8:14; Gal. 3:26; Jn. 1:12; 1 Jn. 3:2; cf. Mt. 5:9). The second was after the Transfiguration experience. If we have correctly connected this event with Jesus' messianic role, the first usage would apply.

It can be noted that the most common use of the term in the Hebrew Bible is usually in the plural, *sons of God (or god, or the gods)*, designating either angels or the deities of pagan polytheism. But this meaning is not applicable in the case of Jesus.

Son of Man

Son of man is apparently Jesus' favorite term of self-reference in the gospels. Significantly, it is only used once of Jesus outside the gospels in the New Testament (Acts 7:56).

The most common meaning of *son of man* in the Hebrew Scripture is simply *human being*. It is God's favorite form of address to the prophet Ezekiel (e.g., 2:1). In Dan. 7:13, the "one like a son of man" turns out to be almost certainly the personification of the saints of the Most High (7:27). But the introduction of the term in an influential early apocalyptic work probably had an impact. The pseudepigraphic apocalyse of Enoch (see chap. 10) introduces a heavenly savior figure who bears the title *son of man*.

Vermes has shown that in Aramaic writing, especially in letters, from around the time of Jesus, *son of man* was a euphemism for the first-person pronoun, to be used when to say *I* or *me* would sound overly self-important or to avoid linking oneself with language concerning unfortunate events (a common human taboo).[4] This is a particularly impressive point when trying to understand what the phrase may have meant in Jesus' usage, for Aramaic was the common spoken language of Jews in Israel and Babylon in Jesus' time. However, this doesn't necessarily account for every occurrence of *son of man* in the gospels.

It could be that in some cases the phrase is used as a title in the apocalyptic sense already present in Enoch. If so, the issue becomes whether Jesus considered himself the son of man who would return in glory to judge the earth and establish the Kingdom, or whether he used the term in reference to another besides himself who would come later. On this question the debate goes on among knowledgeable interpreters. We will not attempt to resolve it here. Certainly, each occurrence of *son of man* in the gospels should be evaluated in its own context rather than forced into one predetermined pattern.

Lord

Our task in evaluating the titles attributed to Jesus would be much simpler were the gospels written in Hebrew or in the Aramaic in which Jesus taught and conversed. We cannot be certain which Hebrew or Aramaic term lies behind the Greek *kurios* ("lord") that stands in the New Testament texts. Indeed, the Greek word itself apparently came into Aramaic as a loan word and was even used as a surrogate for the Hebrew name for the deity, YHWH, substituting for the Hebrew *'adonai*. The Aramaic *mar* was apparently interchangeable with *'adon* and *kurios* in various senses. *Mar* might also be used interchangeably as the title for a respected person, such as a rabbi. Indeed, the term *rabbi*, as already noted, had as a primary meaning "my great one," "my master," and hence might appropriately be rendered as *mar* or *kurios*. If this were not complication enough, the term *kurios* was the title of the savior deity in some of the Hellenistic mystery cults. But the Greek term, too, could simply be a title of polite or deferential address. The evidence for how the title *Lord* might have been used in reference to Jesus is both complex and confusing. However, some things can be asserted with reasonable confidence.

[4]Vermes, *Jesus the Jew*, pp. 160–91.

First, Jesus' Jewish contemporaries would not address him with the divine name. Unless the gospel pictures of him are grossly in error, it would be quite out of character for Jesus to say that the most holy name for God should be applied to him. Such usages in the Gospel of John that imply a oneness between Jesus and the Father are made in the context of mysticism, not metaphysics. John's view of the nature of Jesus will be addressed in the next chapter.

Second, it is most likely that the application of the term to Jesus partook of two uses. It could have been a form of polite or deferential address, like the American southern *sir* and *ma'am*, or the British *m'lord*. Or it could have been used as a title of honor, either translating or replacing that of *rabbi*, which was also addressed to him by persons within and without his circle.

Finally, it is in the highest degree unlikely that Hellenistic mystery usage affected the language of the Synoptic Gospels. However, the fact that the term *lord* was current in the mysteries of the pagan world probably colored the way it was understood by Gentiles in that world. This might account for the fact that *Lord* became the most popular title for Jesus in the gentile churches. His messianic title in Greek, *Christ,* became something like a proper name (Jesus Christ or Christ Jesus).

CONCLUSION

Jesus was addressed with respect by his followers and others, and his status as a recognized teacher was acknowledged. Some outside his circle apparently regarded him as an eschatological prophet. It was reported that a *bath qol* had confirmed his saintliness. The humility he taught to others he practiced himself, using a polite euphemism (son of man) in place of the first-person pronoun (and when "speaking the unspeakable," as when forecasting his own suffering and death). He understood himself to be the Messiah, the awaited Davidic king who would restore Israel and prepare for the full manifestation of God's reign among people (the Kingdom of God). But he proposed to achieve this through spiritual rather than military force, including vicarious benefits brought about by his own action as God's suffering servant.

Jesus' own intentions as the peaceful Messiah were too far removed from the attractive militant messiah of popular expectation even for his own students to understand his purposes readily or fully. It may have been his challenge to Sadducean priestly authority that led to Jesus' arrest. Perhaps fear of Roman pacification measures in the event that his activities excited a public disturbance caused the High Priest to move against him. Both factors may have been involved. In any case, messianic claims by or for Jesus could be used against him before the Roman procurator, Pilate. To Pilate, *messiah* would have only one meaning: a militant rebel against Rome.

Like the Dead Sea Covenanters, like the other pious priests and innocent folk noted by the rabbis, Jesus fell afoul of Sadducean politics. The trial before the High Priest (Mk. 14:53–72; 26:57–75; Lk. 22:54–71) was not conducted according to rabbinic rules of jurisprudence. The High Priest dominated the Sanhedrin prior to 70 C.E. The charge of blasphemy was a red herring. A rabbinic court would have acquired a much more searching examination to sustain such a charge. In any case, disrespect for an oriental God was no crime under Roman law. And Rome, in the person of her accredited representative, pronounced the verdict and executed the sentence. Rome took the messianic claim literally and seriously!

New Testament documents reflecting a more extensive development of thought after the resurrection reports of the apostles, such as the Letters of Paul, the Gospel of John, and the Letter to the Hebrews, show that the interpretations that ultimately led to the orthodox theological view of Jesus were already in the making during the New Testament period. The resurrection experiences of the first Christians not only confirmed for them the messiahship of Jesus, but they also made him available as an immediate focus of religious devotion and a continuing fount of religious insight for future generations. The rest, as they sometimes say on the sports page, is history.

A life of Jesus, a full biography, is probably not possible. But it is possible to see Jesus as a person in a real time and place. The gospels *can* serve as historical sources to this extent, if they are used carefully. However, they are much more than sources for a reconstruction of the historical Jesus. They are portraits of Jesus, interpretations of the significance of his life, death, and resurrection. To see the gospels in this way we now turn to a literary examination.

SUMMARY

The focus of this chapter was the attempt by historians to reconstruct the life of Jesus. We started from the assumption that although a full biography of Jesus is not possible, we can reconstruct in general the setting in which he lived and establish some facts about his life.

The most important evidence about Jesus from outside the New Testament gospels comes from the Jewish historian Josephus and several Roman historians. These references establish that Jesus was indeed a historical person who lived during the reign of the Emperor Tiberius and was executed under the authority of Pontius Pilate, procurator of Judea. The rest of what can be reconstructed about the historical Jesus comes from the New Testament gospels.

Instead of summarizing all that a modern historian might claim to be able to say about Jesus, after fully evaluating the sources, we demonstrated the general historical, ideological, and sociological settings in which Jesus lived. In general, the portrait of Jesus in the gospels is historically credible. Ideologically, Jesus "fits" what is known about the rabbinic-pharisaic movement, especially its liberal branch. Sociologically, Jesus seems to have been most clearly associated with a charismatic type of Judaism that centered during his lifetime in Galilee.

We also summarized what has been discovered about the most likely original meaning of the titles assigned to Jesus in the gospels—Messiah (Christ), Son of God, Son of Man, and Lord. Although these titles took on other meanings as Christian theologians reflected on the significance of the life, death, and resurrection of Jesus, in each case the title had particular meanings in classical Judaism that may have applied to the historical Jesus.

Discussion of Jesus can be expected to arouse strongly held, conflicting beliefs and opinions that may be difficult to examine rationally. This chapter seeks to create some common ground that will enhance reflection on the ongoing significance of Jesus of Nazareth.

THE CONTEMPORARY WORLD: QUESTIONS FOR DISCUSSION AND REFLECTION

1. We have noted several times that historical (or scientific) methods cannot verify or falsify theological claims. In our world, then, what is the value of historical investigations of religious literature, leaders, movements, and other phenomena? Is it just an interesting pastime for history buffs, or does it have some value for religious thought and practice today?

2. This chapter has explored some of the meanings that the titles assigned to Jesus in the gospels might have had for people in his time and place. It has also suggested how the meanings of these titles might have changed as they passed through time and space. How does such a discussion affect your understanding of Jesus? How are these titles understood in our world today? What other titles might contemporary society appropriately assign to a person like Jesus?

3. Where did Jesus fit in first-century C.E. Palestinian Judaism? Where does Jesus fit today?

4. Discuss the claim that there is a difference between the "Jesus of history" and the "Christ of faith." Do you agree?

5. Various motion pictures have been made about Jesus. Some of the more famous are *The Greatest Story Ever Told* (1965), *The Gospel According to St. Matthew* (1965), *Godspell* (1973), *Jesus Christ Superstar* (1974), and *The Last Temptation of Christ* (1988). Discuss the portraits of Jesus in movies you have seen and the difficulties in attempting to make films about Jesus.

CHAPTER 12

The Proclaimer Becomes the Proclaimed (Mark, Matthew, Luke, and John)

Courtesy of The British Library

Codex Sinaiticus. One of the earliest Greek manuscripts of the Bible (fourth century C.E.) is called *Codex Sinaiticus* because it was preserved by the monks of St. Catherine's monastery on Mount Sinai. It was taken to Russia in the nineteenth century and sold to the British Library (housed in the British Museum) after the Russian Revolution, purchased with money raised by British schoolchildren. This picture shows part of Luke 22.

INTRODUCTION

If the gospels of the New Testament are not merely reconstructions of the life of Jesus, what are they? Why are there four gospels in the New Testament? Are these gospels fundamentally the same, or are there basic differences among them? To answer these questions we must first apply the literary historical method to discovering what we can about the growth of the gospels. Then we will examine the literary world of each one. Finally, we will try to place them in their most likely historical settings.

THE GROWTH OF THE GOSPELS

What a Gospel Is

The term *gospel* comes from the Anglo-Saxon word *god-spell*, a story from or about a god, or about something good, a rendering of the Latin *evangelium*. The Latin term derives from a similar Greek word, *euangellion* ("good news"). As the New Testament employs the term, it connotes the divine announcement of the final stage of God's plan for salvation.

Sometime in the first or second century C.E., Christians gave a literary application to *gospel*. The "Gospel of Jesus Christ" came to refer to a literary work proclaiming the essential role of Jesus, the Christ (Messiah), in God's saving work. To lend credibility and authority to the works, they were sometimes associated (perhaps accurately) with apostles or persons close to apostles of Jesus. A number of gospels were produced, four of which were incorporated into the New Testament canon. Extracanonical gospels include the Gospels of Peter, Thomas, Judas, Mary, and many more. They will be discussed in Chapter 15.

From a literary perspective, *gospel* refers to a genre, a grouping of works of similar form, style, content, function, and perspective. The gospels are not biographies in the modern sense of the term. They are schematic and selective, and their principal concern is theological, not historical. However, they do tell a partial life story of Jesus, from various perspectives. They might be called *mythic biographies*, because their objective is to show that Jesus was the Messiah, the Son of God, the Risen Lord. The Jewish community preserved tales about religious heroes. Other possible antecedents of the gospel genre are Greco-Roman biographies, some of which tell the life stories of "divine men" whose miraculous feats demonstrated divine power, or encomiums, eulogistic accounts of the lives of great men. The four New Testament gospels were incorporated into the canon not so much because they were unique in form, as because their particular perspectives were deemed to reflect apostolic testimony.

The Synoptic Problem

During the last two centuries critical study of the New Testament gospels has yielded a wealth of insights on their origin and development. We now have a widely accepted theoretical picture of the stages of development during the years between the death of Jesus and the writing of the gospels.

First, scholars confronted what became known as the *synoptic problem.* When broad outlines and specific contents of the four canonical gospels are compared, two intriguing features appear. For one, the Gospel of John is quite different from the other three. Important events in the life of Jesus that Matthew, Mark, and Luke recorded are absent from John (e.g., the Gethsemane scene) and vice versa. There are significant chronological and geographic differences as well. At the same time, comparison of the other three gospels shows a common structure underlying the differences. All three share a general chronological and geographical outline, namely:

The baptism of Jesus in the Jordan

A Galilean ministry of teaching and healing

A journey to Jerusalem

The final week in Jerusalem.

Furthermore, long passages are paralleled in all three gospels. Because of their significant agreement in content and outline, Matthew, Mark, and Luke came to be called the *Synoptic Gospels* (*synoptic* means "to take a common view"), and the problem of explaining their interrelationship, the synoptic problem.

Although still challenged from time to time, the most widely accepted solution to the synoptic problem is the so-called *Four-Source Hypothesis.* The first leg of the theory is that the entire gospel of Mark served as a source for Matthew and Luke. Except for a handful of passages, which are largely Mark's editorial contribution rather than substantive traditions, all of Mark is duplicated in the other two synoptic gospels; and, when a Marcan passage is missing from Matthew or Luke, it is almost always found in the other. The outline of Mark also seems determinative for the other two gospels. When Matthew or Luke varies from Mark's sequence, the other follows Mark. Except in a few minor instances, Matthew and Luke do not agree against Mark in wording. Considered together, the evidence for the dependence of Matthew and Luke on Mark is difficult to refute.

The second leg of the hypothesis is somewhat more conjectural but is still almost universally accepted among critical scholars. It is the notion that Matthew and Luke share a second common source besides Mark, the so-called Q source (from the German *Quelle,* meaning "source") or "sayings source." More than one-third of Matthew and one-fourth of Luke consist of material they share in common that is absent from Mark. Although it is possible that Matthew used Luke as a source, or vice versa, the shape of the shared material makes the Q hypothesis more plausible. The common material consists largely of sayings of Jesus such as Mt. 6:22–23; Lk. 11:34–36. The high degree of verbal agreement between Matthew and Luke in Q sections makes it likely that Q was a written, rather than an oral, source. The discovery of the apocryphal Gospel of Thomas (see chap. 15), which is *not* Q, but is a collection of sayings much like scholars think "Q" was, makes this notion increasingly plausible.

The third and fourth legs of the Four-Source Hypothesis are the most speculative, and the least important. To account for the sections in Matthew and Luke that are unique, it is assumed that each gospel had a special source, designated M for Matthew and L for Luke. Whether Matthew and Luke had separate sources or drew on different oral or written traditions circulating in the early Christian Church, M and L are convenient symbols for the special sections of each gospel.

Figure 12–1 is a graphic and helpful summary of the Four-Source Hypothesis.

FIGURE 12-1

The principal critical rival of the Four-Source Hypothesis is the Griesbach Hypothesis, named for the eighteenth-century scholar who devised it. Griesbach argued that Matthew, not Mark, was the first written Gospel (a view first propounded by St. Augustine). According to Griesbach,

Luke used Matthew as a source along with other material at his disposal, and Mark used both Matthew and Luke as sources. The Griesbach Hypothesis is advocated by a thoughtful group of spokespersons who point to alleged weaknesses in the Four-Source Hypothesis, such as the hypothetical nature of the Q source. However, a majority of scholars conclude that the Four-Source Hypothesis solves more problems more simply and raises fewer new problems than does the Griesbach Hypothesis. Both hypotheses represent attempts by modern literary historians to understand in descriptive terms how the Synoptic Gospels assumed their present form. Both remain subject to revision or replacement if and when a better explanation is devised.

The research into the synoptic problem clarified the literary relationship of Matthew, Mark, and Luke, but it left untouched other crucial questions. The traditional view that gospels were eyewitness accounts of the life of Jesus was upset by the realization that the gospels were edited collections of sources and traditions. What evidence is there that these traditions circulated independently before the stage of sources and written gospels? And what situations in the life of the early Christian Church caused these traditions to develop and to be transmitted?

Form criticism was applied to the question of the transmission of the individual traditions about Jesus and their settings in the life of the early Christian community. The assumption of form criticism is that the stories about, and the sayings of, Jesus were not kept alive merely to perpetuate his memory but also to serve the needs of the community seeking to follow him as Lord. In general, these situations would have included communal worship, teaching of children and converts, debate with Jews and Gentiles, community organization and discipline, and reassurance in the face of persecution. This method gives us insight into the general social situation of the early Christian community.

From a literary historical perspective, we have come to recognize that the writers of the gospels were probably neither eyewitnesses nor collectors of sources and traditions. They were creative authors who placed their own distinctive literary and theological stamp on their works. Each gospel is a literary unity with a coherent plan and purpose. This awareness resulted in the development of redaction criticism, which focuses on the stage in the growth of the gospels when they were given their final written shape. This method allows us to appreciate the distinctive theological perspectives of each of the gospels. Redaction criticism can be combined with intrinsic literary study to help us understand the unique worlds of each of the four gospels.

THE LITERARY WORLDS OF THE GOSPELS

Mark: The Secret Revealed Through Suffering

Although the Gospel of Mark is the shortest, and probably the earliest gospel, it is by no means the easiest to understand. One reason is that we cannot, as with Matthew and Luke, examine how the writer has interpreted the sources used. Our understanding of Mark's world depends on finding the key or keys to the gospel's portrayal of Jesus in the writing itself. The problem is that in Mark's gospel Jesus is often portrayed as a puzzling, mysterious presence surrounded by confusion and misunderstanding.

A careful reading of the first chapter of Mark reveals several of the crucial themes recurrent throughout. The opening verse establishes for the reader the truth that is only revealed to the participants in the drama of Jesus at the end of the narrative. This Jesus *is* the Christ, the Son of God. As we shall see, this announcement does not reveal the full truth about Jesus. Even the reader is kept in the dark at first. The rest of the gospel's prologue (1:1–13) identifies a continuity stretching back to the prophet Isaiah. A quote from Is. 40:3 (combined with an adapted text from Mal. 3:1) shows that the prophet prepared the way for John the Baptizer. By his testimony, John prepared the way for "he who is mightier than I" (1:7). Although John gives no special attention to Jesus when he baptizes him in the Jordan, it is made clear to the reader that Jesus is the one for whom John is preparing the way. The theme is power and authority, and their continuity and increase from the prophet Isaiah to the messenger to Jesus. At once, the unfolding drama is given cosmic significance, as Jesus is tempted in the wilderness by Satan and ministered to by angels (1:12–13).

However, the point toward which all is moving is not the earthly Jesus, for he proclaims in a saying that comes as close to a statement of Mark's theme as any in the gospel: "The time is fulfilled, and the Kingdom of God is at hand; repent, and believe in the gospel" (1:14–15). The earthly Jesus prepares the way for the Kingdom of God.[1] The present age is ending; a new age in which God's rule will be fully manifest is imminent. The reign of evil will be replaced by the dominion of God. The time has come to turn away from the path of evil (i.e., repent) and embrace the gospel, the announcement of God's salvation. The earthly Jesus has come to proclaim the good news of the arrival of God's Kingdom with a power greater than earth or heaven has seen.

After the stage of the messenger has ended, with the arrest and imprisonment of John, Jesus at once sets about his work. It soon becomes clear that in Mark, Jesus proclaims the gospel not so much by what he says as by what he does. He begins to gather disciples, who leave their secular lives to follow him. According to Mark, when the call goes out, "immediately" they leave their nets. The recurrence of "immediately" (eight times in the first chapter alone and forty times in the gospel) reflects an urgency in the story being

---

[1]"Kingdom of God" is not a place, but a symbol expressing the apocalyptic hope of a new, final age of peace and righteousness (see chap. 9) or, in a more general sense, God's redemptive activity on behalf of the covenant people. See Wendell Willis, ed., *The Kingdom of God in 20th-Century Interpretation* (Peabody, Mass.: Hendricksen, 1987).

told. The reason for the urgency is eschatological. The end is at hand. The time is now, not only for characters in the story but, by implication, for those hearing or reading this gospel.

The second section of the gospel (1:21–3:6) contains vignettes exemplifying the mysterious power of the man Jesus. He astonishes the people at the synagogue at Capernaum, "for he taught them as one who had authority, and not as the scribes" (1:22). He displays the power to cast out evil spirits and to heal the sick. However, he does not stay in one place long enough to establish a reputation, and he instructs exorcised demons and healed people to keep quiet about him. When word spreads, he flees. Again and again, the question is raised: Why? (2:7, 16, 18, 24). As his ministry continues, the Galilean people respond enthusiastically to him, while the hostility of the scribes, Pharisees, and members of Herod's entourage intensifies.

Mark's next section (3:7–8:21) emphasizes the formation of an inner circle of disciples by Jesus, climaxing in their failure to grasp the significance of their master's teaching. Opposition from the Herodians and the Pharisees forces Jesus to withdraw to the Sea of Galilee, followed, Mark says, by multitudes from what had once been the nation Israel and beyond. In the hills above the Lake, Jesus selects twelve (a symbolic *new Israel*) and sends them out to proclaim the Kingdom of God with acts of power. Then he returns to Nazareth, where he is rejected by the townspeople and even by his own family. Returning to the Sea of Galilee, he tells parables of the Kingdom to the gathered crowds, parables stressing the fact that from meager and sometimes obscure beginnings the Kingdom will grow and ultimately flourish. His explanation of the parables is that to those outside the inner circle everything is in riddles. Only those on the inside are taught directly, with "everything" explained to them. Miracles continue, as does the admonition of Jesus to keep silent about them. The Twelve are sent out again, return, and, with the feeding of the five thousand, begin to show their lack of understanding (see especially 6:51–52). Because of hardness of heart, not even the inner circle, to whom Jesus has explained "everything," grasp the truth. The section climaxes with a rebuke by Jesus to the Twelve: "Having eyes do you not see, and having ears do you not understand?" (8:18).

Now the impending suffering and death of Jesus become the dominant focus. Finally in Caesarea Philippi, one of the Twelve has his eyes opened (after the story of the healing of a man with physical blindness). In response to the question of Jesus, "Who do you say that I am?" Peter gives the answer the readers of the gospel know to be true, "You are the Christ." But again Jesus counsels secrecy.

With this glimmer of understanding, Jesus then reveals to the Twelve that

The Son of man must suffer many things,
and be rejected by the elders and the

chief priests and the scribes, and be
killed, and after three days rise again. (8:31)

But they do not understand. Peter, who has sensed the truth that Jesus is the Christ, rebukes Jesus for speaking of suffering, drawing from him the stinging rebuke: "Get behind me, Satan!" (8:33). The identification of Jesus as the Son of Man has generated intense debate among interpreters (see chap. 11). Some argue that the phrase is a title for the apocalyptic figure who will come at the end of the age to inaugurate the Kingdom of God. If *Son of Man* is an apocalyptic title, the remarkable claim is being made that before the new age begins, the one sent to inaugurate it must suffer and die. The emphasis is on the *necessity* of suffering. Three times this *passion prediction* is repeated by Jesus, emphasizing its importance. Surely it gives us our first clue to Mark's basic interpretation of Jesus. Jesus *must* suffer before the Kingdom of God can come. His ministry of teaching and healing is not sufficient. Acclaiming him as Christ is not sufficient. Not even his disciples grasp the irony. The one who comes with awe-inspiring power and authority will be the one who is humiliated and killed by those whose authority he surpasses. Recognition is more than hearing the words. The bottom line is not only that Jesus must suffer but also that if they are his disciples, they will suffer too (8:34–38). The message they cannot grasp is the irony of his kingship. The man of power will be glorified in suffering! So must they.

This gospel has been called a passion narrative with an extended introduction, not only because the story of the final week in Jerusalem occupies one-third of it (11:1–16:8), but also because, with the passion, the secret is revealed. His entry into Jerusalem is a public pronouncement of the messianic nature of Jesus' ministry. He fulfills a prophecy for the entry of the Messiah into Jerusalem, but it is an entry of humility, not belligerent power. He cleanses the Temple but then refuses to discuss with the chief priests, scribes, and elders the nature of the authority by which he has acted. He makes no effort to use the incident as a catalyst for an open confrontation with the power of these religious leaders or the power of Rome. Only when he has been taken captive, and his fate has been sealed, does he accept the title of Christ. To the end, his closest disciples seem baffled. They desert him when the time comes to suffer and are absent when the empty tomb reveals the vindication of that suffering. At what is usually assumed to be the original ending of Mark's gospel (16:8), the women who have come to the tomb are overcome with awe and keep to themselves what they have seen and heard. On the cross, a suffering Jesus cries out, all alone, "My God, my God, why hast thou forsaken me?" (15:34). When apocalyptic signs herald the new age at his death, it is not the disciples, but a Roman centurion, who makes a confession of faith, "Truly this man was the [a] son of God!" (15:39).

As we look back over Mark's gospel, a pattern emerges behind the shadows. It begins with John the Baptizer. He proclaimed the message of a new age and, as a result, suffered. Jesus, too, announced the coming Kingdom with his words and deeds. But only at his suffering does the Kingdom begin to break into history. In the apocalyptic section of Mark, Chapter 13, we find the prediction that those who follow Jesus will likewise suffer, with the promise that "he who endures to the end will be saved" (13:13). God's plan of salvation is now apparent. The way has been fully prepared by a suffering Messiah. He had to suffer, for this was necessary to God's plan. Now those who truly understand the meaning of his coming must likewise take up their crosses and suffer. Like their master, their suffering will lead ultimately to the glory of the Kingdom.

Matthew: A Higher Righteousness

The structure of the Gospel according to Matthew is nearly as overt as the Gospel according to Mark's is hidden. Interpreters of Matthew have long recognized the fivefold pattern of organization in the gospel, with a Birth Narrative and a Passion Narrative serving as introduction and conclusion.

Introduction: The New Obedience (Mt. 1—2)

I. The Higher Righteousness (Mt. 3—7)

II. True Discipleship (Mt. 8—10)

III. The Kingdom of Heaven (Mt. 11—13)

IV. The New Israel (Mt. 14—18)

V. The End of the Age (Mt. 19—25)

Conclusion: With You Always (Mt. 26—28)

Within each of the five central sections of the gospel, a narrative is followed by a discourse on the same theme. Each of these discourses ends with a phrase such as "When Jesus had finished these sayings..." (7:28; 11:1; 13:53; 19:1; 26:1). Clearly this gospel is concerned, in contrast with Mark, not only with proclaiming the authority of Jesus as teacher and preacher, but also with giving the content of his teaching. The fivefold division of the gospel seems patterned after the Five Books of Moses in the Tanak.

Another pattern in the gospel indicates concern for the relationship between Jesus and the Tanak. Many times Matthew introduces quotations from the Hebrew Bible with a formula that, with some variations, says: "This was done to fulfill what was spoken by the LORD through the prophet..." (see 1:22; 2:5; 2:23; 4:14; 8:17; 12:17; 13:35; 21:4; 27:9–10). According to Matthew's gospel, prophecies of Scripture were meticulously fulfilled in the life and ministry of Jesus.

Having observed some of the main structural characteristics of the gospel, let us attempt to reconstruct Matthew's world, looking for the key to this gospel's portrayal of Jesus. While Mark's gospel begins with the Baptism of Jesus by John, Matthew provides a preface of special material related to the ancestry and birth of Jesus (Mt. 1–2). Careful attention to this introductory section shows that it, like the prologue to Mark's gospel, foreshadows the essence of the gospel.

The genealogy with which the gospel begins (1:1–17) links Jesus to two key figures in the history of Israel, the two key promises in the LORD's relationship with Israel—Abraham and David. He is a son of Abraham, to whom God promised a land, many descendants, and blessing. He is also a son of David, recipient of the promise of an everlasting dynasty, root of the messianic hope. Linking Jesus to these heroes is a way of claiming that through him the promises of God, given to his ancestors, will be fulfilled. Yet into this genealogy breaks the unexpected. In the ancient world, genealogies were typically patrilineal, but in Matthew's lineage of Jesus, five women are included—Tamar, Rahab, Ruth, Bathsheba, and Mary. Moreover, each of the first four women either bore children under suspicious circumstances or were of disreputable character. The point seems to be that behavior questionable from a moralistic perspective turned out to be justified by the fact that God's plan was fulfilled.

Against this background the story of the birth of Jesus is recounted. The first scene focuses on Joseph's response to the pregnancy of his betrothed wife, Mary. Joseph has a dilemma. Knowing that he has not fathered the child, he is obligated by the Torah to separate himself from the shame of Mary. However, as a righteous man, Joseph resolves to divorce Mary quietly and not call public attention to her sin. Already Joseph shows himself to be a humble and compassionate man who does not demand total legal satisfaction. Through a dream (linking him to another Joseph) he learns of a still more radical form of obedience rooted in a new act of God. The child in Mary's womb is of the Holy Spirit, a savior of his people. Joseph is challenged to respond by going beyond the letter of the law to faith, or obedience to God. In the first of the fulfillment formulas, Matthew interprets this event as the realization of Isaiah's prophecy of the birth to a virgin (although it is dubious that "virgin" is what the Hebrew text of Isaiah literally says) of a son who shall be called Immanuel. Because God is present with his people in a new way, a new, radical form of obedience, a higher righteousness, is expected.

The fact that the Gospel of Matthew in a sense ends as it begins, with a call for obedience and the assurance of divine presence in the person of Jesus (28:20), lends support to the view we will now develop more fully. The key to Matthew's world, the gospel's portrayal of Jesus, is a call to a radical obedience, a higher righteousness, linked to the assurance that God is present with those who take this step in a new, definitive way.

Joseph, a Jew, responds to God's new initiative, and so do a group of gentile "wise men from the East." They respond to a sign (the star) that marks a new beginning, even when it requires them to violate their responsibility to abide by the authority of the ruler in whose country they are guests. They too model a new, higher righteousness.

Righteousness, as Matthew uses the concept, means living in a way compatible with God's will, or simply rightness of life before God. It is not a series of things to do to qualify for God's blessing; it is Torah righteousness, a way of life that is the essence of the Kingdom.

In Matthew, Jesus not only calls for a higher righteousness, he models it himself. Although he has no need to be baptized by John, he undergoes this act of repentance, personifying the people he will call together as the New Israel, in Matthew's words "to fulfill all righteousness." In the Temptation in the Wilderness Jesus demonstrates complete and accepting obedience of God's will.

The narrative moves quickly to the Sermon on the Mount. Like Moses, Jesus delivers an authoritative teaching from a mountain, which fulfills the law and the prophets. However, the point is not that Jesus is a new Moses. Whereas at Sinai God spoke through Moses, Jesus teaches on his own, direct, authority. "You have heard of old,…but *I* say to you…" And the teaching is not really a new Torah, but the old clarified.

If there is a single cornerstone to Matthew's gospel it is probably 5:17–20. There the Matthean Jesus emphasizes the continuing validity of the Hebrew Scripture. Until everything has been accomplished, that is, until the Kingdom of Heaven is fully realized, not even the tiniest letter in the Torah may be overlooked. Those who reduce the demands of Torah cannot expect high position in the Kingdom, though they will not be excluded. However, the person who both teaches and does as the Torah commands (a typically rabbinic emphasis on action as well as thought) will be great in the Kingdom. Indeed, Jesus demands that his followers exceed the righteousness of the spiritual elite of the time, the scribes and Pharisees. Later the Gospel of Matthew draws upon a Marcan story to make clear the nature of this higher righteousness that fulfills the Torah (22:34–40). *All* the law and prophets hinge on two commandments—the great commandment to love the one God (Dt. 6:4–5) and the second, to love one's neighbor (Lev. 19:18).

Matthew now turns from word to deed. The second section (Mt. 8–10) begins with ten miracle stories (Mt. 8–9) illustrating Jesus acting in obedience to God out of love for Him. The gospel then moves to the calling of the Disciples and climaxes with emphasis on the response of faith as essential to healing. This sets the stage for the so-called *missionary discourse,* in which Jesus instructs his followers on the nature of true discipleship. Importantly, at this stage of the gospel, the mission is limited to Israel (10:5–6). Only after the Resurrection does the time come for disciples to go to all nations.

The narrative and discourse of the third section (Mt. 11–13) focus on the Kingdom of Heaven. Apparently influenced by rabbinic usage, this gospel avoids the phrase *Kingdom of God* (which Mark uses), substituting the circumlocution *Kingdom of Heaven*. The meaning, however, is the same. The Kingdom of Heaven is not a place but an eschatological situation in which God's sovereignty is fully manifest. In contrast to the portrait Mark paints of reluctant disciples who fail to grasp the truth, Matthew implies understanding and obedience. For example, Mark's rebuke after the parable of the sower (4:31) is given a positive note in Matthew (13:51).

In the fourth section (Mt. 14–18) the Church is highlighted. The Marcan order of stories is rearranged so that accounts of the rejection of Jesus by people of his own home, by his family, and by the scribes and Pharisees can be contrasted with the enthusiastic response to Jesus by those he heals, by a gentile woman, and finally by Peter and the other Disciples. In this section, as elsewhere in the gospel, Peter has a heightened role, in comparison with the other gospels. Jesus also lays down rules concerning discipline within the Christian community, including the possibility of exclusion for those unwilling to repent.

The last of the five Matthean sections has as its theme the final judgment, especially in terms of how this affects the Church (Mt. 19–25). Like the other synoptics, Matthew includes an apocalyptic section stressing the imminence of the end. In Matthew's version an explicit indication of delay in the coming of the end is the insertion of the following statement: "this gospel of the kingdom will be preached throughout the whole world, as a testimony to all nations; and *then the end will come*" (24:14; emphasis added). After the discourse, there is a series of parables counseling watchfulness. For this gospel there is no question that the coming of the end will involve a judgment on the basis of actual deeds of mercy rather than of protestations of faith (25:31–46; cf. 21:28–46; 7:15–23). The test of discipleship is doing God's will, not one's own, as Jesus models in the dramatic conclusion to the gospel.

Matthew's version of the Passion Narrative does not, like Mark's, highlight the actual suffering of Jesus. For Matthew the emphasis is on Jesus' acting out a radical obedience to the will of God. For example, Matthew adds to Mark's account of Jesus accepting the cross (Mk. 14:36) a further affirmation of obedience (26:42). The Resurrection opens the door for the inclusion of all in the Kingdom. During his public career, Jesus' commission to the disciples was to carry the gospel to Israel. Now, the Risen Lord sends his disciples into all the world to baptize and teach the kind of obedience they have learned from his teaching and his life (28:16–20). The descendant of Abraham has now become the fulfillment of the promise to Abraham that through Israel all nations of the earth shall be blessed.

The Gospel of Matthew turns a complete circle. The initial emphasis on radical obedience, introduced in the Birth Narrative, is explained through the earthly teaching of Jesus (3:15; 5:6, 20; 6:33; 7:21; 21:28–32; 25:31–46) and finally enacted by him on the cross. How is such a higher righteousness possible? Because, in the words of the angel to Joseph, Jesus is Immanuel and, in the final words of the Risen Jesus in the last verse of the gospel (28:20), "Lo, I am with you always, to the close of the age."

Luke: Good News for All

With the Acts of the Apostles, the Gospel according to Luke forms a two-volume history of the origin and expansion of Christianity throughout the Mediterranean world (see chap. 13). The gospel is the first volume, containing a narration of the life of Jesus from a distinct theological perspective.

Literary analysis of Luke is assisted by the fact that, unlike either Matthew or Mark, this gospel begins with a preface stating its purpose (1:1–4). The contribution of this gospel, the preface claims, is not originality. Others have compiled narratives of the words and works of Jesus. This is possibly a reference to Mark and Q, the two major sources of the gospel. Luke is aware of the process of transmission of tradition, from eyewitness to ministers of the word to those who, like the writer of the gospel, compile these traditions. The stated purpose of this narrative is "an orderly account" that will seek to point to the "truth" about the story of Jesus. A preface to justify the writing of the work is a common device in Hellenistic historical writing.

Unlike the other gospels, Luke identifies the intended recipient of the work—Theophilus, which means "friend of God." Whether Theophilus is an individual (a Roman official or eminent citizen), a group of persons, or a literary device, Luke's intended audience is clearly (1) gentile, (2) aware of the story of Jesus, and (3) among the so-called "God fearers" who were interested in the Jewish God.

Broadly speaking, Luke adopts Mark's basic order. Although Luke's gospel is a more sophisticated literary work than either Mark or Matthew, the world it creates is another variation of their worlds. Like the other gospels, it weaves a pattern highlighting not only what Jesus once said and did, but also what it all means for those reading the gospel.

As with Mark and Matthew, this gospel begins with a section foreshadowing the major themes that dominate the portrayal of Jesus throughout the work. Like Matthew 1—2, Luke 1—2 is a Birth Narrative. However, Luke draws on an entirely different set of traditions to tell the story of the birth of Jesus. The major Lucan motifs introduced in this "prologue" and developed in the rest of the gospel are universalism, social justice, compassion for those rejected by the Establishment, the crucial role of women in the story of Jesus, the importance of the Spirit, the joy that envelops those who respond to Jesus, and the confession that Jesus is Lord. By examining these motifs and how they function in the infancy account and the gospel as a whole, we can develop a sense of Luke's unique world.

Universalism. Luke places the birth account of Jesus in the context of the events of world history (1:1; 2:1–2), suggesting that here is an event of universal significance. Whereas Matthew traces the genealogy of Jesus to Abraham and David, to emphasize Jesus' role as the fulfiller of the promises to Israel, Luke's genealogy begins with Adam, relating Jesus to all humanity. According to the angels who herald the birth of Jesus, the good news associated with his coming is for "all the people" (2:10).

This emphasis on the universal scope of the salvation Jesus has come to announce is woven throughout the entire gospel. As the story of the ministry of Jesus begins, it is with another reference to the events of world history (3:1–2). In the account of Jesus' baptism, Luke extends Mark's quotation from Isaiah to include the clearly universalistic prophecy that all flesh shall see the salvation of God (3:6; cf. Is. 40:5). In Luke's version of the parable of the banquet (14:15–24), which Matthew had adapted to highlight judgment (Mt. 22:1–10), the emphasis is on the inclusiveness of the invitation. Luke's apocalyptic discourse also adds a phrase stressing the universal implications of the events that will signal the end (21:25). Matthew withholds the universal emphasis until the Risen Christ commissions his disciples. Luke includes such a reference in the final commissioning (24:47), but as the capstone of a theme that has pervaded the entire gospel.

Social Justice. Closely related to the universalistic emphasis is a clear concern for social justice. It is already present in the Birth Narrative in the hymn of praise (the Magnificat) Mary sings (1:46–55). The prophetic theme recurs frequently in the heart of the gospel, as, for example, in the stirring sermon at the synagogue in Capernaum (4:16–30) and in the concern of Jesus for justice for one of the criminals crucified with him (23:39–43). Luke's special concern for justice for the poor and oppressed can most clearly be seen in a comparison of the beatitudes in this gospel with those in Matthew (Lk. 6:20–21; Mt. 5:3, 6).

Compassion for Outcasts. Similar to the emphasis on social justice in the Gospel of Luke is the motif of compassion for those of low social esteem. The Birth Narrative introduces this concern in the account of Mary, who, as a woman without a husband, is of low social prestige in the ancient world. To her the angel Gabriel says, "Hail, O favored one, the Lord is with you!" (1:28). The motif continues with the account of the night of Jesus' birth. The baby himself is born in the humblest of surroundings. He is attended, not by wealthy wise men, but by shepherds who have come from the flocks and who return to them after seeing the baby. Whereas Matthew makes no mention of Nazareth as the family home of Jesus, Luke alludes to the fact that this backwoods hamlet in the hill country of Galilee was indeed Jesus' hometown.

In the body of the gospel there are further references to the concern of Jesus for those of low social station, as well as those despised by "proper" society. The well-known parable of the good Samaritan, also found only in Luke's gospel, focuses on the fact that a social outcast from Samaria is more in tune with the will of God than established religious leaders. Moreover, in the ministry of Jesus as recounted by Luke, it is often those who have been branded with social disapproval who receive his attention (e.g., 7:36–50; 17:11–19; 19:1–10).

The Role of Women.   Luke also demonstrates an interest beyond that of the other gospels in the place of women in the story of Jesus. In the Birth Narrative of Matthew the chief character (besides Jesus) is Joseph, but in Luke's account the focus is on the women of the story. Not only is Mary the principal actor, it is she who grasps the true significance of the birth of Jesus (1:47–56) and who is sensitive to the underlying meaning of events (2:19, 51).

Later in the gospel (and in the continued narrative in Acts), women occupy central positions among the disciples of Jesus. Luke stresses the fact that in the last days of Jesus' life it was the "women who had followed him from Galilee," who stood by him (23:49, 55). Unique to Luke is the account of Mary and Martha, two sisters who received Jesus into their home, Mary becoming a member of Jesus' coeducational seminar (10:38–42).

The Holy Spirit.   The Holy Spirit plays such a crucial role in Luke's account that it is sometimes called, as we have noted, the *Gospel of the Spirit*. During the Birth Narrative the Spirit is frequently mentioned (1:15, 17, 35; 2:25, 26, 27). At the Baptism Luke offers the most graphic and public picture of the descent of the Holy Spirit upon Jesus (3:21–22). Jesus begins his ministry "full of the Holy Spirit" (4:1, 14, 18). Interestingly, there is no further mention by Luke of the Spirit coming upon Jesus or anyone else during his ministry, as though the descent of the Spirit was a singular event in the life of Jesus. Once empowered, Jesus was led by the Spirit. The next, and final, reference to the Spirit in Luke is at the end of the gospel, when the Risen Jesus instructs his disciples to remain in Jerusalem until "you are clothed with power from on high" (24:49). The allusion, of course, is to Pentecost, when, according to the narration in Acts, all the disciples were "filled with the Holy Spirit" (Acts 2:4).

Responses to Jesus: Joy and Recognition of His Lordship.   The most frequent response to the coming of Jesus is simply "joy." When the angels announce the birth of Jesus, they call it an event of "great joy" (2:10; cf. 1:14).

During his ministry (10:17; 15:7, 10) and after the Resurrection (24:41), persons respond with a joy that is sometimes overwhelming. The very last verse of the gospel records the "great joy" of the disciples who had seen the Risen Lord (24:52).

The other typical response to Jesus in Luke is the confession of Jesus as Lord. Beginning with the Birth Narrative (1:43; 2:11), Jesus is acknowledged at least eighteen times in the Gospel as Lord. Like *Son of God*, *Lord* is an acclamation of power and authority that would have been more meaningful in gentile contexts than the Jewish ascription *Christ*.

The "Order" in the Gospel. These recurring motifs help us enter Luke's world, but they do not represent the "order" Luke claims to have found that manifests the truth about Jesus. We come closer to seeing this pattern when we observe the implicit structure of the gospel. In the view of many modern scholars, Luke's "orderly account" is a reinterpretation of the history of God's plan of salvation as "three ages of the Spirit." The first age, presupposed by the gospel's tracing of the lineage of Jesus from Adam, is that which lasted from the creation, when the Spirit hovered over the waters of chaos and life was breathed into Adam, to John the Baptizer. The second age is the ministry of Jesus, beginning with the descent of the Spirit at his Baptism and continuing through the Resurrection and the promise of the Spirit's coming upon the disciples. The third age, the Age of the Church, is the subject of Acts, beginning with the Pentecost account of the Spirit's descent and pointing toward the movement of a spirit-filled church throughout the known world. The purpose of the gospel's account of Jesus is to reveal the nature of the kingdom that will come when all the earth is full of the spirit and Jesus returns in power. During this period Jesus will embody the compassion, justice, joy, and universal scope of the Kingdom.

John: The Journey of Jesus

Like Matthew, Mark, and Luke, the Gospel according to John is a proclamation of the "good news" about Jesus Christ, Son of God, meant to inspire a response of faith. The gospel states this purpose as follows (20:31):

> ...these [signs] are written that you may
> believe that Jesus is the Christ, the Son of God,
> and that believing you may have life in his name.

However, even the most casual explorer of the world of John's gospel senses that it is very different from the Synoptics in content, style, and mood. In 200 C.E. Clement of Alexandria distinguished John from the others as a "spiritual" gospel. That is a good description.

John and the Synoptics. Unlike Matthew or Luke, John has no Infancy Narrative. Instead, this gospel begins with a prologue that takes the story of Jesus all the way back, before the creation of the cosmos. In the interaction with John the Baptizer there is no indication Jesus was actually baptized by John. Instead, Jesus and his disciples are portrayed baptizing people themselves and in tension and conflict with John and his disciples.

Whereas the Synoptics suggest that Jesus made only one journey to Jerusalem and conducted most of his ministry in Galilee, John portrays several journeys to Jerusalem. The Synoptics imply a one-year ministry. Because John refers to three Passovers (2:13; 6:4; 11:55), a three-year ministry is suggested. The Synoptics describe Jesus' last supper with the disciples as a Passover meal. John indicates that it took place on the day before Passover, and the Crucifixion of Jesus occurred on the day the Passover lambs were sacrificed. In the Synoptics the cleansing of the Temple takes place during the final week. In John it is at the beginning of Jesus' ministry (2:13–25).

Most important in comparing John with the Synoptics is the difference in the way the teaching of Jesus is portrayed. In the Synoptics the sayings of Jesus are either individual units or loosely grouped series. The focus is on each saying. In contrast, the teaching of Jesus in John is in the form of long discourses on a single theme such as his relationship with God the Father, and the bread of life. In the Synoptics Jesus talks about his identity as the Son of God only in oblique terms. In John, Jesus declares who he is in bold assertions, using the formula "I am..." These assertions are reminiscent of the form of divine self-revelation used in Exodus 3 and Second Isaiah (Is. 40—55). While parables about the Kingdom dominate the Synoptic portrayal of the teaching of Jesus, there are no parables in John. In the Synoptics the metaphors typically point to the Kingdom of God or of Heaven. John is full of symbols, but they point to the mystery of who Jesus is and the nature of his relationship with those who believe in him.

In the Synoptics there is a mood of expectancy rooted in the hope of the return of Jesus (*parousia*) and the new life to come. In John that hope is maintained, but the tone is dominated by a feeling of realization, not expectancy. For believers the new life has already come. Through belief in Jesus they already experience the power of the Resurrection (e.g., 5:24). John delights in paradoxes such as this, between a sense of *already* and *not yet*. Another paradox is present in John's description of the Crucifixion and the double meaning of the term "lifted up." Although Jesus is "lifted up" on the cross to die a shameful death (8:28), through the same act of "lifting up" he is exalted by God (12:32–34). Sometimes, John seems to be saying, you must look beneath the apparent meaning to see a deeper significance.

The Structure of the Gospel of John. This "layering" of meaning is evident in the structure of John. It follows a rather straightforward outline to tell the story of Jesus. However, at a deeper level, the structure of the gospel is expressed in one of the self-revelations of Jesus: "I came from the Father and have come into the world; again I am leaving the world and going to the Father" (16:28). The gospel can be viewed in terms of three stages of this cosmic journey: the life of Jesus with the Father from whom he comes; his life in the world, revealing the glory of his Father to those who believe; and his return to the Father to a life of glory. The gospel focuses especially on his life in the world. Chapter 1 begins the story by revealing the origin of the journey and foreshadowing his revelation in the world. Chapters 2—12 contain the seven signs by which Jesus revealed to the world the glory of the Father. In chapters 13—17 Jesus prepares "his own" for his return to the Father. In chapters 18—20 the Son returns to the Father in glory.

This is the *horizontal* structure of the gospel. The journey itself, and the response of "believing" in order to have "life," implies a *vertical* dimension as well. In fact, the journey of Jesus is both vertical and horizontal, from the Father to the world and back. At any point along the journey he manifests the "glory" (full nature) of his Father, so that people can see God's presence breaking into time and space. The "eternal life" he brings is a status of existence through which the believer breaks free from the horizontal continuum of birth, life, and death. Through transformation wrought by God, the believer shares the unity that the Son has with the Father. We will now look more closely at the stages of Jesus' journey as presented in John.

The Journey: Stage One (John 1). The Gospel of John begins with a poetic midrash (free interpretation) on the creation account in Genesis 1, as if to say, "To tell the real story of Jesus, we must begin at the *very* beginning." Genesis 1:3 says that creation began as God said, "Let there be light." This poem looks into that verse to explore the nature and significance of the divine utterance. The key term is Word (*logos*), which has a background in Greek philosophy and also a variety of possible biblical and rabbinic references, all of which the poem could very well be affirming.

In Greek philosophy, especially Stoicism, the logos was the principle of order, or reason, lying beneath the seeming chaos of the world. Jewish philosophers like the Platonistic Philo of Alexandria had associated logos with the personified Wisdom of Jewish wisdom speculation. In that tradition, Wisdom is portrayed as the agent of God's creative power, present at the origin of the cosmos, bringing order out of chaos. The Torah plays a similar role in rabbinic thought. In the prophetic tradition, the Word of God was a means of revealing the divine will, as was the Word in the Torah tradition (as in the Ten Words [Commandments]). Thus, logos is a term with a number of layers of meaning that bring together basic themes from both Greek and Jewish intellectual traditions.

For the poem this synthesis is a starting point; it opens up an even fuller range of meaning than the Greek and Jewish traditions suggest. The Word is paradoxically with God, yet "is" God. The logos to which this poem points is not merely a cosmic principle or agent of God; the Word mysteriously shares a common identity with the one God, yet it is also mysteriously present in the creation as "life."

The prologue and other passages in the gospel dealing with the motif of light reflect John's apparent contact with Jewish *Creation Mysticism* (see chap. 10). But John is not a gospel merely for mystics. It is also a gospel by a mystic for a larger Christian community. The full significance of the creation of light is that "darkness" (a symbol for the chaos and evil threatening the divine order and will) is held in check. Darkness is present, but it cannot overcome the light, and by implication, the life that is the source of the light.

A brief narrative interlude (vv. 6–8) introduces the motif of witnessing to the life-giving light and begins to intertwine the mythic with the historical. For the witness is not a divine being but a man sent from God, named John. He recognizes the light in a *person*, but he is not himself the light.

In verses 9–10 the poem resumes. The light-Word is a person who has come into the world. In verse 10 "world" takes on a double meaning as the creation but also as that which fails to recognize the "true light." The focus narrows from the "world" to "his own home" and "his own people," who do not receive him. Chapters 2—12 of the gospel develop this motif of rejection by "his own." In contrast, those who do receive him "by believing in his name" (which means not merely verbally acknowledging but also trusting in who and what he is) will become "children of God," not in the apparent, physical sense, but at the deeper, spiritual level. Chapters 13—17 focus on the community of those who respond in this way.

Now comes the climax toward which the poem has been moving. How is the logos present in the world? The Word is incarnate (in-fleshed), in a way in which "we" can see it. "We have seen his glory" points to a community bearing witness to the glory of God manifest in this person. In Jewish tradition the glory of God was said to dwell in the Temple. There the believer could behold, indirectly through the High Priest, the holiness of God. This poem is saying that the Word-made-flesh manifests the divine reality. The stage is set for a confrontation between the Temple and the Son. The comment (vv. 17–18) makes clear that in this gospel's view, the effect of the Word becoming flesh is that a new means of access to God has been opened. Finally, he is named: Jesus Christ.

The Journey: Stage Two (John 2—12).   John tells the story of the public ministry of Jesus through seven accounts of miracles by which Jesus manifests his glory. Typically, the miracle is followed by a dialogue between Jesus and someone else, then a monologue by Jesus. The seven miracles are

Turning water into wine at the marriage feast in Cana (2:1–11)

Curing an official's son at Cana (4:46–54)

Curing a paralytic in Jerusalem (5:1–15)

Feeding the five thousand in Galilee (6:1–15)

Walking on water (6:16–21)

Curing the blind man in Jerusalem (9)

Raising Lazarus from the dead in Bethany (11).

Scholars call this section of John the *Book of Signs.* The first, third, sixth, and seventh miracles have no parallels in the Synoptics, while the rest do. There are no exorcisms in John. The signs are woven into a narrative by inclusion of transitional segments that move Jesus from place to place.

As the prologue has indicated, those who believe are empowered to be born of God and receive new life. This is developed in a dialogue between Jesus and Nicodemus, a Pharisee and member of the Sanhedrin, on the theme of being born "anew" or "from above" (both translations of 3:3 are possible) and in a monologue on the theme of the power of the Son to give eternal life to those who believe in him (3:1–21). In the latter, the future expectation of judgment and the hope of new life are brought into the present. Jesus' reference to being born of the water and the spirit almost certainly means the Church's rite of Baptism with the laying on of hands, symbolizing the gift of the Spirit. Elsewhere John alludes to both Baptism and the Lord's Supper (Eucharist), usually referring to the elements of water, bread, and wine.

Balancing the dialogue with Nicodemus, one of the rulers of Israel, who does *not* grasp the real behind the apparent, is a dialogue with a Samaritan woman who recognizes who Jesus is (John 4). A drink of water becomes the occasion for the revelation that Jesus brings the water of eternal life. And a comment by the woman about worship becomes an opportunity for a monologue about true worship in "spirit and truth."

The third through sixth signs are grouped together around the theme of Jesus and the Jewish festivals. First, Jesus and the Sabbath are taken up in chapter 5. While in Jerusalem, Jesus heals a paralyzed man on the Sabbath. As in the Synoptics, this causes a controversy. Rabbinic practice authorized emergency, but not elective, medicine on the Sabbath, the day that prefigures the Kingdom of God. John typically generalizes the interaction between Jesus and religious leaders, so that here "the Jews" chastise him for working on the Sabbath. This becomes the occasion for Jesus to reveal his identity as the son of God who does the work of his Father. The Son has the power to give life and to judge. He makes clear that to honor the Father, one must honor the Son.

In chapter 6 Jesus and the Passover are the subject. The synoptic miracles of the feeding of the five thousand and the walking on water occur. Again, a distinction is drawn between the real and the apparent. The *real* bread of life is not that which the Israelites received in the wilderness, Jesus says, for "I am the bread of life." Those who receive the true bread are those who believe in him. In chapters 7—10 the Feast of Tabernacles and the Feast of Dedication (Hanukkah) are used to reveal who Jesus is.

Periodically, John has mentioned the intention of "the Jews" to kill Jesus (5:18; 7:1). Now the death of Jesus moves to the fore as the concern dominating the narrative. In a "rounding off," the public ministry of Jesus is described as ending (11:54) where it began, at the place where John baptized (10:40).

The last sign, the raising of Lazarus, leads to the Crucifixion (11:45–53) and Jesus' revelation that "I am the resurrection and the life" (11:25). In a deeply ironic statement, the High Priest, Caiaphas, unwittingly affirms the significance of the death of Jesus (11:49–50). And Jesus is symbolically anointed for death (12:1–8). As the Book of Signs draws to a close, Jesus literally "cries out" the significance of what he has done and the response of belief his acts should elicit (12:44–50).

The Journey: Stage Three (John 13—20). The public ministry and the revelation of his glory to "the world" complete, Jesus turns to his disciples to prepare them for his "glorification" and return to the Father (Jn. 13–17). At a last supper with his disciples he washes their feet, in an act of humility, as an example of how they should act and a prelude to his own action on the cross.

In a farewell discourse (Jn. 14–16) Jesus tells his disciples that he is going to "prepare a place for you" (14:1–2). In John's world the journey of the believer should model the journey of Jesus. Jesus uses journey imagery, saying "I am the Way, and the Truth, and the Life; no one comes to the Father, but by me" (14:6). If the believer wishes to follow Jesus, he must "do the works that I do" (14:12) and "keep my commandments" (14:15). To guide and teach them, God will send the Holy Spirit (helper, advocate) to dwell in the believers (14:16–17; 26). Using the image of a vine, Jesus speaks allegorically of "abiding in me" like branches in a vine, which are to "bear fruit" (15:1–11). The believers are to enter into a relationship of love with one another (15:12–17) and to separate themselves from the "world" (15:18–27). They are to expect persecution, even death (16:1–4). He then reveals to them the journey he is on (16:28).

Turning now to heaven, Jesus offers a "high priestly prayer" (John 17). He prays for himself, that the Father might glorify him with "the glory which I had with thee before the world was made" (17:5). He prays for his disciples, asking not that they be taken "out of the world," but kept from the "evil one"

(17:6–19). Finally, he prays for all believers everywhere (17:20–26), asking that they might share in the unity he has with the Father so that the world might believe.

Although the Passion Narrative in John roughly follows the same order as in the Synoptics, there are significant differences in emphasis. For one thing, the role of Jewish leaders in the death of Jesus is heightened, while the role of the Roman procurator Pilate is softened (see 19:11). In fact, in John, Pilate is portrayed as a sympathetic figure who is only interested in the welfare of Jesus. In addition, Jesus moves through his trial and crucifixion without a sign of anguish or despair. This is the moment of his glorification, according to John.

At the trial before the High Priest we encounter a disciple (18:15), who is the so-called "beloved disciple" (20:2) referred to elsewhere in the gospel (13:23–26; 19:25–27; 21:7; 20–24). In 21:24 this disciple is identified as the source of the tradition upon which this gospel is based.

Missing in this gospel are any of the apocalyptic signs associated with the Crucifixion. At the Crucifixion, Jesus says, with dignity, "it is finished," and dies. In the Resurrection appearances, the emphasis is on seeing Jesus as a spiritual presence. Thomas is reprimanded for insisting on physical proof in order to believe. "Blessed are those," the Risen Jesus says, "who have not seen [physically] and yet believe." Once Jesus has returned to his Father he can no longer be seen. Belief must be based on the testimony of others. The gospel ends with a statement of its basic purpose (20:31).

Balancing the prologue is an epilogue (John 21) that narrates a post-Resurrection appearance of Jesus in Galilee. It highlights the restoration of a chastened Peter, after his earlier denial, to a position of leadership in the community, taking the role of shepherd. It also refers to the "other disciple" and his role as a writer of the traditions about Jesus.

THE HISTORICAL SETTINGS OF THE GOSPELS

We return now to the historical world. On the basis of available evidence, what are the most likely historical contexts in which the four canonical gospels were written?

Mark

We have already accepted the theory of the development of the Synoptic Gospels that holds that Mark was the earliest. Traditions that can be traced to approximately 150 C.E. attribute authorship of this gospel to John Mark, the companion of the apostle Paul and, perhaps, of Peter. This tradition influenced the titling of this work as "The Gospel According to Mark." However, we must realize that this gospel, like the others, is anonymous if only internal evidence is considered. None of the gospels includes the name of the author. All the titles came from later church traditions, which may or may not have historical validity. Association with apostles or those close to apostles gave credibility and authority to the gospels and was a common practice in the ancient world. It is possible that John Mark wrote this gospel, but it is by no means certain.

According to tradition, the gospel was written after the death of Peter and Paul in Rome about 64 C.E. The gospel itself seems to indicate that the destruction of Jerusalem is either imminent or has just taken place (13:2; 14), so that the most common date suggested for the writing of Mark is about 70 C.E. The tradition of origin in Rome is credible, for Mark seems to have a gentile Christian audience in mind. (The gospel assumes that readers are not aware of Jewish practices; see 5:41; 7:3-4, 11, 34; 15:22). As we have seen, the necessity of suffering is a crucial theme. Persecution of Christians in Rome in the mid-60s by the Emperor Nero is documented by the historian Tacitus and others. Like other apocalyptically oriented works, Mark was probably written to publish the secret of the end time in expectation of its imminent arrival. This sense of urgency seems a more likely reason for the gospel's composition than the more general contention that, with the passing of the apostolic generation, there was a need to write down the traditions about Jesus. Additionally, as noted before, in rabbinic Judaism religious traditions were preserved in oral form out of deference to Scripture. The earliest Church may have shared this practice until it drifted away from its original moorings near the Hebraic Jewish center.

Matthew

Like other gospels, Matthew has no direct reference within the work itself to its author or place of origin. A report usually dated about 130 C.E. seems to attribute origin of the gospel to the apostle Matthew, although the reference is to a Hebrew writing (the original Q?), and this gospel (like the others) was almost certainly composed in Greek. Because it used Mark as a source, it is hard to accept that the Gospel as it stands is an eyewitness account of an apostle, even though it is the only one to name the tax collector called by Jesus as Matthew (9:9; 10:3). The familiarity of the gospel with Jewish law and customs and its concern over the "law and prophets" have caused some to view the author as an anonymous Christian scribe or perhaps a member of a school of Christian interpreters. The concern for church order and discipline suggests someone active in the leadership of a Christian community.

Because the gospel seems to assume the destruction of Jerusalem (22:7), a date after 70 is likely. If Mark was composed about 70, then Matthew could date to 80 or later. Because the earliest witness to Matthew's gospel is

Ignatius, Bishop of Antioch in Syria about 110 C.E., and because Antioch was an important center for early Christianity, with a mix of Jewish and gentile Christians, it seems a likely place of origin for the gospel.

The gospel clearly presupposes tension between Jews and Christians, and perhaps between Jewish and gentile Christians, so the need to define Christian teaching as distinct from traditional Judaism is one obvious motive for its being written. As we have suggested, it may have served as a manual of instruction and discipline for a Christian community. Our observation that Matthew may have been a sort of Christian scribe or rabbi suggests that the author would have needed to defend his authority against the rising influence in the Jewish world of the rabbinate centered in Yavneh. The intended audience surely included Jewish Christians who needed to be reassured that the Christian gospel was not a negation of their heritage, but rather a fulfillment of it.

Luke

The oldest tradition about the Gospel according to Luke (from about 200 C.E.) claims that both it and Acts came from the same author. There is no reason to doubt this tradition. However, the author must be considered anonymous, in spite of the tradition (which gave the title to the gospel) that Luke, a physician who accompanied Paul, wrote the gospel. Based on its language and style, we can be certain that the author was an educated gentile or Hellenistic Jewish Christian.

Like Matthew, Luke seems to presuppose the destruction of Jerusalem. Because the preface looks back at two earlier stages of the development of the tradition, we can assume a date roughly the same as Matthew's, about 80 C.E., but possibly as late as 100 C.E.

The only real evidence for a place of origin is negative. The gospel seems not to have a clear grasp of Palestinian geography; thus a gentile Christian setting outside Palestine is likely. Of all the gospels, Luke seems to be addressed to a general audience to explain the universal implications of the story of Jesus, especially to educated Romans aware of and drawn to the Christian message.

John

According to this gospel the traditions upon which it is based stem from the "beloved disciple" (21:24). The Christian Church traditionally has assumed that this was John, the son of Zebedee, who went to live in Ephesus, where he wrote the gospel. However, the epilogue to the gospel hints that this disciple did not live too long (21:23). A more general problem with identifying John, or any of the immediate disciples of Jesus, as the author is that the gospel seems to reflect a process of theological development. It is difficult to believe that the level of theological sophistication present in this gospel would have been reached so quickly.

An attractive theory of authorship is that of a *Johannine School*, which perhaps began with the beloved disciple and his reflections. As was the custom in Judaism, followers may have been attracted to this teacher and preserved his teachings about Jesus. The Johannine School theory is supported by the existence of other Johannine writings—the Letters of John. These are similar enough to the gospel in language, style, and thought to suggest common origin. We have already witnessed the phenomenon of a school preserving and developing a master's teachings in the Isaianic school associated with the Book of Isaiah (see chap. 6).

If the gospel was written in the context of a "school," then there is not necessarily a single date of composition. The question remains of the time frame within which it developed. The latest evidence of a date comes from a papyrus fragment of several verses of the gospel (18:31–33, 37–38) found in Egypt and dated by scholars to the first half of the second century C.E. If the gospel was circulating in Egypt by about 125 C.E., it must have been written by about 100. In addition, a reference to expulsion from the synagogue in 9:22 probably reflects a ruling not adopted until 80 or 90 C.E. This points to a date for the final redaction of John about 80–100 C.E. However, earlier editions of the gospel may have existed prior to this time. An early time of origin for the gospel in some form is supported by some of the evidence concerning its intended audience.

In its final redaction the intended audience is surely the general Christian Church. However, there is a good possibility that there was originally a unique Christian community in which the gospel circulated in some form. Was there a Johannine community composed of "children of light," which, like the Qumran sect, withdrew from the world to prepare for the coming (again) of the Messiah and a new age? If there was, it probably did not withdraw into the wilderness, nor was it as exclusive as the Qumranian Covenanters. John indicates that there is antagonism with the world, and the community is not "of the world," but, like Jesus, the community is sent into the world to bear witness to Jesus. The community is not restricted to the purified, but is open to all willing to "come and see"—Jew and Gentile alike. Moreover, it was apparently not an apocalyptic community awaiting the end, as was the Qumranian sect. The parousia was, as we have seen, deemphasized, and the stage was set for the community to exist for some time. If anything, its orientation was mystical, teaching persons how to experience the presence of God through the Church sacraments and meditation on his Son, who was, after all, the unmediated light of creation (1:4–5). Some members of the community may have practiced a Christian version of Creation Mysticism (see chap. 10).

The Gospel of John portrays Jesus as the Redeemer who came from the Father to reveal his glory on earth and then returned to the Father. On the surface this is a gnostic interpretation of Jesus, for Gnostics spoke of a divine figure who descended from heaven in order to liberate a selected group of spiritual people from their entrapment in the evil material world. However, it is clear that the gospel uses gnostic imagery in a polemical manner, to attack the gnostic point of view. Gnostics viewed the world as inherently evil, created by a fallen divine being. And they viewed the Redeemer as a divine being who entered the evil world but was not part of it. The gospel makes clear that the world as created is not evil. It is the creation of God through the Redeemer himself. And the Redeemer is not purely a divine being, for the Word became flesh. Although there is a dualism between spirit and flesh, good and evil, life and death, the world and the heavenly realm, the gospel portrays Jesus as the mediator between these polarities so that they lose their power.

In a more positive sense the gospel was written not to counter, but to enhance, a school of thought with its roots in the Hebrew Scriptures—Jewish wisdom. As observed in Chapter 8, one dimension of Jewish wisdom was speculation on the principle of order in the world. In Proverbs 8 and Sirach 24, Wisdom is portrayed as a "person" who participated with God as an agent of creation and who "dwelled" in Israel. She is also the communicator of the divine will and purpose. In the Wisdom of Solomon this is especially apparent (9:9–10). Although John shifts from the feminine Sophia (Wisdom) to the masculine Logos (Word) to speak of Jesus (and draw in Greek philosophical imagery), the gospel is squarely within the wisdom tradition. As Sirach 24 developed Proverbs 8 to identify the place of Wisdom's dwelling as the Torah, John 1 takes a step beyond to assert that the Word-Wisdom had become human and "dwelled among us."

So the intended audience of the gospel was probably originally a mixed community of Jewish Christians who withdrew from Temple worship to form a new community of believers in Jesus, led by the Spirit. They were perhaps joined by Gentiles. It is certainly possible that this community and its gospel existed very early in Christian history. In its first stages John may have been the earliest gospel!

SUMMARY

The previous chapter analyzed the New Testament gospels as historical sources for the life of Jesus of Nazareth. In this chapter we summarized the results of literary historical study of the gospels and offered interpretations of the literary worlds of each of the gospels. We also considered the original historical settings of the gospels.

Gospel is a type of literature that developed in the first century C.E. as Christian writers sought appropriate ways to interpret the meaning of the life of Jesus. Comparison of the four canonical gospels reveals close similarities among Matthew, Mark, and Luke; hence we call them the *synoptic* gospels. The most widely accepted theory of how the synoptic gospels are interrelated is the four-source hypothesis, which holds that Mark and a *sayings source* (called Q) were the main sources used by the authors of Matthew and Luke.

Although similar in many ways, each synoptic gospel has a unique interpretation of Jesus. The theme of Mark's gospel seems to be that the secret of Jesus' identity was revealed only when he suffered as a part of God's apocalyptic plan. Matthew stresses the radical obedience exemplified by Jesus and expected from those who would be his disciples. Luke emphasizes that the gospel is intended for all and highlights special concern for social outcasts, the poor, and women.

The Fourth Gospel (John) is significantly different from the synoptic gospels in content, style, and mood. In this chapter we argued that John's portrait of Jesus follows the pattern of a three-stage cosmic journey, through which the Word (Logos) of God became flesh, revealed the Father's glory, and returned to the Father to be glorified.

We concluded this chapter by speculating on when, how, why, and by whom the four canonical gospels may have been written. The inclusion of four canonical gospels in the New Testament suggests that the early Christian community recognized the inevitability, and perhaps desirability, of different interpretations of the meaning of Jesus. Still other perspectives on Jesus will be found in other New Testament books. The refusal to accept other gospels being written (see chap. 15) implies limits to the range of interpretations of Jesus that early Christian leaders were willing to acknowledge. Readers would do well to reflect on and discuss the question of the range of interpretations of Jesus current today, and how broad the criteria of legitimate perspectives should be.

THE CONTEMPORARY WORLD:
QUESTIONS FOR DISCUSSION AND REFLECTION

1. Our analysis in this chapter shows how each gospel interpreted the significance of Jesus in a somewhat different way. Which of these literary worlds seems to have the most points of contact with the world of your experience? Which of these gospels has, or should have, the

greatest impact on contemporary understanding of Jesus? What other views of Jesus are current?

2. To what extent should the four gospel portraits of Jesus be harmonized into a single interpretation of him? How important is it to recognize and respect the different portraits as we seek to understand the significance of Jesus today?

3. Some contemporary interpreters think that the significance of the Resurrection of Jesus is found in the transformed lives of the disciples, the birth of Christianity, and the continuing potential of the resurrection faith to change persons and the world. They feel that it is not important whether the Resurrection was an actual, historical event. Its importance is as a symbol. Others argue that if the Resurrection did not actually happen, then the Christian faith has no basis and therefore no place in the contemporary world. Discuss these two ways of interpreting the significance of the gospels' Resurrection accounts.

4. Our literary analysis of the gospels is framed between a literary historical account of gospel origins and an attempt to understand the historical setting to which each of the gospels was first addressed. How important are historical observations such as these to understanding the gospels? Or to understanding a Shakespearean play? How important is it to understand the history and historical setting of the writing of any play, novel, poem, or other literary work, and the historical setting to which it was addressed?

5. Obtain a copy of a gospel "harmony" or "parallel" from a library or bookstore. (This is a document that arranges corresponding passages of the Synoptic Gospels, and perhaps the Gospel of John as well, in parallel columns to facilitate study and comparison.) Try to make up your own mind which hypothesis concerning the synoptic problem is best supported by the evidence of the texts: the Four-Source Hypothesis, the Griesbach Hypothesis, or the notion that each of the gospels is an independent composition? Does the Gospel of John seem to use the same source material as the Synoptic Gospels, or does it seem to represent an independent tradition?

CHAPTER 13

The Birth of Christianity
(The Acts of the Apostles)

Photograph by Robert Seelinger

The Acropolis, Athens. The Acropolis was the ancient citadel of Athens. In classical times it became the great cultic center of the city, graced with a number of elegant temples and crowned by the Parthenon, which was dedicated to Athena Parthenos ("Athena the Virgin"), patroness of Athens. By the time Paul preached on the nearby Areopagus (Acts 17), Alexandria had eclipsed Athens as a center of learning. But Athens' symbolic status as a fountainhead of culture endured.

THE UNITY OF LUKE-ACTS

As their introductions indicate, the Gospel according to Luke and the Acts of the Apostles are two volumes of the same work. Acts also begins with a preface addressed to Theophilus that refers to the "first book" that dealt with the words and deeds of Jesus through his Resurrection and Ascension. Together they are a history of the birth of Christianity. In this chapter we will examine the literary world of Acts and use the evidence from this historical narrative and other sources to reconstruct the life of the early Christian community in the decades after the death of Jesus.

As we noted in discussing Luke (chap. 12), Luke and Acts together also form a historical narrative reinterpreting the history of salvation. According to Luke-Acts there are three epochs in the history of God's plan of salvation. Each of these is marked by the descent of the Holy Spirit: at creation, on Jesus, and on the Apostles. The latter two periods both begin with baptism—of Jesus in the Jordan and of the Apostles in a baptism by fire (Acts 1:5).

The first period is the subject of the "law and prophets" (the Hebrew Bible, with the third section of the canon still open). The Gospel of Luke tells the story of the middle age, the time of Jesus and his manifestation of the life of the Kingdom (see chap. 12). Acts tells the story of the third phase of salvation history, from the descent of the Spirit at Pentecost in Jerusalem through Paul's carrying of the gospel throughout the Mediterranean world, ending with Paul preaching "openly and unhindered" in the heart of the empire, Rome.

By the standards of historical writing of the time, Luke-Acts is good history. Like other historical works, it is not a mere recounting of events but also an attempt to find the underlying meaning and purpose of them. Before using Acts as a historical source, let us examine the literary world it creates.

THE ACTS AS LITERATURE

The title *Acts of the Apostles* is drawn from Hellenistic literature, where narratives recounting the deeds of great leaders (like Alexander the Great) were common. Acts does focus on the activities of two principal leaders of early Christianity after the death of Jesus—Peter and Paul. However, it is more than a chronicling of the lives of these two men. It is a historical-theological essay that weaves narratives of the lives of these and other leaders into a story of the spread of the Christian message from Jerusalem to Rome.

The structure of the narrative is geographical. Paralleling the journey motif of Luke (the journey of Jesus from Galilee to Jerusalem), Acts portrays the journey of the message about Jesus from Jerusalem to Rome. After the prefatory note to Theophilus, Acts links up with the end of the Lucan narrative (Lk. 24:51) by recounting the Ascension of Jesus (1:6–11). This passage establishes both the theme and the mood of the work. Jesus tells the disciples that once they have been empowered by the Holy Spirit they will be "my witnesses in Jerusalem and in all Judea and Samaria and to the end of the earth" (1:8). This is the theme of Acts, the carrying of the message of Jesus to the "end of the earth" under the guidance and power of the Holy Spirit. In response to the disciples' question of when Jesus will return, they are told that it is not for them to know the time (1:6–7). The concern of the disciples is not to be the return of Jesus but the work of carrying the gospel throughout the world. The expectation of the parousia is maintained (1:11), but emphasis is shifted from preparing for the end to mission in the world. The apocalyptic urgency of some other New Testament writings is not the mood of Acts.

The descent of the Spirit at Pentecost (2:1–42) closely parallels the beginning of the ministry of Jesus as narrated by Luke. It has been called a baptism (1:5); so the Church begins as did the ministry of Jesus—with baptism and the descent of the Spirit. The gift of tongues is a vivid symbol of the reality of the Spirit's presence and the worldwide implications of what has begun here. The image of the Tower of Babel (Gen. 11:1–9) is reversed. Language will become a means of bringing unity to mankind rather than separation. Description of the event gives way to an illustration of the unifying power of language—a speech purportedly given by Peter on the occasion (2:14–36, 38–39). This is the first of a number of speeches by Peter and Paul in Acts. In fact, nearly one-third of the content of Acts is comprised of such speeches. When the speeches are compared, it is apparent that a number of themes are repeated, regardless of who is speaking. These include

Jesus is descended from King David.

Jesus' ministry was validated by mighty acts performed in the Spirit.

Jesus was put to death in fulfillment of the Scriptures.

God raised Jesus from the dead and exalted him as Messiah and Lord.

God sent the Holy Spirit through Jesus.

All people should repent and receive salvation through the name of Jesus, who is the judge of all mankind.

The similarities between these speeches suggest that they were not exact transcripts of the things literally said on each occasion. The frequent occurence of all or most of the aforementioned elements in most of these speeches and in other early Christian writings such as the letters of Paul (cf. Rom. 1:1–6; 1 Cor. 15:3–11), where the subject is the preaching of the early

Church, has led many modern critical scholars to conclude that these elements made up the earliest Christian proclamation. The Greek word *kerygma* (meaning "proclamation") is used as a technical term for this early Christian preaching. We will note the probable historical settings of such preaching later. Hellenistic historiography sanctioned the use of such appropriate and typical speeches, particularly when the historian was not aware of a speaker's exact words. They might also serve to underscore an author's perspective on the significance of the narrative.

The first summary statement (2:43–47), like the others, describes the success of the Church in carrying out the commission of the Risen Jesus. Just as the earthly Jesus had done (as recounted in Luke), the apostles performed signs and wonders that demonstrated their authority, we are told. A community was created that broke down social and economic distinctions (as Jesus had called for in Luke), and their numbers grew.

Empowered by the Spirit, the apostles continue in Jerusalem the ministry of Jesus. Like him, they participate in the Temple ritual. They heal the sick (3:1–10). They are persecuted by the Sadducean religious leaders (4:1–31; 5:1–24), but they "obey God rather than men" (5:29). They speak the Word of God with boldness (4:31). They share their goods and care for those in need (4:32—5:11). The account is rich in detail of name and place, giving it the appearance of an account based on eyewitness testimony. Whether this is actual realism or part of the "real-life" style of the essay is debated by interpreters. As a result of the apostles' ministry, the community grows from about 120 (1:15) to several thousand (2:41). The point is clear: Empowered by the Holy Spirit, the Church is growing.

Although Acts paints an idyllic picture of Christian life in Jerusalem, the narrative acknowledges disputes, the most prominent between the Hellenists and the Hebrews (Jews who spoke Aramaic or Hebrew, and were more conservative in keeping the traditions of their native culture).

Among these Nazarean Hellenists was Stephen, whose eloquence in debate sparked the emnity of certain other Hellenistic Jews in Jerusalem, whose accusations brought about his arrest and trial. But Stephen's own defense, presented as an inflamatory sermon not unlike the propaganda with which later Hellenistic Christianity sought to descredit Judaism, was his real undoing. What began as a trial ended as a lynching, with the young man Saul an approving bystander (Acts 6:8—8:1).

Stephen's death sparked persecution (in which Saul was one of the Jewish leaders). The Hellenists seem to have been the main targets. Ironically, persecution provided the opportunity to begin the movement of the Christian message into Judea and Samaria (in fulfillment of Jesus' instruction). As Jesus had reached out to draw social outcasts into the Kingdom, so do the leaders in Acts. The most marginal of the Jews, the Samaritans (cf. Lk. 10:25), hear the gospel. A eunuch hears the message and is baptized (8:30–40).

Saul, a young Pharisee from Tarsus in Asia Minor, had a vision of the Risen Messiah while on his way to Damascus armed with letters from the Sadducean High Priest to facilitate his persecution of the Nazareans there. This illumination changed him from a persecutor to a partisan of the fledgling messianic community. This is such a crucial turning point in the narrative that it is repeated in three slightly different versions (9:1–30; 22:3–21; 26:9–23). It is Saul (also known by the Latin name of Paul) who will carry the gospel to the Gentiles (9:15). In contrast with Paul's own account in Gal. 1:1–20, Acts maintains that Saul went soon after his illumination to Jerusalem and began to preach there. At first he was suspected, then apparently supported by, the Twelve Apostles (9:26–30).

With the Church established in Judea, Galilee, and Samaria (9:31), the Christian gospel moves into the completely gentile world. Acts portrays Peter converting the first Gentiles, showing that from the outset he did not disagree with a separate mission to the Gentiles that was not based on strict observance of the Torah (10:9–16; 11:1–18). The first church in the gentile world was established at Antioch (11:19–30). There Paul came at the urging of the Jerusalem church's delegate, Barnabas. In Antioch, according to Acts,

Photograph by Arthur C. Young

The Areopagus, Athens. The Areopagus ("Mars Hill") rose near the Athenian Acropolis. It was the original meeting place of an important Athenian council. According to Acts 17:21–33, the Apostle Paul spoke to the "men of Athens" from the Areopagus.

those who followed the Way (of Jesus) for the first time were called "Christians" (11:26). The harmony between gentile and Jewish Christians is illustrated by the Antioch church's sending relief to the "brethren" in Judea, where famine had struck (11:27–30).

The rest of Acts focuses on the missionary activities of Saul (now known as Paul). This work is presented by Acts as three distinct missionary journeys (13—14:28; 15:36—18:21; 18:23—19:19). Given Luke-Acts' penchant to organize the narrative by journeys, it is an open question whether these three journeys are a literary device to structure the presentation of Paul's work or an accurate description of what actually happened.

According to Acts' patterning of events, Paul and Barnabas left from Antioch for the first missionary journey into Asia Minor. Paul preached in synagogues where "God fearers" were especially responsive to his message. When challenged by Judean teachers who said that unless a man was circumcised he could not be saved, Paul and Barnabas returned to Jerusalem. There, according to Acts, certain Christian Pharisees argued the necessity of keeping the law of Moses, but Peter opposed them, and his support of accepting Gentiles without prior condition won out. Once again, Acts shows Peter and Paul in full agreement, in keeping with the harmonious mood in the Church that dominates the work.

The second journey carries Paul, joined by Silas and later by Timothy, back through Asia Minor and on to Macedonia. He preaches in synagogues and is received by God fearers, but he is persecuted by the leaders of the Jewish community, who accuse him of treason before Roman authorities. This is another aspect of Acts' concern to blame Jewish, not Christian, leaders for the emerging split between Judaism and Christianity. Led by the Spirit, Paul takes the gospel into Europe, via Macedonia, at Philippi. Then he moves to Greece, where he makes a rational defense of the gospel in Athens (17:22–31) and establishes the church at Corinth. The narrative makes clear that Paul commits no offense against Rome (18:12–17).

On the third journey Paul goes to Ephesus for a long period (over two years), then back to Macedonia, Greece, and, finally, Palestine.

Led like Jesus in Acts by the Spirit, Paul resolves to go to Jerusalem and then on to Rome (19:22). Just as Jesus carried the gospel to the heart of the Jewish world, Paul will take the message to the center of the gentile world. Like Jesus, he has a hearing before the Sanhedrin (22:30—23:10) and the Roman governor (24:1–27). Like Jesus, he is accused of blasphemy and profaning the Temple. Unlike Jesus, Paul mounts a defense that convinces the scribes (Pharisees) in the Sanhedrin but not the Sadducees and the Roman governor. Only when Paul insists on his right as a Roman citizen to appeal his case to the emperor is he sent to Rome for trial.

The narrative shifts without warning to the first-person plural and uses it especially in the last phase of the story (16:10–17; 20:5–15; 21:1–18; 27:1—

28:16). From a literary perspective these so-called "we" passages heighten the excitement of the description by giving first-person authenticity and drawing the reader into the story. Whether this is a literary device or an indication of the inclusion of a section of Luke's (or someone else's) travel diary is a historical issue. Certainly, the detail and realism of these passages is impressive.

The narrative concludes with an air of confidence and anticipation. Paul is active in the imperial capital, even though under house arrest. His work continues and the promise of the gospel's reaching the "end of the earth" is on the verge of fulfillment. The theme, stated in 1:8, has been fully developed.

Luke-Acts tells a story in which the gospel is carried from "nowhere" (Nazareth) to the city that is the greatest power center in the world (Rome) in journeys by persons led by the Spirit. Christianity should now be recognized as a legitimate world religion that reluctantly broke from its Jewish heritage. To its readers, Luke-Acts gives examples of how to live in the world by presenting heroes to emulate—Jesus, Peter, Stephen, Paul, and others.

THE EARLIEST CHURCH

The Resurrection experiences of the immediate followers of Jesus gave them both a message to proclaim and the courage to proclaim it. The main documentary source for this earliest stage of the Christian Church is Luke's book of Acts. As we have noted, the portrayal in Acts, although an excellent example of Hellenistic historiography, is selective and schematic. Luke is supplemented by the letters of Paul, other early Christian writings, and such archaeological data about the early Church as exists (though very little can be pushed back this far).

This section will review the history of the Church down to about 70 C.E., a few years beyond the coverage of Acts. It will reserve comment on Paul for the following chapter. But 70, the year the Romans destroyed Jerusalem and its Temple, serves as a significant watershed for both Jewish and Christian history. The events of that year probably hastened the estrangement of the early Christians from their original Jewish matrix. The flourishing community life of prewar classical Judaism could afford the richness and variety of the numerous denominations and sects that prospered to a greater or lesser degree (see chap. 10). The community that emerged from the crisis was besieged and threatened. The rabbis at Yavneh, who inherited the task of reconstruction, had less room for toleration and maneuver. And on the Nazarean side, where it had been advantageous to be identified with the Jewish community before the war, it became desirable to be recognized as distinct after it began. The increasingly gentile composition of the Christian group in the Roman world outside the Jewish homeland probably made separation inevitable over the long haul. In any case, once the Church spread beyond Israel and opted for gentile conversions, this outcome was a demographic inevitability. The process was nevertheless a lengthy one, and developed at different rates depending on occasion, situation, and the respective Christian and more or less traditionally Jewish groups involved.

FIGURE 13–2

Events Related to the New Testament
Before 70 C.E.

Date	*Event*	*Roman Emperor*
B.C.E.		
44	Parthian Invasion	
40–4	Herod the Great appointed "King of the Jews" in Judea by Romans	Augustus Caesar (30 B.C.E.–14 C.E.)
20	Temple rebuilt by Herod	
Between 8 and 4 B.C.E.	Jesus born	
4 B.C.E.–39 C.E.	Herod Antipas (son of Herod the Great) tetrarch of Galilee	
4 B.C.E.–6 C.E.	Herod Archelaus (son of Herod the Great) ethnarch of Judea	
C.E.		
18–36	Caiaphas High Priest	
26–36	Pontius Pilate procurator of Judea	Tiberias (14–37)
27–29 (?)	Ministry of John the Baptizer	
Sometime between 27 and 33	Ministry of Jesus	
Sometime between 30 and 33	Crucifixion and Resurrection of Jesus	

FIGURE 13–2 *(cont.)*

Events Related to the New Testament
Before 70 c.e.

Sometime between 33 and 45	Conversion of Paul	
		Caligula (37–41)
41–44 (?)	Herod Agrippa King of Judea imprisons Peter	
41–49	Jews banished from Rome	
		Claudius (41–54)
About 47–56	Missionary activity of Paul	
About 49	Jerusalem Council	
56	Paul arrested in Jerusalem	
Between 60 and 63	Paul under arrest in Rome	
About 64 or 65 (?)	Peter & Paul martyred in Rome Nero (54–68)	
About 62	James, brother of Jesus, martyred	
64–65	Christians persecuted under Nero after Rome burns	
66–73	Jewish Revolt against Rome; Christians flee Jerusalem	
70	Jerusalem captured; Temple destroyed	Vespasian (69–79)

The Jerusalem Church

The earliest Jerusalem church was centered around Galileans who had come to Jerusalem with Jesus and remained in the holy city, the most logical place to await the return of the Davidic messiah. The gospels suggest that Jesus had also acquired Judean followers prior to the crucifixion, including Joseph of Arimathea, a member of the Sanhedrin who provided the tomb in which Jesus was buried. The community organized itself in a fashion that was apparently an accepted model for Jewish sectarian communities. The Dead Sea Covenanters shared some of these same customs, which proves nothing more than that both were roughly contemporaneous Jewish groups. The churches of Galilee, and of the Diaspora, opted for the model of a synagogue congregation.

One of the first actions of the Jerusalem group was to replace Judas, the lapsed member of the Twelve, by lot from among the original disciples. One Matthias was chosen. The Twelve, the inner circle of leadership established by Jesus, was, as noted, symbolically related to the twelve tribes of Israel, emphasizing further the Jewishness of the community. From the time of Jesus, there had been an inner-inner circle of three within the Twelve, Simon Peter and the two sons of Zebedee (probable cousins of Jesus), James and John. They apparently continued to hold positions of particular importance. Peter, who had been the spokesman and leader of the Twelve in Jesus' public ministry, became the chief figure in the Jerusalem group. After James, the son of Zebedee, was executed on orders of Herod Agrippa (37–44), James, the brother of Jesus, appeared as one of the three "pillars" of the Jerusalem church. In due course, James seems to have been recognized as the chief leader of the community, with Peter assuming the role of itinerant missionary. The group practiced a community of goods, pooling all their property in a common fund. Their Jewishness was further evidenced by their continued frequenting of the Temple, a custom going back to Jesus' ministry.

Luke attributed a sudden surge of growth in the community to a miraculous occurrence, the speaking "in other tongues" at Pentecost described in Acts 2. What may be behind the story is the astonishment that unlettered Galileans, noted for their strange accent and limited literacy, were speaking such a message. The first Hellenistic Jewish converts may date from this time.

The Jerusalem church was never a wealthy community. If the later Jewish Christian group called the *Ebionites* ("poor folks") were their descendants, they probably prided themselves on their poverty (as did the Dead Sea Covenanters). But their need for a relief offering like those collected in the gentile churches by Paul was due to the ravages of famine, not the failure of their communal and collective economic practices. Still, if the Jerusalem church was not affluent, it was influential. Other churches looked to it as the mother church, the arbiter of difficult issues.

Gentile Converts

Did Gentiles who wanted to enter the Way, the Christian circle, first have to become converts to Judaism? That was a question with which the Jerusalem church was asked to wrestle. Two matters must be grasped to understand the issue and its ultimate resolution. First, how did these first Christians understand their situation? The early Jewish Christians apparently understood the *kerygma*, the basic proclamation of their community, to be that the long-awaited Messiah, the once and future Davidic ruler, had appeared in the person of Jesus. All doubt was removed by the fact that, although he had been killed by his enemies, God had raised him from the dead, proclaiming him once and for all his agent of redemption. The Risen One would return to restore the fortunes of Israel and usher in the full realization of the reign of God on earth. Those who signified their trusting confidence in the Messiah thereby established their citizenship in the messianic kingdom.

This is almost certainly the way the kerygma was understood by early Jewish Christians and by their early gentile converts who had been "God fearers" and, hence, were conversant with Jewish modes of thought. The dominant Jewish view of the destiny of non-Jews was enunciated in the generation after Paul by the great Rabbi Joshua: "The righteous of all the nations have a portion in the world to come." This view was inherent in the Hebrew Scriptures and had been expressed in the school of Rabbi Hillel. Its gist was that, while God held the Israelites to their covenant promises, he expected of those without more detailed revelations only that they would behave according to their best lights. Still, for the gentile proselyte, there must have been a sense of special belonging to God's people through the step of conversion.

As the Church moved further afield and made converts among Gentiles whose acquaintance with Jewish lore was more limited or nonexistent, the kerygmatic proclamation was heard more in terms of personal salvation— deliverance from a decaying world, from death, and from demonic powers. Familiarity with the revealer-redeemers of gnostic myths and the savior deities of Greco-Roman mystery religions colored the way the gracious offer of the kerygma was (and to a large extent still is) understood. Paul's mystical and highly personal formulation of Christian revelation lent particularly to this more Hellenized form of understanding (see chap. 14). The identification of the *kerygma* does not imply the existence of a unified orthodoxy at this early stage. The Gospels and letters of the New Testament and much extra-canonical literature, including the New Testament Apocrypha (cf. chap. 15), make it clear that a variety of interpretations of the significance of Jesus as the Messiah flourished in the early Church.

However emphasis in the early Church's understanding of its basic message may have shifted, there was the common belief that the Church was in, or at least on the threshold of, the messianic age. This leads to the second matter relating to gentile converts. As we have noted, Judaism had always accepted converts. Before the Exile, it had been more a matter of assimilation into a national population. After the Exile the customs of proselytism evolved more as a religious exercise. But from the time of the prophets, and above all in texts with messianic, or at least eschatological, overtones, the notion had been abroad that, in the ideal future, the pagan nations would turn from their idolatry and to the God of Israel without ceasing to be

Gentiles. (The terms *Gentile* and *nations* are the same.) The Messiah had come. Gentiles were showing an interest in the Way. Scripture was being fulfilled.

By linking the first gentile converts to Peter, inspired by a vision, Acts diverts any allegation that the mission to the Gentiles initiated by the church in Antioch was a conspiracy. The mass gentile conversions by Paul and his associates were also regularized in Acts by the Jerusalem church (Acts 15). The only Torah-like observance required of gentile Christians resembled the rabbinic *Covenant of Noah;* that is, a few general moral and dietary observances.

Persecution

It appears in the early chapters of Acts that the principal adversaries of the Church were the Sadducean High Priest and his cohorts, who resented public attention being called to their role in the judicial lynching of Jesus. The pharisaic leadership, according to Luke, opposed the Sadducees on this score and urged toleration. The stoning of Stephen smacks of a spontaneous outburst of mob violence after he was interrogated by the Sanhedrin. It was not typical. Persecution was mainly directed against Hellenists like Stephen. The High Priest Ananus' killing of James, the brother of Jesus, and Herod Antipas' action against James, the son of Zebedee, were also isolated actions, the former act condemned by many influential Jews.

A similar judgment must be made in connection with the treatment accorded to the Church after it spread into the Roman world. The Greco-Roman world was generally tolerant and pluralistic. But Judaism, and its emerging daughter-religion, sat ill with the easygoing polytheism of that society. Neither would trade at the pagan temple butcher shops. Neither would participate in public occasions in which pagan religious overtones were too obvious. Neither would sacrifice to the divine emperor.

It is sometimes said that the unforgivable sin is to be *too* different from everybody else. In the Roman world, Jews and Christians were guilty of that sin and paid a price for it. The price was not constant violence and harassment, though it occasionally came to that. For the Church in the latter part of the century and later, failure to participate in the emperor cult became a serious problem and resulted in individual arrests and executions and occasional local or regional persecutions, such as the one in the eastern provinces that led to the writing of the Revelation to John during the reign of Domitian (see chap. 15). A famous exchange of letters between Pliny the Younger, governor of Bithynia in the early second century, and the emperor Trajan sanctioned Pliny's policy toward the Christians. Pliny held that the Christians were a relatively harmless lot, and he could not see that much really needed to be done about them. Still, he did his duty and executed the hardheads among them. Though the sufferings of those Christians who did end up in the arena or in the hands of the executioner are not diminished, it does not seem to be the case that the baptism of blood and fire of popular legend really belonged to this period.

The vicious and systematic persecutions occurred on the threshold of the Church's final triumph, after it had become prominent enough to constitute a serious force in the Roman order. The persecutions began under Decius in 250 C.E., with the last and worst being mounted by Diocletian until he abdicated in 305 C.E. In 311 there was an imperial decree of toleration followed by Constantine's Edict of Milan in 313, which legalized Christianity. Within a few decades Christianity was the established imperial religion, and non-Christians were persecuted! But all this lies far beyond the horizon of the biblical period.

Leadership

We have seen that the Twelve were the prominent leaders of the Jerusalem church, with the smaller number of three "pillars" exercising even greater influence. But the somewhat larger group, known as *apostles*, were the preeminent figures in the spread of Christianity through the Roman world. To clarify, the pillars and the Twelve were apostles, but the total company of apostles was more numerous. There is no clear indication of how many apostles there were. They were not identical with the disciples, the apparently larger number yet of Jesus' students and later, apparently close followers of the apostles.

The thing that made a person an apostle was a personal commission by the Lord Jesus. The Greek word *apostolos* means "one sent." Apostles were ambassadors of King Messiah, understood to have extraordinary authority in the Church. Later Church teaching associated *apostolic succession* with a power passed from Jesus to the apostles, then to the bishops. But documentation from the earlier history of the Church shows that the concern was not for the passing of power, but for correct teaching.

In the world beyond Jerusalem, the Church generally assumed the structure of a synagogue, that is, a congregation. The Greek word for church (*ekklesia*) means a group of people called together. They were governed by a group of elders (Greek, *presbuteros*), one of whom was chief. The organizing apostle would appoint the first *presbytery* (company of elders). With the passage of time, the office of chief elder evolved into that of *episcopos* ("overseer" or "bishop"). Ultimately, the bishops of the most important churches began to exercise authority over lesser churches in their neighborhoods (although this takes us beyond the period covered in this text).

Ephesians 4:11 lists prophets, evangelists, pastors, and teachers after apostles among the spiritually gifted leaders of the early Church. Apostles stand first in 1 Cor. 12:28, followed by prophets, teachers, miracle workers, healers, helpers, administrators, tongue speakers, and presumably interpreters thereof (see 1 Cor. 14:1–9). In keeping with the order of both rosters, Paul assigned particular honor to the office of prophet. Acts 11:27–28, 15:32, and 21:10–11 show prophets in action among the early Christians. The authority of the apostle was derived from a connection with the Lord Jesus, while that of the Church prophet was entirely charismatic. Apostles could also be charismatic, but their authority did not depend on it. The apostles were, of course, irreplacable. In keeping with the development noted between First Corinthians and the later Ephesians, the charismatic offices in the Church apparently waned progressively. This, as observed by anthropologists and sociologists, is in keeping with the typical development of leadership in religious organizations.

A Time Whose Idea Had Come

Traditional theology has held that Christianity arose providentially at just the right time to prosper. Even disbelievers in providence are obliged to agree that circumstances in the Roman world were rather well-suited for the spread of a new religion of personal salvation at the time Christianity came on the scene. The legacy of Alexander in the east, combined with the fact that Rome had used many Greek slaves as teachers and the mobility of free Greek traders, all meant that Greek could be understood in every quarter of the Roman empire. The Roman highway system remains legendary. The Pax Romana (Roman peace) enforced by Rome's legions and navy meant that travel was safer than it had ever been before. The Roman peace also created a common market extending on both sides of the Mediterranean from Arabia to Spain and northward into France, the German lands south of the Danube and west of the Rhine, and Britain. Cities grew as commerce waxed. Thus, Roman peace also brought Roman prosperity. People had places to go, business to conduct, and the relatively safe means to do so. Missionaries of the new faith could get about the world and count on making themselves understood with greater facility than at any earlier time. And not least, as noted before, Judaism had preceded the early Christians into the Greco-Roman realm. There were nuclei of people throughout the empire who knew the Scriptures, in most cases the LXX, and grasped some basic concepts of Judaism.

Cultural factors also favored the introduction of new religious options. The conquests of Alexander, followed by those of Rome, cut the roots to the past in a way that the predecessor empires had never done. They introduced attractive new cultural options, whereas the emperors of Persia, Babylon, Assyria, and Egypt had been content to let people rock along in their conventional ruts so long as tribute was paid on time.

Old religions also suffered from the new order. Most ancient religions were either the state cult of a kingdom or, in the case of the Greeks, a *polis* ("city-state") or family or tribal affairs. Even the victors were vanquished, for the old cult of the city of Rome proved quite inadequate to the needs of the empire. The emperor cult arose as the needed surrogate, glue for a disconnected entity. Increasing numbers of people were moving from the countryside into the growing and prosperous cities. For many, the move was not voluntary; they came as slaves or displaced workers. Urban folks have always been rootless in comparison with rural populations, and, in this case, they provided a ready market for new religious ideas.

To judge from both the religious and the philosophical options exercised, as well as the superstitions cultivated, the age of the early Roman empire was an age of anxiety. The blind goddess, fate, and the faceless goddess, chance, were figures of iconography. Astrology and augury flourished. It was widely assumed that not just these impersonal forces menaced human existence, but that potentially capricious gods and a variety of malign spiritual entities (including the "principalities" and "powers" of Rom. 8:38 and Eph. 3:10) threatened life and welfare both in this life and the hereafter.

If any single category summarizes the intellectual outlook and religious perspective of classical antiquity from the time of Alexander onward, it is *dualism*. This notion divides reality into two opposite and irreducible essences, the mental (or intellectual or spiritual) and the material. In the Greek version, the former is greatly to be preferred over the latter. It was Plato who drew the distinction most decisively, but the odds are it would have been drawn even if he had never lived. This characteristic attitude stood in stark contrast with the world-affirming optimism of the Hebrew Scriptures and Judaism, thus also of Jesus. The world, created by God, including people, sex and all, was pronounced in the Jewish tradition "very good."

The most popular philosophies of later classical antiquity shared a concern with personal salvation. Cynicism liberated people from stultifying convention. Epicureans sought the higher (intellectual) pleasures. Stoicism, particularly in its Roman versions, taught self-control, devotion to duty, and salvation through harmonizing one's own inherent *logos* (reason) with the cosmic logos that permeated the entire universe. Originally Pythagoreans combined a celibate, highly ascetic, coeducational monastic rule of life with a mystical quest that began with mathematical knowledge. Neo-Pythagoreanism was eclectic. Neoplatonism, with its theory of overflowing being, taught a mystical discipline designed to work through the levels of being to God. Although it did not emerge as a distinct movement until after this period, the work of Philo of Alexandria shows that the fundamentals of Neoplatonism were already well in place.

The term *mystery religions* is used to describe a class of religions that flourished in Greco-Roman culture. They all promised the gift of immortality (or at least profound illumination) from a benefactor deity who had achieved the gift in question and had the right to distribute it. Persons were initiated into the mystery in rituals often adapted from ancient fertility cults. Some were not unlike modern fraternity, sorority, or lodge initiations. The Great Mystery was the cult of Demeter and Persephone at Eleusis in Greece. Two of the more widespread and popular mysteries, celebrated throughout the empire, were those of Isis and Mithra. Isis, the great Egyptian goddess, was the archetype of the faithful wife, and her cult was especially popular with women. The cult of Mithra, the Persian hero-god and bullslayer, was especially popular in the army and was dominated by males.

Later Christian apologists heaped abuse on the mysteries, calling them inventions of the Devil. However, the mystery cults almost certainly influenced the way people in the pagan world understood Christianity, and Christian missionaries may have borrowed mystery terminology to interpret their message to pagans unfamiliar with Jewish ideas.

Gnosticism stands somewhere between religion and philosophy. It took a variety of forms, but the common element in all was the notion that an esoteric *gnosis*, transcendental knowledge, was the vehicle of redemption. Gnosticism took one of the most radically dualistic viewpoints in late classical antiquity. Gnostic mythology understood the creation of the physical world to be a catastrophe that led to the entrapment of good spirits (souls) in the depraved and evil realm of matter. As noted earlier, redemption came to these imprisoned souls when a being from the spiritual realm entered the material world, bringing the mystical gnosis, the secret of escape. Some Gnostics believed that only the higher and more spiritual souls were capable of understanding the gnosis, though some lesser souls might also be delivered by their trust in gnostic truth. We have already discussed the influence of Gnosticism on the Gospel of John (chap. 12).

Thus, just as Christianity was not spawned amid a sterile and moribund Jewish matrix, but within a richly creative one, so it did not emerge into a pagan world bereft of vital spiritual options. Christianity, like the other newer religions and philosophies, found its market in the burgeoning cities of the Roman Empire and made its original urban inroads among Hellenized Jews and God fearers. But it found the largest number of recruits among the urban masses of the gentile cities. The conversion of the countryside was slower (*pagan* comes from the term meaning *country person*). Christianity's competitors during this stage were probably not so much the philosophical schools as the mystery and gnostic sects, popular local cults, and purveyors of various forms of astrology and occultism.

In a well-populated religious environment, Christianity prevailed and ultimately became the religion of the empire. Faith attributes the outcome to providence. Anthropologists point out that Christianity turned out to be the most adaptive competitor. History simply notes the outcome. In the next chapter we will take a somewhat closer look at the process, and in Chapter 15 we will carry it through the end of the biblical period.

SUMMARY

This chapter dealt with the birth of Christianity as portrayed in the Acts of the Apostles and in light of available historical evidence.

The literary world of Acts includes the Gospel of Luke, for the two are part of a single historical work. The two volumes combined tell the story of the spread of the Christian gospel from its origins in the isolated hill country of Galilee to the very nerve center of the vast Roman empire. Luke recounted the role of Jesus. Acts is an account of the creation and growth of the community that proclaimed Jesus the Messiah and their Lord. Both stress the role of the Holy Spirit.

Like other historical sections of the Bible, Luke-Acts is more concerned with lifting up the underlying pattern of divine purpose in events than in merely describing them. Acts stresses that the early Christian church was a community of social justice and universalism, embodying what Jesus himself taught according to Luke's gospel. Acts also emphasizes that the spread of the message about Jesus into the gentile world carried the endorsement of the original apostles, including the first leader of the emergent Jerusalem church—Peter. Paul, first a persecutor and then a partisan of the church, is used as the vehicle to portray the Gentile mission. Much of Acts relates the missionary journeys of Paul and various companions throughout the Mediterranean world, climaxing in his arrival in Rome.

Our historical analysis in this chapter covered the period from the death of Jesus to about 70 C.E. We focused on the Jerusalem Church; the conversion of gentiles; early persecution of Christians; leadership in the early Christian churches; and the political, economic, cultural, and religious factors that enhanced the development and spread of Christianity throughout the Roman world. We discussed the reasons for the split between the followers of Jesus and the Jewish community and the various philosophies and religions of the Roman Empire, such as Cynicism, Stoicism, the mystery cults, and Gnosticism, which are significant for an understanding of this period. The important role of the Apostle Paul in the development of Christianity will be treated in the next chapter.

Although Acts presents an idealized picture of the early Christian church, it can be interesting to compare the characteristics of the first Christian communities with those of churches today. As any movement matures it becomes more and more institutionalized. This happened to Christianity, as we shall later see. At various times revitilization and renewal groups spring up, seeking to restore the original vitality of the movement. This is also true in Christian history.

THE CONTEMPORARY WORLD:
QUESTIONS FOR DISCUSSION AND REFLECTION

1. What was the "social world" of early Christianity? What is the social world of modern American Christianity? How does a social setting affect the forms of expression of Christianity or any other religion?

2. Evaluate Acts as a source for a modern historian writing the history of early Christianity. Identify both strengths and weaknesses.

3. Acts was written, our analysis suggests, to portray the spread of the early Christian Church from Jerusalem to Rome and to show that both Jewish pharisaic authorities and Roman authorities were friendly to it whenever all the facts were before them. What might have been the purpose of this? How do modern writers, musicians, and film makers achieve their creative purposes?

4. How did the early Church establish its footholds in the Greco-Roman world? What sort of treatment was it generally accorded by the larger public of the Roman Empire? How are groups that are "different" treated in our world? Have you ever been affiliated with a group that was regarded as weird? How were you treated?

5. Do we live now in a period of greater institutionalization or revitilization of the Christian Church? Discuss recent news stories about events that bear on this issue.

CHAPTER 14

Paul: Apostle to the Gentiles (The Letters of Paul)

Photograph by Ozark-Engle, Fulton, Mo.

Ephesus: the main street between the harbor and marketplace. The marketplace (agora) was the hub of life in any ancient city. It was probably in the agora of Ephesus that the uproar recorded in Acts 19:23–41 began. Ephesus was apparently a center of activity of the Apostle Paul in Asia Minor and Greece.

INTRODUCTION

It is both easy and extremely difficult to exaggerate the importance of the Apostle Paul. It is easy to exaggerate his importance in his own time. He is the central figure in over half of the Book of the Acts of the Apostles. Traditionally, he was considered the author of thirteen or fourteen of the twenty-seven books of the New Testament. He did write at least seven, and probably more, in the judgment of literary historians.

Legend has Paul preaching the gospel as far away as Spain, Gaul, and even Britain. A superficial reading might lead to the conclusion that Paul was a sort of apostolic Lone Ranger, single-handedly spreading Christianity throughout the Roman world. Paul himself never made such a claim. His own letters make it quite clear that he was only one among many early Christian missionaries. Romans, ordinarily considered his most important letter, was written to a church he had not founded or visited at that point. In the context of his times, Paul was an important and controversial leader in the Church from sometime in the 30s until his death in 65 C.E. But he did not dominate the Church of that time.

It is extremely difficult to exaggerate Paul's importance in the history of the interpretation of the New Testament and the development of later Christianity, particularly in the Western Church (Roman Catholicism and Protestantism). St. Augustine was deeply influenced by Paul, especially in his relatively pessimistic view of human nature. Not only was Augustine the official doctor of the Western Church through much of the medieval period, but also Pauline-Augustinian thought has fired many of the revitalization movements and many of the great leaders of Western Christendom. A partial list would include the Protestant Reformation, the Jansenist movement in seventeenth-century Roman Catholicism, Neo-orthodoxy in the twentieth century, and leaders such as Martin Luther, John Calvin, Blaise Pascal, John Wesley, Karl Barth, and Reinhold Niebuhr.

It was once easy to write a life of Paul. The historian simply took the account of Paul's activities in Acts and harmonized it with the contents of his letters as much as possible. Then there was a period of extreme skepticism concerning the historical reliability of Acts. Today, historians feel that they may lodge in Acts qualified confidence (see chap. 13). But at best Acts covers only a small part of Paul's life. It does not supply as many chronological anchors as one might like. It is not clear how the letters that can be attributed to Paul with some confidence correlate with the Acts narrative. It is difficult, if not impossible, to square what Paul says about his visits to Jerusalem in Galatians with the visits mentioned in Acts. This chapter will follow the lead of the primary witness, Paul's letters, in cases of apparent divergence. But when all has been said, we simply lack the information to write a biography of Paul, just as we lack the information to write a biography of Jesus.

However, as in the case of Jesus, there are some things that can be said with confidence even if a "life" is beyond our reach.

Indeed, it is in some respects becoming easier to place Paul in his original historical context. In the past many critical studies of Paul emphasized the Apostle's background in Greek thought, especially Stoicism and the mystery religions. Recently, scholars have recognized more fully Paul's debt to his Jewish heritage. That will be apparent in our treatment of where Paul fits in the first century C.E. We will honor his own claim to being "of the people of Israel…as to the law a Pharisee" (Phil. 3:5).

THE QUEST FOR THE "HISTORICAL" PAUL

Paul and Judaism

There is no reason to doubt the assertion of Acts (9:11; 22:3) that Paul was born, and probably grew up, in Tarsus. Tarsus was an important Roman city, the gateway to the hinterland of Asia Minor (Galatia), a seaport and a university town. Paul's Hebrew name, as mentioned, was Saul. His Latin name doubtlessly related to the fact that he was by inheritance a citizen of Rome, and not just a citizen of a prominent provincial city. Our narrative will use his Latin name, simply because it is more familiar.

Paul's background made him a native of the Hellenistic world of the Roman Empire. His family must have retained a grasp of its Jewish heritage and genealogy, to judge from some of Paul's later autobiographical remarks. It is impossible to ascertain, however, whether Paul's was a family of Hellenistic Jews or a family of displaced rabbinic loyalists. Two things are plain, though. Whatever his original Jewish loyalties, Paul was a child of the Roman-Hellenistic world, and he was, or became, a very devoted Jew. According to the Book of Acts, he sought higher Jewish learning in Jerusalem at the feet of Rabbi Gamaliel, the presiding officer (*nasi*) of the now-Hillelite academy.

At this point, anomalies begin to emerge. Both by his own testimony and by that of Luke in Acts, Paul was a fanatical persecutor of the earliest Christian Church. But Luke shows Paul's teacher, Gamaliel, defending the apostles against the murderous intentions of the Sadducean High Priest and his cohorts (Acts 5:33–39). Here Luke the historian reveals a grasp of the standard pharisaic-rabbinic operating procedure toward religious deviants. Luke also quickly acquaints his readers with the fact that the young fanatic from Tarsus sought and received credentials to root out the Nazarean deviants in Damascus from the Sadducean High Priest, not from his teacher, the leader of the pharisaic academy. For whatever reason, the bright young student from the provinces had broken with the more tolerant policies of his teacher and made common cause with the Sadducees, even if he was "...as to the Law, a Pharisee."

Another anomaly concerns Paul's attitude toward the Law-Torah. Here let it be noted that Paul wrote in Greek, not Hebrew. When he wanted to refer to the Mosaic Torah, he did so by the Greek word, *nomos*, which comes into English as "law." *Nomos* is not quite so rich and comprehensive a term as *Torah*, but certainly closer to the Hebrew than the inadequate English term *law*. Moreover, a careful reading of Paul's letters suggests that he did not use nomos univocally. Sometimes, as in Romans 7, he seemed to use the term in two or more senses. However, the problem is more than one of ambiguity. For Paul seemed clearly to suggest that he once believed that the Torah was an instrument of salvation, that, by keeping the Torah, one could be saved. This assertion is puzzling, because, as we have seen (chap. 10), rabbinic Judaism never claimed that the Torah *was* an instrument of salvation. Rather, Torah was God's gift to the people, Israel, whom he had already taken to himself. It was one of God's gifts of love to his people and a means of responding to that love, not a device for gaining God's acceptance.

It may be that Paul's notion of "salvation by works of the Law-Torah" was an idea he brought with him to Jerusalem from his Hellenistic background. This possibility gains credibility from the widespread popularity of such views in Hellenistic gentile Christianity from the late first century onward. Romans 7:7–25 implies that Paul was, and to some degree remained, deeply vexed by his near success and inevitable failure to live a perfect life of Torah-faithfulness. The revelatory awareness that in Jesus the Messiah (Christ) God had freely given all that Paul sought and more, not only resolved his personal religious problems but also changed his perspective on the Torah, though not his respect for it. Following his revelation, Paul's notion of the function of Torah was in some respects closer to that of Hillelite phariseeism than it had been before. English-speakers may be misled by the usual translation of the Greek word *telos* in Rom. 10:4, "Christ is the end [*telos*] of the law." This word means goal, purpose (including, continuing purpose), or fulfillment. A scholar who has led the way in study of Paul's background in rabbinic Judaism, W. D. Davies, has suggested that, for Paul, Messiah Jesus embodied the Torah. Paul's new understanding of Torah would hardly be fully congenial to his mentors in Judaism, whether Hellenistic or rabbinic. But it should be equally clear that his experience of the Risen Christ did not lead him to the out-of-hand rejection of Torah encountered in some oversimplified accounts of his thought.

Another possibility for understanding Paul's attitude toward the Torah arises from analyzing his relationship to mysticism. Although too much should not be made of it, the deliberately veiled reference to himself in Second Cor. 12:1–10 seems to connect Paul with the practice of Chariot-Palace Mysticism (see chap. 10). His affinity with early kabbalism suggests two possible explanations for Paul's attitude toward Torah.

The notion developed in regular rabbinic circles and, with the passage of time, became particularly strong in Jewish mysticism, that the coming of the Messiah could be hastened by devoted living of the Torah. Had Paul as a younger man tried to force the messianic age into being by living a perfect life of Torah, only to have the Messiah come graciously to him while he was still a fully self-conscious sinner? It cannot be proven, but it is a provocative possibility that should not be ignored.

A second and related possibility arises from the fact, noted in Chapter 10, that intensive study of Torah was an important part of mystical discipline. Was it in a profoundly personal way that the Torah, conventionally approached, failed Paul? Unable to achieve mystical illumination in the prescribed fashion, had he received his mystical vision unbidden, at the hands of the Risen Messiah Jesus? Again, a confident answer is not possible. But this conjecture, based on recent progress in research, warns against oversimplified views of Paul.

Paul never renounced his own Jewishness or the Jewish people as a whole. His own love was encompassing enough to include both Israel after the flesh and Israel after the spirit, those "honorary Jews" God had grafted onto the root stock of Israel through Messiah Jesus. He was confident that God's love and providence were equally comprehensive.

Paul, the Apostle

Luke's account of Saul/Paul's vision of the Risen Messiah on the road to Damascus (Acts 9:1–22) is one of the most colorful narratives in the book of Acts. Popularly known as "the conversion of St. Paul," it has become a favorite theme of western art, and the model of true Christian conversion for the more devotional forms of Christian piety. But in truth, the term *conversion*, in its usual sense, is a misnomer. It misrepresents Paul's experience, dramatic as it was. And it is anachronistic at this stage of history.

Paul did not stop being a Jew, or stop thinking of himself as a Jew, when he recognized Jesus as the Messiah of Israel. He seems rather to have thought that he was a *better* Jew as a consequence. Both his own writings and Luke's portrait in Acts make this quite evident. Further, it would be decades after Paul's time, centuries in some circles, before it was considered that a Jew who became a Christian thereby ceased being Jewish. It would be much more accurate to speak of Paul's transforming experience as an *illumination*, particularly in the light of his probable connection with Jewish mysticism.

Luke narrated his version of Paul's illumination twice more (Acts 22:4–16; 26:9–18) after his initial account. Paul's own description of what most historians take to be the same event (Gal 1:11–17; 1 Cor. 15:8) is much more modest. Luke had Paul launching his missionary career the moment he recovered from his trauma. Paul himself was less specific. He said simply that he went into Arabia and later returned to Damascus (Gal 1:17). These data would counsel caution in the use made of the Acts narratives. In any case, it is dubious that either Paul or Luke would have described his experience as a "conversion" from Judaism to a different and distinct faith.

Paul's illumination apparently took place in the early to mid-30s, that is, not too many years after the first Resurrection experiences. Whether or not he ever saw or heard Jesus before his death is beyond demonstration, though most Pauline experts think not.

A chronology of Paul's subsequent career is also difficult, though Luke's narrative portrays an itinerary and implies a chronology. But even Luke does not explicitly name three missionary journeys that can be shown on a map with dotted, dashed, and dot-and-dashed lines. That is a product of the interpretation of Acts. We simply do not know how many missionary journeys Paul made. It may have been more than three, probably not less.

The one event in Paul's career that seems to be closely datable is his death. The tradition that Paul and Peter were jointly martyred in Rome during Nero's postfire persecution of 65 C.E. is supported by a number of early sources, including the First Letter of Clement, then bishop of Rome, to Corinth in about 95 C.E. Whether Paul's death was the outcome of the imprisonment and forthcoming trial at the end of Acts is disputed by experts. There are legends that he was acquitted and released on that occasion, resuming his missionary activities. Some think that the contents of the so-called "prison letters" (to be discussed) demand two Roman imprisonments and another lengthy jailing in the east, probably at Ephesus.

Despite our inability to reconstruct a chronology, there can be little doubt what Paul was doing in the years between his illumination and death. He journeyed by land and by sea, from city to city in Syria, Asia Minor, and Greece. He had planned to visit Rome, which he eventually did as a prisoner, on his way to Spain (Rom. 15:24), and perhaps his travels eventually led there. Arriving in a town, he would take his stand in a public place and begin his proclamation or visit the synagogue, if there was one. There he could be sure of a nucleus of persons familiar with the Hebrew Scriptures, if only in the Greek version, and conversant with Jewish messianic hopes. These forays into Jewish congregations probably created friction, for though messianic enthusiasm was not unheard of, and certainly was not against the Torah, Paul's activities would almost certainly have appeared as a challenge to local leaders and, in due course, an attempt to split the congregation or make off with members and fellow travelers (the God fearers). But through whatever approach, Paul's goal was the establishment of a Christian church, probably meeting in the homes of adherents and attracting to itself additional members. Paul's stay in a community was usually governed by circumstances. If

Photograph by Ozark-Engle, Fulton, Mo.

Ephesus: the theater. Ephesus seems to have been a hub for the work of the Apostle Paul in Asia Minor and Greece. According to Acts 19, some of Paul's colleagues were dragged into the theater at Ephesus by an irate mob, disturbed that sales of copies of the famous image of Artemis (or Diana) might be hurt by Paul's preaching.

things went well, he might remain to instruct converts or perhaps move on, leaving the task to colleagues.

Paul was at least as likely to run afoul of public hostility and government zeal from gentile quarters as he was of Jewish resentment, any of which could lead to a hasty departure. Acts 19:9 may be taken to mean that Paul rented a hall during his rather long stay in Ephesus and lectured after the manner of a Stoic teacher. Luke noted two occasions when Paul got into trouble because his activities infringed on local business interests (Acts 16:16–24; 19:23–41).

Paul tried to revisit the churches he had established, though, as we learn from his exchange with the Corinthian church, he was not always welcome. Paul's letters were almost certainly intended as his surrogate presence with the churches he had established. He took care not to interfere in the affairs of congregations he had not started, his letter to the Romans being the one known exception to his rule of writing only to his own congregations. At least one letter is mentioned in the Pauline corpus that seems to have been lost, Laodiceans (Col. 4:16). It is quite likely that more were lost than survived.

No physical description of Paul survives in credible sources, though his remarks about himself to the Corinthians suggests that he was neither an imposing presence nor an impressive orator. He suffered from some sort of chronic illness or disability. He alluded to it as a "thorn in the flesh" that prevented him from becoming too intensely affected by his mystical experiences (2 Cor. 12:7–10). With the passage of years, he doubtless bore more and more visible signs of the physical hardships he had endured in pursuit of his holy vocation: beatings, stonings, shipwrecks, prison terms, years on the road in all kinds of weather. Whatever his physical limitations may have been, Paul more than made up for them through his courage, tenacity, and enthusiasm.

Paul comes across in his letters as a man of passion. His wrath blazed when he felt himself crossed, and his vocabulary of invectives knew few bounds. But he relished reconciliation and forgiveness more than victory. He seems to have been more of an intuitive thinker than a logical and discursive reasoner.

As we have seen in Chapter 13, the rank of apostle was the most prestigious office in the early Church. Paul insistently maintained his claim to apostleship. To make his claim, he appealed to two basic arguments (see Galatians 1—2). Like all other true apostles, he was directly commissioned by the Lord Jesus, but in a revelatory encounter with the Risen Messiah, not during Jesus' physical ministry. And the most important leaders of the mother Church in Jerusalem accepted him and his gospel. He could also have a dispute with them and win, he says, reporting his showdown with Peter over making Gentiles observe the dietary restrictions of the Torah (Gal. 2:11–14).

Paul also strongly maintained that he had received his gospel not from any human agency, but directly from God through the Messiah. It was this gospel that received the approval of the Jerusalem church (again Galatians 1—2). This does not mean that Paul was claiming direct revelation as the source of everything he knew or taught. He quotes and cites sayings of Jesus. Twice in the latter part of First Corinthians alone he appeals to tradition (11:23–26; 15:1–11).

Paul, along with John, stands as one of the two most creative thinkers in the early history, perhaps the entire history, of the Church. In terms of influence, Paul stands next after Jesus himself. But to portray Paul as the "real" founder of Christianity, the one who turned the religion of Jesus into a religion about Jesus, is a misrepresentation. It misunderstands both the impact of Paul and the timing of that impact, as well as the other currents flowing in the early Church. By the time Second Peter was written, Paul's letters were being read with respect in the Church, but he was not the only authority (2 Pet. 3:15–16). It is also true that Paul's formulation of Christianity lent itself particularly to the shift away from the Jewish messianism of the earliest church to the emphasis on personal salvation of later Christianity. One may suspect, though, that in his own mind, Paul was not so far removed from the traditional Jewish view of things as later readers have perceived.

Sir Christopher Wren's epitaph in the great London cathedral he rebuilt, of which Saint Paul is claimed patron, reads: "If you would see his monument, look about you." Something of the sort might equally be said of Paul himself, the Jewish-Christian apostle to the Gentiles.

LETTERS AS LITERATURE

Of the twenty-seven books of the New Testament, twenty-one take the form of letters. Thirteen are attributed to the Apostle Paul, seven are general ("catholic") letters attributed to James, John, Peter, and Jude, and one is anonymous, bearing the title "To the Hebrews." Most are "occasional" letters, that is, written to a particular person or group in response to a specific situation. All of the letters that designate Paul as author (except Ephesians and perhaps Colossians) are occasional letters. Third John is the only other occasional letter. Most of the rest of the letters can be called general because they are not addressed to any particular audience but to a broad group (such as "the saints" in the case of Ephesians or "the twelve tribes in dispersion" in James). Two of the letters (Hebrews and First John) are "open letters" or tracts, not addressed to any specific or general group, and called letters only because of their closing salutations.

The form of the New Testament occasional letters was similar to that used in the correspondence of the period. Consider, for example, a typical Greek papyrus letter of the first century C.E.

> Irenaeus to Apollinarius his dearest brother, many greetings. I pray constantly for your health, and I myself am well. I wish you to know that I reached land on the sixth of the month of Epeiph and we unloaded our cargo on the eighteenth of the same month. I went up to Rome, on the twenty-fifth of the same month and the place welcomed us as the god willed, and we are daily expecting our discharge, it so being that up till today nobody in the corn fleet has been released. Many salutations to your wife and to Serenus and to all who love you, each by name. Goodbye.[1]

The writer begins by identifying himself and the one to whom the letter is being sent (salutation), prays for the well-being of the recipient (prayer), and talks of his own situation. The message is communicated (body), and the letter closes with greetings to others, more wishes, and a final word to end the letter (conclusion). The letter is a substitute for the more preferred form of oral communication; thus its language is informal and free flowing (except

[1] C. K. Barrett, *New Testament Background* (New York: Harper & Row, 1961), p. 29.

for the stylized opening and closing). In contrast with a narrator, the author of a letter is an onstage participant in the writing. The "world" of the letter is the relationship presumed by the letter, and the letter is like a snapshot showing us the status of that relationship at a particular time. To understand the world of the letter, it is essential to know the nature of the relationship and the expectations of sender and recipient.

The occasional letters of Paul adapt this common form to the relationship between an apostle (Paul) and the Christian churches he has founded or intends to visit (Romans). The letters also assume a broader relationship between God and these churches and individuals, which has been established, both sender and recipient assume, through the Crucifixion and Resurrection of Jesus Christ. In his role as apostle (one commissioned by Christ to proclaim the gospel authoritatively), Paul presumes both his relationship to the churches and the relationship he and they have entered into with God through Jesus Christ. The modifications in the form of the typical Greek "familiar" letter reflect this broader relationship. Thus, Paul incorporates into his letters extended discussions of what God has done through the Crucifixion and Resurrection of Jesus and the implications of these events for his readers and others. He also includes exhortation (called *paraenesis*) concerning the obligations of this relationship. This was the counterpart of the behavioral advice given by rabbis.

Paul's correspondence is not very carefully patterned for literary effect. Where literary polish is evident (as in Phil. 2:6–11), it is usually the result of inclusion of a sacred song from Christian worship. The letters read, not surprisingly, like letters; that is, like a conversation between persons who know each other. The Pauline letters show a refinement of this conversational style, especially when making points about the nature of the divine-human relationship, and Romans reflects a more carefully patterned structure, as we shall see. But we should not try to make the letters more literary than they are, for, in Greek, Paul was a master of the run-on, or life, sentence. The basic elements of Pauline letters can be outlined as follows:

Salutation (identification of sender and recipient and greeting)
Thanksgiving (prayer)
Body
Closing commands (paranaesis)
Conclusion (peace wish, greeting, kiss, benediction).

We should try to place ourselves within the context of the relationships, so that we can imagine what Paul is trying to say and why, and what his audience is hearing.

THE LETTERS OF PAUL IN CONTEXT

In our discussion of the letters we will combine literary and historical observations in an effort to understand the particular relationships forming the context of each letter. We have arranged the letters in the order of their most probably historical development.

First Thessalonians: Like a Thief in the Night

This is Paul's earliest surviving letter, which makes it a likely candidate for the oldest book in the New Testament. It was written about 50–51 C.E. to the church at Thessalonica, capital of Macedonia (in northern Greece), which Paul, Timothy, and Silas (Silvanus) had recently founded (see Acts 17:1–10), after Paul's imprisonment at Philippi (1 Th. 2:2). Paul had been forced to flee from Thessalonica (Acts 17:7), so he was naturally concerned about the well-being of the fledgling church. He sent Timothy to Thessalonica (1 Th. 3:1–10), and this letter is based on what he learned from his co-worker about the congregation and their concerns.

FIGURE 14–1

Suggested Dates for New Testament Writings
(Before 70 C.E.)

Date	Writing
50–52	1 and 2 Thessalonians
53–54	Galatians
54–55	1 Corinthians
55–56	2 Corinthians
56–57	Romans
58–60	Prison (Captivity) Letters of Paul (Philippians, Colossians, Philemon)

In his thanksgiving (1:2–10) Paul praises the Thessalonians for being an example to other believers (1:7) and hints at the themes he will develop in the letter—the validity of their ministry among other Thessalonians, the ethical implications of the gospel, and the coming again (parousia) of Jesus.

Apparently Timothy had brought word of opponents who challenged Paul's work, saying that he was motivated by guile and a desire for gain, for the Apostle mounts a vigorous defense of his work among them (2:1–16). Next he turns to what is bothering the Thessalonians (4:1—5:11). First, he exhorts them to "abstain from immorality" in order to attain "holiness" (4:1–8). Then he reassures them that those who have died before the parousia will be raised from the dead when Christ appears (4:17). But he cautions them against trying to determine exactly when this will happen, for Christ will come when he is least expected, "like a thief in the night" (5:2). Therefore, Christians should be ever ready, armed with faith and love (5:8). This apparently is to counter the view of some that they should sit back and wait passively for the end to come.

After a final exhortation to "respect those who labor among you" (5:12), "admonish the idle" (5:14), "rejoice always" (5:16), and not "quench the Spirit" (5:19), he closes with his typical blessing and a request to have the letter read to the whole church (5:27–28).

The letter is delicately balanced between encouragement and chastisement. Paul both applauds their exemplary faith and warns them about failure to respect his ministry and giving in to the vices of the world and laziness in the belief that the end is at hand. Paul makes use of apocalyptic imagery to describe his position on the parousia (4:16–17; 5:5), yet seems to reject the penchant to identify when the end will come, apparent in Daniel and other apocalyptic works.

Second Thessalonians: Stand Firm

Not all scholars agree on the date of this letter. Some think it was written shortly after (perhaps even before) the previous letter. Others argue it is not a Pauline letter at all but was written in the style of one and attributed to Paul after his time. Regardless, its major concerns—encouragement of the Thessalonians and correction of their understanding of the parousia—echo those of First Thessalonians.

Apparently a spurious letter has come to the Thessalonians claiming to be from Paul, saying that the day of the Lord has already come (2:2). In response, Paul lays out some specifics about the signs of the end that seem to contradict his teaching in First Thessalonians that the end will come unexpectedly. He says that before the end there will be a "rebellion" and a "son of perdition" who will occupy the Temple of God. He has not come because there is someone who is "restraining" him. When the "man of lawlessness" comes, many will be deceived. Paul gives thanks for the Thessalonians' faith and exhorts them to "stand firm." As in the first letter, his final exhortation relates to those who refuse to work, apparently believing that the end is near.

First Corinthians: Unity in the Spirit

Corinth was one of the most important cities of Greece. It was a wealthy port city, a commercial center where all the cultures and religions of the

Mediterranean world collided. Paul had established a church there, spending about a year and a half in the city. He worked principally among the poor. After leaving, Paul settled in Ephesus, across the Aegean Sea from Corinth. While there he wrote a letter (see 1 Cor. 5:9) that is now lost (or perhaps partly represented in 2 Cor. 6:4—7:1) in which he expressed concern about immoral behavior in the church. In response he received word that the church was perilously close to rupture because of rival factions within the community who made claims to have the only truth. He also received a letter from the congregation with questions about marriage, contact with the world, worship, the Resurrection, a collection for the church in Jerusalem, and a Christian teacher named Apollos who had followed Paul to Corinth.

First Corinthians is Paul's response to both the oral and the written correspondence. At the same time as he sent the letter by sea, he dispatched Timothy to act with an oral message by land (4:17). On the question of factions Paul urges the Corinthians to put aside dissensions and recognize that Christ is not divided (1:10—4:21). He reminds them of the gospel he preached,

> ...Christ crucified, a stumbling block to Jews and folly to Gentiles, but to those who are called, both Jews and Greeks, Christ the power of God and the wisdom of God. (1:23–24)

Although neither the Corinthian Christians nor Paul are wise or strong on worldly standards, God has chosen them both to show up the learned and powerful of the world. Factions are the result of their acting like "ordinary men" or, in Paul's vocabulary, "of the flesh" (3:3). Leaders like Paul and Apollos should be seen as "fellow workers" (3:9) in God's field, stewards of the "mysteries of God" (4:1). All the work of the leaders will be tested on the final day; it is not up to the Corinthians to judge.

A recurrent theme is the "unity" of the community. Paul uses the human body as a metaphor to describe the church as the "body of Christ" in which all are members though with various functions. Ideally, all work together for the common good. The parts of the body that seem the weakest are often the most indispensable (12:12–31). His concern about the ecstatic spiritual gifts, especially "speaking in tongues," is that this mysterious utterance be used to build up the community as much as other more intelligible gifts (14:1–12). According to Paul, the best way to unity is not through any of the various gifts, but through self-giving love, which he extols in his famous "Ode to Love" (1 Corinthians 13). Unity is also his concern when he condemns the Corinthians for turning the meal that commemorates the death of Jesus into a drunken orgy, making the problem of factions worse. Apparently the wealthier members would arrive early and consume too much, leaving nothing for the poorer members who came later. He reminds them of the instructions for observance of the meal and of its sacred significance that "I received from the LORD" (11:23).

In this letter Paul gives his clearest statement of his view of life after death. In keeping with his pharisaic roots, Paul affirms resurrection of the body at the last judgment. Perhaps influenced by Greek teaching on the immortality of the soul, the Corinthians have questioned Paul's teaching. Paul's vigorous defense shows how important he considered this teaching. In his view, if there is no resurrection from the dead, then Christ has not been raised, and if Christ has not been raised "your faith is futile" (15:17). But if Christ has been raised from the dead, this is the "first fruit" of the resurrection of all believers. Paul explains the resurrection by using the argument of different types of bodies, including the "spiritual" bodies of the resurrection. Only when the resurrection occurs will the final victory over death be won.

Second Corinthians: From Bitterness to Joy

The majority view of scholarly opinion today is that Second Corinthians is not one, but at least two letters editorially combined. The principal reason is a markedly different tone in Second Corinthians 10—13 from that of 1—9. We can also reconstruct a chain of events that accounts for two letters.

Upon Timothy's return to Ephesus, Paul learned that First Corinthians had failed to turn the community away from factionalism. Instead, new Christian missionaries hostile to Paul had come and made the situation worse (2 Cor. 11:1–15). In Paul's view these interlopers were "false apostles" (11:13) who preached "another Jesus" (11:4). They apparently performed "signs and wonders" to claim authority for their message, and they accused Paul of being forceful in his letters but inarticulate and uninspiring in person (10:10). Paul's response was to rush to Corinth himself, but it was by his admission a "painful visit" (2:1). He had been insulted (2:5–8; 7:12) and forced to leave in humiliation.

Against this background it is easy to understand the anguished and bitter tone of the letter he wrote in response (2:3–4, 9; 7:8–12). Most interpreters believe this letter is preserved at least in part in Second Corinthians 10—13, the "severe letter." Here Paul sarcastically attacks his opponents and boasts of his own apostleship. His defense of his Jewish background (11:21–22) suggests that the opponents are Jewish Christians. His claim of mystical experiences (12:1–10) implies that the opponents claim heavenly visions.

The response to the "severe letter," brought by Titus, was encouraging. The opponents had been dealt with and a chastened church had new zeal for Paul's leadership (7:6–7). Paul then sent them another letter (8:16–24), which also might very well be partially preserved in Second Corinthians 1—9. These chapters climax in an expression of joy by Paul at the restoration of his relationship with the church (7:2–16).

In this letter Paul develops his view of the "spiritual body," which he had mentioned in First Corinthians 15. He had spoken of the spiritual body that the faithful would inherit in the resurrection. He qualifies this position somewhat by speaking of a process of ongoing spiritual renewal (4:16—5:10) that begins in the earthly life, so that when the time comes to put on the "heavenly dwelling," "we may not be found naked" (5:3). This point of view relates to becoming a "new creation" in Christ, a concept he will develop in other letters, and taking up the "ministry of reconciliation" (5:16–21).

Galatians: "The Gospel Which Was Preached by Me"

The origin of this letter is disputed, although there is consensus that it is an authentically Pauline writing. The uncertainty surrounds the location of the recipients and the date of its writing. "Galatia" could either be the old tribal kingdom in north central Asia Minor or the Roman province further south. Wherever they were, Paul had started the Galatian churches when he was confined by sickness to the area (4:13). Because of similarity to the major themes of Romans, many scholars think it was written about 54 C.E., perhaps while Paul was at Ephesus. Other scholars date the letter to 48–49 C.E., making it the earliest extant Christian writing. This dating resolves apparent conflicts with the Book of Acts on the place of the Jerusalem Council in the Pauline chronology (see Acts 15).

The letter is a vigorous defense of the legitimacy and basic themes of the gospel Paul is proclaiming. However, his presentation is, as usual, shaped by the situation he is addressing. The situation in Galatia is grave, Paul feels. These churches have turned to a "different gospel" (1:6) from that which Paul had taught them. There is an urgent need to reaffirm the true gospel, which is from Jesus Christ, not man. So Paul dispenses with his typical flowery thanksgiving and instead begins abruptly. For several verses the words pour out and Paul's ire is painfully evident.

Apparently his opponents have accused Paul of preaching a message received from men, specifically the apostles in Jerusalem (1:16–17). In response Paul describes his dramatic encounter with Jesus Christ and his commissioning by God to preach to the Gentiles (1:11–24). His is not a gospel of men, but from God via his son Jesus. His apostleship was recognized by the Jerusalem apostles, and he was entrusted with the gospel to the uncircumcised (Gentiles), as Peter was entrusted with the gospel to the circumcised (Jews) (2:1–10). He intrudes an account of a confrontation with Peter over kosher customs that occurred earlier at Antioch, perhaps to underscore his own apostolic authority (2:11–14). He moves smoothly from his experience with Peter to a basic theme of the letter: "a man is not justified [made right with God] by works of the law but through faith in Jesus Christ" (2:16).

As we shall see when we turn to Romans, "justification by faith" is one of the key concepts in Paul's interpretation of the significance of Jesus Christ.

To the "foolish Galatians" Paul appeals to Scripture to defend "justification," by quoting Gen. 15:6, Hab. 2:4, and other proof texts. The true heirs of Abraham, he maintains, are not those who keep the law, but those who live by faith. That was already true in Abraham's time; now through Christ this truth is to be universally proclaimed. The law had a purpose, to restrain people (be a "custodian") until Christ came, opening to all the way of justification by faith. Christ's coming, Paul says, frees people from bondage to sin and the law and allows them to become sons of God, heirs of the promises made to Abraham. To make the point, Paul uses the allegorical method to interpret Scripture (4:21–31). Developing the theme of "freedom," he confronts the issue of whether being liberated from the law means license to do what the law forbids. He argues that freedom from the law leads to life in the Spirit, which is a life, not of gratifying physical desires, but of "love, joy, peace" (5:22–23).

From Paul's concerns we can assume that his opponent(s) at Galatia had tried to convince the gentile Christian men that they must be circumcised in order to be heirs to the promises to Abraham in the Scriptures (see Gen. 17:9–14). Because this position was based on Scripture, Paul put to use his skills as an interpreter of the Bible to refute it. He also let his anger boil over (5:12).

In addition, some Galatian Christians were returning to worship of "elemental spirits of the universe" and to observance of pagan festivals (4:9–10). Paul appeals to the trust they once placed in him and begs them to listen to him and return to the true gospel.

Uncharacteristically, in the closing he signs his own name (6:11) and reiterates the basic themes of the letter in a postscript (6:11–18).

Romans: The Power of God for the Salvation of All

Unlike Paul's other letters to churches, Romans was written to a church he had not founded himself. It was a church he had not even visited. So Romans does not read like the other correspondence. Missing are the answers to specific questions and the responses to particular problems. Paul wanted to enlist the support of the important Roman church in his planned mission to Spain. Because this is a "letter of introduction," it is a more carefully developed basic statement of Paul's understanding of the Gospel of Jesus Christ than we find in his other letters. It was probably not written until about 56–57 C.E., from Corinth, so it also reflects a maturing of Paul's thought.

The general nature of Romans should not be overemphasized. Paul was certainly aware of the dynamics of the Roman church, and his message to them is shaped by that church's situation. In particular, Paul knew of the disputes between Jewish and gentile Christians in the Church. The Jewish Christians would have emphasized observance of the commandments of the Torah, while the gentile Christians (who were in the majority) would have stressed freedom from these regulations and placed their emphasis on faith in Christ. The Jewish Christians would have labeled certain gentile practices immoral, and the Gentiles would have considered the Jewish members of the church overscrupulous and too wedded to the traditions of the past. In Romans, Paul addresses this conflict.

Paul begins his letter with an expanded greeting (1:1–6), to establish his right to communicate with the Romans (he is an apostle to *all* the nations) and his basic understanding of the Gospel of Jesus Christ (of Davidic ancestry, Jesus was designated Son of God by the power of the Resurrection). The thanksgiving (1:8–15) includes a petition that he and the Romans may be "mutually encouraged by each other's faith" (1:12).

In 1:16–17 Paul in effect states the theme of the letter. He will demonstrate to the Romans that the gospel is the "power of God for salvation to every one who has faith, to the Jew first and also to the Greek." In Paul's world there are only two types of people: Jews and others (Greeks). Thus, in Romans he will make clear that everyone (Jew and Greek) with faith (trust) in the power of God will have salvation (be delivered from that which holds them in bondage). He will show how God's power for salvation has been made available—to the Jew first and then to everyone else—through faith and what it is that holds everyone in bondage. Through the gospel the "righteousness of God" (a state of harmony in which there is a proper relationship between God and mankind) is made available through faith.

First, why is salvation needed by "every one"? In 1:18—3:20 Paul states his understanding of the fundamental human dilemma. Through the creation, God has revealed himself to all mankind, but to no avail. For humans fail to honor the God they instinctively know. All are aware of the proper way to live to honor God. Gentiles have an inner law written on their hearts (conscience), and Jews have the revealed law (Torah). The basic problem is that "both Jews and Greeks are under the power of sin" (3:9). This Paul substantiates with a list of no less than seven quotations from the Tanak. His conclusion is that, "no human being will be justified in his [God's] sight by works of the law, since through the law comes knowledge of sin" (3:20). For Paul, sin is an insidious force, whose power thwarts the human ability to live as God intends (according to the natural or revealed law). Because of sin, a proper relationship between God and mankind is impossible.

If humans cannot justify themselves, how is a proper relationship with God possible? In 3:31—4:25 Paul explains that harmony with God is available as a free gift (by God's grace) through faith in Jesus Christ. For in Christ there is redemption (a buying back or ransoming of someone in bondage) through the expiation of his blood (the Crucifixion), seen as a sacrifice for sin, with the death of Christ wiping out the effect of sin on humanity. Thus the way is open to justification. Neither Jew nor Greek has cause to boast. The gospel is not a new innovation, according to Paul. Abraham, father of the Jews, through whom blessing was promised to all nations (Gen. 12:1–3), which makes him in a sense father of all nations, was justified by faith before he received the sign of the Jewish covenant, circumcision. Therefore, all who have faith are the true descendants of Abraham, not just the heirs of the Torah. Paul again shows his mastery of rabbinic methods of scriptural interpretation in Romans 4, with an extended commentary on Gen. 15:6.

Having established the necessity of the gospel and how it is accessible to all, Paul describes the consequences of "justification by faith" in 5:1—8:39. As one man's disobedience (Adam's) brought death, one man's righteousness (Jesus') leads to "acquittal and life for all" (5:18). Where sin increased, grace abounded all the more. Paul can hear the Romans asking whether this means Christians should keep on sinning so that grace will increase, and he preempts the question by developing the theme of "new life in Christ," which begins with baptism (symbolically dying with Christ and being raised with him). This "death" that leads to new life brings freedom from sin, replacing the bondage of sin with "righteousness for sanctification" (a harmony with God that leads naturally to ever greater devotion to him).

The new life also involves death to the law. This does not mean the law is evil. On the contrary, the law is holy. It is sin, Paul says, that dwells in my flesh (my human nature, which is not per se evil), making me incapable of following the law and doing good. When, by the grace of God received in faith, we are delivered from sin and death, we are also freed from having to try to follow the law, for instead we will act according to the Spirit of God, which dwells in us. By the Spirit we are God's children. The Spirit's regenerative power is present in all creation, which will, like God's children, be set free from its bondage (to decay, in the case of the natural world). In conclusion, Paul summarizes the gospel as he understands it and, in a rhetorical flourish, the consequences of the gospel (8:31–39).

In chapters 9—11 Paul turns to the problem his Jewish roots cannot let him avoid. Does his message not imply that God has turned his back on the unconditional promises he made to the nation Israel? Paul follows several lines of argument to explain what God is doing, buttressing his views with frequent biblical quotations: (1) he reiterates his contention that the true heirs of father Abraham are spiritual, not physical, descendants—those who live by faith; (2) he defends God's right to choose whomever he will; (3) the missing ingredient in Israel's response to God was the realization that righteousness is through faith, not works of the law; and (4) the Jewish failure to respond in faith is providential, for through the disobedience of Israel the door has been opened to the Gentiles. In any case, God has not rejected his people whom he foreknew (11:2). The time will come when "all Israel will be saved" (11:26), for the gifts and the call of God are irrevocable (11:29). In the meantime, gentile Christians, wild branches grafted onto the rootstock of Israel, are warned not to exalt themselves over their hosts. The paradox at the center of Paul's interpretation is that "God has consigned all men to disobedience, that he may have mercy on all" (11:32).

Moving to practical advice and exhortation (Romans 12—15), Paul echoes the body metaphor used in 1 Cor. 12:4–8. He urges respect for those civil leaders "to whom respect is due," saying that God creates governments. Human relationships should be guided by but one law: Love one another. He urges the strong in the community to respect the scruples of the weak and bear their burdens.

The letter closes with personal notes, greetings, and a benediction. The extended greetings in chapter 16 seem out of place in a letter to a church Paul has not yet visited. It may be that they were part of a different letter (to the Ephesians?) and were appended here editorially.

Philippians: My Joy Complete

Paul's letter to the Philippians is one of his "captivity letters" (as are Colossians, Philemon, and perhaps Ephesians). He wrote it either while in jail at Ephesus (before 55) or Rome (about 56–58 or 61–63). If written during his final imprisonment in Rome about 62, it is his last surviving letter.

Philippi was probably Paul's favorite church, as this letter implies (4:1). He was undoubtedly proud of it, because it was the first in Europe (Acts 16:11–45). It was the only community from which Paul accepted financial support. In contrast with the anger and bitterness he often felt in his relationship with others of his churches, Paul felt affection for the Philippians, which makes this his warmest letter.

When the Philippians received word that Paul was in jail, they sent Epaphroditus with money to aid him and to remain with him as a helper (4:18). When Epaphroditus became ill, Paul sent him back, perhaps with this letter (2:25–30).

The words that characterize the Apostle's mood throughout this letter are "rejoice" (1:18–19; 2:28; 3:1; 4:4; 4:10) and "joy" (1:4; 1:25; 2:2; 4:1). He "rejoices" knowing that whether he lives or dies, Christ will be honored through him. He rejoices that those who oppose him still proclaim Christ. He calls on the Philippians to "complete my joy" by living a life of humility, following the example of Christ. His exhortation is to "rejoice in the Lord" as he does. Even though he is in prison, Paul is confident about his present situation, for even in jail he is advancing the gospel.

In his call for unity and humility among the Philippians, Paul utilizes a Christian hymn (2:6–11) that (according to our own translation) speaks of

Christ as the "servant who though in the form of God emptied himself and took the likeness of man and was totally obedient, even to the point of dying on the cross. Therefore, God exalted him and gave him the name above every name—Lord."

While he rejoices, even in his opponents' preaching, Paul nonetheless has a word of caution about those who are misleading the Philippians. His joyful tone lapses as he denounces as "dogs" (3:2) those who "mutilate the flesh" (who insist that gentile men must be circumcised in order to be Christians), those who renounce the cross (3:18), and those whose god is their belly (who participate in the gluttonous rites of pagan, probably mystery religions, 3:19). It is difficult to see these oponents as one group, for some seem to argue for stricter observance of the Torah and others advocate self-indulgence.

For Paul, the process of salvation is not yet complete. His present sufferings are a sharing of the suffering of Christ, and they will ultimately lead to a sharing of Christ's glory (3:10–14). He is concerned that the Philippians not claim too much too soon in their faith, as a result of false teachers, and instead "imitate" him (3:15–17). Thus Paul stresses that whether in poverty or plenty he is content.

Philemon: No Longer a Slave

While he was in prison Paul met a fugitive slave named Onesimus. Paul converted him to the Christian faith and became his spiritual father (10). Apparently Onesimus had been the slave of a man named Philemon, who had become a Christian himself as a result of Paul's preaching (19). Onesimus had fled Philemon's home, taking money with him (18).

Paul writes to Philemon, not to instruct him, but to appeal to him out of love (8). Although Paul would like to keep Onesimus with him, he is sending him back to Philemon. His appeal is that Philemon receive him no longer as a slave but as a beloved brother (16). Paul appeals to his relationship with Philemon as a "partner" (a fellow servant of Christ), to receive Onesimus as he would receive Paul himself, and to charge any debt the slave owes "to my account."

Paul uniformly showed respect for the ordering of society. He did not challenge the institution of slavery. But he did direct a Christian slaveholder to a higher law, the law of love, which should cause him to forgive a runaway slave and accept him as a brother in Christ. This letter shows how Paul put into practice in a particular instance his belief that in Christ there is neither slave nor free person (Gal. 3:28).

If this letter was written during Paul's final imprisonment in Rome, it dates to 60–62 C.E. However, it could also have been written during another, earlier confinement.

Colossians: Christ Is All in All

In most of the Pauline letters, the Apostle focuses on the Crucifixion and Resurrection of Christ as the heart of the gospel. Paul stresses individual believers' conforming to the image of the one who gave himself fully for others that they might receive new life through Him.

In this letter to a church in a small town in Asia Minor, about 100 miles from Ephesus, Paul emphasizes another aspect of his understanding of who Christ is. To the Colossians, Paul writes that Christ is not merely the firstborn of believers, to whom obedience unto death opens the way to their salvation. He is also the firstborn of all creation. In fact, he is the goal of all creation, for "all things were created through him and for him" (1:16). This portrait of a "cosmic Christ" in whom "all things hold together" (1:17) adds a new dimension to the Pauline view of the nature of Christ and causes some scholars to question whether Paul really wrote Colossians.

The reason for appealing to this different understanding of Christ was the nature of the opposition in the Colossian church. Apparently, there had sprung up a group who worshiped the "elemental spirits of the universe" and taught an elaborate system of festivals and rules as to what believers must avoid, even to the point of injuring themselves, in order to attain "wisdom" (2:8, 20–23). This may have been an early form of Gnosticism, which taught that the world is under the control of spiritual powers hostile to God that must be placated if their influence is to be overcome. Gnostics believed that a redeemer had brought a true knowledge of God and that only those who purified themselves from this evil world and its powers would experience it.

Colossians challenges this teaching by attacking the "elemental spirits" themselves with a different understanding of the cosmos. The world has been brought into existence through Christ and continues to exist through him. There is no place for "elemental spirits." To be in Christ is to die to such beings (2:20) and to recognize any philosophy based on them as "empty deceit" (2:8). The true mysteries of the cosmos and knowledge are not in such speculation, but in Christ (2:2–3). Cleverly, Paul adopts the imagery of the teaching of his opponents and applies it to Christ (as the authors of the Tanak had done with the mythologies of their day).

As in Philippians, Paul again adapts an early Christian hymn (1:15–20) speaking about who Christ is. However, its theme is almost the opposite of the theme of the hymn in Phil. 2:6–11. There Christ was praised as the one who "emptied himself." Here Christ is praised as the one in whom "all the fullness of God was pleased to dwell" (1:19). "Fullness" is the Greek term *pleroma*, possibly a key Gnostic concept.

The exhortation to the Colossians (3:1—4:6) follows from this teaching. If they have died with Christ through baptism (2:12), then they should be concerned not with earthly matters (the rules and regulations opponents are teaching), but with living a life in Christ, reflecting a "new nature." The ethics of the new life focus, not on rituals and rules, but on the virtues of human relationships. Their ritual should be simple, teaching one another and singing sacred songs (3:16). In the exhortation Paul adapts a literary form typical of Hellenistic moral teaching—a list of virtues for ordinary people. Except for the references to "the LORD" there is nothing particularly Christian in them, although they are clearly adapted to the purposes of the letter.

A case can be made for challenging the traditional assumption that Paul wrote this letter, in part because it portrays a development of church offices beyond his time (1:7, 23, 25). However, an equally strong case can be made for the view that Paul did indeed write it. Unless and until clear evidence emerges to resolve the issue, the vote should probably go to the Apostle.

Ephesians: He Is Our Peace

Although the Letter of Paul to the Ephesians is similar in many respects to Colossians, it is also quite different, not only from that letter, but from any attributed to Paul. In terms of literary form, Ephesians is not an occasional letter like the rest of the Pauline correspondence. It is an *epistle,* that is, a general letter, which, instead of responding to particular concerns or opponents, develops a theme of its own. The greeting in the earliest known manuscripts is not even addressed to the Ephesians but to the "saints" in general. In its earliest form, Ephesians was probably an open letter addressed to no one church in particular.

The verbal parallels with Colossians are so pervasive (73 out of 155 verses) that many literary historians think Ephesians used Colossians as a source. Missing, however (except for 4:21, which is virtually the same as Col. 4:7), are the personal references and responses to specific opponents that make Colossians an occasional letter. Because of these many parallels with Colossians and other Pauline letters, some scholars feel that Ephesians was a sort of "cover letter" attached to the collected Pauline letters when they began to be circulated as a collection sometime toward the end of the first century. If this be the case, the letter may not have been written until 90–100 C.E. Others would identify it with the otherwise lost Letter to Laodicea (Col. 4:16).

The theme this epistle develops is that the unity of the cosmos through Christ (Ephesians 1—3) should be reflected in the unity of the church (Ephesians 4—6). Echoing Colossians, this letter asserts that the hidden mystery now revealed is that "things in heaven and things on earth" are united in Christ (1:10). To this it adds the Pauline view of "justification by faith" (2:5, 8–9), giving a rounded "introduction" to Paul's theology.

The letter looks upon the unity of Jews and Gentiles as an accomplished fact (2:11–12), utilizing a Christian hymn that begins

For he is our peace,
   who has made us both one,
and has broken down the dividing wall
   of hostility…(2:14)

This is the mystery of Christ now revealed (3:4–6). This "dividing wall" could be an allusion to the wall in the Jerusalem Temple that separated the Court of Israel from the Court of the Gentiles. It was physically destroyed in 70 C.E. According to this letter's interpretation of the hymn, it was symbolically destroyed when obedience to the Torah was abolished as a condition for being a part of God's people. Because division among Jews and Gentiles was an unsolved problem in Paul's time, its "resolution" implies a later era.

The theme of cosmic unity, now revealed in the unity of Jew and Gentile (that is, everyone) in Christ, leads smoothly to the exhortation. First there is an appeal for unity in the Church (4:1–16), where there is but "one LORD, one faith, one baptism" (4:5). Second, there is a call to live according to the "new nature," renouncing the ways of the Gentiles in favor of being "imitators of God" (4:17—5:20). Third, there will be unity in the home (5:21—6:9) if all live by the principle: "Be subject to one another out of reverence for Christ" (5:21). Finally, there will be victory in the battle against the "principalities and powers" of this world and the spiritual world (6:10–20), achieved by putting on the "whole armour of God" (6:11).

SUMMARY

Next to Jesus, the Apostle Paul is the most prominent character in the New Testament. He is a main figure in the Acts account of Christian origins. According to tradition he was the author of over half of the books of the New Testament.

In this chapter we assessed Paul's importance in the historical world of the New Testament and in subsequent history. We placed the Apostle in his original historical context, emphasizing the importance of his Pharisaic and Hellenistic background and his self-understanding as an Apostle of Jesus. We explained the difficulty of reconstructing the life of Paul. Instead of a detailed account of his life, we characterized his missionary work in general.

Our literary analysis began with the issue of whether the twenty-one letters in the New Testament should be considered literature. Most of them are occasional letters written in response to specific situations and to a particular audience. Others are more closely argued treatises intended for broader audiences. We suggested that the most fruitful literary approach to the occasional letters is to combine literary and historical observations in an effort to recreate the relationship between sender and recipient implied in the correspondence.

We treated those letters that are most likely authentically Pauline, following a likely chronological order of composition. This enabled us to see in general the development of Paul's thinking as he worked to spread the Christian message, but to respect the particular situation implied by each letter.

Interpreters disagree on the relevance of Paul's understanding of the meaning of Jesus for our age. In the following questions we will raise some of the more significant issues.

THE CONTEMPORARY WORLD:
QUESTIONS FOR DISCUSSION AND REFLECTION

1. Some interpreters call the Apostle Paul "the second founder of Christianity" (Jesus being the first). Evaluate this claim on the basis of your study of the historical Paul.

2. How do you think Paul's letters would be viewed if they, like the Dead Sea Scrolls, had not been found until recently, instead of being part of the New Testament?

3. Paul went through several "career changes" in his early life. He was a rabbinic student whether or not he was ever accredited as a rabbi, he became an agent for the High Priest, and he became a Christian apostle. If Paul were alive in our world today, how would he fare and what would he be doing?

4. Which of the teachings in Paul's letters do you find most compelling? Which do you have the most trouble with? Which seems most important for contemporary individuals? Which is out of step with the modern world?

5. Some interpreters appeal to Romans 13 in arguing that Christians should not work to change existing civil governments. How do you feel about this interpretation of what Paul was saying?

6. On the basis of Paul's instructions to first-century C.E. churches about the role of women (e.g., 1 Cor. 14:33b–36), some contemporary churches do not allow women to be ordained ministers or priests or to lead worship. How do you feel about this interpretation of what Paul was saying?

7. How is Paul's interpretation of the significance of the life, death, and resurrection of Jesus similar to and different from that in the Gospels?

If you note different interpretations, do you think Paul or the Gospels is the most relevant today?

8. Romans 1:18–27 often is cited in the discussion of biblical teaching about homosexuality. Discuss the passage and its relevance to contemporary debate about homosexuality and the rights of gay people.

CHAPTER 15

The Growing Church (The Pastoral and General Epistles, Hebrews, and the Revelation to John)

Photograph by the senior author

Armageddon. "The Mountain of Megiddo" was designated by the Revelation of John as the site of the climactic "final battle." This view from the ancient fortress of Megiddo is to the south, toward the mountain range that gave rise to the symbolism. Megiddo controlled the most strategic passes through this range and thus the main route of trade and conquest between Egypt and Mesopotamia. Many historic battles took place here.

INTRODUCTION

In this chapter we will continue the story of the developing Christian Church, in the period known to historians as the postapostolic era (70–125 C.E.) We will then survey the group of writings known as the Pastoral Epistles (First and Second Timothy and Titus) and the General (or Catholic) Epistles (James; First and Second Peter; First, Second, and Third John; and Jude). Although the Pastorals are attributed to Paul, there is a strong case for associating them with a later period. We will also examine the Letter to the Hebrews and the one apocalyptic book in the New Testament, the Revelation to John.

TOWARD A POSTAPOSTOLIC CHURCH (70–125 C.E.)

Internal Changes

Church tradition held from an early period that John the son of Zebedee was both the youngest of the Twelve Apostles and the last to die. Irenaeus of Lyon, a great Christian writer of the second century C.E., cited the eyewitness authority of Polycarp for John's residence at Ephesus in Asia Minor. Irenaeus seemed to imply that John died during the reign of Trajan (98–116). The fourth-century historian Eusebius says so explicitly. It really does not matter for our immediate purposes whether this tradition is totally accurate. It is in any case a clear reminder that, as the Church moved forward through time, there was an inevitable change in its form of organization and leadership. The apostles, unique in their authority because of their relationship to the Messiah-Christ, the bearers of treasured firsthand testimony to gospel events, inevitably had to pass from the scene. John's brother James died early on. Peter and Paul were martyred about 65. By the crisis of 70, four decades after the Crucifixion, the majority were probably gone. If one apostle survived to near the century's end, that would have been as remarkable as those two American architects of the Declaration of Independence, Jefferson and Adams, living until July 4, 1826, a half a century beyond the great event.

Loss of the apostles would not have been the only change. With the passage of time, less and less is heard of prophets in the Church. And some of what is heard is not favorable. The Pastoral Epistles reflect developments in Church offices beyond the data of Acts, First Corinthians, and Ephesians. The office of bishop became very significant (1 Tim. 3:1–7; Tit. 1:7–9). It is not clear whether the offices of bishop and elder were yet differentiated the way they eventually would be (1 Tim. 5:17–22; Tit. 1:5–9). The order of deacons had also apparently been regularized (1 Tim. 3:8–13).

Ignatius, who was martyred at Rome in 115, wrote letters to churches he knew or visited on his relatively leisurely journey to meet his destiny. Among other things, in his letters he urged fidelity to the bishops, who had received the authentic traditions from the apostles and who passed them on to true and faithful Christians. It appears from Ignatius's writings that by the early second century C.E., though the emergence of bishops over large areas, let alone a papacy or ecumenical patriarchate, remained a future development, the outline of the ministry in three orders (deacons, elders or priests, and bishops) was progressively defining itself. The bishop of each community was definitely the chief over the elders and deacons, as well as the laity, in Ignatius's view. This pattern would become the norm for most of Christendom thereafter.

The Teaching of the Twelve Apostles, also known by its Greek title, *Didache* (Teaching), is a church instruction book that probably emerged in Syria toward the end of the first century C.E. It expresses suspicion of itinerant prophets and suggests moral tests of their authenticity. Apparently, various sorts of crooks were exploiting the faithful. Of particular interest are the detailed instructions for executing such ritual actions as baptism and the regulations for ritual meals. These would strike many moderns as excessively meticulous. Some think that the first section of the document, a collection of moral teachings emphasizing the theme of "two ways, one of life and one of death," was the nucleus around which the remainder of the text was collected.

The gist of these data, and other facts that could be added, is that, in sociological terms, the Church was developing in a less charismatic, more bureaucratic direction. This should not be understood as a negative observation. Ideas and aspirations, however noble they might be, require institutional embodiment to survive beyond one generation, if indeed they make it that far on a spontaneous basis.

The Church and Judaism

Recent research suggests that the process leading to the ultimate divorce between the Church and traditional Judaism was much lengthier than was once supposed, and developed at different rates depending on local conditions and the particular communities involved. Paul's letters reflect a situation in which Church and Synagogue had drifted some distance apart, but there remained a sense of common relationship. By contrast, the Gospel of Matthew, while recognizing the historical fact of Jesus' Jewishness and the Jewish context of gospel events, reveals substantial hostility toward the pharisaic rabbinic leadership of post-70 Israel. The friction is not over theology (Matthew recognizes the validity of the "law and prophets"), but over ultimate authority. The "Christian rabbinate" of the Matthean circle challenged the rabbinate of traditional Judaism while recognizing their right to "sit in Moses' seat." Meanwhile, the Johannine circle adopted the Samaritan term *the Jews* to reject traditional Jewish authority.

At the official level, the 30s of the second century C.E. probably mark the break in a great part of the Roman world. Still, a sort of symbiotic relationship may have continued. Some historians suggest that, up to the fourth century, Christianity only took root in those parts of the Roman empire where Jewish communities already existed. And in the Jewish home-land, coexistence, if not cordiality, was the rule in parts of Galilee well into the Byzantine period between various mixtures of Jewish and Gentile Chris-tians and more traditional Jews. But this carries us well beyond the purview of this book.

Rabbi Gamaliel II, while leader of the major academy of rabbinic Judaism, attempted to deal with the problem of deviancy (Christian and otherwise) in a manner worthy of his distinguished namesake (Acts 5:34–39). He enacted the addition of a nineteenth prayer to the Eighteen Benedictions, the prayers that, along with the Shema (Dt. 6:4–5), constitute the core of the synagogal liturgy. It is sometimes called the *exclusionary benediction*. It prays, "For apostates may there be no hope, and may the Nazareans and the deviants suddenly perish." No Christian, Samaritan, or other deviant could lead in prayer or, in good conscience, worship with a congregation where such a curse was part of the liturgy. Thus in a skillfully nonviolent manner such potential troublemakers were excluded.

Such nonviolent solutions were not to be found during the time of the Jewish revolutionary Simeon bar Cocheba, who accepted messianic acclaim for himself. During his abortive uprising, the Second Jewish War with Rome (132–135), devotees of other messiahs were given a simple choice: Recant or die. Christians were not the only skeptics where Simeon's claims were concerned, and they were thus not the only non-Roman victims of his wrath. But they were the advocates of a countermessiah and thus objects of special attention. Following Simeon's defeat and death, and the widespread ruin that befell Judah as a consequence, Christians had their revenge, mocking the catastrophes produced by false messiahs.

The Church and Rome

Difficulties with the Roman administration also increased with the passage of time. We noted earlier that the Romans had originally regarded the first Christians as simply more Jews, which most of them were. Frictions between Christians and traditional Jews were likely to be seen as "domestic quarrels." But as Christians grew more numerous, and gentile converts came to outnumber Jewish adherents by a growing percentage, such confusion was no longer possible.

Although some historians have tried to find in Roman law the reasons why the government began to pay more attention to the Church, the simple fact is that the Christians were probably regarded as up to no good, whether or not they violated any specific legislation. Those officials who took time to investigate usually came to the conclusion that these Christians were a bit daft, but not dangerous.

Christians were objects of prejudice, which inclined the government against them. From the standpoint of the conservative aristocrats who occupied many of the seats of power in the Roman world, they were an oriental import, and that was damning enough. The satirist Juvenal exclaimed, "The Orontes [a river near Antioch, where Christians first emerged outside the homeland] has emptied into the Tiber [in Rome]." At least metaphorically, he held his nose.

Street gossip accused both Jews and Christians of atheism, because they had no images in their shrines. Christians were alleged to worship an ass. They were also alleged to be cannibals, no doubt a garbled understanding of the Lord's Supper. Such popular prejudice tends to encourage and justify official repression.

Still, the reaction of Roman officialdom was not generally vicious. Trajan, one of the legendary "good" emperors, endorsed the policy followed by Pliny the Younger of not seeking Christians out but of dealing with them if they were accused before him or one of his officials.

On one point devout Christians were obdurate in their resistance to Roman policy. This was the cult of the divine emperor. Actually, the emperor cult was a bit of an anomaly. Augustus had built a temple to the Divine Julius in the Forum, but his uncle and patron was long-since dead. The cult of the emperor was more popular in the provinces than in Rome itself. Augustus himself was honored with provincial shrines, and Claudius had a temple dedicated to him, the podium of which still supports the medieval castle at Colchester, in England. Caligula, his predecessor, had insisted on divine honors and claimed to be Zeus. The emperor cult enjoyed its greatest popularity in those provinces with a history of divine kingship, particularly in the eastern Mediterranean. And these were the areas where Christianity had a substantial foothold.

To most inhabitants of the empire, accustomed to polytheism, the offering of a pinch of incense to the emperor was an act as innocuous as saluting the flag today. Not so to Christians. And their refusal elicited a reaction not unlike a public refusal to salute the flag today. Their loyalty was under heavy suspicion. Despite the opportunities to be persecuted, and the Church's honoring of its victims, Christians were discouraged from seeking out persecution and martyrdom. The martyr's crown was a gift to be received with joy, but if one went out of the way to get martyred, it did not count.

Other changes were occasioned by a shift in the apocalyptic orientation of the Church. From its foundation, Christianity had been more charismatic and eschatological than rabbinic Judaism, because of the belief that the Messiah had come and would return soon to initiate the Kingdom of God on earth. This is not to say that all early Christian communities were whipped up in apocalyptic frenzy. Such sects are usually shortlived or experience a high rate of membership turnover, and neither seems to be true of early Christianity. Probably not all were quite as literal about apocalyptic symbolism as that. Almost certainly, though, many early Christians expected a relatively early return of the Messiah and the consummation of the Kingdom. Some may have perceived the First War with Rome as the messianic woes of common expectation, "the birth pangs of the Messiah," as they were called by the rabbis. In the aftermath of the war (after 70), the realization must have settled in with almost everyone that the Church might just be in business in this world for quite some time.

Religious movements that attract members of the lower orders of society to a more disciplined mode of life frequently have the effect of producing upward social mobility among their members. In the case of "personal improvement" cults, the effect is deliberate. But in most cases it is probably serendipitous, and in some cases, contrary to the wishes of the leaders. We have noted that the appeal of the Church in the Roman world was principally to the disenfranchised of the urban centers. But the Roman world was a prosperous world and one that had been experiencing extensive social change, an ideal environment for upward social mobility. Thus, it is likely that with the passage of time, not only did the Church attract more affluent members, but it also moved up in the world with the improved condition of its previous members, which would render membership more palatable to persons of higher status.

No less a person than Augustus had legislated against social mobility, especially the rights of freedmen (freed slaves), who were often persons of talent and enterprise. The two older aristocratic orders of the city of Rome, the senatorial class at the top and the equestrian class immediately beneath, were not destined to restrain the tide. The conflicts accompanying the demise of the Republic and the rise of the Empire, the savaging of the aristocrats by the more eccentric emperors of the Julio-Claudian line, and subsequent upheavals must have exacted a substantial cost. Further, the demands of administration in the complex world of empire were such that a man who might occupy a seat in the Senate, live in a big house, or look good on a horse was completely beyond his depth. The recruitment of the provincial nobility, who of course remained persons of note if they were not expropriated by the Romans as an allied class, some of whose members were ultimately elevated to the equestrian or senatorial rank in Rome itself, was not adequate to stem the inevitable.

Beneath the aristocracy in Rome were the plebians (the local proletariat), freedmen, and slaves. The latter two groups, gathered by Rome's conquests, were particular repositories of talent. The most gross of all the gross characters in Petronius's *Satyricon* (dating from the age of Nero) was a noveau riche old freedman who was also the wealthiest character in the story. Other denizens of the lower ranks (again, especially freedmen) made their way upward by proven ability as administrators in the machinery of

---

FIGURE 15–1

Events Related to the New Testament After 70 C.E.

Date	Event	Roman Emperor
70	Temple destroyed Major Rabbinic Academy and 　Sanhedrin at Yavneh (Jamnia)	Vespasian (69–79)
		Titus (79–81) Domitian (81–96) Nerva (96–98)
	Some persecution of Christians	Trajan (98–116)
107 (?)	Martyrdom of Ignatius	
132–135	Jewish Revolt of Bar Cocheba Rabbinic Academy moves from 　Yavneh to Ussha	Hadrian (117–138)

Suggested Dates for New Testament and Other Christian Writings After 70 C.E.

68–70	Mark
75–100	Ephesians
85–100	Matthew
85–100	Luke-Acts
90–100	John (Gospel)
90–95	First Peter
90–95	Hebrews
90–95	Revelation
90–110	Letters of John
90–100	James
95	First Clement
100–130	Didache
100–130	Pastoral Epistles
100–140	Shepherd of Hermas
110–117	Epistles of Ignatius
110–130	Jude
130–150	Second Peter

empire. And what was true in Rome was also true in the provinces. The introduction of new blood into the higher orders, by wealth or by title, and the introduction of foreigners into the official aristocracy probably made it easier for Christians and others who would have been objects of contempt to Cicero or Tacitus to rise to very high status, which made it easier for others who enjoyed similar backgrounds to join them. But in the last analysis it was Christianity's mass appeal that led Constantine to conclude that it was the perfect element to supply coherence to an empire.

The Outcome

It is probable that most of the books of the New Testament had been completed by 100, and all of them by 150. Hadrian, whose plan to rebuild Jerusalem as a pagan Roman city helped to touch off the Second Jewish War with Rome (132–135), had succeeded Trajan as emperor. The apostles had passed from the scene, replaced by an increasingly ordered ministry under the bishops. Clement of Rome and Ignatius of Antioch in their writings pointed toward the new class of gentile Christian intellectuals. In the second century these would include the troublesome Marcion; the immensely influential Tertullian, whose dogmatic tendencies ultimately led him into heresy; and such champions of orthodoxy (as they understood it) as Justin Martyr, Irenaeus, and Clement of Alexandria. By the end of the second century, the main part of the New Testament canon would be established. That is an appropriate point at which to draw the line in this historical survey.

THE PASTORAL EPISTLES: BE STRONG IN THE FAITH

The Letters to Timothy and the Letter to Titus are attributed to Paul and included in the canon (with Philemon) as Pauline letters to individuals (after the letters to churches). These letters are usually called the *Pastoral Epistles* because they express pastoral concern for the well-being of churches and their leaders. They are similar in structure. After compact introductions and before brief conclusions, the bodies of the letters consist mostly of warnings against false teachers and advice on the organization of the churches.

Because the letters differ markedly from other Pauline letters in vocabulary, style, and mood, and especially because of the developed church structure the letters imply (bishops, elders, and deacons), they were almost certainly not written by Paul himself. Rather, they were written by a person or persons appealing to the authority of the Apostle to deal with general developments among Christian churches in the period after 70 C.E. By their being addressed to companions of Paul, the literary device of pseudonymity (writing in the name and spirit of some earlier figure) is given greater plausibility. "Timothy" and "Titus" are effective symbols of church leaders trying to preserve the traditions of the past in a new situation. "Paul" is the voice of apostolic authority in a postapostolic age.

These letters are not personal, despite their personal addresses and isolated references. They are general tracts written in response to the problems of a growing church.

First Timothy

This epistle takes up the problem of false doctrine focused on "myths and endless genealogies" (1:4), suggesting the gnostic view of hierarchies of spiritual beings with which humans must cope. Either the same, or other, teachers distorted the Jewish law (1:6–11). Like the troublemakers of Colossians, they practiced various forms of abstinence (4:1–3). To counter this false teaching, "Timothy" is to be an example and teach the true doctrine he has received (4:6–16). He is to be guardian of the faith entrusted to him (6:20–21).

To serve as a "pillar of the truth" there must be a well-ordered Church with officers—bishops, elders, and deacons are here mentioned—who live exemplary lives. And the various types of church members—such as widows, slaves, masters, heads of household, and other women—must recognize their places and submit to the proper authority.

Second Timothy

Of the three pastorals, this letter is closest in tone to the authentic Pauline letters. Like the other pastorals, it focuses on false teaching and urges "Timothy" to be true to the faith he has received (3:14–15). However, it gives more of a sense of an actual relationship between sender and recipient.

The letter is written to urge "Timothy" to "rekindle the gift of God that is within you through the laying on of my hands" (1:6). He is urged to testify to Christ without shame (1:8–18) and be willing to suffer as a "good soldier of Christ Jesus" (2:1–13).

Two false teachers are named who teach that the Resurrection is past (and therefore salvation has been fully attained and we may "do what we please"). In particular, concern is expressed about "stupid, senseless controversies" which only breed dissension (2:23). In the final age there will be great stress. Men will be "lovers of self" (3:2) practicing the form of religion while denying its power (3:5). People of "counterfeit faith" will mock the truth. They are to be avoided.

To combat error, "Timothy" is urged to attend to "the sacred writings [Hebrew Scriptures] which are able to instruct you for salvation through faith in Christ Jesus" (3:15). This suggests that a more formal attitude toward Scripture was developing both in Jewish and Christian circles.

The letter ends with a personal note (4:6–8) and greetings (4:9–18), which give it a realistic tone.

Titus

According to this letter, after accompanying Paul (Gal. 2:1, 3; 2 Cor. 8:6), Titus was entrusted with the organization of a church on the island of Crete (1:5). However, like "Timothy," "Titus" is probably a symbol for the *church leader* in general.

As in First Timothy, the two concerns of this letter are church order (elders and bishops) and false teachers. It is frustrating to church historians that, as in First Timothy, the focus is less on what these officers did than the moral qualifications for those who serve. Here, the two names seem to describe the same position, suggesting a stage in the growth of the Church when they were not clearly separated. Bishops, at least, are to be able to give instruction in "sound doctrine" by holding firm to what they have been taught.

The false teachers are variously described as "empty talkers," members of the "circumcision party" (who insist that Gentiles must be circumcised before they can become Christians), and people who teach for base gain (1:10–11).

THE LETTER TO THE HEBREWS: CHRIST AS HIGH PRIEST AND MEDIATOR OF A NEW COVENANT

Except for an ending that reads like the closing of a Pauline letter (13:18–25), the Letter to the Hebrews makes no pretense of being a letter at all. It begins abruptly with a prologue stating the theme, then develops what may be the longest sustained argument in either the Old or New Testaments. Much of the argument is subsumed in two extended artistic allegories or typologies drawn from the Tanak, the figure of Melchizedek (Gen. 14:17–20; Psalm 110) and the priestly directions for the observance of Yom Kippur, the Day of Atonement (Lev. 16:6–34). The Platonic contrast between the heavenly realm of eternal realities and the physical world of transitory phenomena is also discussed. Much of this is reminiscent of the approach of the Jewish philosopher Philo and of later Alexandrian biblical interpretation. The author's Greek is, along with Luke's, the best in the New Testament. The rhetorical skills of Hebrews are similarly well-honed. All of this is quite un-Pauline, though later Christian tradition ascribed the "letter" to Paul at a time when an apostolic connection had become an essential factor in canonical credentials. The main body of the work makes no such claim.

The closing was probably appended by an editor, and it was probably classed as a "letter" simply because the great majority of other New Testament books are letters. In fact, it is a religious treatise or sermon that was written to encourage Jewish Christians who were on the verge of giving up on the Christian faith and returning to traditional Judaism. It mixes proclamations about Jesus with exhortations. It probably originated during the period when there was not yet a clear distinction of Church, Synagogue, and Temple or between Christianity and Judaism; perhaps even before the Temple was destroyed in 70 C.E.

The theme of Hebrews is the supremacy of God's revelation through his Son, "whom he appointed the heir of all things, through whom also he created the world. He reflects the glory of God and bears the very stamp of his nature, upholding the universe by his word of power." He is the heavenly priest who made "purification for sins" and is "superior to angels." In former days God spoke through prophets; in the "last days he has spoken to us by a Son" (1:1–4). With this imagery Hebrews relates Christ to the priestly tradition, the prophetic tradition, and the wisdom tradition. In each case Christ is superior to his precursor.

In subsequent sections, Hebrews supports these contentions with evidence to show that (1) Christ is superior to the angels (1:5—2:18); (2) he is superior to Moses (3:1–6); (3) Jesus is the great High Priest (4:14—9:10) who is in the line not of the Aaronid or Levitical priests but of the great Melchizedek (7:1—8:13); and (4) the sacrifice of Jesus on the cross is incomparably superior to the sacrifices at the Temple (9:11—10:18). Alongside the argument there are exhortations to renewed faithfulness, maturity in the faith, and endurance (2:1–4; 3:7—4:13; 6:1–20). The work ends with admonitions to constancy in faith and endurance (10:19–39; 12—13), supported by a listing of the Jewish heroes and heroines who exemplify living "by faith" (Hebrews 11), climaxing with Jesus "the pioneer and perfecter of our faith" (12:1–2).

To defend the assertion that Christ is superior to the angels, Hebrews begins with a list of seven quotations from the Old Testament, asking the rhetorical question, "For what angel did God ever say…?" After an exhortation to "pay the closer attention" to the message "declared at first by the Lord, and…attested to us by those who heard him" (cf. Lk. 1:2), Hebrews interprets Ps. 8:4–6 as a veiled reference to Christ, emphasizing the paradox that the one whom God made Lord over everything was "for a little while" (a translation that agrees with the LXX, but not the Hebrew, text of the Psalm) lower than the angels. This opens the way for a discussion of Christ's suffering, its saving purpose, and the necessity of Jesus' becoming human. We see here the early stages of theological reflection that ultimately led to the assertions of the two natures of Christ—fully divine and fully human.

Hebrews then introduces the phrase that dominates the treatise—Jesus as "high priest." In the organization of the Jerusalem Temple, the High Priest represented the people before God and God before the people. On the yearly

Day of Atonement (Yom Kippur), the High Priest entered the Holy of Holies with the blood of the atonement sacrifices, thus assuring God's pardon and the reconciliation of the people with God for another year (see Leviticus 16). This gave the High Priest a special role as mediator of the covenant between God and Israel and an aura of divinity that no other human shared. According to Hebrews, Jesus perfects both the human and the divine in the office of the High Priest. He is in the very image of God and has "passed through the heavens" (4:14); thus he is superior to any other in representing God to mankind. Yet, because of his humanity and his suffering, he is able to "sympathize with our weaknesses" (4:15).

Again Hebrews employs scriptural exposition to reflect on Jesus as a "new" High Priest. In the patriarchal narratives, a mysterious figure, Melchizedek, the priest-king of Salem (later Jerusalem) makes a brief appearance (Gen. 14:17–20). No ancestors or descendants for Melchizedek are named in the Genesis text. Psalm 110:4 names the Davidic king "a priest forever, after the order of Melchizedek." Hebrews uses both texts to argue that Jesus, the Davidic Messiah, is therefore an eternal priest, not in the line of the Israelite priests, the heirs of Levi, but after the order of the eternal priest, Melchizedek.

As an eternal priest, Jesus offered one sacrifice effective for all time. Thus the sacrifice of Jesus, not with the blood of animals but with his own blood, replaces the Temple ritual. Just as the covenant through Moses was ratified by blood, Jesus has become the mediator of a new covenant (9:15). The perfect priest has made one perfect offering in the perfect (heavenly) tabernacle. The assurance of what Jesus, the heavenly High Priest, has done should give the faithful confidence and hope even in the face of persecution.

Alongside the dualism of time (the limited duration of the earthly High Priest versus the eternal nature of the priesthood of Jesus), there is a dualism of space in Hebrews. The earthly Temple is a copy of the heavenly Temple where Jesus serves as High Priest. This distinction between seen and unseen, appearance and reality, material and spiritual, temporal and eternal might reflect the influence of Greek philosophical thought on Hebrews. However, as we have seen, dualism is a characteristic of the apocalyptic (and mystical) traditions that sprang up within Judaism itself. Although the polished Greek style of Hebrews suggests an author familiar with Hellenistic culture, there may have been a tendency to overemphasize the Greek nature of the writing. Like the writings of Philo, it exemplifies Hellenistic Jewish thought.

Adapting the Jewish practice of appealing to a catalog of heroes (see Sirach 44), Hebrews names men and women from the Tanak who were given promises by God but did not live to see them fulfilled (Hebrews 11). This illustrates the definition of faith as the "assurance of things hoped for, the conviction of things not seen" (11:1). The fulfillment was, Hebrews has shown, to come through Christ. This list of heroes and, above all, the example of Christ should inspire the faithful to "run with perseverance the race that is set before us" (12:1).

Balancing the positive assurances in Hebrews are stern warnings based on the analogy of what happened to those who ignored the old covenant (see 12:25–29).

THE GENERAL (CATHOLIC) EPISTLES:
FOR THE WHOLE CHURCH (James; First Peter; Jude;
Second Peter; First, Second, and Third John)

Several "letters" are grouped together because (except for Third John) they take the form of letters but are written to Christians in general, not to specific churches or individuals. In this context *catholic* refers to the *universal* church. Grouping them together is somewhat misleading, for, from a literary perspective, they are quite different. What they share is a relatively late time of origin in comparison with other New Testament writings. Because Second Peter probably used Jude as a source, we will consider Jude out of its canonical order, before Second Peter.

The Letter of James

A one-verse salutation (1:1) gives this writing the form of a letter from James to the "twelve tribes in the Dispersion." The reference is to the "new Israel," the Christian Church spread throughout the Mediterranean world. In fact, the work is an anthology of admonitions and observations on various topics, with no single theme. This style and its concern with wisdom (1:5; 3:1–18) place it within the tradition of the wisdom literature of the Tanak and Apocrypha and the Greek tradition of ethical exhortation. It includes the Greek literary device of diatribe (a dialogue between the writer and an imagined questioner) in 2:18–26 and 5:13–15.

Despite its attribution to James, the brother of Jesus and a leader of the Jerusalem church, the work makes almost no mention of Jesus or the gospel. It apparently presumes that its readers are already familiar with who Jesus is and the meaning of his coming and focuses instead on the question of how Christians ought to live. Its closest parallel in the New Testament is probably the Sermon on the Mount. Throughout, the tone is pragmatic. In contrast with the theological concerns of the Pauline letters, the Pastorals, and Hebrews, James is practical advice without much theological reflection. Jesus is, in fact, mentioned only twice in the work (1:1; 2:1), causing some to speculate that it was originally a non-Christian work adapted to a Christian setting.

Although there is no overarching unity to the collection, some topics receive repeated emphasis. In contrast to the Pauline stress on "justification by faith apart from works of the law," James observes that "faith by itself, if it has no works is dead" (2:17). Because James quotes the same passage from the Abraham story that Paul uses in Romans to defend "justification by faith" to support justification by works "and not by faith alone" (2:24; cf. Rom. 4:1–8), it is possible that this is a self-conscious response to a perceived overemphasis on faith that might have resulted from Paul's teaching. The contrast, however, in James is not really the same as in the Pauline correspondence. In James, faith means *belief*, and the contrast is between merely believing and acting on that belief. In Paul's letters, faith is trusting in God's grace revealed in Christ, and the contrast is between trying to attain justification, reconciliation with God, through one's own efforts (works) and recognizing that it is only by faith (confident trust) in God's power that anyone can be justified. For James it is not enough merely to hear the gospel; the hearer must act on the gospel, which James calls the "perfect law, the law of liberty" (1:25). Practically, James and Paul seek the same end.

What sort of works should Christians undertake? James emphasizes acts of compassion for the weak and poor as the essence of true religion (1:26–27; 2:15–16). The letter also stresses, in traditional wisdom fashion, restraint in speech and control of anger and the passions (1:19–20, 26; 3:1–12; 4:1–12). Like Ecclesiastes, James highlights the transcience of life (1:9–11). As in the prophets and the sayings of Jesus, there are warnings to the rich who oppress the poor (1:9–11; 5:1–6). James also counsels patience in the face of trials and sufferings, coining the phrase the "patience of Job" (1:2–4; 5:7–11). There is also advice on the practical benefits of prayer (1:5–8; 5:13–18). James advises Christians to keep themselves "unstained from the world" (1:27; 4:4–8).

It is difficult to determine a time of origin for a work like James. It could be an early response to misunderstood Pauline teaching or a later compilation.

First Peter

This work presents itself as a letter of the Apostle Peter, written from Rome (Babylon in 5:13 is a symbol for Rome; cf. Rev. 17:5, 9) to Christians in Asia Minor at a time of persecution. This means that it would have been written about 64–65 C.E., during Nero's persecution of the Christians in Rome. Many modern literary historians have questioned whether the letter originated with Peter at such an early date. The strategy of the letter, whoever wrote it, is to take a theological foundation stone, by reminding readers what God has done in Christ, and build on it with exhortations on how Christians are to live in the world. Some historians suggest that the letter was actually a baptismal sermon (see 3:21).

In the first section (1:13—2:10) readers are reminded of their having been "born anew to a living hope through the Resurrection of Jesus Christ"

(1:3). Thus, they are called to a new life of holiness. Structurally, 1:21–25 rounds off the first section by returning to the image of 1:3. This is the gospel the letter is proclaiming (1:25). On this basis the challenge is made to come to the "living stone" (Christ) and, like "living stones," be built into a spiritual house, a new Israel. The letter applies the imagery of the Sinai Covenant (Ex. 19:5–6) to the Church.

The next section (2:11—4:11) is an appeal to good conduct that even Gentiles (which has come to mean non-Christians, because the Church is the new Israel) will recognize as good (2:12). Like Paul in Romans 13, this letter counsels submission to the state. A recurrent theme in this section and throughout the letter is that endurance of unjust suffering at the hands of evil people is a necessity for Christians, and that through suffering they win God's approval, because they are following the example of Christ (2:20–23; cf. 1:6; 3:13–18; 4:1, 12–19; 5:10).

The final section (4:12—5:11) appears to be an afterthought or an addition after the letter has been ended (4:11). It reiterates the theme of enduring unjust suffering (4:12–19) but with the implication that it has already begun. The letter concludes with exhortations to the "elders among you" to lead through example, not domination (5:1–5).

Like Paul and Mark, First Peter reflects the apocalyptic view that the present age will end soon (4:7), and Christ will be revealed (1:7). During this time before the end, there will be persecutions that Christians must endure, but those who have been persecuted will receive a crown of glory (5:4). This apocalyptic perspective might help explain the enigmatic reference to Christ's preaching to the fallen angels who disobeyed at the time of Noah (3:19; cf. Gen. 6:1–4). This is a theme developed in such apocalyptic works as Enoch (where the fallen angels are the heavenly counterparts of earthly rulers). Because the apocalyptic perspective was popular early in the development of the New Testament, this may support an early dating for First Peter.

Jude

Presented in the form of a letter from Jude (the brother of James and Jesus; cf. Mk. 6:3) to Christians in general (v. 1), this work is a polemic against a group of false teachers who have made their way into the Church. Because the letter looks back on the time of the Apostles (v. 17), it is almost certainly pseudonymous, assigned to Jude to lend it authority. It probably was written in the early second century C.E.

The heretics are described only in general terms. They are immoral men who reject authority, spurn the angels (vv. 4, 8), and carouse during the "love feasts" (v. 12). It is possible that they were Gnostics who argued that, because they were liberated from the flesh, they were free to engage in any actions.

In good polemical style, Jude is more interested in denouncing these heretics than debating with them. Their wickedness merits the punishment inflicted on the Egyptians, the fallen angels, and Sodom and Gomorrah (vv. 5–7).

Jude alludes once directly (vv. 14–16) and twice indirectly (vv. 9, 13) to the Jewish apocalyptic works, the Assumption of Moses and Enoch. The heretics are so perverse that they revile angels (v. 8). The Assumption of Moses includes the midrash that when Moses died, Satan came to claim his body, and the angel Michael rebuked him, but not with a "reviling judgment." So not even Satan deserves the kind of abuse from a fellow angel that these mere mortals are directing against good angels. Enoch assures the judgment of the wicked when God appears at the end of history. The motif of fallen angels (v. 16) is also apocalyptic.

Second Peter

This "letter" is a manifesto against false teaching and a defense of the return of Christ despite the delay. After a stereotypical greeting from Peter to Christians in general (1:1–2), there are no more characteristics of the letter form. For several reasons, this letter is often judged the latest of all New Testament writings, possibly composed as late as around 140 C.E. It uses Jude vv. 4–16 as a source in 2:2–17. It seems to know the Pauline correspondence as a collection, equating it with "other scriptures" (3:15–16). It also quotes the synoptic account of the Transfiguration (1:17–18; cf. Mt. 17:1–8). It also knows First Peter (3:1).

A key motif is the "knowledge of God and of Jesus Christ" (1:2, 3, 5, 6, 8; 2:20; 3:18). The authentic "knowledge of God" is manifest in righteous living (1:3–11), while the claimed knowledge of the false teachers shows it is inauthentic because of the perverse behavior of those who claim to have it (2:20–22). Apparently, the false teachers Second Peter is concerned about, like those condemned in Jude, are Gnostics who claim to be purified from the world but are in fact entrapped in it through their immoral behavior. They apparently twist the letters of Paul to support their views (3:15–17). Quoting a proverb, Second Peter calls them dogs who return to their vomit (3:22).

The letter uses the device of a Petrine origin to give validity to its teaching, reminding readers that "we were eyewitnesses of his majesty" (1:16). Peter has had a mystical experience of true divinity every bit as powerful as the Gnostics claim to have had, and he teaches not licentiousness but purity.

The Gnostics would also have disputed the parousia, saying that the full revelation from Jesus had already come. So Second Peter reemphasizes the coming judgment by fire (3:7, 10). It will come in God's good time; its delay is so that more may repent and be saved (3:8–9). Christians must lead blameless lives so that they will be prepared when the new heaven and the new earth come.

Interestingly, Second Peter reflects the development of the canonical process. In quoting Jude, it purges all references to works outside the Hebrew canon, expunging the allusions to the Assumption of Moses and Enoch.

First John

This writing lacks even the pretense of being a letter, having no opening or closing greetings. Only the title, added later, claims that this is the first "letter" of John. It is actually a tract or sermon on the incarnation of Jesus, his coming in the flesh. Like a letter, it is written in the personal style of direct address (cf. 2:12–14, 26; 5:31). It may very well have been written to counter a teaching (called *docetism*, from the Greek word for "appear") that held that Jesus was fully divine, but only appeared to be human. This point of view was apparently associated with Gnostic forms of Christianity. The vocabulary, literary style, and theological perspective of this letter (and Second and Third John) are similar enough to those of the Fourth Gospel to cause many to conclude that the letters and the gospel came from the same author, or from the Johannine School. Although attributed to the Apostle John, it is now widely agreed that this is a pseudonymous claim. The actual author is unknown and the time of origin disputed, although the scholarly consensus favors the first decade of the second century C.E. Tradition holds that all the letters of "John" were written in Ephesus.

The tract moves between instruction and exhortation, with no apparent unity of structure. In the prologue (1:1–4; cf. Jn. 1:17), the Incarnation is affirmed, and a mood of closeness with the readers is established. Apparently the opponents have claimed that they are free from sin, for the tract begins by saying that those who claim not to have sinned are liars (1:5–10). The ultimate goal of Christian living is to avoid sin, but that is possible only by keeping the commandments of God. The opponents presumably thought they were liberated from such obedience.

The opponents are called antichrists, whose appearance shows that the end is near (2:18). The term *antichrist* is unique to the letters of John (1 Jn. 1:2, 18, 25; 4:3; 2 Jn. 7), but the idea of an opponent or opponents of God (or his Messiah) appearing as a prelude to the coming of the end is fairly common in Jewish and Christian apocalyptic writing. The teachers about whom First John is concerned show themselves to be the antichrists by their denial that Jesus is the Christ and that he has come in the flesh (that is, the Incarnation). These are the "children of the devil" who, in contrast with the "children of God," persist in sin and hatred toward fellow Christians.

In perhaps the most famous passage, First John challenges readers to "love one another; for love is of God, and he who loves is born of God and knows God. He who does not love does not know God; for God is love" (4:7–8).

Thus, the letter establishes a twofold test (summarized in 5:1–5) for distinguishing between truth and error—obedience to the commandments of God, which are centered in the command to love, and adherence to the true teaching that Jesus Christ has come in the flesh. The distinction is not only between truth and error, but also between life and death (5:12).

The dualism of the Gospel of John, between truth and error, life and death, the "world" and the believer, light and darkness, the spirit and the flesh is quite apparent throughout.

Second John

This writing claims to be a letter from one called "the Elder" to the "Elect Lady" (either the whole Church or a single church). All the thoughts of this letter echo First John: truth, love, following the commandments, the antichrist (false teachers who deny Jesus came in the flesh), eternal life. Here the "lady" is advised to deny membership in the Church to any who deny true "doctrine." This suggests the development of standards of belief in the Christian churches and, therefore, a rather late date.

Third John

Here "the Elder" writes to an individual (Gaius) on specific matters of church life. There are no references to the motifs of First and Second John (except for v. 11). The Elder commends Gaius for receiving hospitably traveling missionaries (perhaps in order to ensure a good reception for another, Demetrius, named in v. 12). He contrasts another leader, Diotrephes, who refuses to acknowledge "the Elder's" authority or receive his emissaries. Apparently, when this letter was written, lines of authority were not yet clearly established, and church leaders competed with one another.

There is evidence of a church leader named Elder John who lived sometime during the late first or early second centuries C.E. It is tempting to see him as the author of the Johannine letters (and perhaps the Gospel of John), but there is too little evidence to establish the connection with confidence.

THE REVELATION TO JOHN: WHAT MUST HAPPEN SOON

The Revelation to John is the one complete apocalyptic work in the New Testament. There are apocalyptic sections in other works (such as Mark 13 and the parallel chapters, Matthew 24 and Luke 21) and an apocalyptic mood in many of Paul's letters (especially First and Second Thessalonians) and other writings (Second Peter and Jude especially). But, like Daniel 7—12 in the Tanak, the Book of Revelation is a report of highly symbolic visions purporting to reveal the secrets of the end time to a seer.

In at least two respects, the Book of Revelation is unique in literary form. Superficially, it presents itself as a letter. After a prologue that makes clear its apocalyptic thrust, there is an opening greeting (1:4–6). In addition, the work closes with a benediction (22:21) similar to Pauline closings. The first full section is composed of "letters" to seven churches in Asia Minor (2:1—3:22).

Unlike most apocalyptic works, Revelation is not pseudonymous. The writer identifies himself as a man named John who had been exiled to the tiny Aegean island of Patmos because of his Christian faith (1:9). According to tradition this John was the son of Zebedee mentioned in the gospels. However, there is no internal evidence to support this assumption. Nor is there solid evidence for the view of some modern interpreters that the author was the John the Elder who lived in Ephesus around 100 C.E., as the early church historian Eusebius maintained. The fact is we do not know who "John" was. He obviously wrote during a time of persecution that he himself had experienced. He may have been banished during the persecution of the Emperor Domitian in 95 C.E. At this time Christians were under attack for their failure to worship the emperor as god, an act implied in Revelation 13. Finally, the work claims to reopen the tradition of prophecy (1:3; 22:6, 9, 19) that had been closed in rabbinic tradition. Like Isaiah (Isaiah 6), John's visions of heaven validate the message he is announcing. As in other prophetic works, the Word of God is received in the present and reveals what is about to unfold. The device of an ancient worthy who predicts the course of history up to the author's actual present time and beyond is not used.

The theme of Revelation is "Persevere!" The writer's visions reveal that the present evil epoch of history will end soon. Jesus will return. Although the forces of evil seem to prevail, they will be vanquished by the returned Messiah. After the final battle, a new age will begin. If the faithful continue to resist the powers trying to force them to compromise, they will be rewarded, as certainly as the evil will be punished. The impact of the visions as a whole is to assure the faithful that God has the course of history firmly in hand. His plan is for the judgment of evil and the reward of righteousness.

In keeping with apocalyptic style, the "action" of the visions is at the heavenly level, with the effects felt on earth. This results in graphic but cryptic imagery that only the "initiated" would be able to understand. It also makes the Book of Revelation an exceedingly rich and enigmatic piece of literature. The substance of the visions reflects imagery from a variety of canonical (Daniel, Ezekiel, Joel, Zechariah, and Jeremiah) and noncanonical sources. By the end of the first century C.E., the apocalyptic tradition had a large stock of symbols and images, and Revelation includes many of them.

It also reflects the liturgy of the early Christian Church, drawing on hymns and prayers probably current in Christian worship (e.g., 1:5–6; 4:8, 11; 5:9–10; 7:10, 12; 11:15, 17–18; 12:10–12; 15:3–4; 19:1–2, 5–8; 22:13).

The structure of Revelation is so complex it has inspired many varying and conflicting interpretations. As with other subtle and imaginative literary works, there may be a variety of structures at different levels. We have already observed the letter structure of the whole work and the first section. In the rest of the book, after introductory visions of the heavenly court (4:1—5:14) and before the epilogue, interpreters generally see seven (the perfect number) visions; (1) seven seals (6:1–8); (2) seven trumpets (8:7—11:19), (3) the Dragon's (Devil's) rule (12:1—13:18); (4) those who worship the Lamb (Christ) and those who honor the beast (14:1–20); (5) seven bowls of divine anger (15:1—16:21); (6) Babylon's (Rome's) fall (17:1—19:10); and (7) the end of Satan's power and the creation of a "new heaven and a new earth" (19:11—21:8).

The symbol of triumph over oppression in Judaism is the seven-branched lampstand, the *menorah*, which goes back to the time of Solomon's Temple (1 Kgs. 7:49; cf. Ex. 37:17–24). The menorah was particularly associated in later times with the festival of Hanukkah, which commemorates the rededication of the Jerusalem Temple in 164 B.C.E., at the end of the persecution of Antiochus Epiphanes. The menorah was a popular Jewish symbol during the first century C.E. Archaeologists have discovered menorahs in synagogues and as decorations in funerary contexts. Revelation may be a Christian menorah, symbolizing in its sevenfold structure the end of the persecution of the Church. The clue may be the several references to lampstands in Revelation (such as 1:12–13).

The seven churches to which John writes symbolize the whole Church. In general, the letters commend, exhort, and chastise, like the Pauline letters. However, in all the letters, John singles out from the churches the righteous few who will persevere in the face of persecution—like the prophetic "remnant." "He who has an ear let him hear…" is present in each letter, indicating that only a few get the message (2:7, 11, 17, 29; 3:6, 13, 22). The letters allude to those who "conquer" (2:7, 17, 26; 3:5, 12, 21), promising the blessings of the new age to them—eating of the tree of life (2:7); escaping the second death (2:11); receiving the hidden manna and a new name (2:17); power over the nations (2:26); the morning star (2:28); white robes (3:5); becoming a pillar in God's temple (3:12); and sitting with Christ on the throne (3:21).

Against this background, the visions that follow become a validation of the seer's authority to make these promises and a preview for those righteous few who have "ears to hear" of the rewards beyond the present and impending struggle.

Like others in the prophetic tradition (see First Kings 22, Isaiah 6, and Ezekiel 1), John speaks of being transported "in the Spirit" to the heavenly throne room, where he experiences directly the majesty of the Divine King surrounded by beings who glorify him with hymns (Revelation 4). Then he sees the slain Lamb (Christ), who has already conquered and who is worthy to open the scroll (containing the divine plan).

Then come the three sets of seven visions, with the seventh vision of the first two sets transitional to the next. Their imagery is much too complex to explore in detail here. Some of the more famous images are the "four horsemen," who symbolize warfare, slaughter, famine, and pestilence (6:1–8); the dragon (identified as Satan), described in imagery reminiscent of the beasts of chaos who oppose the Divine King in myths such as those found at Ugarit and Babylon (12:1–17); the beasts who do the dragon's bidding on earth (Revelation 13), one of whom is given the symbolic number 666 (13:18); and the drunken harlot (Revelation 17).

The demand for submission to the beast and the order that those refusing to worship the image of the beast are to be slain (13:15) strongly suggest the cult of the Roman emperor and the requirement that all in the empire pay homage to his statue. Not all emperors ordered such worship, as we have seen, so there are a limited number of circumstances available as a context for this demand.

The course of events as revealed in the subsequent visions is the reign of the beasts, followed by a series of disasters climaxing in the last great Battle of Armageddon (a Greek transliteration of the strategically located Mount Megiddo; see chap. 1). Then Babylon (Rome) will fall, Satan's forces will be defeated, and he will be thrown into the "pit" for a thousand years (the millennium), during which Christ and the martyrs will reign. Satan then will be loosed and defeated forever. There will be a final judgment, and death and Hades (the temporary abode of the dead) will be destroyed. This reflects the pattern of rabbinic eschatology in which "the days of the Messiah" prepare the way for "the world to come," the eternal kingdom. Thus, there will be a new heaven and a new earth in which God will "wipe away every tear from their eyes, and death shall be no more, neither shall there be mourning nor crying nor pain any more, for the former things have passed away" (21:4). Then John sees the heavenly Jerusalem coming to earth and the river of the water of life.

In the epilogue John is told *not* to seal up the words of this "prophecy," for the "time is near" (22:10). This contrasts with the instruction to Daniel to seal up his visions until the end (Dan. 12:4).

The enigmatic symbolism of the visions of Revelation has inspired persons in every generation, including the current one, to see their time as the end time prophesied by the seer. In any age, impressionable people can be led to read current events into the symbols of the visions. These interpreters are especially successful during times of high anxiety. Given the very real possibility of nuclear annihilation today, it is not surprising that many have sought reassurance through interpreting Revelation as an ancient, inspired prediction of what is happening now. The authors will leave it for readers to discuss and decide whether this type of interpretation, similar to the way in which the sectarians of the Qumran Community read the Hebrew prophets in the first century C.E., is a proper way to read Revelation in the closing decades of the twentieth century. The alternative is to read Revelation as a prophecy to persons living in the first century, announcing God's judgment on wickedness and reassuring the faithful of God's ultimate Lordship in history.

Regardless of its historical reference point, Revelation dramatizes a world in which the conflict between good and evil ends with the triumph of goodness. In any circumstances in which evil seems triumphant, it is reassuring to feel such a world can still be projected. Jewish victims of the Nazi Holocaust framed similar worlds. It is not surprising that visions like those of John, of Tolkien in *Lord of the Rings*, and of modern movies like *E.T.* and the *Star Wars* saga strike such a responsive chord among so many.

THE NEW TESTAMENT APOCRYPHA

There are a variety of early Christian writings that did not attain canonical status. Unlike the Old Testament Apocrypha (Deuterocanon), the New Testament Apocrypha is not considered canonical by any major contemporary branch of the Christian Church. This was not always the case. Most, if not all, of these writings were considered authoritative by the communities that preserved them. However, with one or two exceptions, none was ever considered a part of the canon by the larger Christian Church.[1]

Most of these writings reflect the same literary categories as the canonical books: gospels, letters, apostolic "acts," and apocalypses. Some seem to bridge these categories. Most were written later than, and were probably inspired by, the New Testament books, but a few probably contain traditions as old as any in the New Testament. Most are known to us by name only or are preserved in fragmentary form, sometimes through quotations in other documents. A relatively few are preserved complete. Rather recent discoveries (such as those found in 1946 at Nag Hammadi in Egypt)[2] have greatly increased the available texts; so there is a great deal of current study of these writings and the light they shed on the New Testament and Christian origins. We can only survey them very briefly here.

---

[1]Wilhelm Schneemelcher, *New Testament Apocrypha* (2 vols.), R. McL. Wiltson, ed., trans. A.J.B. Higgins and others (Philadelphia: Westminster, 1963, 1966).

[2]James M. Robinson, ed., *The Nag Hammadi Library in English* (New York: Harper & Row, Pub., 1987).

Gospels

The preface to Luke's gospel (1:1–4) implies the existence of many narratives about Jesus. Indeed, we know now of a number of other works presenting stories about him and collecting sayings attributed to him. Thus, they are gospels. (Unfortunately, some of the apocryphal works called gospels are not, while others that do not carry the title *gospel* are similar to the canonical gospels.) A recent study has identified sixteen important noncanonical gospels, including five collections of sayings of Jesus and eleven gospels telling stories about him. The former include the Gospel of Thomas, the Dialogue of the Savior, the Gospel of the Egyptians, Papyrus Oxyrhynchus 840, and the Apocryphon of James. The traditions of stories about Jesus include the Secret Gospel of Mark, Papyrus Egerton 2, the Gospel of Peter, the Gospel of the Hebrews, "John's Preaching of the Gospel," the Gospel of the Nazarenes, the Gospel of the Ebionites, the Protoevangelium of James, the Infancy Gospel of Thomas, the Epistula Apostolorum, and the Acts of Pilate.[3]

The Protoevangelium of James is actually more about the birth, infancy, and youth of Jesus' mother, Mary, than about Jesus himself. It is apparently the earliest (second to third century C.E.) witness to the doctrine of Mary's perpetual virginity, a notion alien to the Jewish world of the canonical Gospels but much treasured in the Hellenistic world.

Probably the most important noncanonical gospel is the Gospel of Thomas, a collection of sayings and parables attributed to Jesus, many of which are similar to sayings in the canonical gospels, but in a less edited, perhaps earlier, form. They claim to be "secret sayings" that Jesus spoke, which enable those who understand them to "not experience death." Although the Gospel of Thomas has been stereotyped as a gnostic gospel because of its concern with a saving knowledge Jesus taught, it may indeed preserve authentic sayings of Jesus which enhance our understanding of the historical Jesus and the composition of the gospels.

The apocryphal gospels that include stories generally offer incidents from the infancy of Jesus or his Passion and Resurrection. They seem on the whole to be imaginary elaborations of canonical traditions and lacking any value as authentic historical sources for the life of Jesus. They do, however, help us understand the variety of interpretations of Jesus that developed in the early Christian Church.

Other Works

There are a variety of "acts" of the Apostles among the apocryphal writings, such as the Acts of Paul, John, Peter, Andrew, and Thomas. They

---

[3]Ron Cameron, ed., *The Other Gospels: Non-Canonical Gospel Texts* (Philadelphia: Westminster, 1982).

typically describe the heroic activities of the Apostle and end with an account of his martyrdom.

Only a few letters are included among the works of the New Testament Apocrypha. Like some of the New Testament letters, most are tracts and treatises rather than actual correspondence.

There are apocalypses in which figures like Peter, Mary (the Mother of Jesus), James, Stephen, and Thomas are transported into the realms of heaven and hell to see the fate awaiting the faithful and the unbelievers. An Apocalypse of Paul was probably inspired by Paul's reference to the experience of being taken up into the "third heaven" (2 Cor. 12:2).

There has been prejudice even in modern scholarship about the value of these works as historical sources. Indeed, many *are* fanciful writings. The story in the Infancy Gospel of Thomas describing Jesus as a child making clay sparrows on the Sabbath, then commanding them to fly away when he is chastized for playing on the Sabbath, hardly sounds realistic. However, each writing should, and now is, being carefully studied by itself to determine its value as a source for early Christian piety. Studies are also needed of the literary worlds of these writings.

In addition to the works classified as *New Testament Apocrypha*, some other writings of the early Christian Church were close to the New Testament both chronologically and in terms of their importance for the Christian community. A few were apparently considered canonical for a time. For example, one of the best ancient New Testament manuscripts (the *Codex Sinaiticus*) includes the Shepherd of Hermas (a visionary composition). Hermas was so popular that some scholars think it would have achieved canonical status were it not so clearly post-apostolic. Hermas, the Didache (Teaching of the Twelve Apostles, a manual of church discipline), and the Epistle of Barnabas (a moral treatise purportedly written by Paul's traveling companion) appear alongside the canonical works, in an index. The early church leader Clement of Alexandria considered the Didache canonical. Indeed, it may preserve traditions dating to the apostolic age.

SUMMARY

In this chapter we completed our historical overview of the New Testament period with a description of the postapostolic era (70–125 C.E.). We discussed the significance of the passing from the scene of the original apostles and the growing institutionalization of the church. We also reflected on the growing split between Christians and Jews during this period and the treatment of Christians by Roman authorities.

Although attributed to Paul, the Pastoral Epistles (First Timothy, Second Timothy, and Titus) reflect the postapostolic situation, especially the more complex church structure. The majority view in modern scholarship is that attributing authorship to Paul and identifying the recipients as young colleagues of Paul was a literary device used to heighten their authority. While they certainly reflect a Pauline perspective, they probably were written by followers of the Apostle after his death. The Pastorals give advice on church leadership and warn against false teachers.

The Letter to the Hebrews is actually a religious treatise directed to Jewish Christians who are faltering in their newly proclaimed Christian faith. Drawing astutely on Hellenistic philosophy and biblical interpretation, the anonymous author of Hebrews skillfully crafted a defense of the superiority of Christ to the angels, Moses, the priesthood and high priest, and Temple sacrifices.

The catholic (general) epistles are a group of compositions of various literary styles, considered together because they are by tradition directed to no one church, but to the universal (i.e., catholic) church. James is the New Testament example of a Wisdom book. It is an anthology of advice and observations, attributed to James, the brother of Jesus. Its most frequent theme is putting faith into practice by caring for the poor and hungry. The two letters attributed to Peter and a Letter of Jude (another brother of Jesus) concern themselves with Christian conduct and false teaching. Three short letters of John may come from the same school or tradition in which the Gospel of John originated.

The last book of the New Testament is its one fully apocalyptic work—the Revelation to John. Our treatment explained its unique literary form, touched on the question of authorship, speculated on the basic theme and structure of the work, and highlighted some of the more intriguing sections of this enigmatic writing. We left open for your discussion the question of how the fantastic visions of Revelation relate to our world.

The chapter concluded with a brief overview of early Christian writings not included in the New Testament canon.

Having completed this journey into the literary and historical worlds of the Bible and having reflected on and perhaps discussed issues in the contemporary world of the Bible, what are your main impressions? Has the journey been exciting, challenging, confusing, enlightening?

In the final chapter we will discuss in general how the Bible has impacted our world. We suggest that before reading Chapter 16 you consider how the Bible and this study of it has affected you.

THE CONTEMPORARY WORLD:
QUESTIONS FOR DISCUSSION AND REFLECTION

1. According to some interpreters, the Book of Revelation should be seen as a prediction of events taking place now. This is similar to the way the Dead Sea community read the prophets, like tomorrow's newspa-

per. How does the analysis in this chapter affect your view of this type of interpretation?

2. We have noted that pseudonymity was not regarded as fraudulent in antiquity. The purposes of pseudonymous writings were often to promote the goals of the earlier worthy, as in the Pastoral Epistles. Modern writers sometimes do the same thing by making historical persons characters in novels, plays, or movies. If you were going to assume the role of Paul, Peter, James, or John in the modern world, what art form or medium would you select and what ideas would you emphasize? How would you state them?

3. The early Church criterion for including a work in what became the New Testament canon was apparently that it contained the apostolic testimony, not necessarily that it was *written* by an apostle (though the notion of apostolic authorship later became important). Do you know any modern books (or record albums, or films) that seem to embody apostolic testimony that you would offer as candidates for inclusion in an enlarged New Testament canon? (For instance, some would argue for certain writings of C. S. Lewis, Tolkien's *Lord of the Rings*, etc.).

CHAPTER 16

Journey On!

The Annunciation. The story of the Annunciation (Luke 1:26–38) has been a favorite theme of artists through the centuries. The modern American painter Henry O. Tanner (1859–1937) registered the psychological complexity of the situation: an innocent, young, unmarried woman called to the hazardous role of queen mother in a revolutionary regime. Tanner's madonna shows a mixture of awe and skepticism. And how *does* one picture an archangel?

We began this journey into the three worlds of the Bible by suggesting the metaphor of a student going abroad to study. The modern reader venturing into the historical and literary worlds of the Bible is like the student who studies in a foreign country. Having completed this study, you (like the student who has gone abroad for a term) should now have a basic familiarity with the territory. You are ready to move on toward more advanced investigations, perhaps at some point even to become a tour guide yourself! In the bibliography we offer you a few suggestions on how to continue your journey into the literary and historical worlds.

If our discussion questions have done their intended job, you will not only understand the first two biblical worlds better, but will also have begun to develop a sensitivity to the variety of ways that the Bible enters into the world of modern experience. We will end our discussion of the three biblical worlds by suggesting ways in which you might explore the impact of the Bible on the values, institutions, and culture of Western civilization in general and the United States in particular.

The most obvious way in which the Bible impacts upon the modern world (in the West and beyond) is as the Scripture of Judaism and Christianity. No study of these religions, or any particular segment of them, is complete without attention to the way in which the Bible functions in shaping the life, teaching, and worship of their various communities. For example, what is the role of the Tanak in Reformed Jewish settings in comparison with its function in Conservative or Orthodox Jewish communities? Or, how is the Bible used in a Roman Catholic mass in comparison with its function in a Baptist revival? Every minute of every day the Bible is being read, studied, taught, and used in religious contexts. It is virtually impossible to overestimate its importance within the religious communities that honor its authority, although there is widespread disagreement on the nature of that authority.

However, the Bible shapes the contemporary world in many other ways beyond the groups that consider it canonical. For example, the impact of the Bible on Western law and government is so pervasive that most people do not realize it. The principle that governments are of laws, not men, upon which Western European and American societies are based, is biblical. According to the Bible, God, and not any human ruler, is the source of laws. Even kings and emperors cannot ignore the law, as King David learned. Although secularized, the principle that no one is above the law is a fundamental premise of Western legal systems.

Another biblical principle pervading our system of values in the West is the worth and dignity of the individual. It is rooted in the view of human life expressed in the first chapter of Genesis and reaffirmed throughout the rest of the Tanak and the New Testament. Other social systems put the highest value on the good of the entire society, at the expense of the rights, freedom, and sometimes the life of the individual or on the well-being of some privileged elite. Although individuals are not permitted to compromise the common good for their own advantage, Western societies reflect a commitment to the worth and dignity of the individual citizen that traces ultimately to the Bible. In the latter part of the twentieth century, liberation movements throughout the world have been inspired by the Bible's special concern for the poor and oppressed.

The impact of the Bible on Western art is also almost incalculable. A visitor to any major art museum in the world will be struck at once by the substantial amount of art based on biblical themes. Much of this, like Michelangelo's famed rendition of creation on the ceiling of the Sistine Chapel at the Vatican in Rome, was executed for religious leaders or houses of worship. Some of it still is. But the great themes themselves seem to challenge the artistic imagination.

The stained-glass windows of Marc Chagall in a small synagogue at the Hadassah Hospital, Jerusalem, bring the poetic language of Genesis 49 and Deuteronomy 33 to life in images that speak in the mystical accents of eastern European Hasidic Judaism. A poignant realism informs the American artist Edward Tanner's *Annunciation*, now in the Philadelphia art museum (see page 345). The British artist Edwina Sandys, a granddaughter of Winston Churchill, has sculpted a twentieth-century feminist version of the Crucifixion entitled *Christa*, with a female body. It is an interpretive work inspired by issues of our day. The point is that painters and sculptors today continue to draw from the rich reservoir of biblical images in the styles and with the meanings to which the present age points.

The Bible has also inspired some of the most memorable musical creations in history. To cite but one familiar example, the entire text of Handel's *Messiah* is drawn from the Bible. Today, contemporary musicians continue the tradition. For example, Arnold Schoenberg is not usually thought of as a composer of religious music. But his opus 50 is a beautiful *de profundis*, that is, Psalm 130. Thus, he joins Ralph Vaughn Williams and a host of other modern composers who have set the Psalms and other biblical texts to music.

The great English and American writers have also dealt extensively with biblical themes. Critical editions of Shakespeare often contain footnotes revealing the biblical allusions of the bard. Similar notes are necessary to capture all the ways in which modern poets use the Bible. T.S. Eliot's *The Wasteland*, a poem written in the 1920s and expressing the desolate mood of the twentieth century, weaves a number of allusions to biblical poetry together with hints of various oriental scriptures. The American poet Wallace Stevens used the apocryphal story of Susanna and the Elders in his "Peter Quince at the Clavier." Without an awareness of the biblical allusions, the reader's appreciation of these and other modern poems is hampered.

Even without notes, the biblical connections of a substantial amount of modern poetry, drama, and fiction spring out at the reader with a solid background in the study of the Bible. The great nineteenth-century American writer Herman Melville drew on the Bible, especially the Book of Job, in telling his intricate tale of the search for the great white whale *Moby Dick*. Many interpreters feel that *Moby Dick* is, at least on one level, Melville's dialogue with the Bible, especially Job. He captured the impact of the mysterious meaning of that book for America in the early nineteenth century. In his later novella, *Billy Budd,* he wrestled with the theme of the fall from innocence in the story of Adam in Genesis and the New Testament question of redemption through suffering. In ways we are only beginning to recognize, Melville is one of the most important American interpreters of the Bible.

Another New England writer, Henry David Thoreau, not only quoted the Bible extensively in his works but he also, like Melville, tried to understand its significance for the times in which he lived. Although Thoreau signed off from membership in the church and disparaged the church's teaching about Scripture, he found in the Bible truths he felt his fellow countrymen needed to learn. In his masterpiece, *Walden,* Thoreau drew on biblical sayings and images well over 100 times in unique and imaginative ways. Twentieth-century writers have also engaged in imaginative interpretations of the Bible. Obvious examples would include Thomas Mann's rendition of the Joseph story from Genesis and Archibald Macleish's retelling of the story of Job in dramatic form in *J.B.* Much of the ambience of John Steinbeck's *East of Eden* is lost on those who miss its roots in the early chapters of Genesis. So also is the impact of the title of William Faulkner's *Absalom, Absalom.* Recent novelists like John Updike (a Protestant), Graham Greene (a Catholic), and Bernard Malamud (a Jew), to name but a few, have used biblical themes in their works. They are often more subtle than the direct allusions to the Bible of earlier writers, but they are no less important to a full understanding of these authors' works.

Even pop culture offers us examples of imaginative use of the Bible; for instance, the hit musical shows based on the gospels, *Jesus Christ Superstar* and *Godspell.* Science fiction sometimes offers unorthodox interpretations of the Bible, as, for example, Robert Heinlein's *Stranger in a Strange Land.* The so-called *Christ figure* has become virtually a stock character in post-World War II literature and films. One was the convict of the title in *Cool Hand Luke,* effectively portrayed by Paul Newman. Other, more explicit movies about Jesus, such as *The Last Temptation of Christ,* have inspired heated discussion and led to public demonstrations.

These examples of the Bible's influence on the arts only scratch the surface. As you read fiction and poetry, as you go to plays and movies, be sensitive to the presence of biblical themes and allusions, and ask yourself how they contribute to the meanings of the works. It will be a rewarding endeavor, leading to a fuller appreciation of modern culture and the manifold ways in which the Bible is still influencing our perception of ourselves and our world.

Another interesting area in which the Bible is shaping modern life was opened up for exploration by Robert Bellah's provocative essay, "Civil Religion in America" (1970). As a social scientist, Bellah realized that all political states develop some organized set of symbols to legitimate the nation. The nations of Europe drew on traditional Christianity in the form of established churches to achieve an underlying symbol system. But the diverse religious affiliations present at the birth of the United States made the establishment of any particular church denomination impossible.

Thus, by happenstance or design, a religious symbol system began to emerge that cemented and celebrated the national identity of America. Important aspects of this symbol system drew on biblical themes, especially from the Hebrew canon. These include the Exodus (from oppression in Europe) and the coming to a promised land in the New World. To the founders of the United States, America was a "new Israel" chosen by God to be his people in a noble new experiment. According to Bellah, the early versions of American civil religion avoided any allusions to the New Testament. However, the Civil War introduced such New Testament ideas as redemption through suffering, sacrifice, and rebirth. Many interpreters feel that this biblically based civil religion, which is apart from any particular denomination, is still an important ingredient in understanding the special dynamics of American life. It could be an area for you to explore, for, since Bellah's article, there has been a stream of analyses of American civil religion.

The final conclusion must therefore be that the third world of the Bible is very much alive and well. An awareness of the Bible and its continuing influence remains essential for anyone who desires to grapple with the question of where we are and where we might be going. Whether from the perspective of a religious community or a more neutral vantage point, the Bible cannot be avoided, not merely for its historical and literary value, but for its continuing role in shaping our world. Journey on!

Annotated Bibliography

No one book or type of book can encompass all the information that an explorer, even a beginning explorer, in the various biblical worlds might wish to have. We have assembled here a limited list of resources for further study of the three worlds of the Bible. Our intent is to be suggestive rather than exhaustive.

DICTIONARIES

A Bible dictionary is an extremely useful tool for students of the Bible. It gives definitions of, and short articles about, words, topics, persons, and events in the Bible. A one-volume dictionary such as *Harper's Bible Dictionary* (San Francisco: Harper & Row, Pub., 1985) can answer many questions quickly. Another useful one-volume dictionary is the *New Bible Dictionary* (Wheaton, Ill.: Tyndale, 1982). *The Interpreter's Dictionary of the Bible* (five vols.) (Nashville: Abingdon, 1962, 1976) is really an encyclopedic dictionary, offering longer and more detailed articles, each by a recognized expert. It is probably the most useful single reference work in English on the Bible. Any serious student will be rewarded by a familiarity with it.

CONCORDANCES

A concordance is an alphabetic listing of the words occurring in a particular corpus of literature (such as the works of Shakespeare, Marlowe, or Goethe, or the Bible), that also cites where the words are located (by book, chapter, and verse in the Bible). A complete concordance gives an exhaustive list of all the words in the corpus and locates every occurrence. Such a work is a great help in studying a particular concept (such as *righteousness*) or in running down a particular person, word, or idea. An analytic concordance contains additional linguistic information.

Because all concordances are essentially word lists, only one in the original language of a document is universally useful. A concordance in translation must of necessity be keyed to a particular translation and be of limited value with any other translation. At the present, *Nelson's Complete Concordance of the Revised Standard Version Bible* (Nashville: Thom. Nelson, 1973) is probably the most useful. The older Young's analytic concordance, keyed to the King James Version, is also helpful.

COMMENTARIES

A commentary is an extremely valuable tool to have on hand when actually reading the Bible closely. Commentaries usually contain introductory articles on a number of relevant topics, followed by verse-by-verse explanatory notes to clear up difficulties in understanding the text at hand. A good one-volume commentary should meet the ordinary needs of most readers. Four excellent ones are currently available: *Peake's Commentary on the Bible* (Nashville: Thom. Nelson, 1962); *The New Jerome Biblical Commentary* (Englewood Cliffs, N.J.: Prentice-Hall, 1990); *The Interpreter's One Volume Commentary on the Bible* (Nashville: Abingdon, 1971); and *Harper's Bible Commentary* (San Francisco: Harper & Row, 1988).

Some commentaries devote an entire volume or more to a single biblical book. Such works are of most use to serious students or persons engaged in research projects. Some are freestanding works, but many more are parts of multivolume series. Among the more valuable sets, one should note *The Old Testament Library; The New Testament Library; The Anchor Bible* (translations and notes); *The New International Commentary; Word Biblical Commentary; Interpretation;* and *Hermeneia. The Interpreter's Bible* has been the most widely used modern commentary in English, and is generally quite sound.

INTRODUCTIONS

German scholars have developed a genre known as *Introduction* to either the Old or New Testament. Typically, these works introduce readers to the literary history of each biblical book, often with extensive bibliographies. The now classic introductions to the Old Testament by German scholars are

Georg Fohrer, *Introduction to the Old Testament* (trans. David Green) (Nashville: Abingdon, 1968), and Otto Eissfeldt, *The Old Testament: An Introduction* (trans. Peter Ackroyd) (New York: Harper & Row, Pub., 1965). One of the most widely used New Testament introductions is Werner Kümmel, *Introduction to the New Testament* (trans. A. J. Mattill, Jr.) (Nashville: Abingdon, 1966). More recent entries into the field include Brevard Childs, *Introduction to the Old Testament as Scripture* (Philadelphia: Fortress, 1979), which advocates an approach that recognizes the canonical context of biblical works, and Helmut Koester's very thorough *Introduction to the New Testament* (2 vols.) (Philadelphia: Fortress, 1982).

The results of research on the historical world of the Bible are summarized in other introductions for beginning students. Bernhard Anderson, *Understanding the Old Testament* (3rd ed.) (Englewood Cliffs, N.J.: Prentice-Hall, 1975) has won a well-deserved reputation as an excellent textbook introduction to the Hebrew Bible. Howard Kee, *Understanding the New Testament* (4th ed.) (Englewood Cliffs, N.J.: Prentice-Hall, 1983) is an excellent companion for the beginning New Testament student. Another recent introduction to the Tanak, emphasizing social scientific study, is Norman Gottwald, *The Hebrew Bible—A Socio-Literary Introduction* (Philadelphia: Fortress, 1985).

John Rogerson and Philip Davies, *The Old Testament World* (Englewood Cliffs, N.J.: Prentice Hall, 1989) is a brilliantly illustrated, up-to-date college textbook introduction that clearly distinguishes between geopolitical and historical concerns on one side, and literary matters on the other, making use of the recent methodological developments discussed in this text. One-volume introductions to the Bible have tended to emphasize the historical world. One example is John Hayes, *Introduction to the Bible* (Philadelphia: Westminster, 1971). An exception is Leonard Thompson, *Introducing Biblical Literature: A More Fantastic Country* (Englewood Cliffs, N.J.: Prentice-Hall, 1978), a work that focuses on the literary world of the Bible in an innovative and enlightening way.

An introduction to the literature "between the testaments," discussed in Chapter 10, is G.W.E. Nickelsburg, *Jewish Literature Between the Bible and the Mishnah: A Historical and Literary Introduction* (Philadelphia: Fortress, 1981).

HISTORIES

There are a number of histories that draw on the Bible as a source for the study of ancient Israel and the early Christian Church. The two now classical histories of biblical Israel are John Bright, *A History of Israel* (3rd ed.) (Philadelphia: Westminster, 1981), and Martin Noth, *The History of Israel* (rev. trans.

Peter Ackroyd) (New York: Harper & Row, Pub., 1960). J. Maxwell Miller and John H. Hayes, *A History of Ancient Israel and Judah* (Philadelphia: Westminster, 1986) is the most recent comprehensive effort. Now dated, but still a good general orientation to the New Testament world, is Floyd Filson, *A New Testament History (Philadelphia: Westminster, 1964).*

Recent interest in the application of social scientific models to the study of biblical history and ancient society is represented by Robert R. Wilson, *Sociological Approaches to the Old Testament* (Philadelphia: Fortress, 1984); David L. Petersen, *The Roles of Israel's Prophets* (Sheffield: JSOT Supplements 17, 1981); John Gager, *Kingdom and Community: The Social World of Early Christianity* (Englewood Cliffs, N.J.: Prentice-Hall, 1975); and Wayne Meeks, *The First Urban Christians: The Social World of the Apostle Paul* (New Haven: Yale, 1983); Robert B. Coote and Keith W. Whitelam, *The Emergence of Israel in Historical Perspective* (Sheffield: Almond Press, 1987); David C. Hopkins, *The Highlands of Canaan* (Sheffield: Almond Press, 1985); and Frank Frick, *The Formation of the State in Ancient Israel* (Sheffield: Almond Press, 1985). Much of the best work in this area remains scattered in journal articles (much in *The Journal for the Study of the Old Testament*). Students should be warned that not all works purporting to apply social scientific insights to an understanding of biblical materials would win the approval of professional anthropologists and sociologists.

LITERARY STUDIES

Modern study of the literary world of the Bible is still in its infancy. Recent works that might prove to be foundational in this type of study include Northrop Frye, *The Great Code: The Bible and Literature* (New York: Harcourt Brace Jovanovich, Inc., 1982), and Robert Alter's *The Art of Biblical Narrative* (New York: Basic Books, 1981) and *The Art of Biblical Poetry* (New York: Basic Books, 1985). These works deal with the formal structure of texts, the approach we have followed in this work. A good example of this type of literary analysis in practice is found in Michael Fishbane, *Text and Texture: Close Readings of Selected Biblical Texts* (New York: Schocken, 1979).

An introduction to "reader response" and other recent literary approaches is Edgar McKnight, *The Bible and the Reader: An Introduction to Literary Criticism* (Philadelphia: Fortress, 1985). Those who wish to pursue the *deep structures* (see chap. 2) of biblical texts should consult such works as R. Barthes et al., *Structural Analysis and Biblical Exegesis: Interpretational Essays* (Pittsburgh: Pickwick, 1974), and D. and A. Patte, *Structural Exegesis: From Theory to Practice* (Philadelphia: Fortress, 1978).

An introduction to literary analysis for general readers is found in Tremper Lingman III, *Literary Approaches to Biblical Interpretation* (Grand Rapids, Mich.: Zondervan, 1987).

ATLASES AND GEOGRAPHIES

Historical atlases on the Bible wed geographical and historical considerations and provide both maps and a narrative bringing the two into conjunction. The work that does the best job of providing graphic placement of each biblical event is *The Macmillan Bible Atlas* (New York: Macmillan, 1968), edited by Y. Aharoni and M. Avi-Yonah. It offers a separate small map illustrating each notable event, covering almost every one mentioned in the Tanak, the Deuterocanon, and the New Testament. *The Oxford Bible Atlas* (3rd ed.) (New York: Oxford, 1984), edited by H.G. May, illustrates very well the climate, geography, and physical features of Bible lands.

Hand in hand with the historical atlas is historical geography. Historical geographies are simply more detailed narratives correlating history and geography. The most authoritative work in this field at present is the second edition of Y. Aharoni, *The Land of the Bible* (rev. ed.) (Philadelphia: Westminster, 1979). The best source on the physical geography and the geology of Israel remains D. Baly, *The Geography of the Bible* (rev. ed.) (New York: Harper & Row, Pub., 1974).

ARCHAEOLOGICAL BOOKS

Archaeology constitutes a fundamental source of data for biblical study. Y. Aharoni, *The Archaeology of the Land of Israel* (Philadelphia: Westminster, 1982) is one of the more recent works in this area. The most comprehensive work on the subject is the four-volume *Encyclopedia of Archaeological Excavations in the Holy Land*, edited by M. Avi-Yonah (Englewood Cliffs, N.J.: Prentice-Hall, 1975–78). Eric Meyers and James Strange, *Archaeology, the Rabbis, and Early Christianity* (Nashville: Abingdon, 1981) is also an important work.

The most important texts discovered by archaeologists that relate to the study of the Bible can be found in *Ancient Near Eastern Texts Relating to the Old Testament* (3rd ed.) (Princeton, N.J.: Princeton University Press, 1969), edited by James Pritchard, and in *The New Testament Background* (New York: Harper & Row, Pub., 1961), edited by C. K. Barrett. A wealth of illustrations are found in J. B. Pritchard, *Ancient Near Eastern Pictures Relating to the Old Testament* (2nd ed.) (Princeton, N.J.: Princeton University Press, 1969). A briefer selection of texts and pictures is available in J. B. Pritchard, *The Ancient Near East* (Princeton, N.J.: Princeton University Press, 1975).

PERIODICALS

The most recent research in biblical studies, as in other scholarly disciplines, appears in learned journals. These will be of use to students engaged in specific research projects. The most prestigious journal in English is the *Journal of Biblical Literature*. The *Catholic Biblical Quarterly* publishes high quality biblical research from Catholic and non-Catholic scholars. The *Bible Review* publishes well-illustrated articles by scholars, but written for general readers. British journals include *New Testament Studies* and the new and innovative *Journal for the Study of the Old Testament* and *Journal for the Study of the New Testament*. *Vetus Testamentum* is a trilingual (English, German, French) international journal of research on the Tanak. *Novum Testamentum* is its New Testament counterpart. *Zeitschrift für die altestamentliche Wissenschaft* and *Zeitschrift für die neuestestamentliche Wissenschaft* are German journals that frequently contain articles in English.

Reports on archaeology related to the Bible appear in *Bulletin of the American Schools of Oriental Research*, *Biblical Archaeologist*, *The Israel Exploration Journal*, and *Biblical Archeology Review*, to name but a few.

THEOLOGICAL BOOKS

Students interested in theological interpretation of the Bible might wish to consult the two most widely read works on Old Testament theology: G. von Rad, *Old Testament Theology* (2 vols.) (New York: Harper & Row, Pub., 1962–65), and W. Eichrodt, *Theology of the Old Testament* (2 vols.) (Philadelphia: Westminster, 1961–67). A recent, innovative theological interpretation of the Tanak is Dale Patrick, *The Rendering of God in the Old Testament* (Philadelphia: Fortress, 1981). A now classic, and still very controversial, New Testament theology is R. Bultmann, *Theology of the New Testament* (2 vols.) (New York: Scribner's, 1951–55). A much different view is found in the recently published L. Goppelt, *Theology of the New Testament* (2 vols.) (Grand Rapids: Eerdmans, 1981–83). A recent general work on biblical theology is S. L. Terrien, *The Elusive Presence: Toward a New Biblical Theology* (New York: Harper & Row, Pub., 1978).

METHODOLOGICAL BOOKS

There are many books available on methods of interpreting the Bible. A recent introductory survey on various modes of biblical analysis is John Hayes and Carl R. Holladay, *Biblical Exegesis: A Beginner's Handbook* (Atlanta: John Knox, 1987). Another is O. Kaiser and W.G. Kümmel, *Exegetical Method: A Student's Handbook* (rev. ed.) (New York: Seabury, 1981).

A series of works on the various methods, intended for general readers, is available from Fortress Press, Philadelphia. The series includes works on literary criticism, form criticism, redactional criticism, traditions criticism, and structural criticism.

Glossary

Note: Most proper names in the Bible and biblical books are not included in this glossary. See the Index for appropriate page references.

Adam Hebrew for "(hu)man." Formed by God from the earth (Hebrew *ᶜadamah*), according to Genesis 2. In Paul's letters (see Rom. 5:12–21), "first" Adam (of Genesis) contrasted with "new" Adam (Christ).

Agape A Greek term for "love." Used in New Testament to refer to the unconditional love shown by God to humankind in the sending of his son. See First Corinithians 13.

Alexandria Egyptian city named after Alexander. Largest Jewish population outside Palestine by the first century C.E. Tanak translated into Greek from Hebrew and allegorical method of biblical interpretation perfected here. Philo and other important Jewish and Christian philosophers worked in Alexandria.

Allegorical Referring to a narrative or method of interpretation in which the elements of a literary composition serve as symbols for other religious or moral truths. The allegorical method of interpretation is evident within the Bible (see, for example, Romans 4).

Amarna The modern name assigned to the ruins of the ancient Egyptian city of Akhentaten, capital in the fourteenth century B.C.E. In the ruins, archaeologists discovered over 350 letters, many from rulers of cities in Palestine (including Jerusalem and Megiddo). During the Amarna Age the Egyptian king Akhenaton experimented with the worship of a single god, the sun god Aten.

Anthropology The social science that focuses on the study of human origins, and the development and dynamics of human cultures.

Antichrist The final opponent of Christ. Found in the New Testament only in the Letters of John.

Antioch A Syrian city to which the Christian gospel was brought by Hellenists about 40 C.E. The name "Christian" first used here (Acts 11:26). Center of mission to Gentiles.

Apocalyptic From the Greek for "an uncovering." Refers to literature and movements that speak of the "uncovering" of the secrets of the end of history, the vanquishing of evil, and the beginning of a new age of peace and righteousness.

Apocrypha From the Greek for "hidden." A group of books or portions of books not found in the Jewish canon but included in the Septuagint and early Christian versions of the Old Testament. Most Protestant groups do not consider these works canonical. The Catholic Church considers them a deuterocanon ("second" canon) to distinguish them from the Jewish canon. In Catholic usage "Apocrypha" refers to the writings that have become known as the Pseudepigrapha, but which we suggest calling the Larger Apocrypha.

Apostles Greek for "one sent out." In the New Testament the inner circle of followers of Jesus commissioned to carry on his ministry. The "Apostolic Age" in early Christianity is usually dated from the death of Jesus to the Fall of Jerusalem in 70 C.E.

Aramaic A Semitic language closely related to Hebrew, evident from the ninth century B.C.E. onward. Several Tanak passages are in Aramaic (especially Dan. 2:4—7:28). In common use by the first century C.E., so it was the language spoken by Jesus.

Archaeology The scientific study of the material remains of the human past.

Archetype A literary term used to designate recurrent situations, characters, images, symbols, or plots. Often function in opposites. Recognition of the archetypes in a literary work such as the Bible enhances understanding of the literary world of that text.

Ark of the Covenant The container for the tablets upon which the Ten Commandments were inscribed. A symbolic throne for Yahweh, and thus representative of the divine presence and protection. Placed in the Jerusalem Temple's Holy of Holies.

Armageddon Hebrew for "Mount Megiddo." Transliterated into Greek in Rev. 16:16 as a name for the place of the final, cosmic battle of the forces of good and evil.

Ascension The departure of the risen Jesus into heaven. See Acts 1:2–11.

Asia Minor The western peninsula of Asia, from the Black Sea to the Mediterranean, where Turkey is now located.

Assyria A major ancient near Eastern empire, located in Mesopotamia, which dominated Israel and the entire region from the ninth through the seventh centuries B.C.E.

Atonement, Day of Ten days after the Fall New Year, a day set aside to confront and remove the sins of the past year. In the Jerusalem Temple the High Priest entered the Holy of Holies only on this day, symbolically placing the sins of the people on an animal called the "scapegoat." See Lev. 23:27–32 and Hebrews 8—9.

Baal "Lord, Husband." A Canaanite deity associated with thunderstorms, god of fertility. Opposition to worship of Baal is a recurrent theme in the Tanak.

Babylonia Ancient near Eastern empire, located in southern Mesopotamia, which dominated Judah in the later seventh and sixth centuries B.C.E.

Babylonian Exile See **Exile.**

Baptism From the Greek for "immerse in fresh water." A rite of religious purification and regeneration.

B.C.E. Before the Common Era. A neutral designation for the Christian B.C.

Bishop Translation of Greek word (*episcopos*), meaning overseer, guardian. An early Christian office mentioned in Phil. 1:1 and the Pastoral Epistles.

Canaan Name for the region and inhabitants of the land of Palestine, prior to its becoming "Israel." Grandson of Noah (Gen. 9:18–27).

Canon From a Greek term for "rule" or "standard." Any list of religious writings deemed authoritative. The process through which the writings become accepted as authoritative is called *canonization.*

Capernaum The town on the northwest shore of the Sea of Galilee that served as the center of the Galilean ministry of Jesus.

Catholic Epistles See **General Epistles.**

C.E. Common Era. A neutral designation for the Christian A.D.

Charismatic From the Greek word for "gift." In general, refers to a spiritual power, and by extension, to the qualities of leadership that come not from office or inheritance, but that mark a particularly powerful, inspiring person. In the New Testament refers to the particular gifts of the Holy Spirit (see First Corinthians 12 and Romans 12).

Christ From the Greek term *Christos,* which translates the Hebrew term *mashiach* (messiah), which means "anointed one." Specifically, the one anointed by God from the house of David to restore the nation Israel. Became a title associated with Jesus of Nazareth. (See **Messiah.**)

Circumcision The removal of the foreskin of the male's penis. In ancient Israel a sign of God's covenant with Israel (Genesis 17). The merits of the necessity of the ritual were debated in early Christianity. See Acts 15, for example.

Corinth A major Greek city, with ports on both the Aegean and Adriatic seas. Site of an important Christian congregation. Visited by the Apostle Paul for the first time in 50 C.E.

Cosmic Referring to the entire universe considered as an ordered whole, as opposed to the chaos that precedes and stands against cosmos.

Covenant A formal, sacred treaty or agreement between two parties with each assuming obligation. Refers especially to the relationship established by God with the nation Israel. Several covenants are important in the Bible, including the Noahic Covenant (Genesis 9), the Abrahamic Covenant (see Genesis 12—17), the Sinai Covenant (see Exodus 19—20), the Davidic Covenant (see Second Samuel 7), and the "new" covenant mentioned in the prophetic books (e.g., Jer. 31:31) and understood in the New Testament as the new relationship between God and humans begun with Jesus Christ (see, e.g., Mk. 14:24).

Cultic Having to do with the organized, institutional aspect of religion.

D A designation by Source Critics for the book of Deuteronomy, considering it one of the written sources of the Torah.

Deacons One of the types of ministry and apparent officers in early Christian communities.

Dead Sea Scrolls The writings discovered in caves along the northwest shore of the Dead Sea, beginning in 1947, near a site called Qumran, including at least fragments of almost every book of the Tanak and many documents from the apocalyptic religious community that resided there. Important for understanding Palestinian Judaism and Christian origins as well as providing the earliest evidence of Hebrew texts of the Tanak.

Decalogue The Ten Commandments.

Deuterocanon From Greek for "secondary canon." See **Apocrypha.**

Deuteronomic Code The legal section of the Book of Deuteronomy (Deuteronomy 12—26).

Deuteronomistic History The historical narrative that runs from Deuteronomy through Second Kings. Many modern scholars think the framework of the narrative reflects a pattern of judgment by God on Israel because of the people's failure to follow their covenant obligations. Called Deuteronomic because of stylistic similarities, and because this theology is found in that book.

Diaspora From Greek for "scattered." The Jews who lived outside Palestine after the Babylonian Exile (587 B.C.E.)

Divided Kingdom The period between 922 and 722 B.C.E. when the once united Israel became a Northern Kingdom (Israel) and a Southern Kingdom (Judah). Ended with Assyrian conquest of Israel.

Documentary Hypothesis The theory advanced by modern source critics that the Torah came into existence through the combination of several originally separate "documents." See **J, E, D,** and **P.**

Dualism A perspective that divides a subject into two opposite categories such as good and evil, light and darkness, life and death, matter and spirit.

E The "Elohist," one of the hypothetical sources of the Torah. So named because of the preference for the divine name Elohim. Supposedly deriving from Northern traditions about the origins of Israel and dated to the eighth or ninth centuries B.C.E. Genesis 22:1–19 is a famous "E" passage.

Ebla Modern Tell Mardikh in Syria, site of an important ancient city state, where a library of tablets were discovered in excavations beginning in the 1960s. The relevance of the finds for the study of the Tanak is debated by scholars.

El The common word for "God" in ancient Semitic languages like Hebrew. The father god and head of the Canaanite pantheon. Appears in personal names in the Bible, such as Elijah ("Yahweh is my God"). Worship of El in pre-Israelite Canaan is suggested in names for God that appear in the patriarchal narratives (e.g., Gen. 16:7–14).

Elders In ancient Israel, the notable persons of a tribe who were responsible for the maintenance of justice. In the New Testament, either Jewish leaders or officers in Christian communities (translating the Greek *presbuteros*.)

Election A theological term used to refer to the belief that God chooses a particular agent (Israel and/or Christ) as an instrument and bearer of divine salvation. In the New Testament the "elect" are those who respond to Christ.

Elohim Hebrew for "gods" or "God." Common name for God in Tanak (occurring over 2,500 times).

Enuma Elish The Babylonian story of creation of the cosmos, resulting from divine combat. So named after the account's first words, in the original language of the text.

Envelope Structure A pattern in which the opening and closing of a literary unit are similar in form, serving to round off and enclose the composition.

Ephesus An important port city in western Asia Minor. Visited on more than one occasion by the Apostle Paul, once for more than two years, according to Acts. Fourth largest city in Roman Empire in the first century C.E. The city has been extensively excavated, revealing many first-century structures.

Episcopos See **Bishop.**

Epistle From Greek *epistole*, letter. Modern scholars distinguish between the more personal and informal "letter" and the more literary, impersonal "epistle" that uses the form of a letter as a literary device.

Eschatological From Greek *eschaton,* last or final. A term used by modern scholars to refer to ideas about the end of history.

Essenes A Jewish apocalyptic group in existence from mid-second century B.C.E. until about 70 C.E. Most scholars think the group at Qumran that possessed the Dead Sea Scrolls were Essenes. Mentioned as one of several Jewish groups by Josephus.

Eve The first woman (Gen. 2:21–22). Meaning uncertain, but resemblance to Hebrew word for "living" relates to identification as "mother of all living" (Gen. 3:20).

Exile See **Babylonian Exile**. The period during the sixth Century B.C.E. when part of the population of Judea was taken into captivity in Babylon.

Exodus The escape of Semitic residents of northern Egypt from forced labor under the leadership of Moses, described in the book of the same name. Becomes a powerful biblical symbol for God's deliverance of his chosen people from bondage. The "New Exodus" refers to the anticipated restoration of the people from Exile in Babylon.

Faith Trust in or reliance on God, in response to God's trustworthiness. One of the most basic and important biblical themes, found in both the Tanak and New Testament.

Forgiveness The "sending away," "covering," "removal," or "wiping away" of human sins.

Galatia Both the ancient territory in north central Asia Minor and the Roman province that included this area and others to its south. Thus, New Testament references to Galatia and the Galatians might be to either the territory or the province.

Galilee The forty-five mile (north to south) region in northern Palestine in which Jesus grew up and conducted most of his public ministry.

Gehenna Hebrew term, meaning Valley of Hinnom, a place near Jerusalem where human sacrifices were once conducted. In the New Testament it was the city dump and thus a symbol for the place of judgment on sinners.

Genealogy A history of the descent of a person or group from an ancestor, or showing the boundaries of a kin group.

Genre A literary term designating literature according to basic, distinctive types.

Gentile From the Latin word for *nation.* A non-Jew.

Gilgamesh Epic A legend about the Mesopotamian king Gilgamesh (ca. 2650 B.C.E.). The legend includes a flood account similar to the narrative in Genesis.

Gnostic Referring to a variety of religious movements of the early Christian period that claimed salvation came through *gnosis* (Greek for "knowledge").

God Fearers Gentiles who were attracted to the monotheistic teaching of Judaism and/or the Christian gospel in the Roman world.

Gospel English translation of Greek *euangelion*, "good news." Used in the New Testament to refer to the good news of God's Kingdom proclaimed by Jesus and the good news of what God accomplished for humanity through Jesus. By the second century C.E., referred to the literary genre represented in the New Testament canon by Mark, Matthew, Luke, and John.

Grace In general, that which brings joy or happiness. In the Bible refers to the divine mercy shown toward humans.

Habiru (or Khapiru) Sumerian term for "outcasts." In ancient near Eastern texts from the third and second millennia, the term refers to various ethnic groups who stood outside the feudal system. The possible association with the "Hebrews" of the Bible is hotly disputed.

Hades Greek word used to translate Hebrew term *sheol*, the abode of the dead.

Haggadah Jewish term for interpretations of Tanak that are devotional, not legal in character (contrast *halakah*). Often supplement the scriptural narrative with stories about principal characters.

Halakah From the Hebrew term for "to walk, go." Refers to the rules that guide the faithful person's life, derived from interpretation of the Torah. The New Testament portrays Jesus engaged in *halakic* discussions with Pharisees (e.g., Mt. 12:1–8).

Hannukah The Jewish festival of dedication, celebrating the purification of the Jerusalem Temple during the Maccabean revolt (164 B.C.E.). During the eight-day festival, a candle is lit each night remembering the miraculous relighting of the Temple menorah (lampstand).

Hebrew The Semitic language in which most of the Tanak was written. Also used to designate the people of the nation Israel. Typically used by foreigners when speaking about Israelites and as a self-designation by Israelites when speaking to foreigners (e.g., Gn. 40:15, 41:12, 1 Sam. 13:3).

Hellenistic Referring to the Greek culture that spread throughout the Mediterranean world (including Israel) beginning in the late fourth century B.C.E.

Hellenists A term found only in Acts 6:1 and 9:29, which probably denotes Greek-speaking Jewish members of the early Christian community in Jerusalem.

Heresy Deviation from accepted teaching or practice in a religious community.

Hermeneutics An area of study dealing with the principles and process of interpretation of the Bible or other literature.

Herod In general, a family that ruled Palestine from about 55 B.C.E. until the late first century C.E. The most famous was Herod the Great (40–4

B.C.E.), who was named "King of the Jews" by Roman authorities. His son, Herod Antipas, was ruler of Galilee from 4 B.C.E. until 39 C.E.

Holy of Holies The most sacred portion of the Jerusalem Temple, which housed the Ark of the Covenant. Entered only once a year on the Day of Atonement, and only by the High Priest, during the Second Temple period.

Holy Spirit The mysterious power and presence of God within and among humans and nature.

Hymn Any poetic composition praising God. Found in the Book of Psalms and elsewhere in the Tanak (e.g., Ex. 15:1–18). In the New Testament some hymns honor Christ (e.g., Phil. 2:6–11).

Immortality Endless existence, life beyond death. A Hellenistic idea that influenced some biblical writers. See also **Resurrection.**

Incarnation Literally, "to become flesh." Refers to the Christian teaching that the Son of God was present with God at creation, indeed *was* God, and "became flesh" in the person Jesus. See John 1.

Inerrancy The belief that God inspired the writers of the Bible in such a way that their words are without error.

Irony A literary term for the incongruity that results when words are used to convey a meaning opposite of what they literally mean, and when what happens is contrary to what might logically be expected. A frequent literary device in the Bible.

Israel The name for the twelve tribes that the Tanak says descended from the patriarch Jacob (also called Israel). A political designation for the nation and people who inhabited the land of Canaan. After the division of the nation in 922 B.C.E., "Israel" referred to the Northern Kingdom. Also a synonym for the Jewish people. (See also Palestine and Canaan.)

J The designation used by source critics to refer to the Yahwist (from the German transliteration "Jahweh"), one of the hypothetical written sources combined to create the Torah or perhaps Hexateuch. Dated to the tenth century B.C.E. and thus the earliest of the sources of the Pentateuch.

Jehovah See **Yahweh.**

Jericho A city in the Jordan River Valley, just north of the Dead Sea.

Jerusalem Literally, "city of peace." The key city of ancient Israel, located in the central hill country on the edge of the Judean desert. Under King David it became the religious and political symbol of the unity of the covenant people. Referred to as *Zion* in the Bible.

Jew A designation for the people of the Judean Kingdom, later province, and those in the Diaspora. Came into use after the Babylonian Exile. In the New Testament, used to distinguish descendants of Israel from the Samaritans and Gentiles.

Josephus   A Jewish historian (ca. 37–100 C.E.) whose works strive to make Jewish history and traditions understandable to Hellenistic readers.

Judah   1) A son of Jacob and Rachel, ancestor of the Tribe of Judah; 2) the region in southern Palestine associated with the tribe; 3) after the division of the nation Israel in 922 B.C.E., the Southern Kingdom, ruled over by the Davidic dynasty until the Babylonian conquest of the early sixth century.

Judea   Greek for *Judah.* A political designation first used to describe the Jewish province created by the Persians around Jerusalem in the sixth century B.C.E. Under the Maccabeans came to refer to the whole of Palestine; later under the Romans to the area ruled by Herod the Great, then to the limited area around Jerusalem administered by procurators. Also one of the three geographic regions in Israel, in addition to Samaria and Galilee to the north.

Judgment   God (or his Messiah's) punishment of the wicked and reward of the righteous, either during history or at a Day of Judgment at an "end time."

Justification   To make or declare righteous. A recurrent concept in both the Tanak and New Testament. Refers to the bringing of persons into proper accord with one another and/or God, overcoming that which thwarts the right relationship. In the New Testament, used to explain what God accomplished through the sacrifice of Jesus, accessible to persons through faith.

Kerygma   A transliteration of a Greek term, meaning "preaching." In the New Testament the focus is on the content of the preaching, the Gospel.

Kingdom of God/Heaven   The sovereignty or rule of God. A rabbinic and New Testament phrase, rooted in the Tanak's claim of God's universal kingship. The synoptic gospels portray the announcement of the nearness of the kingdom and the necessity of repentance in order to prepare for it as the basic message of Jesus. It is sometimes used in apocalyptic contexts as a symbol for the expected new age. As a symbol it relates also to God's redemptive activity for the covenant people.

Lament   A literary term denoting personal and communal songs that cry out in anguish to God, imploring God to act to deliver the individual or people from the situation of distress.

Larger Apocrypha   See **Pseudepigrapha.**

Levite   In general, members of the priestly tribe of Levi. In the Book of Deuteronomy, a term for the priests, who conducted sacrifices and administered the law. After centralization of worship in Jerusalem, the Levites were apparently reduced to a position subordinate to the Aaronide Temple priesthood. After the Exile, however, certain Levites constituted the Temple choirs.

Light Often a symbol for the presence of God and spiritual illumination.

Logos Greek for "word." In Stoic philosophy, reason. The principle that gives the world coherence and order. In the New Testament, Jesus is called the *logos* (John 1).

Lord A title of respect and authority, used for God and prominent persons in the Tanak and applied to Jesus in the New Testament.

Lord's Supper The last meal shared by Jesus with his disciples. Became the central sacrament in the Christian community.

LXX See **Septuagint.**

Maccabees A family that led the revolt against Seleucid rule in Israel (167–164 B.C.E.) and established the Hasmonean dynasty, which governed throughout much of the second and first centuries B.C.E.

Marduk (or Merodach) A Mesopotamian deity, chief god of the city of Babylon. A storm deity portrayed as creator in the Babylonian creation poem (see **Enuma Elish**).

Mari An ancient Mesopotamian city that served as a center of trade in the third millennium. Archaeological excavations have revealed texts that shed light on the cultural background of some biblical customs.

Megiddo A city in northwestern Palestine in the Plain of Esdraelon, in a very strategic location controlling two major trade and military routes, above all the mountain passes leading to the coastal plain.

Melchizedek Hebrew for "my king is righteous." King of Salem (Jerusalem) called in Genesis 14 a priest. Interpreted later to mean "King of Righteousness." Came to be regarded as the ideal priest-king, a supernatural figure whose priesthood is eternal. (See Hebrews 5—7.)

Mesopotamia The geographical region bounded by the Tigris and Euphrates Rivers, now modern Iraq. The Sumerian people occupied southern Mesopotamia around 3300 B.C.E. Later, the Babylonians were centered in this area, while the Assyrian Empire dominated northern Mesopotamia.

Messiah Hebrew for "anointed one." In general, anyone inducted into an office or given a responsibility through the ceremony of anointing with oil. In particular, the king of united Israel, or the Davidic monarchy of Judah. After the fall of the Davidic monarchy, associated with the notion that God would restore the Davidic line in the person of an ideal king. Some Dead Sea Scrolls also speak of a Messiah of Aaron, a restored high priesthood (Lev. 9:30).

Midrash Biblical interpretation of the type found in rabbinic literature, in which the text is carefully explained, often verse by verse. Midrashic interpretation assumes the text has an inexhaustible store of meaning to be mined by the careful reader. May be halakic or haggadic.

Millennium In general, a thousand years. In the Bible, a thousand-year reign of peace. In Revelation, associated with a period in which Satan would be defeated and Christ would rule, before a final onslaught by Satan and the final defeat of evil (Rev. 20:1–3). Corresponds to the rabbinic "days of the messiah."

Mishnah Rabbinic/Pharisaic Judaism claimed that its oral traditions (in the New Testament, the "traditions of the elders") constituted an oral Torah, equal in antiquity and authority to the written Torah. Mishnah refers specifically to the written version of the rabbinic Oral Torah, completed in Palestine by about 200 C.E. Became the basic stratum of the Talmud.

Monotheism The belief in one all-powerful god to the exclusion of other deities.

Moses The leader of the people of Israel out of bondage in Egypt and the mediator between Yahweh and the people, through whom God entered into the Sinai covenant with Israel. Considered the lawgiver and archetypal prophet.

Mystery Religions Hellenistic groups associated with various deities, all with the belief in initiation rites that united believers with the deity, with the promise of immortality. The influence of these groups on the formation of early Christian teaching is disputed.

Mysticism A disciplined quest for direct experience of the divine presence.

Myth In a narrow sense, an account of activities of the gods in eternity or in the spirit realm, though may also denote accounts of divine–human interaction. In a more general sense, stories that embody the foundational traditions of a culture. May be reenacted in worship.

Nag Hammadi A town in Upper Egypt where (beginning in 1945) a cache of texts (such as the *Gospel of Thomas*), which shed light on early Christian history, were found. Some documents provide primary evidence for Gnostic teachings.

Nazarene A Greek term used to refer to Jesus and his followers in the New Testament (e.g., Acts 24:5). The Hebrew form "Nazareans" was a rabbinic term for the early Christians.

Nazareth A small village of lower Galilee, near the major trade route to Egypt, where Jesus grew up.

Nineveh Capital of Assyria during the height of its power.

Nuzi A Mesopotamian city, where a collection of texts that aid the reconstruction of the cultural context of early biblical history, were unearthed by archaeologists. The texts date to about 1450 B.C.E.

Oracle A message from a god.

Oral Torah See **Mishnah**.

P A term used by source critics to designate the Priestly Source, one of the hypothetical sources of the Torah. Called "priestly" because of a special concern for ritual and the Aaronide priesthood. Thought to be the latest of the four "sources," dating from about the fifth century B.C.E.

Palestine From the Greek name for the area along the eastern coast of the Mediterranean Sea (after the Philistines). Also called Canaan, Israel, and the Promised Land.

Parable Brief stories that point beyond their literal meaning toward another truth or truths. The synoptic gospels record over twenty-five parables of Jesus.

Parousia Greek for "coming," almost always referring to the expectation of the coming again of Jesus to judge the earth.

Passion Narratives The stories of the suffering and death of Jesus in the gospels.

Passover The Jewish festival commemorating God's deliverance of the people of Israel from bondage.

Patriarchs The male leader of a family or clan. In the Tanak, refers to the ancestors of Israel described in Genesis.

Pentecost Greek for "fiftieth," designating the Jewish Festival of Weeks (Shavuot) held fifty days after Passover, which came to be associated with the giving of the Torah on Mt. Sinai. Because of events on Pentecost narrated in Acts 2, Pentecost has become an important Christian festival.

People of the Land In Tanak, originally notables among the lay yeomanry with militia responsibilities. Later, the humbler classes. Pharisaic-rabbinic term for the Jewish masses who were careless or indifferent in their religious practices.

Pharisees A predominantly lay-scholarly religious movement of particularly pious and influential Jews, in the classical period, described by Josephus and the New Testament.

Philippi A city in northeastern Greece, visited by Paul in about 50 C.E. Site of the first European Christian community.

Philistines A group that migrated to the southern coast of Palestine in the twelfth century B.C.E., and became one of the principal rivals of the Israelites.

Phoenicia Land of the Phoencians; the name given to the coastal area to the north of Israel during the first millennium B.C.E. Tyre and Sidon were the most important cities in the region; known for its extensive trade.

Presbyters See **Elders.**

Prophet One who serves as an instrument of communication between God and humans.

Proverb A brief statement that communicates a familiar truth.

Psalm From the Greek *psalmos,* translating a Hebrew word meaning "song." However, among the 150 psalms of the canonical Book of Psalms, one finds prayers and other types of religious poems, in addition to songs.

Pseudepigrapha Approximately sixty-five noncanonical Jewish writings from roughly the third century B.C.E. until the second century C.E. They are called the pseudepigrapha ("false writings") because many are connected with persons who are not the authors. However, this designation is being questioned by many modern scholars who consider it unnecessarily misleading in its suggestion that the works constituted an ancient collection. The term *larger apocrypha* is preferred in this text.

Pseudonymous A literary convention in which an author assumes the name of another person, perhaps a famous person, to lend authority to the work.

Purim A Jewish holiday based on the Book of Esther.

Q A designation used by New Testament scholars for the material common to the Gospels of Matthew and Luke, but not found in Mark. From German *Quelle* (source). It is commonly assumed that the Q material comes from a source used by the writers of the Gospels of Matthew and Luke.

Qumran The site of a settlement along the northwest shore of the Dead Sea, where the Dead Sea Scrolls were found.

Rabbi Hebrew title that came to mean "my master" or "teacher." A title denoting respect for Jewish teachers. Used in New Testament in direct address to Jesus.

Redemption The release of someone or something in exchange for payment. In the Bible, also refers to the action of God in restoring sinful people.

Remnant In the Bible, the remainder of faithful people left over after divine judgment on a nation's sins.

Repentance Turning around from the wrong way toward the proper path. In the Bible, turning from sin to the Lord and the path in harmony with God.

Resurrection New life beyond death. In the Bible, a complete transformation of the human being or nation after the experience of death. For people, an event to take place at the end of history when the dead are raised and brought under divine judgment.

Retribution The idea of repaying in kind. A principle that applies in various biblical writings both to human and divine justice. The belief that God will reward or punish people in proportion to their degree of loyalty to divine law.

Revelation Unveiling or disclosing. In the Bible, the making known of truths from God about enduring realities or the divine plan for the future. Often associated with apocalyptic teaching.

Righteousness The state of being right, or in proper relationship. In the Bible God is portrayed as righteous, indicating the divine intent and action to bring humans and all creation into a state of harmony. Humans are also described as righteous, when they are living in obedience to God or trusting in the divine righteousness. A pervasive theme in the Bible.

Sabbath   From the Hebrew *shabbat,* seventh. The weekly seventh day of rest mandated for Israelites by God in the Ten Commandments. Observed as a memorial of God's resting after creation and to give workers an opportunity to rest. From sundown on Friday to sundown Saturday.

Sadducees   An aristocratic Jewish group that existed from the second century B.C.E. until the late first century C.E. Usually described as opponents of the Pharisees and thought to be from the priestly and wealthy families.

Samaria   The capital city of the Northern Kingdom from the early ninth century B.C.E. until its destruction by the Assyrians in 721 B.C.E. Also, a district in the central hill country, north of Judah and south of Galilee.

Samaritans   A religious community centered in Samaria, near Mt. Gerizim, which Samaritans consider the holy mountain (in contrast to Mt. Zion in Jerusalem). Although Samaritans and Jews shared a common heritage, differences in beliefs and traditions led to the animosity reflected in the New Testament. The community continues to exist today.

Sanctification   Making holy or dedicating someone or something to God. Transferred from a secular, profane state to a sacred one.

Sanhedrin   A Greek term for a council of leaders. The term may refer to a series of councils of courts, but principally the council of Jewish notables who were responsible for Jewish relations with Rome. In the Bible the most famous sanhedrin is the council of Jewish leaders in Jerusalem during the New Testament period. The precise composition and powers of the Jerusalem Sanhedrin are the subject of intense scholarly debate.

Satan   Hebrew for "adversary." Depicted in the Tanak as a member of the divine court whose duty is to report to the heavenly king on the faithfulness of humans. By the time of the New Testament, perhaps as a result of Persian influence, Satan (also identified as Belial, Beelzebub, or simply the devil) is portrayed as the leader of forces hostile to God.

Second Temple   Refers to the Jerusalem Temple from its rebuilding following the Babylonian Exile, until it was destroyed by the Romans in 70 C.E. The Temple was in fact refurbished several times, and completely rebuilt on the orders of Herod the Great.

Semitic   A term developed by scholars to describe a group of peoples of the ancient near East whose cultures and languages were very similar. Includes Assyrians, Babylonians, Canaanites, Hebrews, Phoenicians, Arabs, and others. Often refers to the languages of these peoples.

Septuagint (LXX) The Greek translation of the Tanak from Hebrew begun in Alexandria, Egypt in the third century, to which the Deuterocanon was added. From the Greek for *seventy*, reflecting the tradition that the translation was done by seventy elders.

Sheol The place where the dead go. See also **Hades.**

Sinai, Mount The mountain in the Sinai Wilderness where, according to the Exodus narrative, God revealed the Torah to Moses and Israel entered into covenant with God. Also called Mount Horeb.

Social Sciences Disciplines that study the dynamics of psychological, social, and cultural organization and change.

Sociology The social science that focuses on the communal dimension of human behavior, whether in families, clans, tribes, nations, or the hosts of institutional settings in which humans are grouped.

Son of God In general, a person or community with a special relationship with God. In the Tanak, angels or divine beings. Became a title applied to Jesus to denote his special relationship with God, and ultimately shared identity.

Son of Man A phrase with meanings varying from simply "a human being" to an apocalyptic title for the one coming to judge the world. Also a euphemism for the first-person pronoun. In the New Testament, the meaning of Jesus' reference to himself as "son of man" is a subject of intense scholarly debate.

Stoicism A school of Greek philosophy established in the fourth century B.C.E., emphasizing the logos that orders all things, and a life of discipline and duty.

Structure In this text used as a literary term for the pattern or patterns discernible in a literary unit.

Sumerians A people who inhabited southern Mesopotamia and developed the first ancient near Eastern civilization in the fourth millenium. According to Genesis, the ancestors of Israel came from Sumer.

Synagogue Greek for "assembly." A Jewish place of gathering for prayer, reading and studying Scripture, and hearing its teachings expounded.

Synoptic From the Greek for "from or with a similar perspective." Refers to the first three canonical gospels (Matthew, Mark, and Luke), which share a similar view of Jesus' public career.

Talmud The authoritative compilation of rabbinic lore not directly dependent upon Tanak. Consists of Mishnah (see definition in this glossary) plus Gemara—comments and elaborations on the Mishnah. There are two editions of the Talmud: the Babylonian, edited in the rabbinic academies of Babylon, and the Yerushlami, edited in the academies of Galilee, the former being more authoritative. Completed about 500 C.E.

Tanak An acronym created from the Hebrew words for the three canonical sections of the Hebrew Bible: Torah, Neviim (Prophets), and Kethuvim

(Writings). Used in this text in preference to other possible designations, such as Old Testament or Hebrew Bible.

Temple The house or palace of a god. A place of sacrificial worship. In the Bible, especially the place of worship constructed in Jerusalem, first by King Solomon, which was the center of the nation Israel and came to symbolize God's dwelling with his people.

Theology The application of human reason to the study of God and divine revelation in an attempt to explain their meanings.

Theophany The manifestation of God. In the Bible a number of stories about and poetic allusions to appearances of God are found. See, for example, Ex. 3:1—4:18; 19:1—20:21; Is. 6:1–8; Mt. 17:1–8; Rev. 4:1–11.

Torah Hebrew for "instruction, teaching." Refers to God's instruction to the covenant people as well as to the first five books of the Tanak. In its broadest sense refers to all of the divine commandments, from both the Tanak (the written Torah), the Mishnah (the Oral Torah), and other religious teaching, and thus to the total divine revelation of how the covenant people are to live.

Transfiguration The event narrated in the synoptic gospels when the "true nature" of Jesus was revealed to his closest followers. See Mark 9:2–8 and parallels.

Ugarit An ancient city-state located along the Mediterranean coast in Syria opposite Cyprus, now known as Ras Shamra. Twentieth century archaeologists discovered a library of texts at Ugarit that provide important information for the linguistic, cultural, and religious background of ancient Canaan, and of the Tanak.

Versions Translations of the Bible into other languages, ancient and modern.

Virgin Birth Refers to the tradition that Mary gave birth to Jesus by the power of the Holy Spirit rather than human agency.

Way In general, a term used in the Bible to refer to the path of action in harmony with God's intentions. Also, one of the earliest designations for the Christian community (see Acts 9:2).

Yahweh (YHWH) The name for God, which according to the narrative in Exodus, was revealed to Moses, and thus was the "special" Israelite name for God. Jewish tradition considered the name too holy to pronounce; whenever the name appeared in the text another Hebrew word for Lord (*adonai*) was pronounced. When vowels were added to the consonantal text of the Tanak, the vowels for *adonai* were placed with the consonants YHWH to remind readers not to pronounce the divine name. Some English translations therefore render Yahweh as Jehovah, reading YHWH with the substituted vowels. Represented in English versions in uppercase type, usually LORD, but also Lord GOD.

Zealots Refers to opponents of the Roman occupation of Israel, who sometimes engaged in violent revolution against the Romans.

Ziggurat A Mesopotamian stepped tower, usually with shrines both at its base and on its top, connected by a processional ramp. The Tower of Babel described in Genesis 11:1–9 was probably a ziggurat.

Zion Name of the "mountain" on which the Jerusalem Temple was located, hence Mount Zion.

Index

Josiah, 86–87, 115–16, 136
Josiah's reform, 86–87
"J" source, 45, 55, 364
Judas Maccabeus, 207
Jude, Letter of, 333–34
Judges, Book of, 26, 90–100
Judges, major, 97
Judges, minor, 97
Judgment, 130–31, 365
Judith, Book of, 220
Justin Martyr, 326
Juvenal, 323

Kenites, 93
Kerygma, 286, 365
Kingdom of God (Heaven), 198, 244, 253, 259, 365
Kings, First Book of, 101–3, 108–12
Kings, Second Book of, 108–16
Kurios, 243 (see also Lord)

Laban, 63–65, 68
Lachish, 32, 89, 95, 133
Lament, 128, 148–49, 155, 160–61, 365
Lamentations, Book of, 160–61
Language, biblical:
  characteristics, 39–42
Larger Apocrypha (see Pseudepigrapha)
Law, ancient Near Eastern, 83–84
Law, biblical:
  law codes, 82–83
  types, 81–82
Leah, 64, 68
Legends, biblical, 36, 38
Letters in the New Testament, 302–3
Letters of Paul, 304–16
Leviathan, 164, 171, 176
Leviticus, Book of, 83
Literalism, 16
Literary history (see History, literary)
Literary world, 2–8, 30, 33–43
Literature, types of biblical, 35–39
Logos (Word), 265–66, 273, 366
LORD (see God, names of)
Lord, 243–44, 366
Luke, Gospel of:
  audience, 271
  authorship, 271
  date, 271
  literary world, 260–63
LXX (see Septuagint)

Maccabees, 200, 204–10, 366
Maccabees, First and Second, 219–20
Macleish, Archibald, 348
Malachi, Book of, 144
Manasseh, 115
Manasseh, Prayer of, 221
Mann, Thomas, 348
Mar, 243 (see also Lord)
Marcion, 326
Marduk, 56, 118, 186, 366
Mark, Gospel of:

historical world, 269–70
literary world, 252–56
Mary, 257, 262
Masada, 209–10, 216
Matthew, Gospel of, 236
  historical world, 270–71
  literary world, 256–60
Megiddo, 26, 113, 116, 319, 366
Megilloth, 156–57
Melchizedek, 329–30, 366
Melville, Herman, 348
Mendenhall, George, 93
Menorah, 338
Merneptah, 76, 79
Merton, Thomas, 147n, 150n
Mesha, 114
Mesopotamia, 17, 20, 23–25
Messiah, 123, 125, 144, 238–41, 244, 246, 286, 297, 337, 366
Methods of biblical study, 33–51
Micah, Book of, 142
Micaiah ben Imlah, 112
Michael, 199
Michelangelo, 347
Midrash, 212, 223, 366
Mishnah, 155, 212, 223, 234, 367
Mithra, 291
Moab, 97–98, 106
Monotheism, 134, 367
Mordecai, 195–96
Moses, 74–82, 367
Motifs, 43
Mystery religion, 290–91, 367
Mysticism, 137, 213, 266, 272, 297–98, 367
Myth, 36, 38, 249, 367
Mythology, 69, 129, 164, 171, 174–76, 314

Nabi (Prophet), 120
Nabonidus, 186
Nahum, Book of, 142
Naomi, 193
Nathan, 102–3, 123
Nazareans, 218, 282, 322, 367
Nazareth, 21, 232, 367
Nebuchadnezzar, 116, 137
Necho II, 116
Nehemiah, Book of, 192
Neoplatonism, 290
Neo-Pythagoreanism, 290
Nero, 230, 284
Nicodemus, 267
Nineveh, 142, 367
Noah, 58, 367
Northern Kingdom (Israel), 108–16
Numbers, Book of, 80–81

Obadiah, Book of, 141
Omni, 114–15
Onesimus, 313
Oracles, prophetic, 37–38, 127–28
Oral tradition, 44

Palestine, 17, 368
Parables, 38, 236, 254, 368
Parallelism, poetic, 39–40, 151

Paranaesis, 303
Parousia, 264, 305, 368
Parthia, 210
Passion narrative, 255, 259, 269, 368
Passover, 82, 264, 268, 368
Pastoral Epistles, 326–28
Patriarchs, 25, 61–70, 71, 74, 80, 368
Paul, 279–81 (see also Saul)
  apostle, 298–302
  attitude toward Law-Torah, 297–98
  biography, 295, 298–302
  death, 299
  and Judaism, 296–98
  letters of, 262, 304–16
  missionary journeys, 281–82, 299–300
  persecution of Christians, 296
  physical description, 301
Pax Romana, 289
Pentateuch, 42, 45, 74, 81, 216
Pentecost, 82, 140, 278, 368
"People of the Land," 216–17, 367
Persecution, 287–88
Persians, 24
Peter, 233, 236, 277, 281–82, 284, 308
Peter, First Letter of, 332–33
Peter, Second Letter of, 334
Pharisees, 211–13, 234–36, 368
Philemon, Letter to, 313
Philippi, 304, 368
Phillipians, Letter to, 312–13
Philistines (Sea Peoples), 17, 20, 80, 99–100, 106, 368
Philo, 192, 214, 217, 265
Plato, 290
Plebians, 324
Pleroma, 314
Pliny the Younger, 287, 323
Poems, biblical, 37–38
Poetry, biblical, 39–41
Polycarp, 320
Pontius Pilate, 229, 269, 283
Praise, songs of, 149
Prehistory, 56–61
Presbytery, 288
Priestly Code, 83
Prophecy:
  origins, 122–23
  as a social phenomenon, 119–22
Prophet, definition, 119, 368
Prophetic literature, 126–30
Prophetic oracles, 127–28
Prophetic poetry, 128–30
Prophetic themes, 130–31
Prophetic visions, 126
Prophets, 119–45
  former, 7, 89–117
  latter, 7, 119–45
  minor, 138
  types, 120
Prose, biblical, 41–42
Protoevagelium of James, 341
Proverbs, Book of, 166–69

SHARED READING
My First
I Can Read!

Pete the Kitty
AND
THE THREE
BEARS

by Kimberly
& James Dean

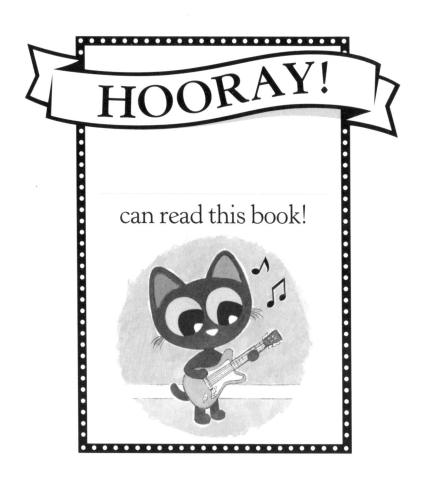

HOORAY!

can read this book!

harpercollinschildrens.com

US $5.99 / $7.25 CAN
ISBN 978-0-06-309607-3

Dear Parent:

Your child's love of reading starts here!

Every child learns to read in a different way and at his or her own speed. Some go back and forth between reading levels and read favorite books again and again. Others read through each level in order. You can help your young reader improve and become more confident by encouraging his or her own interests and abilities. From books your child reads with you to the first books he or she reads alone, there are I Can Read Books for every stage of reading:

SHARED READING
Basic language, word repetition, and whimsical illustrations, ideal for sharing with your emergent reader

BEGINNING READING
Short sentences, familiar words, and simple concepts for children eager to read on their own

READING WITH HELP
Engaging stories, longer sentences, and language play for developing readers

READING ALONE
Complex plots, challenging vocabulary, and high-interest topics for the independent reader

I Can Read Books have introduced children to the joy of reading since 1957. Featuring award-winning authors and illustrators and a fabulous cast of beloved characters, I Can Read Books set the standard for beginning readers.

A lifetime of discovery begins with the magical words **"I Can Read!"**

Visit www.icanread.com for information
on enriching your child's reading experience.

I Can Read® and I Can Read Book® are trademarks of HarperCollins Publishers.

Pete the Kitty and the Three Bears
Text copyright © 2024 by Kimberly and James Dean
Illustrations copyright © 2024 by James Dean
Pete the Cat is a registered trademark of Pete the Cat, LLC., #5118017

Library of Congress Control Number: 2023937487
ISBN 978-0-06-309608-0 (trade bdg.) — ISBN 978-0-06-309607-3 (pbk.)

Book design by Jeanne Hogle

24 25 26 27 28   LB   10 9 8 7 6 5 4 3 2 1   First Edition